Rabbis and Lawyers

RABBIS

and

LAWYERS

THE JOURNEY FROM TORAH TO CONSTITUTION

Jerold S. Auerbach

INDIANA UNIVERSITY PRESS

BLOOMINGTON & INDIANAPOLIS

The paper used in this publication meets the minimum requirements of American
National Standard for Information Sciences—Permanence of Paper for Printed
Library Materials, ANSI Z39.48-1984.

⊗™

Manufactured in the United States of America

Library of Congress Cataloging-in-Publication Data

Auerbach, Jerold S.
Rabbis and lawyers : the journey from Torah to Constitution / by Jerold S.
Auerbach.
p.   cm.
Includes bibliographical references.
ISBN 0-253-31085-7 (alk. paper)
1. Jews—United States—Cultural assimilation.   2. Jews—United States—Iden-
tity.   3. Judaism—United States.   4. United States—Ethnic relations.   I. Title.
E184.J5A94   1990
305.8'924073—dc20   89-46008
CIP

For

Shira and Rebecca

With Love,

אבי

CONTENTS

Preface ix
Introduction xv

Preface

This book continues, from a different angle of vision, my protracted exploration of the intriguing relationship between Jews and American law. Twenty years ago, during my research for *Unequal Justice*, I was startled to discover how deeply entrenched anti-Semitism once had been in the American legal profession. (So were some readers, who found ingenious ways to deny what abundant historical evidence confirmed.) Yet the astonishing success story of Jewish lawyers, as they erased the stigma of professional ostracism, alerted me to the boundless adulation that Jews bestowed upon American law. I wondered, as have others, whether some powerful affinity between Jewish tradition and the rule of American law might help to explain the passionate commitment of Jews to the American legal system.

The question lingered, and sharpened, while I wrote *Justice Without Law?*, about Americans who had chosen to resolve their disputes entirely outside the American legal system, without judges or lawyers. As several reviewers detected, I was especially fascinated by the dispute-settlement patterns of Jewish immigrants from Eastern Europe, who preferred their own indigenous alternatives to American litigation. That provoked my first excursion into Jewish law, with glimpses of the ways in which rabbinical legal authority had sustained the oldest continuing legal culture in the world.

Somewhere along the way, far from scholarly inquiry and quite unexpectedly, I came to the realization that *two* legal traditions, one American and the other Jewish, had claims upon my allegiance. That insight deepened my comprehension of the tormenting struggle of so many American Jews, during the last century and a half, to forge an identity that reconciled their American and Jewish loyalties. While the ideas for this book germinated, I lived for a (second) year in Jerusalem. I cannot yet unravel the timeless mysteries of that holy city, but it surely focuses mind and soul upon Jewish history and memory, even in the most mundane daily encounters, in ways that continue to leave me incredulous. Although it became evident, finally, that I would not leave the United States to live in Israel, there was some consolation in learning why I had always felt, as an American Jew, that I was living in someone else's country. How ironic to discover that I was doubly a stranger: (as a Jew) in my American home and (as an American) in the Jewish homeland.

I returned to the United States with a different perspective on American Jewish history. I was no longer persuaded by the conventional wisdom that attributed the ideological foundations of American Judaism, and the political behavior of American Jews, to some imagined continuities with Jewish tradition. Nor did it seem self-evident that Judaism had converged quite wondrously with American values because they were inherently compatible. Instead, from within the framework of Jewish history, the terms of American Jewish acculturation appeared in bold relief: American identification required the radical modification, if not complete renunciation, of the most distinctive and enduring commitments within Judaism, to the sacred law and holy land.

A story is told of the rabbi who was called to resolve a dispute between two Jews. After hearing one, he said, "You are right." Then, after hearing the other, he said, "*You* are right." "But rabbi," asked a puzzled witness, "How can they both be right?" The rabbi paused for a moment before responding, "*You* are right!" The story has historical resonance. Ever since biblical times, and especially during the prolonged dispersion of the Jewish people, Jewish law defined normative Judaism. Then, in the modern era, Zionism reasserted the normative claim of Jewish life in the land of Israel. To paraphrase: the rabbis are right; normative Judaism is prescribed by Jewish law. The Zionists are also right: geographically, normative Judaism is in Israel. (Indeed, without an understanding of the intricate relationship between law, land, and people, Jewish history becomes all but incomprehensible.) And if they are both right, American Jewish history has something significant to reveal about the ways in which a people relinquishes its past while claiming to affirm it.

If the synthesis of Judaism and Americanism is a historical fiction, as I believe, its endless reiteration is nonetheless quite revealing. I do not, in any way, wish to imply that its proponents were (or are) disingenuous. They have genuinely and fervently believed in the fortuitous convergence of the Jewish and American traditions. This does not prove the truth of their assertion, but only the passion with which they have affirmed it. The persistence of the claim underscores the fundamental imperative of American Judaism: to integrate two historical traditions lest American Jews be forced to choose between them.

To question the claims of convergence and compatibility, as I do, invites reconsideration, from a perspective largely foreign to the writing of American Jewish history, of the most fascinating theme in the American Jewish experience: how Jewish immigrants became American Jews. Among the most creative encounters between Jews and American society were those that redefined Judaism in American terms. In the United States the chosen people became the people who demanded the freedom to choose how to be Jews, while insisting upon the Jewish legitimacy of their individual preferences.

I should emphasize that I make no plea for a fundamentalist reading of Jewish texts and traditions, which those very texts and traditions actively discourage. Rather, I suggest that Jewish history asserts its own claims, quite apart from the fanciful reconciliation with the American experience that American Jews have so often proclaimed. The timeless demands of law and land do not lose their normative authority within Judaism, nor are they converted into options that have no greater sanction than any others, merely because American Jews disregard them.

This book is explicitly addressed to American Jews, and to others who may wish to ponder the meaning of their remarkable history in the United States. But I hope that it may also encourage a wider audience to consider acculturation as the inevitable consequence of immigration and, therefore, the inheritance of every American, no matter how remote or recent an immigrant. Whether acculturation should be celebrated or lamented, and in what measure, is—along with so much else in American life—a matter of individual judgment. My own rendering of losses and gains surely will be disputed. My purpose is to encourage, not foreclose, careful analysis and vigorous discussion of a subject that is destined to linger as a definitive attribute of the American national experience and, consequently, of American Jewish history.

It may be my personal fate to live in two worlds, Jewish and American, constantly pulled between their competing demands and unable to reconcile them. I suspect, however, that this has long been the historical burden of American Jews; and that the more insistently they have asserted the compatibility of traditions, the more clearly they have demonstrated the difficulties of harmonizing them. Some accepted the duality as the inevitable consequence of being a Jew in the diaspora, and struggled with it; most submerged Judaism in Americanism, precisely as they were instructed to do by the rabbis and lawyers who are the subject of this book. Whatever their choice, the conflict endures as the legacy of the dual legal tradition of American Jews.

During the years that I struggled with these issues, I received institutional and personal support that made scholarly solitude bearable and this book possible. Wellesley College funded a sabbatical leave and awarded grants for research and typing expenses. The Hebrew Union College Library in Jerusalem gave me unrestricted access to its fine reference collection. Upon my return, I enjoyed similar privileges at the American Jewish Historical Society in Waltham, where Bernard Wax and Dr. Nathan Kaganoff graciously tolerated my prolonged presence and responded to my endless requests for assistance. Librarians and archivists in the various archives listed in the Bibliographical Note were unfailingly attentive, and I am grateful to all of them. A fellowship from the National Endowment for the Humanities and a grant from the Lucius N. Littauer Foundation afforded an additional year of freedom to write the first draft. I am especially indebted to William Lee Frost, president of the Littauer Foundation, for his early demonstration of support for my project, when it was most needed and least available.

I enjoyed several opportunities to share my ideas with other scholars, who were encouraging even when I was least confident about my direction and destination. The Israel American Studies Association invited me to address its members. An invitation from the Aranne School of History at Tel Aviv University, to deliver the Kenneth Keating Memorial Lecture in 1986, not only brought my subject into sharper focus but returned me to the institution where, ten years earlier, I had enjoyed the most rewarding teaching year of my academic career. Near the end of my research and writing, during a bout of weariness induced by overexposure to my subject, an invitation from Prof. Marc Galanter, and the thoughtful responses of participants in the Interdisciplinary Legal Studies Colloquium at the University of Wisconsin Law School, provided a welcome boost to my intellectual morale. I am grateful to the editors who granted permission to reprint those portions of this book that originally appeared in their journals: *American Jewish History, Commentary, Forum on the Jewish People, Zionism and Israel, Judaism,* and *Midstream.* As my manuscript meandered toward publication, Jean Proctor and Thelma Pellagrini typed successive drafts, and Wendy Gelberg prepared the final manuscript expertly and with good cheer. Elsa Stanger was an enthusiastic and valuable research assistant. Peter Corbett gently introduced me to some of the mysterious wonders of computerized legal research. At Indiana University Press, Lauren Bryant displayed reassuring interest in my project; and Stephen Cole skillfully copyedited the manuscript.

In ways that I could not possibly have imagined at the time, the quest that culminated in this book began in a seminar for academics, in Israel, sponsored by the American Jewish Committee. The seminar expressed the creativity of Yehuda Rosenman and his exuberant commitment to Jewish learning and to the Jewish State. Although he and I argued endlessly, I think he suspected that even my obduracy would be moderated, in time, by my experiences in Israel. He was right; and long before we saw each other in Jerusalem for the last time, it was evident to both of us what an extraordinary gift he had given to me. The generosity of friends in Israel remains vivid. Moshe and Chava Wagner gave so much of themselves and their family to Susan, Shira, and me that hardly a *Shabbat* or holiday passes without some reminder of their loving-kindness. Haggai and Adina Hurvitz, once again, sustained us with their enduring friendship. Ruth Rubin provided astonishing glimpses of the subtleties of the Hebrew language, while cheerfully enduring my ineptitude as a student.

Friends offered appropriate measures of encouragement and, above all, the respite that I desperately needed. My warm appreciation to Janet Burstein, Helen Epstein, Michael and Sharon Haselkorn, Arnie and Ellen Offner, Michael and Judy Rosenthal, and Steve Whitfield; and especially to Stanley Fisher, Artie Goren, Fred Konefsky, Jon Levenson, Michael Meltsner, Avi Soifer, and Mel Urofsky for reading the manuscript with sympathetic understanding and critical acumen. Haggai Hurvitz and I have shared so much for so long that Shira was prompted to declare that we must be brothers. I am more grateful than I can say to all my friends in the Newton Centre Minyan, whose welcome into a quite wonderful *kahal* has been a blessing in the best and worst of times.

Within my family, Pammy and Jeff provided comforting reassurances from past experience that their father's prolonged disappearances into his study were not only a tolerable idiosyncrasy but likely, later if not sooner, to produce tangible results. Shira and Rebecca, who experienced them for the first time, were less certain. Shira wrote so many books, all delightfully illustrated (usually on my notepaper), while I was writing only this one, that I often came close to sharing her preference for crayons and magic markers. Fulfilling her name, she is a song of joy. Rebecca, for whom life began in Israel, offered daily (and often nightly) reminders that writing a book cannot compare to hugs, kisses, and smiles, nor to the loving companionship of Roary. Susan, as always, responded with wisdom, patience, and love.

J. S. A.
Newton, Massachusetts
September 1989
Elul 5749

Introduction

Ever since 1841, when a *chazan* in Charleston, South Carolina, declared "this happy land our Palestine," American Jews have located their Zion six thousand miles west of the biblical promised land. Uprooted from Europe, they survived a passage to freedom as perilous as the biblical exodus. In the United States they were inspired and comforted to discover that the legacy of the Torah converged with American democratic promise, miraculously fusing ancient Jewish tradition to their adopted American homeland.

Not only was the United States the land of promise but the land where promise was fulfilled. Jewish immigrants, their children, and the generations that followed found ample reason to be thankful for their opportunities and proud of their achievements. Their stunning success has aptly been cited as the "greatest collective Horatio Alger story in American immigration history."[1] American Jews responded to the blessings of abundance and freedom with boundless gratitude. Who but a Jew (Irving Berlin) would have composed "God Bless America," the popular hymn of praise to the United States as "home sweet home"? (And who else would so quickly have become an American that he would soon be "dreaming of a white Christmas"?) Even the occasional suggestion that an American Jew might yet be a "stranger at home," or uneasy there, still implicitly affirmed that the United States indeed was home for a people whose history was exile and wandering. The sharp edges of a profound cultural dislocation, as Jewish immigrants became Americans, have worn smooth with time. Jews are now so thoroughly integrated into American society, and their accomplishments so endlessly celebrated, that it is all but inconceivable that they once had to struggle to secure their American birthright. By now a nostalgic glow suffuses Ellis Island and Hester Street as portals to freedom, opportunity, mobility, prosperity, and security.

Yet the *goldene medine*, according to those European rabbis who warned Jews not to emigrate, was *trefe*—an unclean place, not fit for Jewish habitation. Judaism, after all, contained its own historical imperatives, which bound Jews across time and space to a shared history and, some would claim, to a shared destiny. It transmitted an abiding sense of the distinctiveness of the Jewish people, based upon the covenantal relationship between God and Israel. According to the biblical tradition, God had chosen Israel from among the nations to be his own "treasure" people; in turn, they assumed the obligation of obedience to divine command, revealed in the Torah given to Moses at Sinai. Faithful performance would assure a bountiful national life in the promised land of Israel. These memories and yearnings were endlessly reaffirmed in sacred texts, ritual observance, and historical experience. They molded an extraordinary consciousness of peoplehood, undiminished by defeat, dispersion, and disaster. Even the devastating destruction of the Second Temple, followed by exile from the land, did not diminish its vitality. In a remarkable burst of creativity, the rabbis constructed a legal system that sustained Jewish autonomy for nearly two thousand years after national sovereignty had ended.

But the Jewish sacred-law tradition, a blend of divine revelation and rabbinical interpretation, could not easily be transplanted to the United States. It had been severely weakened by emancipation, with its promise of legal and political equality, which accelerated the transfer of legal loyalty to the state, and by immigration, which relocated Jews far from their self-governing communities in Europe. The obligations of Jewish law were evident impediments to their absorption in a Christian country, even if the immigrants had been determined to abide by them—which most were not. But Jewish tradition still exerted its claim, too powerful to be completely ignored. That left American Jews in a quandary. Uneasily suspended between the covenantal traditions of *two* chosen peoples, they were legitimate heirs of *two* legal traditions, with title to *two* promised lands. The task for American Jewish leaders, then and since, was to reconcile the Jewish past with an American future, teaching immigrants how to remain Jews while becoming Americans.

Deeply embedded in Judaism were conceptions of law and land that seemed sharply at variance with the obligations of American citizenship. Jewish memory, after all, was framed by God's promise to Abraham concerning the land of Israel ("To thy seed will I give this land"), and the command to Moses regarding the law of Israel ("Observe thou that which I command thee this day").[2] To be sure, Jews had not always observed the law nor lived in the land, even when it was possible for them to do so; but the divine promise and command had not been abrogated either. That was the challenge of American Jewish life: to transform enduring Jewish commitments to land and law into indisputably American sources of Jewish obligation, proving that in the United States Jews had finally eluded the debilitating stigma of divided loyalties. Only then could they be home at last, at home in America.

From the mid-nineteenth century, when German Jews first arrived in the United States in significant numbers, there was no more urgent issue in American Jewish life. The security of American Jews depended upon their unconditional commitment to American, rather than Jewish, conceptions of land and law. It is not surprising, therefore, that rabbis and lawyers, as custodians of their respective legal traditions, devised the most persuasive synthesis between Judaism and Americanism. As they redefined Jewish legitimacy in American legal terms, they fused Torah and Constitution as the sacred texts of a Judeo-American legal tradition, which pointed to the biblical origins of the American rule of law. By the end of the nineteenth century, rabbis had all but dismantled the authority structure of Jewish law; by World War I, lawyers had defined a new legal identity for American Jews.

Yet even as rabbis and lawyers relied upon a biblical idiom, they demonstrated the strength of their American identification. America, after all, had been conceived in biblical imagery: the seventeenth-century errand of English Puritans into the wilderness of New England pointed unerringly to the fulfillment of biblical destiny in the American Canaan. Centuries before Jews found their Zion in America, zealous Christians had already envisioned America as the stage for their own salvation drama. Eager to find a place within the American creation story, Jews absorbed the Puritan rendition of biblical history as their own. With the Hebrew Bible as the primary source of American civilization, Jews could become as indisputably American as the Puritan pioneers.

If the biblical heritage shaped the American experience, so that American and Jewish history converged, there could be no conflict between Jewish and American values. To take that claim at face value, however, forecloses exploration of some fascinating issues in American Jewish history. Once its content and context are carefully examined, it is easy to detect beneath the confident rhetoric of compatibility some nagging doubts about the place of Jews in American society. Those doubts generated unrelenting pressure upon Jews to rewrite their own history to conform to American patterns. The ingenuity of rabbis and lawyers in synthesizing Americanism with Judaism was a decisive contribution to American Jewish acculturation. As the role of law in Jewish life was transformed, Jews found a "secure resting place" within the American legal system and "a home in America as lawyers."[3] As lawyers became the law men of American Jewish life, the loyalty of Jews to the American constitutional tradition was assured. But their constitutional faith did not express values in the Jewish legal tradition. Rather, it was a decisive step in the repudiation of Jewish legal authority in the modern era.

This book does not celebrate the American Jewish success story (which hardly needs further documentation). Neither is it a nostalgic lament for a lost edenic paradise, located back in the misty realms of the European *shtetl*. Instead it seeks to understand the process of American Jewish acculturation and the rhetoric that was offered to justify (or conceal) it. I try to be explicitly attentive to Jewish history, traditions, and meanings. (Yet I recall Cynthia Ozick's terse observation: "English is a Christian language.

When I write English, I live in Christendom."⁴) I recognize, of course, that critical scrutiny of the terms of American Jewish acculturation is likely to encounter substantial resistance. It cuts sharply against the grain of conventional understanding, reinforced by a century of reiteration, which proclaims the synthesis of Judaism and Americanism as a statement of literal truth. But historical accuracy has its claims, even if these must override comforting fictions.

Perhaps it is time to begin to write American Jewish history outside the ideological constraints of acculturation myths. The synthesis of Judaism and Americanism, correctly understood, was not the fortuitous discovery of convergent traditions but the expression of a sustained effort to obliterate their divergence. To appreciate the significance of this crucial point, it is necessary to step outside the conventional boundaries of the discipline of American Jewish history. American Jewish historians (demonstrating how thoroughly American they are) usually confine their subject within narrow conceptual and chronological limits. Once the immigrants reach American shores, anything non-American seems virtually un-American. Historical analogies with Jewish communities elsewhere, in time or space, are highly suspect and rarely, if ever, drawn. One historian has explicitly rejected the premise that "American Jews in the last decades of the twentieth century sufficiently resemble other Jewries centuries ago to draw analogies." Not only does she consider "of questionable value the process of seeking historical lessons in the distant past" but "by turning to history for lessons . . . we risk engaging in polemic" to advance a "political agenda."⁵

It is not, of course, as simple as that. The exclusion of the past, no less than its inclusion, is a "lesson" that may serve a "polemical" purpose within a "political agenda." The Jewish past is not only relevant but necessary for an understanding of American Jewish history. It provides a framework for grasping the very essence of the history of Jews in the United States: their extension of, *and* radical departure from, Jewish historical norms. To treat American Jewish history in isolation is, of course, to implicitly endorse a fundamental American idea, the uniqueness of the American experience. That serves the purpose of legitimating the full integration of Jews into American society, exclusively on American terms. I reject this approach; as my chapters on Jewish sacred law and Hebrew prophecy indicate, I believe that American Jewish history can only be comprehended within the full sweep of Jewish history.

The essence of acculturation, after all, is that a distinctive people relinquish its language, memory, calendar, ritual, and even diet to become like everyone else. Whether this measures freedom, or servitude, remains an open question. The answer notwithstanding, a fascinating, complex and prolonged exchange of cultures should no longer be disguised, or misunderstood, as historical continuity. The synthesis of Judaism and Americanism all but obliterated Jewish historical imperatives from American Judaism. Rabbis and lawyers insisted, instead, that law secure the allegiance of Jews to the United States, where the promised land would be designed according to American specifications. So they taught Jews how to become Americans.

Jews, struggling like all immigrants to reconcile their ancestral past with their American future, were attentive to this lesson. Yet the adaptation of Jews to the United States, while remarkably successful, seems to have been characterized by uncommon, and persistent, anxiety. Understandably so. For historical Judaism was not merely a religion, or a national identification, but a combination of both. Jewish immigrants not only relinquished forms of worship and left a country behind. Compelled to demonstrate their loyalty as Americans, they also placed in jeopardy their unique history as a distinctive people and the covenantal relationships with God and each other that had defined and sustained it.

Especially for Jews, American law offered enticing rewards, beyond financial security and professional status. Law afforded Jews a rare opportunity to define themselves as patriotic Americans. As lawyers and judges, Jews were empowered to interpret the traditions and explicate the rules of American society; to become, that is, respected custodians of American culture. All immigrants learned how to become good Americans: in school; from sports, movies, newspapers; from the myriad of social cues that street, neighborhood, factory, and office provided. But law was special, and Jews, among all immigrants, were powerfully drawn to it. Law, quite uniquely, could link Jewish history to American destiny. So Jews could claim fidelity to the spirit of their own sacred-law tradition precisely as they replaced it with the rule of American law. Their journey from Torah to Constitution is the story of this book.

DIVERGENCE: LAW & JUSTICE

American Zion

T he Hebrew Bible framed the American experience even before the Puritans first sailed from England in 1630. Their apprehension must have been palpable: to anticipate a hazardous voyage to an uncertain fate in an unknown land would stretch even the capacious boundaries of their evident piety and determination. As the Rev. John Cotton delivered his farewell sermon, he set their journey in the only context that could have eased their trepidation. Comparing their departure from England to the deliverance of Israel from Egypt, he reminded them of God's promise to "appoint a place for my People Israel"—a special "place of their own" where, physically and spiritually secure, they would "move no more."[1]

On board the *Arbella*, sailing toward their promised land, John Winthrop defined their "due forme of Government both civill and ecclesiasticall"—in familiar covenantal terms "between God and us." He recalled their task: "to serve the Lord and worke out our Salvacion under the power and purity of his holy Ordinances." Failure assured divine wrath. To "avoyde this shipwracke," Winthrop warned (choosing a chillingly apt metaphor for the ocean voyagers), they must "followe the counsell of Micah, to doe justly, to love mercy, to walke humbly with our God." So doing, they would surely "finde that the God of Israell is among us." Winthrop, in his peroration, repeated the parting words of Moses, "that faithful servant of the Lord in his last farewell to Israel, Deut. 30": to love God and obey His commandments so that God would bless them in "the good land whither wee pass over this vast Sea to possesse it." Therefore Winthrop admonished, in the words of Moses: "lett us choose life . . . by obeying his voyce, and cleaveing to him, for hee is our life, and our prosperity." So the Puritans moved backward in time as they crossed the Atlantic. Their journey to the American wilderness was inexplicable, especially to themselves, without the "sacred significance" that it derived from ancient Israel.[2]

Faithful to their mission, the Puritans designed a Bible commonwealth in Massachusetts Bay whose theology, rhetoric, law, and literature were infused with allusions to the biblical experiences of Israel. There were traces everywhere in New England throughout the seventeenth century: in the names the Puritans gave their towns (among them Salem, Canaan, Hebron); in sermons referring to the "New England *Zion*" and the "American *Jerusalem*"; and in devotion to the Hebrew language (a required course at Harvard College). The Plymouth legal code rested upon the "right judgments and true lawes" of ancient Israel, while in New Haven "the judicial laws of God, as they were delivered by Moses" were binding. The Hebrew Bible was the blueprint for the wilderness Zion in America, an unquestionable assurance that providential destiny favored "God's New Israel" in the promised American Canaan. "We are the people that do succeed Israel," Thomas Thacher would proclaim, "We are Jacob."[3]

The metaphor of Israel and "the language of Canaan" pervaded Puritan discourse, defining a public identity, linked to messianic destiny, that remains characteristically American more than three centuries later. The Bible was not merely an ancient religious text. It was literally a historical model, prefiguring the Puritan experience, illustrating divine intervention in the affairs of his covenanted peoples. "The people of God," John Robinson explained, were leaving "Babylon" for "Jerusalem," there to build "a spiritual house, or temple for the Lord to dwell in." The Puritans, according to a Cambridge minister, were "Abraham's children, a people in covenant with God." The theme reverberated through New England sermons to the end of the century. "*Jerusalem* was, *New England* is, they were, you are God's own, God's covenant people," proclaimed Samuel Wakeman. As a colleague explained, "The Historie of the Old Testament is Example to us." Puritan governors were likened to Joshua or Nehemiah, leading their people from exile to the American "Holy Land." There, as Cotton Mather declared, "You may see an Israel in America."[4]

Mather, more than anyone, entwined the Hebrew Bible with the New England experience. After the restoration of the monarchy in England in 1660, all hope for a Puritan commonwealth there was extinguished. The American Puritans, isolated and despairing, renewed their purpose with a deepened identification with ancient Israel. Events abroad had strengthened their sense of themselves, less a new England than a new Israel. Mather's *Magnalia Christi Americana*, his turn-of-the-century recapitulation of the Puritan experience, brought to fulfillment the enduring themes of biblical typology in Puritan thought.

Mather understood the New England experience as a reenactment of the biblical return from Babylonian exile. Governor John Winthrop was "Nehemias Americanus," the Puritans' own "New English Nehemiah" who led his people to their promised land and governed "the public affairs of our American Jerusalem." With his "exacter parallel" to the biblical narrative, Mather's redemptive history converted the Jerusalem of antiquity into a prefiguration of the Jerusalem of Mather's New England. So intimately identified were the two Israels in Mather's mind that he concluded, after a sermon delivered as he brought the *Magnalia* to completion: "My hearers . . . know not, whether I am giving an Account of *Old Israel*, or of *New England*: So surprising has been the Parallel!" But Mather could hardly have been surprised. "Like every preacher before him," a student of seventeenth-century New England sermons has written, " Mather integrated the history of New England with the history of Israel so completely that it became one unified narrative."[5]

The interweaving of American history with biblical text has profoundly molded the self-conceptions of the American people. American destiny has been inextricable from divine blessing. The theme of "God's New Israel" has served as an assurance of divine election, an invitation to become a light unto the nations. Taken as fact, faith, or myth, it remains the irreducible essence of the national credo (or civil religion) of the American people. It has enabled Americans to understand themselves and to validate their yearnings and actions as a people. Israel endures in the American mind because "the Judaic heritage flowed through the minds of America's early settlers and helped to shape the new American republic."[6] With the Hebrew Bible endlessly cited as a formative influence upon American values and institutions, it might even be said that biblical promise reached fulfillment in the American national experience.

But the Puritans, it must be remembered, were above all else zealous Protestants, whose fervent attachment to the Hebrew Bible was inextricable from their devout Christian piety. God's "new Israel" in America, for them, was intended to hasten fulfillment of a Christian salvation drama in which they assigned themselves the leading roles. Their venture into the American wilderness belonged to "the realm of sacred history"—a realm securely bounded by Protestant theological imperatives. The Massachusetts Bay Commonwealth, Urian Oakes preached, was designed as "a little model of the kingdome of Christ upon Earth." The Puritans, as Cotton Mather knew, were "the people of the Lord Jesus Christ," drawn to New England for one reason only: to fulfill their Christian mission. Any attribution of spiritual compatibility between ancient Israel and the American promised land implicitly absorbs the Christian triumphal assumptions that unerringly guided the Puritans from biblical text to American context.[7]

The Puritan fondness for biblical analogies climaxed more than a millennium of Christian history. It can be traced as far back as the apostle Paul, who first conceived of the Hebrew Bible as a prefiguration of the formative events in the emergence of Christianity. His purpose was clear: to eradicate the normative legal content of the "old" testament, transforming it instead into the prophetic anticipation of the Christian Savior. The life and death of Jesus had fulfilled, and thereby annulled, the "old" testament; with its laws and rituals abolished, it retained only prognostic value. In this way, the new Christian faith could accommodate itself to the Jewish setting in which it arose. The early church constantly referred to the Hebrew Bible, even if only to repudiate it. Church fathers, followed by medieval theologians, imaginatively developed the possibilities of typology. So the *Akedah*, the binding of Isaac, prefigured God's sacrifice of His son in the crucifixion; the days that Jonah spent in the belly of the whale anticipated the entombment of Jesus; Noah's Ark was the "type" for the early church (and, to Puritans, for their own Congregational churches in New England); the rebuilding of the Temple foreshadowed the resurrection of Jesus. As St. Augustine explained: "in the Old Testament the New lies hid; in the New Testament the meaning of the Old becomes clear."[8]

For the Puritans, biblical language merged into the larger currents of philo-Semitism that swirled through seventeenth-century England. Reformation theologians had emphasized reading and understanding the biblical text as the word of God, suggesting that biblical narratives provided "instructive examples of God acting in history, if not illustrations which foreshadowed the future glory of the fully reformed Christian faith." Hebrew Bibles, grammars, law codes, and rabbinical commentaries circulated widely in England. And "the highly biblical wash over the language of the period," so evident in Puritan discourse, located those pious Protestants even more securely in the millennial spirit of Christian redemption that pervaded English society. But such "bibliolatry" should not be confused with any fondness for Jews, or Judaism. Jews had been excluded from England for more than three hundred years, since 1290; even the mounting pressure for their readmission during the first half of the seventeenth century was not a demonstration that Christian hostility had abated, nor that toleration was a virtue. Rather, it was a concession, fully consistent with Christian dogma, that until Jews were readmitted they could not be converted, a prerequisite for the imminently expected second coming of the Messiah.[9]

The Hebrew Bible was so profoundly significant to the Puritans because Christian redemptive history, in which their own role was so vital, was otherwise incomprehensible. Biblical metaphors enabled the Puritans to link the two testaments, Old and New, through the life of Jesus. Ancient Israel retained its importance, but only for its prefiguration of the Christian church as the true, spiritual Israel. By the seventeenth century, as any Puritan knew, Christ performed his deeds through the Puritan saints in New England, whose struggles were "chronicled before they happened" in the Hebrew Bible. The Puritans turned to the Hebrew Bible as the anticipatory text for their redemptive activities. Their highly refined consciousness of the resemblance between New England and ancient Israel—with Israel, according to one minister, "our glass to view our faces in"—had only one purpose: to transform their mission into the culmination of the Protestant Reformation. For it was, as Samuel Mather wrote, "ordained of God under the Old Testament, to represent and hold forth something of Christ in the New." Typology enabled God to proclaim the Christian Gospel in the Hebrew Bible.[10]

Analogies to the children of Israel defined reality for New England Puritans. As a covenanted people, the Puritans—like the Israelites before them—were a divinely chosen instrument in the process of messianic salvation. Israel had been the first people to demonstrate God's active intervention in human history. But its role ended with the failure to acknowledge Christ as Savior. The new Israel in America confirmed God's continuing involvement, certain to endure until the messiah returned. The New England experience was nothing less than "a providentially controlled reenactment" of the events depicted in the biblical narrative.[11]

Nothing better illustrates the religious content of the Puritan experiment than the decisive role of ministers in defining it. They thundered their jeremiads from the pulpits of New England churches throughout the seventeenth century. They not only located the Puritan mission within a biblical frame of reference but also simultaneously secured their own claim as the authorized interpreters of its meaning. Scripture legitimized their role: one minister, identifying with John the Baptist, saw himself in "the service of our *Lord Christ*, to re-build the most glorious Edifice of *Mt. Sion* in a Wilderness." In their understanding of sacred history, Europe had fallen to the "Antichrist" of Catholicism; their own Church of England had drifted dangerously toward "popery"; so "Christ create[d] a *New England* to muster up the first of his forces in." Ministers were the undisputed leaders of this Protestant vanguard, transforming America into the promised land of biblical prophecy, thereby simultaneously proclaiming their own vital role in the unfolding "drama of Christian eschatology." In their explication of redemptive history, the Hebrew Bible was their most relevant text. Ministers identified the Puritan experience with the biblical narrative; but their purpose was to subsume the history of Jews into its prefiguration of the triumph of Christianity.[12]

The evident Puritan (and Pilgrim) fondness for biblical analogies and Hebrew sources hardly demonstrates the confluence of the biblical and American traditions. Rather, these earliest American settlers were able "to find Christian meaning in Jewish history and ritual." The Puritans transformed the Bible into a superb interpretive structure for their own experience. It made theological sense to them only as the earliest source of Christianity. They were fascinated with the Hebrew language (William Bradford's "longing desire" to comprehend the "holy tongue . . . in which God and angels spake to the holy patriarchs of old time" is a touching example). They strictly observed the Sabbath. Their theology was covenantal. And they named their daughters Sarah and Rebecca. But they were guided by Christian zeal. If the American experiment was truly to enter the realm of sacred history, it must become "a model of universal Christendom." Only then, paradoxically, would it become evident "that the God of Israell is among us," as John Winthrop so fervently wished.[13]

The "language of Canaan," so eloquently articulated in seventeenth-century New England, long outlasted the Puritans. Even as Puritan passion and purpose subsided, and as the bible commonwealth in Massachusetts Bay came to resemble the surrounding colonies, the Hebrew Bible continued to provide a persuasive interpretive structure for the American experience. In the seventeenth century, ancient Israel was the model for a Christian holy experiment; well into the eighteenth century, at least one Bostonian still marveled that "the greater part of the Old Testament were written about us." Before the close of that century, divine blessing had been securely linked to republican government. As Americans drew closer to rebellion and revolution, the fusion of divine election with national purpose explained and justified the struggle for independence. Liberty became the sacred cause of the American people, who inherited the Puritan legacy and reinvested it in their new national endeavor. By 1787, the biblical narrative, as the definition of American national purpose, had framed the formative experiences in the first centuries of American history: settlement and independence.[14]

Biblical precedent and divine purpose were everywhere evident in the revolutionary struggle. A political upheaval was imbued with sacred content; freedom became God's own cause; independence could be understood within the millenial prophecies of the Bible. The divine covenant with Israel was once again recalled, to remind Americans (according to a 1760 sermon) that "what was here spoken and ordered to the Jewish church and people is applicable to all Christian people and societies." Americans read their republican yearnings back into the history of Israel to explain themselves as a divinely chosen people. With Israel recast as "a commonwealth of liberty," it was not difficult to locate biblical authority for opposition to monarchies (despite a long line of Jewish kings). Independence was understood as a reenactment of the Exodus; any resemblance between George III and Pharaoh (or occasionally, Haman) was entirely intentional. George Washington, of course, was the American Moses, divinely dispatched to deliver "the posterity of Jacob" from the "*worse* than

Egyptian bondage of Great Britain." America, wrote two popular revolutionary poets, was the land where the "light of holy revelation beams"; they knew that "the star which rose from Judah lights our skies."[15]

When the colonists faltered in their struggle, a New Haven minister attributed their plight to their own unrighteousness, which made them prone to "act over the same stupid vile part that the Children of Israel did in the wilderness." God, he warned, "is trying us . . . that we may know what is in our hearts, and whether we will keep his commandments." The British Pharaoh, to be sure, was wicked (and his ministers repeated "the same wicked, mischievous plot against the American States, as Haman did against the Jews"), yet "God has a righteous controversy with us in this land." Usually, however, the biblical allusions were more complimentary. John Dickinson compared America to David in his struggle with Goliath; by 1783, it was evident that God's favor had been bestowed upon the American Israel. "By a series of miracles were the Israelites rescued from the house of bondage," recalled David Osgood of Massachusetts. "And by a series of providential wonders have the Americans emerged from oppression, and risen to liberty and independence."[16]

By 1783, the new American Israel was certain of its divine favor as a light of freedom unto the nations. Ezra Stiles, president of Yale, reinterpreted the Deuteronomic promise that Israel would be a holy people as a prophecy of future American glory. Indeed, the structure of government in the Hebrew commonwealth came to bear a remarkable resemblance to the nascent forms of American self-government. Described as a confederacy of "united states or tribes," with a constitution that protected liberty and a congress and president to lead its people, Israel "mirrored to Christian republicans of New England a remarkably clear image of their own developing institutions." The drafting of the Constitution confirmed the parallel, for the new charter of government was understood in biblical terms as a covenant that secured divine blessing for the new nation. Harvard president Samuel Langden recalled the development of Israelite government in the wilderness as it moved "from a mere mob to a well regulated nation" under the rule of law, lacking only a "permanent constitution." The Ten Commandments and Mosaic laws, which rested upon "the plain immutable principles of reason, justice, and social virtue," remedied this deficiency. As, of course, did the American Constitution, a "heavenly charter of liberty." It demonstrated to Langden that "God hath . . . taken us under his special care, as he did his ancient covenant people." Clearly the new nation was, as Israel once had been, at the center of God's redemptive plan for mankind.[17]

The Bible retained its metaphorical power in the United States. Throughout the early years of the republic the New England ministry, with biblical fidelity, defined political virtue as an expression of Christian piety.

But the parallels carried well beyond the pulpit, even to the designs submitted for a new national seal: Benjamin Franklin proposed Moses lifting his arms to divide the Red Sea; Thomas Jefferson suggested the children of Israel in the wilderness, following the pillar of cloud by day and the pillar of fire by night. President Washington, responding to inaugural greetings from the Hebrew Congregation of Savannah, expressed his conviction that the same God who had delivered the Israelites from their "Egyptian oppressors" and led them to their promised land had once again conspicuously demonstrated His "providential agency . . . in establishing these United States as an independent nation." Jefferson, in his second inaugural address, reiterated the parallel, requesting the favor of that divine Being "who led our fathers, as Israel of old," to the promised land. July 4th became known as the "political Sabbath of freedom," its celebration resembling, at least superficially, the covenant renewal ceremonies of ancient Israel.[18]

Biblical allusions still rested upon Christian triumphalist premises. Just as a new testament had supplanted the old, and as the Puritans had identified with Israel in order to supersede it, so divine favor enabled the new American nation to replace its unworthy predecessor in salvation history. As Rev. Langden made clear when he cited "The Republic of the Israelites" as a model for the new American nation, Israel served as a negative reminder of "what will depress and bring us to ruin." For, despite its model constitution, the Israelites had "neglected their government, corrupted their religion, and grew dissolute in their morals." Consequently, God had given to America, "by his son Jesus Christ, who is far superior to Moses," the miracle of independence, a heavenly constitution, and the blessing of divine favor. Washington (when he was not Moses or Joshua) was often referred to as the national "Saviour"; the Declaration of Independence was compared to the Sermon on the Mount; to John Quincy Adams, the American Revolution was nothing less than an extension of "the Redeemer's mission on earth." The true meaning of the American Israel was found in its role as harbinger of the coming kingdom of Christ. In all but name, the United States had become "a republic of Christian virtue."[19]

The blending of Christian and republican themes persisted long after the Revolution. Despite the conventional wisdom, which celebrates the ratification of the First Amendment as assurance of the strict separation between religion and the state, this is largely a retrospective projection of modern secular values. No matter how fervently the "wall of separation" principle (briefly enunciated, and narrowly applied, by Jefferson more than a decade later) is intoned, the United States remained a Christian republic. Both Jefferson and Madison (whose Act for Establishing Religious Freedom and Memorial and Remonstrance constitute the sacred texts of the modern separationist position) acknowledged that only the new national government was constrained by the First Amendment. Madison (who declared Christianity "the best & purest religion") understood the amendment as a limitation of congressional power only; his attempt to restrain the states from infringing the rights of religious conscience was defeated in the Senate. Similarly, Jefferson conceded that only the national government lacked authority to prescribe due forms of religious exercise or enforce religious discipline. States remained free to do so. Indeed, Madison, in 1785, had introduced "A Bill for Punishing Disturbers of Religious Worship and Sabbath Breakers" in the Virginia Legislature; the bill was drafted by Jefferson.

The First Amendment did nothing to moderate "evangelical civic piety," the blending of Protestantism and republicanism that sustained "the long spell of Christendom" in the United States. The amendment did not repudiate the principle of a Christian state; rather, it provided an alternative means toward securing it. Older forms of confessional coercion disappeared (Maryland, for example, ended its established Church of England in 1776), but newer forms of Christian domination emerged (in the new Maryland constitution, religious liberty was secured to everyone who professed Christianity). Three New England states retained their established Congregational churches into the nineteenth century without any sense that they were infringing on religious freedom. It was assumed, according to the Massachusetts Constitution, that "the happiness of a people, and the good order and preservation of civil government, essentially depend upon piety, religion, and morality." The legislature was therefore authorized to require towns and parishes to provide for "the public worship of GOD; and for the support and maintenance of public Protestant teachers."[20]

In the new nation, religious freedom was easily accommodated within the forms of a Christian state. Protestant piety was everywhere evident: in public education, political discourse, and literary expression. At least as far into the nineteenth century as the Civil War, a Christian reading of scripture continued to infuse American history and destiny with religious content. As Herman Melville wrote so evocatively, "We Americans are the peculiar, chosen people—the Israel of our time; we bear the ark of the liberties of the world." In his *Commentaries on the Constitution*, written during the same "era of republican Protestantism," Justice Joseph Story made the point explicit: "it is impossible for those, who believe in the truth of Christianity . . . to doubt, that it is the especial duty of government to foster, and encourage it among all the citizens." Indeed, Story continued, "in a republic there would seem to be a peculiar propriety in viewing the Christian religion . . . [as] the religion of liberty." The United States, Story wrote in an 1843 Supreme Court opinion, was "a Christian country."[21]

With the Civil War, biblical language became more explicitly Christian. Allusions to the Exodus, the wilderness, and Zion yielded to the Christian themes of sacrifice, death, and rebirth. Lincoln's Gettysburg Address has aptly been described as the "New Testament" of American "civil scriptures"; indeed, public comprehension of the meaning of his life and death were located within the Christian metaphors of suffering and resurrection. Like Moses, Lincoln had guided his people through the wilderness of war, only to die with a vision of the promised land of peace. But the closest identification by far was between the martyred president, the Savior of the Union sent to die for his people, and the Christian Savior who died for all mankind. Across the country, on the "Black Easter" following Lincoln's assassination on Good Friday, church sermons noted the remarkable parallel, which was "solemnized by the murder of one who had tried so much to imitate his Divine Master." The terrible national trauma of fratricide had culminated in a death that was only explicable within the Christian imagery at the core of American national self-consciousness.[22]

Just as biblical imagery finally began to recede from American rhetoric, diverted into bombastic statements of American "manifest destiny" in world affairs, Jews embraced it. An influx of German Jews, arriving in the United States by the mid-nineteenth century, became the privileged beneficiaries of the unprecedented economic and civic opportunity that Jews enjoyed in American society. As they climbed the ladder of social mobility to affluence and influence, they began to construct a reformed Jewish identity that was compatible with American values. In a supreme irony of American Jewish history, Jews turned to the Puritans and Pilgrims as the authoritative interpreters of their own biblical heritage. Eager to identify themselves as Americans, they were led back to their own sacred texts as a guide to the American experience. From fragments of seventeenth-century Protestant thought, they constructed a unitary Judeo-American tradition that enabled them, as Jews, to become Americans.

The timing of their discovery was hardly coincidental. The arrival of the first wave of Jewish immigrants from Russia, after the czarist pogroms of 1881, aroused tremors of apprehension among the German Jews, who by then were settled, successful, and culturally integrated. So many impoverished, Yiddish-speaking, religiously observant newcomers, evidently foreign and distinctively Jewish, might call into question the place of all Jews in American society and even their loyalty to the United States.

The Constitutional centennial in 1887 provided an appropriate ceremonial opportunity for the first elaborate affirmation by a Jew of the Hebrew antecedents of American political values and institutions. Oscar S. Straus, one of the German Jewish luminaries of his generation (twice minister, and then ambassador, to Turkey, and the first Jew to serve in a presidential cabinet), was fascinated by the relationship between the Hebrew commonwealth and the American republic. Straus had emigrated from Bavaria as a youngster. Raised in a liberal Jewish family in a small town in Georgia (where he attended Baptist Sunday school), he delayed his entry into L.

Straus & Sons, the lucrative family merchandising business, to attend college. But at Columbia, he recalled, "I was under many disadvantages . . . with no social standing and a Jew." He had, however, absorbed a sense of wondrous fulfillment of ancient Jewish ideals in modern American society—probably from the rabbis of his Reform temple. In 1885, after briefly practicing law, he published a long essay, *The Origin of Republican Form of Government in the United States of America*, which can best be understood as an effort to eradicate some of his "disadvantages" as a Jew.[23]

It was "remarkable," Straus thought, that historians had overlooked the bonds between ancient Israel and the United States. The repeated references that Straus discovered in the revolutionary era to the biblical narrative, especially to the Book of Exodus, demonstrated that the history of Israel had served as "a glorious example and inspiring incentive to the American people" in their own "mighty struggle for the blessings of civil and religious liberty." Straus recognized the Puritan link between Israel and America: "Through the windows of the Puritan churches of New England," he wrote, "the new West looked back to the old East." The Hebrew and American peoples, although separated by two millennia, were united in their commitments to constitutionalism, democracy, and republicanism. Among the numerous parallels that Straus cited were the separation (with Aaron as high priest and Joshua as military commander) of church and state; the principle of federalism (government under the Judges, when each tribe had its own government yet sent "duly elected representatives to the national congress"); and resistance to monarchy (recounted in the Book of Samuel). Above all, there was "the divine supremacy of the law," the primary source of American liberty. To Straus, ancient Israel embodied "the spirit and essence" of American constitutionalism; and, reciprocally, "in the spirit and essence of our Constitution the influence of the Hebrew commonwealth was paramount." Israel had set "a divine precedent for a pure democracy." Truly, "the bright sun of Canaan" had risen again in America, where the spirit of Moses, Joshua, and Samuel, transmitted to Franklin, Washington, and Adams, was expressed in liberty, law, and constitutionalism.[24]

The unity of Americanism and Judaism, proclaimed in Straus's book, molded his own identity as an American Jew. Yet as effortlessly as Straus drew the comparison, his persistent attempts to demonstrate the compatibility of Judaism and Americanism suggest some interior doubts that needed to be overcome—the legacy, perhaps, of the "disadvantages" Straus had experienced as a Jew in a predominantly Christian society. Whether in his writing, or in his commitment to the work of the American Jewish Historical Society and the American Jewish Committee, Straus made certain that "American" and "Jewish" always converged. He succeeded admirably—even to the point where, as a member of the New York delegation to the Progressive party convention in 1912, he could unself-consciously lead the delegates in an impassioned rendition of "Onward Christian Soldiers" as they stood at their political Armageddon and waited for Theodore Roosevelt to lead them into their promised Progressive homeland. When Straus reflected upon American history he frequently returned to the Pilgrims and Puritans, who symbolized the best of the American tradition because they had absorbed the most from biblical Israel. Returning to his central theme in a subsequent book, *The American Spirit*, Straus noted "the Hebrew mortar that cemented the foundations of our American democracy." The United States, he reiterated, is "peculiarly a promised land wherein the spirit of the teachings of the ancient prophets inspired the work of the fathers of our country." So he could confidently conclude that "the American spirit and the spirit of American Judaism were nurtured in the same cradle of liberty, and were united in origins, in ideals, and in historical development."[25] History clearly demonstrated to Straus that Jews were good Americans.

Straus was one of the first Jews to define the terms of convergence between the Jewish and American traditions. What remains of value in his effort is not its historical veracity but the claim itself, which has reverberated through a century of American history since Straus enunciated it. Resting upon a biblical idiom, it unquestioningly absorbed the Puritan self-identification with Israel without any recognition of the Christian triumphalist assumptions that framed it. The Puritan link enabled Straus to connect Israel and America to a common democratic tradition whose origins could be found in the Hebrew Bible. In a fascinating two-step process of identity formation, the Puritans affirmed their divine chosenness through Israel; then Jews affirmed themselves as Americans by reiterating the Puritan identification with the Hebrew biblical tradition. In that way, American Jews could not only demonstrate the inherent unity of the Jewish and America traditions but also claim the Puritans as "their" spiritual forbears. So American Jews became the last Puritans; the last Americans, that is, to take seriously the claim that the United States truly was the fulfillment of divine promise to Israel.

The myth of American biblical origins, woven by devout Protestants to substantiate their claims of providential blessing as the new Israel, ultimately found its most enthusiastic champions among Jews yearning to be recognized as Americans. During the year that Straus's book was published, Rabbi Kaufmann Kohler, the intellectual leader of Reform Judaism, concluded a series of lectures, on July 4th, by describing the United States as "the land where milk and honey flow for all." Rather than lament the destruction of the ancient Temple (as observant Jews would do on the approaching fast day of Tisha B'Av), Jews could fulfill their messianic yearnings in "the Holy Land of Freedom and Human Rights." Kohler heard "in the jubilant tocsin peals of American liberty the mighty resonance of Sinai's thunder." Divine revelation had become the precursor of American patriotism.[26]

American ceremonial occasions provided recurrent opportunities for Jews to demonstrate the compatibility—indeed, unity—of the Jewish and American traditions. David Philipson, a member of the first graduating class of the Hebrew Union College and a nationally prominent Reform rabbi, delivered a Thanksgiving sermon in 1888 in which he proclaimed: "Israel's religion has gained a new foothold in a greater Zion, where the words of its prophets are finding their exemplification." Philipson long retained memories of his own visit to Plymouth where, discovering Hebrew words inscribed on the gravestone of Governor William Bradford, he identified with the very source of American civilization. Several decades later, at a celebration of the three hundredth anniversary of the Pilgrim landing, Philipson described the Pilgrims as "devout and earnest students of Israel's inspired chronicles," who had established "a home of religious freedom . . . for the latter-day children of Israel, outcasts and pariahs in every European land." In that striking demonstration of "poetic historical justice," the Pilgrims thereby repaid their debt to biblical Israel—and, it might be added, Jews repaid their debt to the United States.[27]

Ever since the late nineteenth century, the identification of Judaism with Americanism has depended upon the Hebrew Bible as the source of their compatibility. This has aptly been described as a manifestation of "American Jewish apologetics," designed to justify Jewish legitimacy in American terms (which, earlier, had derived *their* legitimacy from Hebrew texts). Reform Jews were the first, but hardly the last, American Jews who "appropriated for themselves the American national myth of the Republic as the new Zion or Israel." But the biblical heritage, with special emphasis upon the writings of the Hebrew prophets, quickly overspread the Reform movement, inspiring successive generations of American Jews to rephrase Jewish tradition in modern American terms. In the process, the Hebrew Bible came to serve Jews who were least responsive to the claims of biblical authority.[28]

For Jewish radicals, who strayed the farthest from religious tradition, "socialism was Judaism secularized." The fondness of Jewish socialists for biblical allusions might be taken as an indication of their commitment to Jewish tradition. As early as 1883, the poet Emma Lazarus (in her essay on "the Jewish Problem") insisted that socialism was rooted in provisions of Mosaic law that protected the rights of workers, assured a harvest portion to the needy, and restrained the property rights of landlords. Examples abound of Jewish socialists who cited the Bible, especially the prophetic writings, to support their denunciation of class exploitation. "For almost everything I write," a Jewish radical declared, "I have to thank that poet-preacher (Isaiah) who entered my heart and mind with love for . . . oppressed people." "Each era has its own Torah," wrote a socialist poet at the end of the nineteenth century; "Ours is one of freedom and justice." Biblical references aside, the vastly disproportionate number of Jewish socialists in the American (as in the European) movement around the turn of the century seems to suggest a special affinity between Jewish tradition and socialist consciousness.[29]

Did the politics of Jewish socialists truly express deeply rooted traditional Jewish values? Was socialist messianism an adult expression of a youthful immersion in Torah and Talmud, demonstrating attachment to the values of righteousness and justice that may be found there? If so, American Jewish socialists can best be understood, one historian suggests, as "a prophetic minority, responding to biblical norms of social justice, interpreted in a modern context." To be sure, the rhetoric of Jewish socialists often incorporated prophetic and messianic themes. References to the "holy duty" and "sacred struggle" against "sinful" capitalism surely resonated with religious content. Jewish socialists who used such traditional allusions wished, however, to make an altogether different point. David Edelstadt, the Yiddish poet whose Torah was freedom and justice, referred to the "new prophets" who will "deliver us from exile." But he had in mind Karl Marx and Ferdinand Lassalle, not Amos and Isaiah. And Morris Winchevsky, who declared his debt to Isaiah, recalled that his "greatest pleasure" was "proving that Moses did not write the Torah." Benjamin Feigenbaum, a leader among Lower East Side socialists, insisted that "the narrow 'Jewish spirit' has not produced any value that could not have been created—and created better—by the universal human spirit." To Feigenbaum, the greatest blessing, especially for Jews, was assimilation.[30]

Despite the abundant references to Hebrew prophets by Jewish socialists, socialism was a political expression of Jewish renunciation. The prophets of socialism, Marx and Lassalle, had shown the way. Marx, notwithstanding the venerable tradition of rabbinical learning that distinguished his family history (preceding his father's conversion and his own baptism), was explicitly and maliciously hostile to Judaism. Whether Marx was a self-hating Jew or an anti-Semite is an inconsequential distinction. His notorious accusation—"Money is the jealous God of Israel"—and his yearning for "the emancipation of humanity from Judaism" speak for themselves. Lassalle, as a young man, took pride in Jewish religious culture, was attached to Reform, and identified with the struggle of the Maccabees for national independence. But once he rejected Judaism, Judeophobia burst forth as it did for Marx. Judaism, Lassalle wrote, represented "perfect ugliness" as an obsolescent, detestable faith which must be transcended. Lassalle saw in the Jewish people "nothing but the degenerate sons of a great, but long past epoch." For these radical prophets, socialism was less an expression of Judaism than an expression of its denial, pointing toward the ultimate disappearance of Judaism in socialist universalism. That prospect generated vastly more pleasure than sorrow among Jews who heeded their socialist prophets.[31]

For all of its passion for justice, prophetic rhetoric, and messianism, socialism—except for its Labor Zionist variety—offered an alternative to a Jewish identity, an exit from Judaism rather than any modern restatement of ancient Jewish values. Perhaps the biblical idiom expressed a lingering, if tenuous, attachment to Judaism. But socialists, like Reform Jews with whom they otherwise shared nothing in common, used traditional Hebrew sources to break with Jewish tradition. They extracted from the legacy of biblical Israel what they needed to forge a modern identity.

Socialism had widespread appeal among new Jewish immigrants from Eastern Europe, but it was too foreign and shrill to appeal to acculturated German Jews. Their Reform, however, was too thoroughly Protestantized to appeal to the immigrants. Neither an upper-class religion, nor lower-class radicalism, could bridge the vast gulf between old and new immigrants. The reconciliation of Judaism with Americanism depended upon a different kind of synthesis, one that was insufficiently religious to offend the secular majority, but sufficiently American to attract the immigrant newcomers, whose growing numbers were rapidly transforming the demography of American Jewry.

Between 1906 and 1916 that new synthesis emerged as the formative statement of modern American Judaism. Articulated most persuasively by two lawyers, Louis Marshall and Louis Brandeis, it drew upon the centrality of law and justice in the Jewish and American traditions. During that prewar decade, lawyers challenged rabbis as the undisputed public leaders of the American Jewish community. Their professional success, largely as counselors to wealthy and powerful corporate institutions, enabled them to ascend to influence in Jewish communal affairs. The identification of Judaism with Americanism, within a common tradition that emphasized the rule of law and the quest for social justice, was their singular contribution to the self-definition of American Jewry in the twentieth century.

Marshall's forum was the American Jewish Committee, organized in 1906 "to prevent infringement of the civil and religious rights of Jews." Galvanized by czarist pogroms, which cost tens of thousands of Jews their lives and property, the committee was a self-appointed elite of German Jews—predominantly lawyers and businessmen, with some Reform rabbis. Although they wrangled incessantly about how democratic an organization they wished to create, their decision to emphasize civil and religious rights demonstrated their unequivocal commitment to the language of American constitutionalism. That was Marshall's preferred emphasis. A distinguished New York corporate and constitutional lawyer, his Judaism was a religion only, without political or national content. He demanded of Jews unequivocal submission to the legal authority of the state, for respect for law demonstrated one of the abiding virtues of the Jewish people. The American Jewish Committee propelled Marshall to a pivotal position of communal leadership: no one was better able to define and defend Jewish interests within the framework of American patriotic and constitutional values. During more than two decades of his leadership, "Marshall law" governed American Jewish life.[32]

It was Brandeis, however, who forged the most popular synthesis of Judaism to Americanism, through the seventeenth-century New England experience. Brandeis, like so many other German Jews (including Marshall), was deeply concerned about the patriotic allegiance of the new Jewish immigrants. It was virtually the only substantive Jewish issue, before 1914, that elicited public comment from him. By then, Brandeis had earned a glowing national reputation as a progressive reformer (and a considerable private fortune as counsel to corporations). A prominent lawyer and an outspoken liberal, a successful American Jew without any evident familiarity with Jewish tradition, ritual, or texts, he was ideally situated to synthesize Judaism and Americanism.

By 1914, Brandeis, the new leader of American Zionism, had become convinced that the "twentieth century ideals of America had been the age-old ideals of the Jews." No longer questioning the loyalty of immigrant Jews, he embraced the proposition that "there is no inconsistency between loyalty to America and loyalty to Jewry. The Jewish spirit . . . is essentially modern and essentially American." Jews had given to the world "reverence for law and highest conceptions of morality." The prophetic teachings of "brotherhood and righteousness," filtered through seventeenth-century New England (the Puritans, Brandeis believed, were finely honed to their task "by constant study of the prophets"), had become the modern liberal ideals of democracy and social justice. In a circuitous historical and conceptual journey, from prophecy through Puritanism, ancient Jewish ideals had become thoroughly Americanized.[33] Brandeis's appointment to the Supreme Court personified this synthesis. It was not merely that he was the first Jew to serve on the high court. For the first time in American history, a Jew was empowered to determine the final meaning of the American Constitution. The synthesis between Americanism and Judaism, between the biblical heritage of Torah and the American rule of law, had been forged.

Ever since Marshall and Brandeis formulated the compatibility of Judaism and American constitutionalism, rabbis, lawyers, and scholars have offered many variations on the theme. By now, it is virtually impossible for American Jews to understand themselves without locating the origins of American constitutionalism in the Hebrew Bible. This ingenious example of "social memory," with legitimacy defined by an imagined historical model, has taken on a life of its own—the ultimate testimony to its persuasive authority. The Constitution, as the reformulation of biblical ideas in an American idiom, became (even for Jews) the new testament of American democracy.[34] The compatibility theme has become especially audible during wartime crises, when affirmations of patriotism were required, and on national celebratory occasions, to reaffirm Jewish identification with American values.

During World War I, for example, Rabbi Kaufmann Kohler proclaimed the continuity between Hebraic and American democratic ideals. Democracy, he declared, "found its classical expression in Israel's holy writings," where law was proclaimed as "the eternal source of liberty." The synthesis of liberty and law had come to fruition in America, where the Founding Fathers (as spiritual descendants of the Puritans) "took the heroes of ancient Israel as their models for the championship of liberty and democracy, framing their constitution on the principles underlying the Law of Sinai." In a single sentence, Kohler braided liberty, democracy, and law into a strand that connected the divine revelation at Sinai to the principles of American constitutionalism.[35]

Twenty years later, the conjunction of the celebration of the one hundred and fiftieth anniversary of constitutional ratification with the impending crisis of another war, encouraged reaffirmation of the biblical origins of American democracy. "Hebrew learning," it was asserted, had come to America "on the Mayflower." Puritanism and Judaism "spoke the same spiritual language." So the Puritans' "intense, liberal, wholehearted acceptance of the Biblical laws" was transformed into the "sound political maxims" of the new nation, while "Hebraic law and legislation" was the foundation of American constitutionalism. In this way, "the Hebraic and biblical tradition," nourished in Massachusetts Bay in the seventeenth century and in the thirteen colonies during the revolutionary era, was the continuing inspiration for "American ideals and institutions" that must be protected against fascist challenge.[36]

After the Second World War, Jews across the denominational spectrum affirmed the compatibility of the American and Jewish traditions. A Reform rabbi described American revolutionaries as the "heirs of the Prophets"; the Declaration of Independence "had the ring of Prophetic conviction" in its emphasis upon liberty and morality; while the Founding Fathers (concededly the children of the Enlightenment) were inspired by the God of Israel. The president of the Orthodox Yeshiva University denied any "serious conflict between our spiritual heritage and the American way of life, which is itself rooted in Hebraic spiritual values." American Jewish scholarship echoed their pronouncements. One excursion into political theory demonstrated the compatibility of Judaism with the American "democratic ideal." The constitution of ancient Israel was the Torah, under which rulers and citizens alike were "equally bound by the law." The fundamental principles of American political theory—especially "republican government within a democratic context"—were "directly related to the great moral values of Jewish tradition and, indeed, are taken predominantly from that tradition as it is expressed in the Bible."[37]

Scholarly affirmation climaxed in a crescendo of enthusiasm during the bicentennials of the sacred texts of American liberty and law, the Declaration of Independence and the Constitution. Scholars repeatedly cited the affinities of two "Bible-rooted" cultures, noting the pervasive biblical imagery that had molded American democratic consciousness since the earliest Puritan settlements. The ancient Israelite experience of slavery and freedom, culminating in efforts "to build the good commonwealth," was taken as a paradigm for the development of "free American institutions." Americans and Jews shared "strikingly interesting historical affinities." Each people had experienced, at its national birth, "an unsurpassed moment of spiritual exaltation, which found embodiment in treasured and revered written documents." The Ten Commandments and the Declaration of Independence recorded "divinely inspired communications," when "ethical principles, and codes of law which presumably embodied them, were formally adopted." American democracy, "rooted in Judaism," implemented "the laws of justice and the principles of righteousness enunciated in the Torah."[38]

Scattered through the literature of celebration was an occasional hint of uneasiness, a suggestion that, beneath surface affirmations of unity, American Jews might still experience some dissonance as Americans and Jews. One author expressed his discomfort with the idea that American Jews might be culturally schizophrenic, torn between "different and competing" worlds. Nothing in the Declaration of Independence or the Constitution, he insisted, "makes it impossible" to be an observant Jew in America—a revealing denial at a time when the contrary proposition was rarely affirmed. A legal scholar, returning to a subject he had begun to develop more than twenty-five years earlier, reiterated "the intertwining relationship of Judaism and the American Idea"—inalienable rights, equality, democracy, and "the law of justice." As a self-described "Hellenistic Jew," searching for a unified American Jewish tradition, he found it in his discovery that "The spirit, the inner values, the energies of democracy are right at the very heart of Judaism."[39]

The Constitutional bicentennial, a decade later, provided an unprecedented opportunity for Jews to affirm the fulfillment of Jewish values in American constitutionalism. Legal scholar Milton Konvitz reiterated "the confluence of Torah and Constitution," a theme that had preoccupied him throughout his career. Together, he had written earlier, they expressed "the ideal of life under law"; the movement "from biblical covenant . . . to constitution," he now wrote, was the American expression of biblical themes. Political scientist Daniel Elazar (who, appropriately, held academic appointments in the United States and Israel) found a "strong commitment to constitutionalism and the rule of law" at the core of Jewish political consciousness. The Jewish political tradition, he wrote, combined federal and republican values "with strong democratic overtones." Constitutionalism was "central to the study of Jewish political history." Jewish history, for Elazar, was "constitutional history," with the Torah as the "foremost constitutional document" of Judaism. With that reading of Jewish history, the biblical origins of American institutions had all but been inverted into the American sources of biblical norms. No one articulated such patriotic piety, masked in Jewish symbols, more insistently than journalist Anthony Lewis (the son of a family of Jewish immigrants named Oshinsky). Lewis, long a devout worshipper at the shrines of American constitutionalism (especially the Supreme Court and Harvard Law School), climaxed his reverence with a celebration of American law and constitutionalism as "our rock and our redeemer"—terms that can refer, in Jewish liturgy, only to God.[40]

Undergirding the discoveries of a unitary tradition were unabashed expressions of Jewish gratitude for American constitutional blessings. American Jews could find comfort in "the fact that the civilizations share several basic tenets, and that they have borrowed freely from each others." Jews were "overwhelmingly proud and grateful" for the opportunity to participate in "such a majestic and unique experiment in freedom and governance." Jewish gratitude was understandable, for under the Constitution "we have achieved more freedom and more justice than any other country in our history"—including, presumably, the Jewish State of Israel. (American Jews have taken great pains to demonstrate that *their* country, not Israel, is the true legatee of the biblical heritage, precisely as seventeenth-century Puritans had insisted.) With the Constitution duly proclaimed as "another Sinaitic covenant," American Jews could embrace it as the appropriate statement of their undiminished covenantal faith.[41]

The euphoric celebration of the rule of American constitutional law, which climaxed in 1987, should not obliterate the fact that it was never law alone, but law as an instrument of justice, that ostensibly bound the Jewish and American traditions. Justice was a recurrent theme in the American Jewish discourse of compatibility. It was a necessary insertion, for it enabled Jews to submerge "arid" legalism, the part of their tradition with which modern Jews felt least comfortable, in the resounding call of the ancient Hebrew prophets for social justice and moral righteousness. Justice was described as "the golden thread" that Judaism stitched into the fabric of American democracy. A "passion for justice" was part of the "unconscious inheritance" that Jews brought to this country. In the United States they transformed "the quest for social justice" into the truest expression of "Jewish orthodoxy." Jewish "cultural and theological values," which make it "unJewish not to be preoccupied with freedom and justice for everyone," explained the enduring liberal commitments of American Jews.

The social activism of American Jewish lawyers, so conspicuous in liberal causes throughout the twentieth century, was interpreted as a particularly vivid expression of fidelity to the Jewish tradition of justice within a legal order. From Brandeis on, Jewish lawyers had demonstrated a "messianic fervor" which securely attached them to "the Prophetic Tradition." Their "dynamic view of law," reinforced by their "Talmudic style of inquiry," located them within "a jurisprudential tradition" that is "peculiarly American, but still peculiarly Jewish." The literary personification of this hypothesis is Jacob Ascher, the defense lawyer in E. L. Doctorow's *The Book of Daniel*, who struggles valiantly to save the lives of his clients (modeled after the convicted atomic spies Julius and Ethel Rosenberg). Ascher "was said to have worked for years on a still unfinished book demonstrating the contributions of the Old Testament to American law." As the very model of a liberal Jewish lawyer, who "perceived in the law a codification of the religious sense of life," he "could wear a homburg and a tallis at the same time."[42]

As American Jews devised the terms of their integration into American society, Torah and Constitution, prophecy and liberalism, were fused into a single unified tradition. The momentous transformation from the sacred law of Torah and rabbinical legal authority to the constitutional jurisprudence of Brandeis, Benjamin Cardozo, and Felix Frankfurter seemed uncomplicated and inevitable.[43] But beneath the miraculous congruence of Torah and Constitution lies the story of American law as an instrument of Jewish acculturation.

Until the end of the eighteenth century in Western Europe (and much later elsewhere), Jews were tightly enclosed in their language, calendar, ritual, and history. They belonged to island communities that were easily distinguished from the surrounding majority culture. Jews were bound by their shared isolation and especially by the rhythms and rituals that transformed their ancient heritage into a living presence. Judaism defined a people, not merely a religion. It offered an inclusive, coherent way of life that seemed impervious to change.

Yet Jews were hardly inexperienced in the process of cultural adaptation. Ever since Joshua led them into the promised land, they had grafted elements of alien social systems to their own tradition, always struggling to define the permissible boundaries between autonomy and accommodation. Some of the most vivid episodes in Jewish antiquity, from the revolt of the Maccabees against Hellenism to the martyrdom of Rabbi Akiba for teaching Torah over Roman objections, expressed precisely this dilemma.

In dispersion, as a tiny minority everywhere, Jews could not fail to absorb from the surrounding cultures. So their ceremonial objects displayed the architectural history of their host nations, whose styles—from the delicate minarets of the East to the elaborate gothic of the West—they adapted for their own ritual use. Yiddish, the vernacular of Eastern European Jews, reflected the spoken German that surrounded them. For many centuries, a Talmudic axiom—*dina d'malkhuta dina* (the law of the state is the law)—preserved the delicate balance between Jewish juridical autonomy and state legal authority.

The terms of Jewish accommodation always demanded a tenacious commitment to the past. No matter how creatively Jews adapted to their Christian or Moslem environments, the ultimate boundaries of identification could not be transgressed, except by conversion. Jewish life—by any standard of measurement—was profoundly conservative. It was constantly reinforced (and renewed) by the authority of tradition, activated through prayer and ritual, the sanctity of ancient texts, the power of collective memory, the voice of divine command, and the structure of communal life. Ultimately, of course, the rule of Torah, the law of divine revelation contained in the five books of Moses and shaped by two millennia of rabbinical interpretation, not only defined the Jewish people but also, as their "tree of life," sustained them.

The entry of Western Jews into modernity, in response to the enticements of emancipation, left Jews uneasily suspended between old attachments and new attractions. Suddenly free (or perhaps newly obligated) to define Judaism (and themselves), they began the continuing struggle to reconcile a traditional identity with modern opportunity. By the very terms of emancipation, Jews stood alone as free individuals. Their newly won status provided an exquisite mixture of opportunity and vulnerability. Free of traditional constraints, they were simultaneously estranged from the sustenance that only tradition could provide.

The emancipated Jew has been compared to the child of quarreling parents: "He loves both, yet allegiance to one often means, or appears to mean, disloyalty, if not actual treason, to the other." Whether this is labeled "biculturality" or, more sharply, "social schizophrenia" is a matter of personal preference. But the phenomenon itself has been so amply (and poignantly) documented that the history of modern Jewry can hardly be written without acknowledgment of its power or persistence. In the United States, which surely came closer to fulfilling emancipation ideals than any other Western nation, Jews encountered a unique opportunity to participate actively and equally in society. Accordingly, they confronted a special set of dangers, for the very opportunities of integration into American life threatened Jewish survival—not, of course, with active hostility, but with benign absorption. The principles of civil equality and religious toleration enabled Jews to become Americans and permitted them to remain Jewish. But "talk to any thoughtful Jew," it has been suggested, "and back of his earnest soul searching you will encounter the question, what am I essentially—a Jew or an American?"[44] Even the confident assertion, American Jew, has yet to put the question to rest.

For precisely this reason, efforts to overcome the hazards of duality, by connecting a modern American identity to an ancient Jewish tradition, are so integral to American Jewish history. The search for compatibility between Judaism and Americanism can best be understood as the quest by Jews for the internal unity that emancipation shattered, for a measure of coherence between past and present, for an indisputable identification with their chosen American homeland. How tempting to assume that the Hebrew Bible was a preliminary draft of the American Constitution, that the Hebrew prophets were the founding fathers of American liberalism. In this way Jews could continually reassure themselves of the harmony of Jewish and American values.

For Jews who so preferred, and many did, the identification with American law and justice could even provide an escape from Judaism. Among Jews, it has been suggested, "one way of hiding is to choose a universal mask"; as defenders of the American rule of law, and as champions of social justice, Jews located themselves securely within the prevailing liberal precepts of modern America. In the United States, as in other modern Western nations with small Jewish minorities, liberalism came to define Jewish self-interest; law and justice were the universal norms that defined Jewish particularism.[45]

The discovery (or invention) of a unitary Judeo-American tradition of law and justice has enabled Jews to feel genuinely American. But as confidently, and frequently, as Jews assert that Jewish tradition is the source of their American values, the claim deserves careful scrutiny. Can it really be that the values of an ancient Middle Eastern tribal culture have been miraculously revived, three thousand years later, in the United States? Did the national religion of ancient Israel, through some mysterious process of historical alchemy, truly find expression in a modern secular state? How did a covenant binding God and Israel culminate, with evolutionary inevitability, in the American Constitution? Do the urgent cries of the Hebrew prophets truly resonate in the liberal politics of modern American Jews? Did American Jews (like the Pilgrims and Puritans before them) discover the biblical sources of American values? Or have Jews invented a past to suit their needs as Americans, forging an attachment to ancient Israel that ultimately reveals itself as a Christianized rendition of Jewish decline and fall?

If, as these questions imply, the biblical compatibility hypothesis may be largely mythological, it is nonetheless significant for that. It has enabled a tiny Jewish minority to find Zion in America. But it expresses the erosion, not the persistence, of Jewish tradition in the modern era. It reflects the loss of historical memory, not vivid historical recall. It emphasizes the severe, and continuing, Jewish identity dilemmas that emancipation did not resolve, but created and still perpetuates.

American Jews, like the Pilgrims and Puritans who preceded them, found the path to a distinctively American identity by yoking the Bible to American national destiny. The Jewish identification of American values with their own sacred texts continued a process of cultural interpretation that began with John Winthrop on board the *Arbella*. Originating in Christian piety, in Puritan efforts to locate their American errand within a divine plan for Christian redemption, it was revived by Jews who were determined to demonstrate their undivided allegiance to their new homeland. Borrowing the biblical metaphors that had already been grafted to the American national experience, they unconsciously absorbed the Christian triumphalism that was deeply embedded in American history and society. Once Jews came to believe in the compatibility of Jewish tradition with American values, they had become Americans.

To grasp the enormity of that step into modernity, and the profound transformation of Judaism that it required, Jewish law and justice must be considered on their own terms. Only then can the vast disparities between biblical and constitutional concepts be appreciated. And only then does the role of American law in Jewish acculturation become apparent. But acculturation, it must be emphasized, is simultaneously a process of deculturation. In their journey through law to an American identity, Jews abandoned the oldest continuing legal culture in world history. By now, after a century of diligent effort, they have all but obliterated the traces of their journey. By celebrating a unitary tradition of covenant and constitution, American Jews perennially demonstrate how thoroughly American they have become.[46]

The Rule of Sacred Law

Any legal system, virtually by definition, resembles any other. Jewish law, even as sacred law, shares some obvious attributes with familiar secular legal systems of modernity. There is an authoritative rule of law, accompanied by fundamental written texts. Trained experts (whether rabbis or lawyers) struggle to reconcile the claims of tradition with the need for change. Conflict is resolved in designated institutions, according to recognized principles of legal reasoning and procedures of adjudication. There is persistent tension between fixed rules and flexible standards, between the literal reading and expansive interpretation of guiding principles. Judges know how to "find" and to "make" law, assuring stability but permitting change, honoring timeless values while respecting new claims. Functioning like the intricate parts of a fine old clock, these institutions, individuals, and procedures define and validate the norms of society and, above all, the authority of law itself. That perhaps defines the common component of every legal system: it asserts its own rule, the rule of law, as the fundamental principle of social order. Law justifies itself as the alternative to capricious whim or arbitrary power. Law defines legitimacy.

A proper legal order, according to the imaginative insight of Max Weber, emerged from a lengthy process of legal evolution, moving with Darwinian inexorability toward the self-contained, formal, rational legal systems that characterize the modern West. The evolutionary model defined for Weber the necessary transition from the revelation of a charismatic prophet (like Moses) to the rational authority of a legally and logically trained professional class (judges and lawyers). Progression from the "magic" and "irrationality" of "sacred traditions" to "deductive rigor" and "rational adjudication" was the decisive evolutionary step into modernity. Within Weber's conceptual scheme, therefore, Jewish law was an early casualty of the legal evolutionary process. It displayed the worst attributes of religious law, "a lifeless casuistry" in which "living and dead law were thoroughly intermixed, and no distinction was made between legal and ethical norms." Jewish law earned no significant place in Weber's sociology of law other than to demonstrate its evolutionary deficiencies.[1]

For Weber (descended from a line of distinguished Lutheran ministers), the Old Testament ethic, commanding "ritual correctitude," had condemned the Jews to segregation as a "pariah people." Unable to achieve "emancipation from the ritual prescriptions of the Torah," Judaism yielded to the superior truth of Christianity, which liberated itself from "the self-created ghetto" of the Hebrew Bible. Weber's Judaism, encrusted in ritual, was a fossilized artifact of legal *and* religious evolution, with its value restricted to illustrating the higher evolutionary forms of Christianity that superseded it.[2]

Modern understanding of law and religion (and the appropriate distinction between them) still rests upon Weber's categories. Weber's blend of scientific rationality and Christian theology encouraged him to disregard whatever failed to conform to "rationalization," his term for (Western and Christian) emancipation from "magic" and "ritual." His conception of a proper legal order is by now part of the self-legitimating ideology of the rule of law in modern Western society. His consignment of Judaism to the dustbin of religious history, memorable only for its incomplete development of what achieved pure expression in Christianity (especially during the Protestant Reformation), is no longer as self-evident as it was to the founding generation of Bible scholars a century ago. But Weber's impatience with the Jewish (or any other) sacred-law tradition is deeply embedded in the legal ideology of the modern West. An imaginative leap of some magnitude, across two centuries of enlightened thought and many centuries of Christian theology, is required to recapture the Jewish sacred-law tradition on its own distinctive terms. Not yet an obsolete fossil, it never was the first draft of a new testament, nor even (as American Jews have often claimed) the kernel of American constitutionalism.

The fundamental attributes of Jewish sacred law are embedded in the biblical narrative itself, not in any external statement of legal precepts. One episode is so fundamental that it not only forms the centerpiece of the biblical narrative structure but also is vicariously reenacted at periodic intervals of crisis thereafter: the convenantal moment at Sinai, the giving of the Torah, which marks the creation of the Jewish people and defines its relationship to God. That primal experience, subsequently renewed in covenantal ceremonies initiated by Moses, Joshua, Josiah, and Ezra, remains a perpetual reminder to Israel, to the Jewish people, that their law is the law of divine revelation binding them in an intimate relationship with God.

We learn that in the third month after the exodus from Egypt, while the children of Israel camped at the base of Mt. Sinai, Moses ascended to receive the terms of the covenant from God. "If you will obey my voice," God instructed, "and keep my covenant, then you shall be my own treasure from among all peoples." Responding to the divine invitation, "all the people answered together, and said, All that the Lord has spoken we will do." Three days later, amid "thunders and lightnings" and the sounding of the shofar, Moses again ascended the mount, this time to receive not only the Ten Commandments but also the "judgments" (or legal principles of judgment) that Israel must obey. Once again, in virtually identical words, the people assented. Whereupon Moses transcribed "all the words of the Lord," prepared a sacrificial ceremony, and read "the book of covenant," the written code of "judgments," to them. For the third time, now with significantly added emphasis (perhaps suggesting a deeper commitment to faithful performance), the people affirmed: "All that the Lord has said will we do, and obey."³

A moment of such profound historical and theological significance in the consciousness of the Jewish people can be variously (and endlessly) interpreted. An American historian, familiar with the opening words of the preamble to the Constitution ("We the People"), might emphasize the principle of covenantal consent that seems common to both traditions. A lawyer surely would understand that without mutual agreement there could be no binding contract. A biblical scholar, noting that Israel, the special property or treasure (*segulah*) of the Lord, was assured protection and even land of its own in return for obedience, could find instructive parallels to ancient Hittite treaties between lords and vassals. Rabbinical legend, explaining why Israel was chosen to receive the Torah, suggests that God approached other peoples first—but the children of Esau, Ammon, Moab, and Ishmael all found specific prohibitions (regarding killing, adultery, and theft) objectionable. Only the children of Israel, God's fifth choice, promised to obey; freely consenting, they became the covenantal partner.

Yet the covenantal episode at Sinai is more ambiguous than a hasty consensual or contractual reading might suggest. (Even the rabbis hedged their bets.) To be sure, the children of Israel assented. But they acted in a setting so awesome, filled with thunder and lightning in the sky and smoke and fire on the quaking mountain, that fear surely was intermingled with, and perhaps even determined, their choice. They were frightened for good reason. They confronted, more directly than ever before (or since), the majestic and terrifying power of divine authority. It is little wonder that the people "trembled." When Moses recalled the episode, after nearly forty years of wandering, that fear figured prominently in his retelling. The people had shied away from "the voice of the living God," he reminded them, fearful of dying in "the great fire" of divine revelation. Instead, they had urged Moses to be their surrogate, to draw closer to God and to listen; anything he was told, they said with desperate anxiety, "we will hear it, and do it." God surely appreciated the power of fear to motivate. He reminded Moses that all would be well for Israel if "they would fear me, and keep all my commandments always." Fear and obedience became virtually inseparable. There was covenantal consent, to be sure, but what was the alternative? As if to compound the ambiguity of consent, another rabbinical legend recounts that God had already lifted Mt. Sinai and threatened to drop it on the Israelites if they did not accept the covenant![4]

Although God and Israel exchanged mutual promises at Sinai, obedience was endlessly problematic. No sooner had Moses ascended to receive the Torah than the children of Israel, disregarding their pledge, built and worshipped the Golden Calf. Their subsequent journey through the Sinai wilderness was filled with "murmerings" that expressed the difficulties of reconciling freedom from Egyptian servitude with covenantal obligations. Moses was even forced to secure divine assistance to suppress the rebellion of Korah, whose democratic challenge, resting ultimately upon the claim that law is unnecessary when holiness resides in all the people, was summarily rejected: the earth opened to devour his followers. It was made brutally clear that such antinomian challenges, even if they rested upon democratic principles, were incompatible with the exercise of divine legal authority.[5]

Shortly before Moses died, he reminded the people one last time of their covenantal obligations. He instructed them that every seventh year, during the festival of Succoth that commemorated their wilderness experience, all Israel must assemble to hear the reading of the Torah. "Gather the people together, men, and women, and children, and thy stranger that is within thy gates, that they may hear, and that they may learn, and fear the Lord your God, and observe to do all the words of this Torah." The verbs proclaim a succession of interrelated commands: gather, hear, learn, fear, do. The people must assemble; they must listen so that they may comprehend; and they must act. Obedience to divine command, we learn, is anything but a passive process. But why the repetitive ceremonial readings? In part, perhaps (as Moses knew better than anyone), because the tendency to backslide was a rather conspicuous, if altogether human, attribute of the children of Israel. Here was an institutionalized reminder of their assumption of covenantal obligation. Beyond that, surely, was an appreciation that covenantal reaffirmation was simultaneously an instrument of instruction, teaching the substance of Torah (its commandments, statutes, and judgments) while asserting the vital principle of fulfillment through learning and doing. The very word "torah" conveys precisely this duality: it means not only law but also instruction. The covenant renewal ceremony was designed to teach the sacred law and to affirm its binding authority.[6]

Whether or not this was performed every seventh year is unclear. But the Bible does recount several virtually identical covenant renewal episodes at critical moments in the national life of Israel: when Joshua, the last of the desert leaders, transmitted the Sinaitic legacy; again when King Josiah reconstructed his kingdom around the Deuteronomic text and the Jerusalem Temple; and finally when Ezra led the return from Babylonian exile. They provide dramatic illustration that in times of dire emergency, when national life hung in the balance, reconstruction demanded that all Israel gather together to hear, to learn, to fear, and to do—in the biblical phrase, "to walk with God" in obedience to the Torah.[7]

Two historical disasters prompted ceremonies of covenant renewal, which framed momentous attempts to restore national unity and purpose. With the Assyrian and Babylonian conquests, followed by the humiliation of exile (586 B.C.E.), the kingdom of David and Solomon was conquered; the institutions that sustained national life were disrupted; the Temple was destroyed; the people were forcibly removed from their land. Yet these successive tragedies inspired astonishing legal innovations, which enabled the law of divine revelation to remain the core of the national religious life. By the time that Ezra led the Israelites back to Jerusalem from Babylonian exile, Judaism came to depend upon a written Torah, closed into final canonical form, as "a book in which the word of God is fixed and becomes binding on the people." The Torah was the undisputed source that enabled Jews "to know and keep the law of God." Within two formative centuries, framed by political catastrophe and legal creativity, the covenantal principles of Judaism had been reworked into a single text, presented "as one integrated teaching from one specific historical moment," the revelation at Sinai. Its "telling and retelling was a new basis for cultural memory," a memory that endures within Judaism to this day.[8]

The process of covenantal reformation began a century after the destruction of the Northern kingdom of Israel (722 B.C.E.), leaving the tiny kingdom of Judah as all that remained of the vast Davidic empire. The Temple in Jerusalem required extensive repairs, surely a hint of spiritual no less than physical decay. The work of Temple restoration was ordered by King Josiah, determined to invigorate and purify the national religious life of the people. During the renovations, according to the narrative of the Chronicler, Hilqiyyahu the priest discovered "a book of the Torah of the Lord" hidden in the Temple. A scribe carried it back to the king and read it to him. When Josiah heard its contents, "he rent his clothes" in anguish, for he immediately understood how "great is the wrath of the Lord that is poured out upon us, because our fathers have not kept the word of the Lord, to do according to all that is written in this book."[9]

King Josiah hurried to the Temple. Before all the inhabitants of Jerusalem, priests and people, old and young alike, he read "all the words of the book of the covenant that was found in the house of the Lord." Then he covenanted with God, "with all his heart, and with all his soul," to obey the commandments and "to perform the words of the covenant which are written in this book." The people also responded "according to the covenant of God, the God of their fathers." Josiah's affirmation of the covenant in a public ceremony had extraordinary significance for the history of ancient Israel— and modern Judaism. Covenantal renewal, to be sure, was already a familiar expression of loyalty to God and to the sacred law. But the role of a book transformed the ceremony into something altogether unprecedented. Thereafter, Judaism was to be forever defined by the book of law, the Torah.

The book discovered in the Temple in 621 B.C.E., in all likelihood, was Deuteronomy. How it got there remains an unsolved mystery. Perhaps it came from the Northern Kingdom, carried by prophetic disciples who had fled south a century earlier to escape the Assyrians. Since their program focused on Jerusalem as the cultic and political center of a revitalized national community, the Temple was an appropriate location for concealing their book of writings until the propitious moment when national restoration could begin. Its "discovery" provided the opportunity for Josiah to complete the work of restoration. Reviving ancient traditions, he transformed and transmitted them as the written Torah. The book of Deuteronomy gathered the scattered ancient traditions into a single written source, serving as the authoritative statement of divine command that governed Jewish life. All Israel, including kings and prophets, were subjected to its authority, for it declared itself to be the fixed and final statement of divine law: "Every matter which I command you, observe to do it," it records Moses enjoining the people; "thou shalt not add thereto, nor diminish from it."[10]

Historical calamity required the reassertion of ancient covenantal ideals, not the articulation of new principles. Israel was admonished to "love the Lord thy God," to "walk in his ways," and to "keep his commandments." Law, justice, and cultic ritual were inseparable. Indeed, the centralization of worship in the Jerusalem Temple, and the judicial function of the priesthood, were integral to Deuteronomic religious and legal reform. "The priests and Levites" were empowered to resolve difficult cases in "the place which the Lord thy God shall choose." Decisions of the priestly judges were to be obeyed: "according to the sentence of the Torah which they shall teach thee, and according to the judgment which they shall tell thee, thou shalt do."[11] The commandments and statutes, declared the text, defined what was "right and good" in the eyes of God. Josiah's ceremony of covenant renewal, centered around this text, may have been "the first attempt to make the Torah the law of the land" in Israel. As the supreme law of divine revelation, the Torah had become the foundation of Jewish national and religious life.[12]

Yet in less than half a century, despite the reforms of Josiah, the kingdom of Judah was conquered, the Temple was in ruins, and the people were exiled to Babylon. There, as the Psalmist recorded so poignantly, they wondered desperately: "How shall we sing the Lord's song in a foreign land?" The answer, recorded in Lamentations (4:22), was to "renew our days as of old." Renewal took the form of synagogue worship, prayer, and instruction in Torah. Whether or not these practices were initiated in Babylon, or carried there, they functioned amid the disintegration of exile not only as an alternative to Temple worship but also as a vital instrument of national preservation—and, ultimately, national renewal.[13]

After the Persian conquest of Babylon, the king authorized Ezra the priest, "the scribe of the law of the God of heaven," to lead the return to Jerusalem. Ezra may even have brought with him, as "the law of thy God which is in thy hand," the entire Torah, redacted during exile in its final written form. At the very least, he had "prepared his heart to seek the Torah of the Lord, and to do it, and to teach in Israel statutes and judgments." But when he arrived in Jerusalem he found a ravaged city and an "unclean" land. The remaining Israelites had "not separated themselves from the peoples of the lands"; instead, they had worshipped foreign gods and intermarried with foreign peoples. Ezra was implored to renew the covenant with God, "according to the Torah."[14]

Ezra summoned "all the children of exile" to gather in Jerusalem within three days, under penalty of forfeiture of property and severance from the community if they absented themselves. They gathered in the open plaza of the Temple, "trembling because of this matter, and on account of the great rain" (perhaps a natural sign, like the biblical rainbow, of covenantal binding; perhaps a form of communal cleansing). Ezra declared their transgression, demanded confession, and insisted upon separation "from the peoples of the land." The community answered in unison: "As thou has said, so must we do." The people asked Ezra "to bring the book of the Torah of [Moses], which the Lord had commanded to Israel." When Ezra "opened the book in the sight of all the people," they spontaneously arose and he blessed God; the people answered "Amen," bowed their heads, and prayed. Levitical priests joined Ezra in explaining the law to the people: "they read in the book, in the Torah of God distinctly, . . . and caused them to understand the reading." For the entire Succoth holiday of seven days, "day by day, from the first day to the last day, [Ezra] read in the book of the Torah of God." On the concluding day of solemn assembly, the entire people entered into a covenant "to walk in the Torah of God," vowed obedience to the divine commandments, and concluded with the pledge not to "forsake the house of our God."[15]

What is so striking about this prolonged ceremonial ritual of covenant renewal is its enduring familiarity. Not only did it replicate the Sinaitic revelation and the earlier covenant renewals of Joshua and Josiah, but when Ezra opened the Torah in the presence of the community, initiating prayer, reading, and instruction, he performed a ritual that is reenacted to this day, every Sabbath and holy day, as the core of Jewish synagogue worship. With Ezra, the centrality of the legal text in the religious life of the Jewish people was secured. The written law was now "the decisive factor in the way the community understood itself and ordered its life." No less significantly, as the innovative exegetical role of Ezra and the priests suggests, divine revelation had become inseparable from the human interpretation of divine law.[16]

Although the covenant renewal of Ezra was the last such biblical episode, subsequent Jewish history offers persistent variations on the theme of restoration through law. Among the most dramatic, surely, was the Maccabean revolt three centuries later. Under the harsh rule of King Antiochus, the Temple was desecrated, Mosaic law revoked, and the worship of Gentile gods was coerced with swine sacrifice. Jerusalem was sacked, until "Her sanctuary became desolate as a wilderness, Her feasts were turned into mourning, Her sabbaths into shame." Jews who refused to "forget the Law," who observed the Sabbath and circumcised their sons, were condemned to death. There were those, however, referred to as "lawless men," who preferred to covenant with other nations rather than with God. At their instigation, in fact, Antiochus had granted authority to introduce "the customs of the Gentiles." Jewish Hellenizers participated (naked) in Greek games, removed their marks of circumcision, and worshipped foreign idols.

The rebellion against Antiochus was not only a bold demand for freedom from foreign domination, although it was surely that. Jewish assimilation, no less than Hellenistic coercion, incensed Mattathias, provoking his act of resistance that sparked the rebellion—a point that is usually overlooked in the glow of modern celebrations of Chanukah as the Jewish alternative to Christmas. When royal officials came to Modin to compel pagan sacrifice, Mattathias stood firmly on the bedrock of the ancient law. "I and my sons and my brethren walk in the covenant of our fathers. Heaven forbid that we should forsake the law." When a Jew nonetheless stepped forward to obey the royal command to worship, Mattathias's "zeal was kindled, and his heart quivered, and his indignation burst forth." Demonstrating his "zeal for the law," he killed the compliant Jew first and then the royal officer. Then he tore down the altar, calling out: "let everyone that is zealous for the Law and that would maintain the covenant come forth after me!" The rebellion against Antiochus had begun. So, too, had a Jewish civil war, fought between the "zealots for the Law" who followed the Maccabees and the "lawless men" who yearned for full integration into Hellenistic culture. From Antiochus the Maccabees demanded the freedom to observe the law; from Jews they demanded obedience to the law of divine command.[17]

If the obligation to obey divine command was clear, the meaning of divine command was anything but self-evident. During the desert wanderings, Moses had referred difficult issues directly to God for resolution. But once the Israelites reached their promised land, *they* bore responsibility for interpreting the word of God. The Torah itself offered certain guidelines: it called for judges to hold court in city gates (conspicuous places of public commerce and assembly); it instructed them to perform their task "with righteous judgment"; and it provided for difficult issues to be referred to the priests and "to the judge that shall be in those days"— *not* to God. But the historically decisive understanding of that crucial phrase came only after the Roman destruction of the Second Temple. In "those days" of national devastation, which again culminated in the loss of independence and exile, the very rule of sacred law was in doubt. In a momentous assertion of legal authority, rabbis—superseding priests, prophets, judges, and kings—became the law men of Judaism, the judges "that shall be in those days."[18] How did this remarkable transfer, or arrogation, of legal authority occur?

In 68 C.E., with Jerusalem under the terror of prolonged Roman siege, Rabbi Yohanan ben Zakkai implored the Jewish Zealots to end their futile resistance. Despairing of their obduracy, he finally instructed his disciples to remove him from the city. According to legend they carried him in a coffin, safely past the gatekeepers and beyond the city walls, to Vespasian, the Roman commander. To that officer's astonishment, ben Zakkai arose from his bier, proclaiming: *"Vive domine imperator."* Shortly thereafter, Vespasian learned (while bathing at Gophna) that with Nero's death he was indeed the new emperor. In appreciation of ben Zakkai's accurate prediction, he summoned the rabbi and asked for his wish. "I ask nothing of thee, . . . save Yavneh," ben Zakkai replied, "where I might go and teach my disciples, and there establish a prayer house, and perform all the commandments."[19]

There may be good reason to doubt the historical veracity of the episode. Perhaps the Romans (not the rabbi) chose the half-gentile coastal city of Yavneh, not for Torah instruction but to detain ben Zakkai. They were hardly prepared to authorize the establishment of a new national center there. Alternatively, the Romans merely may have granted the limited request of a prominent rabbinical compromiser, a pacifist who had warned the Zealots against the consequences of their continued resistance to Roman rule. There is no doubt, however, about the momentous consequences of ben Zakkai's relocation to Yavneh. There he gathered a number of prominent rabbis, founded an academy for Torah study, and gradually extended its functions to include judicial power, previously exercised by the Great Sanhedrin, or high court, in Jerusalem, the center of national and religious life.[20]

In the Yavneh academy, law was refashioned as the primary instrument of Jewish autonomy in the absence of national sovereignty. Ben Zakkai's reformulation of Judaism proved the key to Jewish survival during nineteen centuries of dispersion. Although Zion as a geographical place was not forgotten, the Torah became the "portable land" of the Jewish people, who carried its commands with them into exile. As the influence of the Yavneh academy spread, and as its legal authority as a *bet din* (rabbinical court) expanded into the diaspora communities, Jews learned how to sustain their faith "outside the land but not outside the Torah." Within a matter of decades after the destruction of the Second Temple, the study of Torah, and acceptance of its binding authority as law, gave Jewish life its form and substance for the next two thousand years. However ben Zakkai may be judged for his flight from Jerusalem (and his departure provides some ground for harsh judgment), his achievement at Yavneh was monumental. His creativity has aptly been described as "a deed equivalent to tying up the nation's vital nerve after it had been severed, or very nearly severed, so that it could continue not only to function, but even to develop." The survival of Judaism after the destruction of its national life and institutions remains "the most remarkable feature of Jewish history."[21]

The rabbis who gathered at Yavneh confronted the momentous task of reconstituting Jewish life without either a sovereign Jewish government or the Temple to sustain it. The loss of both, by 70 c.e., left an enormous void. As long as the Temple had stood, it served as the focal institution for religious and political life. Not only were the priests cultic officials; they were also political leaders and judicial authorities. The destruction of the Temple undermined the political base of the priesthood, enabling the Pharisaic party of rabbis to ascend to dominance. The Great Revolt against Rome had weakened, if not destroyed, their competitors. The Zealots, leaders of the revolt, were defeated and discredited; the Sadducees, their most dangerous rivals, were too closely identified with the priestly cult, which the destruction of the Temple obliterated; the Essenes, notably at Qumran, were isolated and remote; many Christian Jews seemed too ready to jettison the binding rule of law. Only the Pharisees, the rabbis who were prepared to make their peace with Rome to preserve the authority of the Torah, survived to devise the appropriate terms of legal autonomy amid the loss of national sovereignty.[22]

The Yavneh rabbinate, emulating the pattern of accommodation devised by Yohanan ben Zakkai, accepted foreign domination in return for the freedom to study and teach Torah. Ben Zakkai and his followers, willing to submit to the Romans *and* to God, guided Jews from the futile zeal of force to the enduring zeal of faith; in Jacob Neusner's apt phrase, "from politics to piety." The cultic community of the Jerusalem Temple and the Zealot fortress at Masada yielded to the learning community of the Yavneh academy, which taught that "the Torah remained the will of their unvanquished God, and that it remained their duty to obey him." Political revolt was doomed, so Jews wore the mask of political passivity as they pursued their religious activity. The shrewd rabbinical trade-off— political independence for religious piety—enabled Judaism to transcend its worst defeat.[23] In Jewish history, there were few acts of more momentous political consequence.

In the void left by the Temple destruction, national defeat, and exile, the rabbis were free to assert and consolidate their power. They stated their own interpretive authority with unambiguous clarity, positioning themselves directly in the line of succession that began at Sinai: "Moses received the Torah from Sinai and delivered it to Joshua, and Joshua to the Elders, and the Elders to the Prophets, and the Prophets delivered it to the men of the Great Synagogue"—who, in turn, passed it to the rabbis, the final link in the chain of human interpretation of divine revelation. Only the claims of prophecy, rendered all the more menacing by growing Christian reliance upon them, threatened their authority. But the rabbis quickly stifled the danger of prophetic challenges. Ruling that "no prophet may introduce something new from now on," they insisted (citing Leviticus 27:34): "these are the commandments." Interpretation was solely a rabbinical responsibility.[24]

A charming Talmudic story affirmed the historical fact. There was a rabbinical dispute over the cleanliness of an oven. Rabbi Eliezer, firmly believing it to be ritually pure, could not persuade his colleagues. "If the law agrees with me," he said, "let the stream of water prove it." The stream flowed backwards, but the other rabbis were not convinced. Rabbi Eliezer then declared: "If the law agrees with me, let the walls of the schoolhouse prove it." The walls leaned, but when Rabbi Joshua sharply rebuked them for interfering in a legal dispute, they did not fall. Rabbi Eliezer tried again: "If the law agrees with me, let it be proved in Heaven." A heavenly voice immediately cried out: "Why do you dispute with Rabbi Eliezer, seeing that in all matters the law agrees with him?" Again, Rabbi Joshua intervened, citing Deuteronomy (30:12): the Torah, he insisted, "is not in Heaven." What did he mean? The Torah, Rabbi Jeremiah explained, had already been given at Sinai; "therefore we pay no attention to a Heavenly Voice, because You [God] have long since written in the Torah at Mt. Sinai,

'One must follow the majority.'" Some time afterward, Rabbi Nathan asked Elijah the prophet how God had reacted. "He laughed with joy," Elijah replied, saying "My children have defeated Me."[25]

The Torah came *from* Heaven; but once given it no longer was *in* Heaven. With that principle secured, the judges "in those days"—the rabbis in every generation—became the authoritative interpreters of the law. If its language was fixed, its meaning was not. *Halakha*, the term for Jewish law, is related to the Hebrew verb meaning "to go," or "to walk." It is not a static image of self-evident legal command. Rather, it implies purposeful movement along the path that enables Jews to walk with God, a path that rabbinical interpretation defined. For "God Himself, in the act of revelation, handed the deciding authority to man," thereby demonstrating his wish that the children of Israel "live by his word in accordance with its own understanding."[26]

According to Jewish legend, even Moses the great lawgiver came to appreciate the virtues of the interpretive process. When he went to receive the Torah, he found God adding small strokes to its letters. Puzzled, he asked why. Because, God replied, after many generations a brilliant man, Rabbi Akiba, "will expound heaps and heaps of *halakhot* [legal principles] from each and every stroke." Moses asked if God would show him this extraordinary scholar. Suddenly, Moses found himself seated in Rabbi Akiva's academy. Unable to follow the subtleties of the discussion, he quickly became discouraged, to be comforted only when the great rabbi, telling a disciple the source of his teaching, said, "This is a ruling handed down by Moses from Sinai." Moses was reassured. The Torah was fixed, but the meaning of revelation emerged from human interpretation. Following the precedent that Moses himself had set, when by shattering the tablets he emphasized the power of the commandments, the rabbis not only interpreted the law but also were prepared to uproot biblical injunctions, even to dissolve a provision of the Torah, if overriding human need required it.[27]

Rabbis asserted their legal authority and expanded their power in a variety of ways. Rabban Gamliel II, ben Zakkai's successor, rode circuit to the local communities, instructing in matters of law and ritual and extending the range of rabbinical authority throughout Roman Palestine. Rabbinical control over setting the calendar bound diaspora communities to the new center of religious life in Yavneh, thereby extending rabbinical control over holy time. Resort to gentile courts was strictly prohibited. As the Yavneh academy steadily absorbed the liturgical authority formerly vested in the Temple priesthood, and the political and legal authority previously exercised by the Sanhedrin, the rabbinate steadily solidified its power as the authoritative governing institution within Judaism. Against the claim of the Christian Jews, who maintained that Jewish law was superseded because Israel had rejected the Messiah, ben Zakkai and his rabbinical disciples insisted all the more fervently that the old order endured, with the sacred law still at the center of Jewish national life.[28]

During the first centuries of the Common Era, there was considerable pressure for written consolidation. By then, the accumulated legal tradition was vast and diverse. For many centuries, perhaps dating back to Ezra's return from Babylon or even earlier, the Torah had been developed through *midrash*, or interpretation. The written Torah had been supplemented by discussions, interpolations, opinions, and decisions. Known as the Oral Torah, the supplementary commentary had provided interpretive flexibility; yet like the Torah itself, it was located in the Sinaitic revelation. But with the dangers posed by Roman political domination and Christian religious challenge, the very fluidity of the Oral Torah had become a liability.[29]

The decisions, principles, disagreements, and interpretations that comprised that oral legal tradition were gathered into the *Mishna* (meaning "study"). It functioned both as "a complementary legal code" to the Torah and as a stimulus to further study and exegesis. The process of compilation and restatement was carried out over centuries in Babylon and Palestine, until its final redaction in the Talmud. That marked the concluding stage in the reconstitution of Jewish law to render it suitable for a dispersed community deprived of political sovereignty. Under rabbinical direction, a process of oral teaching had evolved into the final canon of authoritative rulings; but the Talmud, like the Torah, was subject to continuing rabbinical interpretation.[30]

The Talmud signified the reformulation and reassertion of the sacred law as the basis of communal order. The very Talmudic passage that had placed the rabbis directly in the line of Mosaic succession also enjoined them to "be deliberate in judging and raise up many disciples and make a hedge for the Torah." The rabbis wove their authority into a virtually sovereign legal system, creating within that hedge a "sacred enclosure" for human contemplation of divine command. The multitude of rabbinic decisions that regulated the minutiae of life—diet, dress, family relations, commercial activity—were designed to apply divine precepts to mundane human relations, "thus to bring the whole of life into conformity with the will of God." The process of creative adaptation was perpetual, for according to rabbinic lore the Talmud—the process of interpretation of divine command—was never completed. Holiness through Talmud Torah (study of Torah) remained the source of Jewish communal cohesion for two thousand years. A community that failed to study Talmud, Adin Steinsaltz has written, "was condemned to attrition." The Torah could thereby fulfill itself as "a tree of life," deeply rooted in the past yet always capable of generating new growth.[31]

The emergence and consolidation of rabbinical legal authority culminated five centuries of creative legal development. From the discovery of the Deuteronomic text in the Temple during Josiah's reign, through the final redaction of the written Torah under Ezra, to Rabbi Yohanan ben Zakkai's innovations in the Yavneh academy, the sacred law was radically transformed. No new divine revelation, or prophetic mediation, would determine its content. There was a fixed written canonical text, with interpretive authority vested in rabbinical hands. "A traditional body of group myths, laws, customs, and half-remembered history" had become "a comprehensive legal framework adaptable to different social settings." The rabbis, like the Deuteronomist before them, reworked old legal materials to fit new circumstances. Locating their authority in divine sanction, they placed their innovations securely within the existing legal tradition. Even within the assumption that divine law was "just and perfect," because it emanated from God, a "fixed and immutable" Torah nonetheless permitted the constant adjustment of law to life.[32]

That reformulation of Jewish law in the centuries following the Roman conquest preserved the vital tension "between text and historical reality." While rabbinical law, by its own imperatives, was bound to precedent and extremely slow to change, the sacred-law tradition legitimized (indeed, mandated) the application of human intelligence to divine revelation. The text was the final word, but its meaning never was final. (Those who clung tenaciously to the Sinaitic revelation were not the rabbis but sectarian heretics known as Karaites.) The Talmudic "hedge" around the Torah, formed during centuries of legal exegesis, was not impervious to new growth, nor to occasional trimming; and it even permitted foreign influences to penetrate into the Jewish legal system. Indeed, it is hardly coincidental that some of the most formative episodes in Jewish legal development occurred on foreign soil, in the wilderness of Sinai and in Babylon, precisely when the need to formulate or restate the basis of Israelite legal authority was greatest. But during each wrenching historical crisis, when the very identity and cohesion of Israel was at risk, the sacred law was reasserted as the foundation of national religious life.[33] Law would adapt to change and to circumstance, but adaptation must remain within the premises and principles of the sacred-law tradition.

There were, to be sure, practical limits to rabbinical legal authority, set by the minority status of Jews in the Christian and Islamic lands of their dispersion. But medieval theory and practice encouraged the self-regulating autonomy of corporate units within the state. Jewish communities took ample advantage of their opportunity. Depending upon the vagaries of local circumstance, rabbinical courts enjoyed far-ranging jurisdiction that included civil, criminal, and religious matters. With recourse to gentile courts largely forbidden, with a wide range of available sanctions (from fines and flogging to excommunication and even execution), and with rabbinical insistence upon the exclusive application of Jewish law, Jewish communities enjoyed a measure of legal self-rule that transformed them, quite literally, into states within a state (even, it has been suggested, "a state beyond the state"). This did not become a term of opprobrium until the modern era, when all citizens were expected to vest exclusive loyalty in the nation-state in return for its guarantees of civic equality and individual rights. Until then, Jewish communities functioned not merely as religious congregations but as political entities, with a measure of legal autonomy that was virtually indistinguishable from sovereignty.[34]

Even the most familiar principle of Jewish accommodation to external authority—*dina d'malkhuta dina* (the law of the state is the law)—sustained the rule of Jewish law. First enunciated in Babylonia in the third century, it necessarily affirmed the power of the state but did so within a very narrow range. The state might regulate affairs (largely regarding taxation and property) between Jews and gentiles, but internal Jewish issues (concerning family, ritual, and communal affairs, even criminal behavior) were beyond its purview. In practice, Salo Baron has written, "it was the rabbi who, by weighing its merits in strictly Jewish legal terms and invoking strictly Jewish precedents, made the ultimate decision." The law of the state might be law, but this was so in practice only "because, and insofar as, Jewish law acknowledged its validity."[35]

Yet Jewish legal development was severely impaired by the loss of national sovereignty and by the prolonged dispersion of Jews as a dependent minority. Portions of the law that were specific to life in the land of Israel were frozen at an early stage of economic development and rendered obsolete by exile. Without Temple worship, substantial segments of the Torah relating to sacrifice and priestly functions were, in effect, suspended. Cut off from important sources of renewal, and deprived of the protection of national sovereignty, Jewish law, increasingly preoccupied with preservation at the expense of innovation, often was reduced to "building fences around communal islands." As its scope narrowed, it became excessively (perhaps at times, exclusively) preoccupied with arcane intricacies of textual exegesis. With the Jews in exile, Jewish law, in "exile from reality," lost much of its capacity for creative growth.[36] The title of Joseph Caro's magisterial sixteenth-century compilation, *Shulhan Arukh* ("set table"), suggested that creative legal development lay mostly in the past.

Well into the twentieth century, however, the sacred law still retained its vitality, if only within a diminishing community of the observant. In their empathetic (if romanticized) portrait of Eastern European *shtetl* culture, Mark Zborowski and Elizabeth Herzog captured its enduring power on the eve of the Second World War. The revealed law of Torah, quite literally, still was the living law of these communities. The Torah itself, as a physical object, was treated "almost as a live being." It was embraced as a dancing partner during the holy day that completed the annual reading cycle; if desecrated, it was wrapped in a shroud, mourned, and buried. In the *shtetl*, there was no distinction between sacred and secular (only between Jew and gentile). Life under Torah still was "one fused whole." Because, according to rabbinical tradition, "there are no dates in Jewish learning," the continual study of ancient legal texts remained appropriate for the resolution of current problems. In this way, law preserved "unity and continuity in time and space," binding *shtetl* Jews to Jews everywhere, and in all times, despite the loss of a common history and territory. The rabbi remained the law man of Judaism, and "those who come before him are judged, not by the law of the land, but by the law of the Promised Land, the sacred Law."[37]

Despite its extraordinary historical durability under the most adverse circumstances, Jewish law long ago was all but dismissed as a vestigial biblical anachronism. Much in Western tradition, whether religious or secular, has been inherently hostile to it. Christianity often defined itself in opposition to the Jewish legal tradition, which provided the necessary negative contrast to the spiritual message of the Christian savior. Christian Jews, the earliest followers of Jesus, assigned demonological status to the rabbis whose teachings they rejected. According to the characteristic complaint, expressed in the Gospel of Matthew, the Pharisees "bind heavy burdens, hard to bear, and lay them on men's shoulders." While they "make their phylacteries broad and their fringes long," and basked in the honor of their rabbinical title and perquisites, they were "hypocrites" who neglected "justice and mercy and faith." The Pharisees made an appearance in each of the Gospels, usually to provide opposition to Jesus, while demonstrating the ultimate futility of Jewish legalism in the face of spiritual truth. (To this day, "Pharisee" remains a derogatory symbol of arid legalism.) By the Middle Ages the Christian critique had broadened to include the Sanhedrin, the institutional seat of Jewish legal authority before the Roman conquest, and the Talmud, the primary text of the post-exilic Jewish legal system.[38]

Modern Bible scholarship, for all of its innovative insights, vigorously reinforced Christian theological dogma. During nearly a century of critical scholarship that began with Julius Wellhausen, every momentous transformation in the legal development of ancient Israel came to be viewed with unmitigated hostility. The elevation of law, according to Wellhausen (whose massive scholarship still casts its long shadow of influence), stifled moral life. Justice and righteousness, the foundation pillars of the old order, collapsed under the weight of "that artificial product, the sacred constitution of Judaism." Filled with "unedifying features," law "thrusts itself in everywhere; it commands and blocks up the access to heaven; . . . it takes the soul out of religion and spoils morality." Law was the source of all that was deplorable in Judaism, for it sustained the power of the priestly cult and stifled the prophetic spirit (until it reemerged in Christianity). Law, at once "a dead work" and "a pedagogic instrument of discipline," transformed Israel into a Mosaic theocracy, which, according to Wellhausen, bore a striking resemblance to "the old Catholic Church, which was in fact its child."[39]

Subsequent developments in the history of ancient Israel, according to Wellhausen's disciples, only compounded the problem. The transition to "legal casuistry" under Ezra, to rules that were extraneous to life, became one of the staples of bible scholarship, as it was in Christian theology. Before Ezra, the commandments had served Israel; thereafter, "Israel had to serve the commandments." With its transformation from a nation-state to a religion of "law and worship," Israel became "a separate and peculiar" (and not very likable) people. The Deuteronomic principles—one God, one revelation, one land, one people, one place of worship, one prophet and lawgiver—left "no doubt" about the "intolerance" of the founding fathers of Judaism. The rule of sacred law left Israel exempt "from all seeking and questioning and doubting." Law had become "an *absolute entity*, valid without respect to precedent, time, or history; based on itself, binding simply because it existed as law, because it was of divine origin and authority." As law became theology, religion was exhausted in legal obedience. Governed by "fossilized laws," Israelites worshipped "dead ordinances and statutes." Addicted to legalism, Israel stepped outside history, transformed by law into "this new thing," Judaism. "Severed once for all from solidarity with the rest of the peoples," it incurred (understandably) the suspicion, even hatred, that became the appropriate historical burden of the Jewish people.[40]

Since the eighteenth century, Western secular thought has offered its own withering critique of the underpinnings of Jewish sacred law. The very meaning of "enlightenment" relegated religious observance to the realm of magic and superstition, far from the respectability afforded to reason. The modern nation-state absorbed the (venerable Christian) dichotomy between religion and nationality. The terms of emancipation required Jews to repudiate the authority of their own legal system. In their encounter with modernity, Jews internalized the criticism of their legal tradition, whose rejection was their entry ticket to Western society. As most Jews readily appreciated, Jewish law rested upon premises that were incomprehensible, if not intolerable, in the modern West.

The distinctive attribute of Jewish law can be succinctly stated: the Torah, both written and oral, is understood to be the revealed word of God. The factual truth of this fundamental axiom may be questioned on theological or historical grounds, but not as a legal proposition. Jewish law is validated by, and only by, its origin in divine revelation. The laws, commands, and statutes (as Moses Mendelssohn wrote at the beginning of the modern era) provide "instructions in God's will." Jewish law is understood as "God's gift to Israel." It is sacred law, which defines holiness, or the right relationship to God. Israel must hear and learn, fear and do, because "the source of authority of the Torah is divine command."[41]

As sacred law, Jewish law comprehensively integrates what is sharply differentiated in the modern West: morality and law; religion and politics; private and public; belief and behavior. There are fundamental distinctions—between holy and profane, or Israel and the nations—but none of the compartments for human activity that Western law requires. In the Torah, indiscriminately mixed, are "legal" principles of trespass and damage, theft and restitution, personal injury and retribution; "religious" precepts regarding sacrifice and festival observance; and "ethical" admonitions regarding due care of widows, orphans, and strangers. Sacred law, because it comes from God, includes social conduct, family relationships, culinary preferences, and ritual obligation. It even regulates thought and feeling—as, for example, in the commands to honor parents and not to covet the possessions of a neighbor. Sexual relations, no less than business relations, fall within its jurisdiction. There are rules for proper dealings with servants, thieves, creditors, and oxen who gore; along with prohibitions against idolatry and the seduction of virgins.

A single paragraph of the Covenant Code of Exodus, probably the most ancient of the several legal codes in the Torah, combines guidelines for loans and pledges, justice in legal proceedings, and Sabbath observance with injunctions not to revile judges, curse rulers, or boil a kid in its mother's milk (the foundation of an important principle of Jewish dietary observance). However odd this combination of civil law and cultic observance, human relations and ritual obligation may now seem, it is integral to the unity of religion and law in Judaism. Because divine will was expressed in legal terms, Jewish law is inherently religious. The ultimate end of Jewish law was holiness, so often expressed biblically as loyalty to God, or walking in His ways.

"This interweaving of the spiritual, the cultic, the moral, and the legal," Nahum Sarna has written, "is one of the quintessential differentiating characteristics of biblical law." Israel was different because it accepted divine revelation (and authority), which necessarily embraced every facet of human behavior. Jewish law formed "an integrated and homogeneous system by which God rules the world." Obedience to such an inclusive range of commands and obligations, the very definition of holiness, enabled Israel to separate itself from other nations, while turning it back toward an exclusive relationship with God. As the Torah commands: "You shall . . . keep all my statutes, and all my judgments, and do them. . . . And you shall be holy to me: for I the Lord am holy, and have separated you from the peoples, that you should be mine." By attending to this task, Israel would demonstrate the "legal piety" that long remained the distinctive attribute of Judaism.[42]

The covenantal relationship between God and Israel remained the framework of Jewish legal obligation. Jews obeyed because God commanded. The theme of submission to divine authority pervades the biblical narrative (although, to be sure, the normative authority of divine law is often illustrated with examples of disobedience). In Jewish tradition, God is *Avinu Malkenu* (Our Father, Our King); Jewish liturgy overflows with blessings to God as *Melech* (King). There are ritualized gestures of respect, even submission: heads are bowed; knees are bent. Scholars have discovered evident parallels with ancient Near Eastern suzerainty treaties, which also required the loyalty of a people to its king, while conveying title to land and assuring special protection in return. This contractual process might even be accompanied by commands, blessings, and curses, as in the biblical text. But despite evidence of cultural borrowing, Jewish law, uniquely, depended upon a covenantal relationship with God, requiring submission to divine, not human, authority.[43]

When Jewish law is compared with American law, the contrast is striking. Modern legal thought compartmentalizes, insisting upon boundaries, limits, separations, and carefully defined spheres. It imposes distinctions—between secular and religious, legal and moral, public and private. When boundaries are transgressed by the "intrusion" of law upon private choice, anger is easily aroused (as recent American examples, including drug testing, abortion restrictions, gun control, and mandatory seat-belts readily demonstrate). The separation of religion and state, of course, is fundamental to modern Western conceptions of law. Sacred space, like moral space, is protected from state legal intervention; while any conception of sacred time is obliterated. The cherished American metaphor of a wall, separating the two realms, expresses the apprehension that each may be contaminated by contact with the other. That wall of separation has no place in Jewish tradition. For Jews, the symbolism of a wall evokes altogether different associations: the Western Wall in Jerusalem remains a tangible reminder of the historic unity of the national religion, with the ancient Temple at its geographical and spiritual center.

Despite persistent efforts to weave them into a common legal tradition, the Torah revealed to Israel and the Constitution ratified by "We the People" have little in common. Indeed, they define two altogether distinctive legal traditions, one sacred and the other secular. The Torah instructs Jews how to live a holy life, while the Constitution is a charter of governance. Consequently, the biblical narrative—often describing the behavior of quite fallible people— is as instructive as the explicit legal rules, perhaps suggesting that the human struggle to comprehend and apply divine command is urgent and timeless. (To be sure, George Washington's shining integrity, like Abe Lincoln's dogged perseverence, may be equally inspirational—but they hardly allow for moral subtlety or ambiguity, nor are they part of the fundamental law.) While the Torah defines an intimate convenantal relationship with God, the Constitution, in many respects, was designed to assure the absence of close relationships: the branches of the national government were separated from each other (and, usually, from the people as well); the principle of federalism separated the states from the new national government; constitutional ratification depended upon a Bill of Rights to insulate citizens from their own national governing institutions. In a legal system governed by divine rule, by contrast, there can be no bill of rights to protect individual autonomy from divine authority; nor can sacred law, divine and eternal, be amended. The Constitution, the legal culmination of a revolutionary struggle against royal authority, all but renders "meaningless and distant" the overriding Jewish metaphor of God as king.[44] Any claims of covenantal compatibility in the Jewish and American legal traditions must rest upon the obliteration of divine authority, the fundamental premise of Jewish law.

Torah and Constitution each define a national community, but the differences between them are overwhelming. The constitutional community rests upon a conception of individual freedom, but the Torah community imposes a collective obligation of obedience. The constitutional emphasis upon personal liberty usually overrides competing communal claims, except in extreme situations of public safety or national emergency. (The notorious Prohibition Amendment, the most significant constitutional intrusion upon private activity except for the abolition of slavery, stands now as a perpetual reminder of the futility of such regulatory efforts.) The Jewish legal tradition, however, strongly asserts the principle of collective communal responsibility, even for intimately private activities. All Jews, those living at the time and those as yet unborn, are assumed to have stood at Sinai to receive the Torah. The giving of the law not only created the nation at a particular moment in time, but bound Jews in perpetuity to that covenantal experience. That conception of command and compliance, embracing all future generations, helps to explain how law could continue to define Jewish life within a communal setting long after the foundations of national sovereignty had been destroyed. The obligation to obey was communal, no less than individual; and the community was expected to assume responsibility, collectively, for individual acts of disobedience, whether willful or unintentional. On Yom Kippur, the day of atonement, Jews declare "We have sinned" and ask divine forgiveness for all Jews, not for themselves as individuals.

The principle of communal responsibility is reinforced by the understanding that the Torah is not only law but instruction as well. It conveyed the obligation to teach its principles so that future generations, "who have not known anything," would learn. As early as the return from Babylonian exile, where Ezra had prepared himself to teach the statutes and judgments of Torah, the priests (as we learn in Nehemiah) "read in the book, in the Torah of God distinctly, and gave the sense, and cause [the people] to understand the reading." The law was not only a written text, but a continuing source of communal instruction.[45] To this day the reading of the Torah, at the core of every Sabbath and holy day observance, affirms a communal obligation to hear, to learn, and to do. Each generation of Jews can thereby return to the covenantal moment and reexperience it.

The Constitution, by contrast, remains far more distant, even inaccessible. It speaks almost exclusively to governing institutions, rather than to the community. It long ago became the virtually exclusive preserve of legal specialists, who continue to monopolize the debate over its meaning. Their intepretive mastery makes it that much less accessible to ordinary citizens, except during relatively rare moments of focused public debate over a controversial issue. A public reading of the Constitution can hardly be imagined; even during the prolonged euphoria of the recent bicentennial celebration, no one seems to have suggested it. Similarly, while Law Day in the United States originated as a patriotic alternative to May Day, and is all but ignored except among ceremonial gatherings of lawyers and judges, the Jewish holy day of *Shavuot*, which commemorates the giving of the law, begins with a night-long period of study, introspection, and commentary to reaffirm the enduring vitality of Torah as the sacred teaching of the assembled community.

The primary substantive values of the Jewish and American legal systems diverge sharply. Because political sovereignty in Judaism has a theological foundation, covenantal rights are rooted in the will of God, not in those self-evident truths of human nature to which the Declaration of Independence refers. Two of the most fundamental American legal concepts, freedom and equality, have entirely different meanings in Jewish law. For Jews, freedom is a national, not a personal, goal. "The right of the individual to deviate from established norms of belief and action is not included in the Jewish conception of freedom." A Jew is not free to choose what to believe, or how to worship God, or (as Deuteronomy reminds) to do "whatever is right in his own eyes." Similarly, the principle of equality yields, in Jewish law, to other priorities. The Torah sharply distinguishes between Jews and gentiles, favoring Jews (who may not be charged usury nor held in permanent servitude); and between men and women, favoring men (in various family law matters, especially divorce). The Law of Return of the State of Israel, enacted by the first Knesset, permits any Jew in the world—but only Jews—to claim citizenship in the Jewish state. There is, then, an overriding conception of Jewish peoplehood, and its distinctiveness, that defines freedom and equality in ways quite foreign to American principles.[46]

If Jewish law resembles any other legal system, it is not American constitutionalism but the law of Islam, the other sacred-law tradition of the Middle East. In Islam, as in Judaism, law based upon revelation is "divine and immutable." Defining a religiously observant way of life, it instructs its adherents in all aspects of behavior; it imposes a conception of sacred time; and it so integrates religion with law that religious officials are simultaneously law men, while places of worship have often functioned as courts of law. There is even a revealing linguistic clue to the compatibility of Jewish and Islamic law. Just as *halakha* is related to the verb "to walk," or "to go," the parallel term for Islamic law, *shari-a*, is literally translated as "the way to a watering place." Like *halakha*, the *shari-a* defines the path that the faithful must follow, the right way to what was, after all, the most vital source of life in a desert culture—literally, of course, water, but spiritually, the authority of divine command.[47]

The American legal tradition, by contrast, is a product of the Christian West. Its essence is political; it confines religion to the narrow realm of private belief; and it rests upon the differentiation of what belongs to Caesar and to God. American Jews, consequently, are the heirs to two vastly different legal cultures. Like other emancipated Jews, they faced the historical necessity of choosing between them. By the nineteenth century, the "competing, authoritative secular legal system" not only limited the scope of Jewish law but also, far more seriously, undermined its authority.[48] The dilemma was acute: Jewish law no longer was binding, but its normative authority in Judaism, as a matter of historical fact, could not easily be denied. American Jews, eager to bridge the widening gap between their two legal traditions, reconciled the irreconcilable and found compatibilities amid incompatibilities. To assure themselves that they could simultaneously be good Americans and good Jews, they invented a unitary Judeo-American legal tradition, which denied the wrenching transformation that occurred as they jettisoned Jewish sacred law and committed themselves, instead, to American constitutionalism.

By doing so, American Jews struggled to resolve the fundamental tension, throughout Jewish history, between autonomy and acculturation. The First Commandment ("no other gods") has been interpreted as a rejection of all "foreign relations"—not only with other gods but, by implication, with the ways of foreigners. But even the authority of the sacred law never completely stifled the attractions that other nations provided in such alluring abundance. Examples abound. Although many of the exiles had returned with Ezra to the land of Israel, the satisfactions of Babylonian life were sufficient to keep many more behind, where they could fondly recall Zion yet not relinquish the bounty of their adopted land. Maccabean zeal for the purity of the law quickly degenerated into Hasmonean accommodation to Hellenism. Josephus, in his *Antiquities of the Jews*, observed, "Our nation does not encourage those that learn the languages of many nations." Rather, Jews attributed wisdom to one "who is fully acquainted with our laws, and is able to interpret their meaning." Josephus, of course, was a Jewish commander turned Roman warrior. He could appreciate, better than most, how the temptation to speak another language might undermine Jewish law.[49]

The American Jewish experience offers its own instructive commentary on this theme. For more than a century, American Jews have tried to demonstrate the compatibility of their two competing legal traditions.[50] Only by obliterating the disparities could they eradicate the nagging duality within their own identity. But the "compatibility" of Jewish and American law has its basis in the yearning for full integration into American society, fed by apprehension lest covenantal distinctiveness undermine the effort. American acculturation demanded the reformulation of the sacred law into the American secular ideal of liberty and justice under the rule of constitutional law. The belief in a unitary Judeo-American legal tradition is one of the cherished myths of American Jews. How they wove Torah and Constitution together comprises one of the fascinating chapters in American Jewish history.

Prophetic Justice

Modern Jews, rejecting the sacred-law tradition, have often found inspiration in the message of the Hebrew prophets, the moral conscience of ancient Israel. "Hate the evil, and love the good," implored Amos, demanding of Israel that "justice roll down like waters, and righteousness like a mighty stream." "I cannot bear iniquity," Isaiah declared, admonishing his people to "relieve the oppressed, judge the fatherless, plead for the widow." Jeremiah severely chastised Israel, for it had "eyes and heart only for thy dishonest gain, and for shedding innocent blood, and for oppression, and for preaching violence." Micah reminded Israel of its continuing obligation "to do justly, and to love mercy, and to walk humbly with thy God," while anticipating the glorious time when "nation shall not lift up a sword against nation, nor shall they learn war any more."[1]

The impact of the Prophets upon ancient Israel, ironically, seems to have been "negligible." The common denominator of their experience may well have been "the bitter fact that no one listened to them."[2] Yet the prophetic denunciation of oppression, exploitation, corruption, injustice, and war has remained an enduring inspiration to our own time. Throughout the twentieth century, the most conspicuous spokesmen for American liberalism—from Louis Brandeis to Martin Luther King, Jr.—have cited the Hebrew prophets to frame their indictments of social ills and their pleas for reform. American Jews still hear in prophecy those timeless truths of social justice that are embedded in their democratic faith and, they imagine, in historic Judaism. But such fidelity to ancient prophecy, among a people not inclined to revere ancient texts or traditions, raises intriguing questions. Are American Jews indeed faithful to prophecy, or do they merely hear in it the echo of their own voices? Did the Prophets say, or mean, what American Jews have attributed to them?

Even to begin to understand the Prophets within their own historical and cultural context requires the literary equivalent of an archaeological excavation. Centuries of interpretive accumulation encrusted the Prophets within Christian theological dogma, which still shapes the modern understanding of their message. From the earliest days of Christianity—indeed from Jesus himself—the Prophets comprised "an essential ingredient of Christian theology, worship, and proclamation." They were venerated by Jesus, his apostles, and the early church for their anticipation of the Christian savior. Isaiah had "predicted" the virgin birth of the Prince of Peace; Hosea provided proof texts for Jesus, who quoted his preference for mercy rather than sacrificial ritual; Jeremiah had spoken of the need for a new covenant. The Prophets had offered Jews an opportunity to repent, but their message of mercy and righteousness (like the savior who proclaimed it) was rejected. The prophetic condemnation of a corrupt, unjust Israelite society offered substantiation for the Christian rejection of Judaism.[3]

In the nineteenth century, the Hebrew prophets were propelled into renewed prominence as the creative innovators of enduring religious truth. A primary thrust of biblical scholarship, in its formative stage, was to depict the Prophets as the founders of a universal religion of moral idealism (which culminated in Christianity). The Prophets broke free of the cultic constraints within Israel to proclaim ethical monotheism as the true religion of the spirit. Their message, elevating ethical behavior above cultic ritual, proclaimed the revolutionary ideal of religious morality. Their spiritual and ethical faith marked the apex of Israel's religious development, while simultaneously preparing the foundation for the culmination of religious truth in Christianity, the most faithful expression of prophetic teaching. So the "exclusivist religion" of Judaism expanded, under prophetic pressure, until "it embraced, in principle, the whole of mankind."[4]

At the core of the new scholarship—and the Protestant faith that sustained it—was a drastic reappraisal of the historical relationship of law and prophecy. According to Jewish tradition the Torah had been divinely revealed to Moses at Sinai, while the Prophets had thundered their denunciation of a morally corrupt society centuries later, during the decline of the Israelite monarchy. This chronology was unchallenged until the nineteenth century, when scholars introduced the claim that the ethical monotheism of the Prophets had *preceded* the development of a national life based upon law and cult. The Jewish national myth of divinely revealed law only arose much later, after Babylonian exile, when Israel needed to reinvent its past in order to compensate for its loss of nationhood. The law "revealed" to Moses was a post-exilic invention, not a pre-exilic reality. The real source of Judaism, therefore, was not law, but prophecy. Indeed, from the lofty heights of prophetic idealism, Israel had slid into a precipitous decline that led inexorably to rigid legalism, and to the Christian New Testament, based upon a true understanding of prophecy, which superseded it. The proper sequence was not from law to prophecy, as Jewish tradition always maintained, but from prophecy to law—from a universal spiritual ideal (ultimately embodied in the teachings of Jesus) to the discreditited ritualism of a tribal cult.[5]

This was no mere scholar's quibble over chronology. It was a frontal assault against the foundation of Jewish religious faith and national self-definition. The foremost proponent of the new interpretation was Julius Wellhausen, whose massive *Prolegomena to the History of Israel* was published in English translation in 1885. It is difficult to exaggerate Wellhausen's impact on biblical scholarship: although few scholars now accept the validity of his findings, many have worked within the long shadow cast by his book. In retrospect, what may be most remarkable about the *Prolegomena* is not the vastness of its scope, nor even its prolonged scholarly dominance, but the single intuitive flash that inspired it.

Wellhausen, the son of a Lutheran minister, had intended to study theology. Along the way, he developed the abiding interest in ancient Semitic languages and documentary source analysis that earned him his enduring scholarly reputation. In his preface to the *Prolegomena* Wellhausen confessed that the pervasive presence of legal material in the biblical text had always impeded his understanding of the Old Testament. Law, he wrote, "intruded itself uneasily, like a ghost that makes a noise indeed, but is not visible and really effects nothing." He had searched in vain for "the light which was to be shed from this source on the historical and prophetical books." Wellhausen sensed that law and prophecy had comprised "two wholly distinct worlds" (the worlds of Judaism and Christianity)—but he knew of no confirming evidence until he learned that an early nineteenth-century scholar, Karl Heinrich Graf, had inverted the accepted sequence of law and prophecy, locating prophecy first. "Almost without knowing his reasons for the hypothesis," Wellhausen concluded, "I was prepared to accept it. . . . I readily acknowledged to myself the possibility of understanding Hebrew antiquity without the book of the Torah."[6]

With that remarkable inspiration, Wellhausen rejected the historical and theological fixation of the biblical narrative on the Sinai covenant as the formative experience in the national life of Israel. Such a religion of law and covenantal obligation, disparaged by Wellhausen as "Mosaism," was a much later historical development. It measured the spiritual decline from the golden age of "old Israel," when "the relation between the people and God was a natural one as that of son to father; it did not rest upon observance of the conditions of a pact." Sadly, however, that edenic existence was eroded by the Israelite monarchy, which left "something rotten in the state of Israel." As the royal court expanded its wealth and power, the administration of justice was corrupted. Social stratification encouraged exploitation of the lower classes. "The times were evil."[7]

Enter the Prophets, on their heroic mission of moral salvation. Cognizant of "right and wrong, truth and falsehood," they were inspired by the knowledge that God hated injustice and demanded righteousness. No longer would He be placated by sacrificial offerings; the ritualized observances of the priestly cult had become obsolete. Wellhausen described, with unrestrained admiration, the volcanic force of prophecy as it burst through encrusted religious institutions that were "fixed and dead." Prophetic ethics "destroyed the national character of the old religion. . . . The first step towards universalism had been accomplished." Prophecy was "the inspiration of awakened individuals," who depended upon no authority beyond "the truth of what they say." The Prophets, to Wellhausen, were "the spritual destroyers of the old Israel," "the founders" of ethical monotheism. For their "progressive step" in religious evolution, Wellhausen bestowed upon them the highest term of praise from a pious Protestant: they had launched "the Prophetic Reformation."[8]

But the prophetic message was doomed in Israel. The people did not heed the Prophets, nor did the priests relinquish their power. National destruction and exile were the appropriate consequences of their moral obduracy. Only upon their return from Babylon, when their national life had been reduced to a dim historical memory, did Israel invent a wilderness tradition based upon divine law to compensate for its loss. "We now find the Book regarded as the foundation of all higher life," Wellhausen wrote. "The cultus with its burnt offerings and sin-offerings, its purifications and its abstinences, its feasts and Sabbaths, strictly observed as prescribed by the Law, is now the principle business of life." With life reduced to the provisions of a legal code, and to priestly ritual, Israel's national downfall was inevitable; but the ancient prophetic wisdom—"the truths and precepts of religion"— would endure as the new universal faith of Christianity. Wellhausen conceded "the persistency of the [Jewish] race," but he was certain that the rejection of prophetic morality for law and ritual ultimately assured "the extinction of Judaism."[9]

To read Wellhausen, even now, is to plunge into a great adventure story, combining history, theology, and myth, propelled into a powerful narrative synthesis. Exuding moral purpose, the *Prolegomena* unequivocally distributed good and evil between Prophets and priests, ethics and law, universalist faith and tribal cult—in sum, between Christianity and Judaism (and, not incidentally, between Protestantism and Catholicism). His book was swept to the pinnacle of scholarly influence by some of the most powerful ideological currents, both secular and religious, of the late nineteenth century. It is easy, now, to identify Wellhausen's bias, so vividly expressed in his model of spiritual decline (law) and regeneration (prophecy). Ethical monotheism, assumed to be the "highest" stage of religious development, naturally was associated with prophetic influence; law represented a retrogressive degeneration from the sublime truths of prophecy.[10]

The religious suppositions that framed the Wellhausen thesis long intruded upon Bible scholarship. Well into the twentieth century, Bible scholars unabashedly proclaimed the prophetic anticipation of Christian doctrine as a matter of undisputed historical truth. As devout Christians, they could hardly do otherwise. For law was "the bony skeleton which supported the warm flesh and blood of prophetic religion." In Jesus, "the great prophets' awareness of God found fulfillment." The New Testament, therefore, "is unintelligible until we have kept company with the Prophets of the Old Testament." The separation of prophecy from law, the inversion of their chronological sequence, and the elevation of prophecy as the final religious "truth," ratified the Christian triumphalism of the New Testament. The Prophets emerged as the first Protestants who, "through the alchemy of the spirit, transmuted base primitive Yahwism into religious gold." We are left to admire "their relevance for the moral claims of Christianity," but little else.[11] With Christian appropriation of the mantle of prophecy, Judaism was relegated to the lowly status of a primitive tribe, whose curious rituals, separatist fetishes, and legalistic obsessions properly consigned it to historical and theological obsolescence.

The liberal Protestant precepts that guided Wellhausen are no longer controlling. Bible scholars have carefully explored the relationship between prophecy and tradition, even the links between prophets and priests (who, according to the Wellhausen school, had been locked in mortal combat). Prophecy has begun to be understood within the sacred-law tradition rather than in opposition to it, as the affirmation, not the repudiation, of the binding covenantal relationship between God and Israel. The Prophets are no longer depicted as inspired Protestants (Weber's "creative outsiders"); rather, they can be located securely within the political and religious institutions of ancient Israel—Temple cult, royal court, covenant, and divine revelation. The Prophets may have initiated an "internal dialogue within Israel," which subjected "accepted ideas and institutions . . . to a seaching scrutiny," but scholars now readily acknowledge "how the prophets rise out of the past, how the traditions of the Mosaic age . . . condition much of what they have to say."[12] The recognition that even the most powerful prophetic insights can be understood within traditional forms has restored the interpretive challenge to the task of understanding prophecy. Did the Prophets deliver a new message, or an old message in new form? Did prophecy repudiate law, or reinforce the obligation to abide by it? Is the familiar disjunction between law and prophecy, so characteristic of modern American Judaism, a legacy of the prophetic tradition or a misreading of that tradition?

History provides a contextual framework for confronting these issues. The Prophets can be understood only if they are located within the domestic and foreign travails that beset eighth-century Israel, for prophecy arose as a form of political judgment in response to the deficiencies of the monarchy and to the social problems that it had failed to resolve. Three cataclysmic historical events tied the Prophets closely to the political realities of their day: the fall of the Northern Kingdom to Assyria in 722 B.C.E.; the Babylonian conquest of Jerusalem in 587; and the restoration of political and religious life in Jerusalem after the return from exile in 538. Prophecy was a response to the catastrophic dislocations—political, economic, and diplomatic—that plagued the first Hebrew commonwealth and ultimately terminated its national existence.[13]

The biblical narrative explicitly defines the function of prophecy during these critical episodes in the history of Israel: to call Israel to obedience to the sacred law. The Book of Kings recounts that during the ninth year of Hoshea's rule (which began in 732 B.C.E.) over the Northern Kingdom of Israel, the king did "evil in the sight of the Lord," while the people "feared other gods, and walked in the statutes of the nations." God warned them "by all the prophets," saying, "Turn from your evil ways, and keep my commandments and my statutes, according to all the Torah which I commanded your fathers, and which I sent to you by my servants the Prophets." Despite the prophetic warnings, the people "hardened their necks." They spurned God's demand, proclaimed by the Prophets, for obedience to covenantal obligations. Instead, "they went after the nations that were round about them, concerning whom the Lord had charged them, that they should not do like them." God, angered by their disregard of His message, "removed them out of his sight." The Israelites of the Northern Kingdom, banished to Assyria, were never heard from again.[14]

The Prophets appeared as messengers of God, determined—as their fervent outrage vividly demonstrates—to call Israel to account for its derelictions and to restore it to its covenantal task. Explanations for terrible national disasters were desperately needed. It is hardly plausible, at such a critical juncture, that the Prophets—or anyone who wanted the attention of Israel—would offer explanations or hope independent of divine will. Every primary experience in the national life of the people, from the covenantal promise to Abraham through the exodus and revelation at Sinai and beyond, had depended upon divine intervention in the history of Israel. So it was in the age of prophecy. The Prophets came to Israel explicitly claiming to bear God's word. The pronouncement "Thus says the Lord" (as each Prophet fervently testified) was the direct, and sole, source of prophetic inspiration. Amos, inaugurating the prophetic era, proclaimed: "The Lord will roar from Zion, and utter his voice from Jerusalem." God, the Prophets insisted, had not ceased to act in history. To the contrary, from the Assyrian conquest through the Babylonian exile to the rebuilding of the Temple in Jerusalem, divine intervention was evident—and Israel must pay heed.[15]

Not merely the fact of divine intervention, but the specific content of God's message to Israel, preoccupied the Prophets. After Sinai, at every crucial juncture in the national life of the people, as the covenant renewal ceremonies indicated, the sacred law had served as an instrument of divine will and as the definition of national purpose. The Prophets could hardly hope to elicit a response from the people without proclaiming loyalty to the fundamental principles of the national faith. For the Prophets "sprang from Israel" and "had their roots deep in its past." Their denunciation of Israel, sweeping and passionate, was securely located in the sacred tradition. Their message is incomprehensible unless it can be heard within "the historical and moral presuppositions . . . of the popular religion." Paramount among these was the singular belief in the holiness of Israel, its land, and its purpose; and the enduring validity of covenantal obligation. Indeed, it was precisely because Israel had violated the terms of the covenant, thereby incurring divine wrath, that the Prophets were sent on their task.[16] Prophecy was an urgent expression of the need for covenant renewal.

It may be tempting to abstract the Prophets from history and nationality, accepting at face value the modern universalization of their role and message. But the temptation should be resisted, for there is little in prophecy to sustain it. The Prophets were exclusively concerned with the relationship between God and Israel. To be sure, they understood (indeed were possessed by) the cosmic, timeless significance of the current events in the land of Israel. But to transform them into fervent preachers of a universal moral order, courageously breaking the shackles of the parochial national religion, is to miss their significance entirely. Not only were they bound by time and place, but also by the sacred-law tradition. The divine message, as Jeremiah transmitted it, reminded Israel, "Ask for the old paths, where the good way is." In a time of supreme travail, when its very existence as God's *am segulah*, or treasure people, hung in the balance, the Prophets reminded Israel that armies and alliances, like material extravagance and ritual practice, were not substitutes for walking (humbly) with God. "Rebellion against the Lord," according to the prophetic jeremiad to Israel, was the ultimate sin.[17]

Prophecy marked no decisive break with the past; no abrupt shift from tribe or nation to universalism. The most universal visions of the Prophets, Yehezkel Kaufmann observed, "are always connected with the glorification of Israel, Jerusalem, and the temple. . . . All of prophetic universalism is suffused with national symbols." Even Isaiah's majestic anticipation of the end of days, when all the nations would come to the mountain of the Lord, is strikingly particularistic (which is why it is still affirmed by Jews in the Torah service): "for out of Zion shall go forth Torah, and the word of the Lord from Jerusalem."[18]

The experience of Babylonian exile vividly illuminates the underlying concern of prophetic "universalism." Exile, of course, was a wrenching trauma of unimagined proportions. The exiled community confronted a terrifying problem: "How shall we sing the Lord's song in a foreign land?"[19] Hidden within that lament was the anxious inquiry: had God accompanied the Israelites into exile, or had they left God behind once they vacated the territorial boundaries of their homeland? The land of Israel was so completely identified as a place of God's presence that the exiles had every reason to conclude (from the very fact of exile) that God had abandoned them— or, worse yet, that He had been sufficiently discredited by the recent national calamity to have left them entirely at the mercies of the gods of their captors.

Confronting a massive crisis of faith, Deutero-Isaiah offered reassurance that God was still with them. The divine reach, truly universal in scope, embraced His children even in the remotest corners of exile. God reassured Israel, through the prophet, that He "will hold thy hand, and will keep thee, and give thee for a covenant of the people, for a light of the nations." God insisted: "Look to me, and be saved, all the ends of the earth. . . . I am God, and there is none else . . . I will place salvation in Zion for Israel my glory."[20] With these words, the Prophet brought God to the exiled community, reassuring the dispirited that God truly was universal, presiding over the destinies of all nations (even Babylonia) and attentive to Israel wherever it might be scattered.

Such prophetic universalism was hardly a new proclamation of faith, or an endorsement of the brotherhood of nations. It served a narrower, Israel-centered, purpose during the period of exile: to restore Israel to God by bringing God to Israel where it dwelt (and, not incidentally, to strengthen Israel against any temptations from its encounter with Babylonian religion, whose gods had only recently asserted their power through military conquest). Deutero-Isaiah, determined to bring God to Israel in exile, reminded the Jewish diaspora of God's unbounded presence and their undimished obligation to obey divine command.

Similarly, to locate the Prophets outside the covenantal tradition, as proponents of a morality independent of covenant morality, is to miss the meaning of their message. The Prophets, as God's "servants," were divinely charged with the responsibility of transmitting "all the Torah" (the laws, statutes, and judgments) which God had commanded to their ancestors. Their link to Moses (the first and greatest prophet) was made explicit by Hosea, who reminded Israel that "by a prophet the Lord brought Israel out of Egypt, and by a prophet was he preserved." The sacred tradition, "a providential history of divine deeds and disclosures and an ancient deposit of custom and law," was severely jolted by invasion and conquest, culminating in the loss of national independence and exile. Such a desperate situation required bold and novel efforts to secure that tradition within new circumstances. The written restatement of the ancient laws, as in the Deuteronomic text discovered in the Temple during Josiah's reign, expressed one such attempt. Prophecy represented a more direct and urgent effort to redirect Israel to its covenantal task. The Prophets were possessed by dire fears, inspired directly from God, that the sins of Israel would shatter the covenant irrevocably. Their message, delivered under the most menacing circumstances imaginable, chastised the Hebrew commonwealth for departing from the sacred tradition. "O Israel," Hosea implored, "return to the Lord thy God."[21]

Sent by God, the Prophets spoke for God. More than any of their contemporaries, they were distinguished by their concern with the convenantal relationship and by their determination to call Israel to its standard at a time when disregard was painfully apparent—at least to them. All around them, the Prophets saw disregard of the covenant, violations of the sacred law, distortions of its purpose. That is why the concept of loyalty is so paramount in prophecy; loyalty to God could only be expressed by covenantal faithfulness. The Prophets knew, and were determined to proclaim, that Israel was subject to "a code of conduct which represented for them the will of their God." Their "unique contribution," accordingly, was to have "actualized the covenant tradition in a situation of crisis, in which the old order had fallen into decay."[22]

The most impassioned prophetic denunciations rested unequivocally upon specific legal commands known to Israel. The prophetic standard of judgment was the sacred law; their social criticism is incomprehensible unless it is connected—as they connected it—to the covenant at Sinai. God's children "rebelled against me," Isaiah declared, reciting an indictment that concluded with the demand for covenantal loyalty and obedience. God wanted "loyal love" from Israel, Hosea pleaded; instead it had "transgressed the covenant." Jeremiah recounted God's message, to be proclaimed in the streets of Jerusalem: "Hear the words of this covenant, and do them." He referred to a "new" covenant between God and Israel; actually, a "renewed" covenant that would write the law in the hearts of the people. Ezekiel, prophesying the return from exile, relayed God's intention "to put my spirit within you, and cause you to follow my statutes." Then Israel would again dwell in its promised land, where (repeating the covenant formula) "you shall be my people and I will be your God."[23]

The prophetic indictment for violations of the sacred law was as sweeping as it was impassioned. Isaiah, Micah, Jeremiah, and Amos were unrelenting in their demands for what, in the modern era, has been transposed into "social justice." Their most memorable accusations condemned oppression of the poor, mistreatment of the disadvantaged (especially orphans, widows, and strangers), and perversions of justice. But these were hardly novel obligations thrust upon Israel by the Prophets. They comprised some of Israel's most ancient legal sanctions, repeatedly found in the various codes within Exodus, Leviticus, and Deuteronomy. Indeed, it is extremely difficult (if at all possible) to find *any* prophetic accusation that is independent of the sacred law. The Prophets knew the sacred law, cited it, and demanded obedience to it. Their denunciations were deeply rooted in the ancient tradition, which they remembered, evoked, and implored Israel to honor.[24]

Israel's demonstrable infidelity to the covenant infused prophetic denunciation with legal metaphors. Isaiah, Micah, Jeremiah, and Hosea all proclaimed God's "controversy" with Israel for violating divine statutes and commandments. Appropriately, God took His people to court for breach of covenant. In a series of divine lawsuits, with the Prophets functioning as God's prosecuting attorneys, Israel was indicted, tried, and convicted for its transgresssions: lying, killing, theft, adultery, bribery, slander, the perversion of justice, the worship of false gods. Litigation was a powerful prophetic metaphor (complementing marriage and harlotry) for the intimate bond between God and Israel and the divine wrath that disloyalty and infidelity provoked. The Prophets called Israel to account for covenantal transgressions before the bar of divine judgment.

The divine lawsuit as a trial for breach of covenant was a highly stylized form of prophetic accusation. It was most fully elaborated by Micah, who summoned Israel on God's behalf, before the hills and mountains as witnesses, to hear "the Lord's controversy . . . with his people." God, the divine plaintiff, recited His "righteous acts" on Israel's behalf. Israel responded with a guilty plea, offering sacrifice, even of its firstborn, in atonement. But God would not be so easily placated, insisting through the prophet that restitution required covenantal loyalty, the willingness "to walk humbly with God." Hosea provided another vivid illustration, beginning with his bold proclamation: "Hear the word of the Lord, you children of Israel: for the Lord has a controversy with the inhabitants of the land, because there is no truth, nor love, nor knowledge of God in the land." There was, instead, swearing, lying, killing, stealing, and adultery. There was idolatry and, furthermore, the priests themselves were guilty of "lewdness" and "harlotry" toward God. For these transgressions Israel was indicted for breach of covenant: "seeing thou hast forgotten the Torah of thy God, I will also forget thy children." In each instance (Jeremiah and

Isaiah provide others, less fully elaborated), Prophets summoned Israel to trial, conveyed the divine indictment, "thought in categories derived from the covenant," spoke "like lawyers quoting the law," and demanded, on God's behalf, that Israel demonstrate fidelity to convenantal norms.[25]

Whether or not the Prophets drew directly upon actual legal proceedings as their model, their choice of legal metaphors revealed something more than a random stylistic preference. It displayed their understanding of the nature of the relationship between God and Israel. The sustained and impassioned prophetic indictments of Israel for breach of covenant pointed to the very essence of the relationship and to the revelation that forged it. For Israel's ultimate sin, according to the prophet Amos, was that "they have despised the Torah of the Lord"; Israel, Hosea reiterated, had "transgressed my covenant, and rebelled against my Torah." Prophecy, therefore, was nothing less than "a call to return to the law." It is hardly coincidental that the prophetic books in the Hebrew Bible conclude with the stern admonition of Malachi, conveying God's instruction: "Remember the Torah of [Moses] my servant, which I commanded him in Horeb for all Israel, both statutes and judgments."[26]

Not only the covenant lawsuit but also the very meaning of "justice" in prophetic discourse demonstrated the prophetic commitment to covenantal fidelity. Justice, of course, was a fundamental, repetitive, thematic plea in prophecy. But the translation of prophetic *mishpat* into the modern Western notion of "justice" has compressed a complex, subtle biblical concept into a political slogan. Biblical *mishpat* has multiple levels of meaning. At its broadest, it conveys a sense of morally right conduct. So Abraham, confronting God's intention to annihilate Sodom, including its righteous inhabitants, inquired: "Shall not the Judge of all the earth do *mishpat*?" In this first biblical usage of the term, *mishpat* suggests divine justice, with God obligated to make right judgments. The term is given more precise legal focus in the covenant code of Exodus, the oldest collection of Israelite laws. There, *mishpatim* refers to the expansive body of ordinances or legal commands, including offenses against persons and property, moral norms, and ritual obligation, transmitted from God to Israel. In Leviticus, however, where Israel is commanded to have "one manner of law [*mishpat*] for stranger and Israelite alike," *mishpat* takes on the meaning of law that is just. The same principle is reworked in the Deuteronomic code as an instruction to Israelite judges (*mishpat* derives from the verb *shafat*, meaning judging): admonished to "judge righteously," they were obligated to respect rich and poor disputants, and large and small matters, equally in their "judgment" (*mishpat*).[27]

In the contextual fullness of its meaning, therefore, biblical *mishpat* embraced the justness of divine judgment, the divine ordinances transmitted to Israel, just law, and the just administration of law by the judges of Israel.

Mishpat commingled divinely revealed law, and divine justice, with procedural fairness and just judgments. *Mishpat*, in sum, defined a justly ordered relationship, based upon covenant obligation, between God and Israel. It conveyed, in the strongest language, the obligation to comply with God's "just ordinances." Justice meant nothing less than obedience to divine law. "God's first inescapable requirement is that the Israelites do 'justice,' Hebrew *mishpat*, a common term for the legal norms demanded by the covenant."[28]

It was this understanding of *mishpat* that the Prophets inherited and communicated. They had no conception of ethical conduct independent of divine command (although they drew sharp distinctions between ethical behavior and cultic ritual). The sum of God's demands upon Israel defined the paired concepts, *mishpat* and *tsedaka*, which appear so frequently in classical prophecy. "Justice" and "righteousness" are loose modern renditions of "judgment" and "rightness," or the right judgment that defines moral behavior. The idea that morality might be independent of "knowledge" of the ways of God was inconceivable to the Prophets who, after all, rested their claim to authority entirely upon divine command. Israel's sin, as God revealed through His prophet Ezekiel, was that "she has rebelled against my judgments" (*mishpat*). The essence of prophecy was its concern to restore "the relation between the God of Israel and Israel." Ethics or morality divorced from religion, or detached from law, were conceptually inconceivable.[29]

Furthermore, the legal injunction to do justice, which the Prophets reiterated, hardly was the innovative "Jewish" contribution to political morality that so often has been attributed to Amos or Isaiah. It replicated similar statutes that have been traced as far back as the Mesopotamian kingdom of 2400 B.C.E. (a millennium and a half before Hebrew prophecy). The Code of Hammurabi, seven centuries later, also protected widows, orphans, and the poor. (But the Torah, it should be noted, added "strangers" to the standard list of protected groups: widows, orphans, and the disadvantaged.) In Canaanite literature, before Israelite settlement, there is mention of a king renowned for "judging the cause of the widow, adjudicating the cause of the fatherless." Whether or not these admonitions were obeyed, they were understood to demonstrate the virtue of local rulers and their concern for the protection of their citizens. Many ancient civilizations had their own kings, or gods, who were guardians of justice and morality. Perhaps the Israelites borrowed this commitment from their neighbors or inherited it from their own ancestors, who may have been exposed to it before they left Mesopotamia, or during the period of Egyptian captivity, or from their contact with Canaanite culture.[30] In any event, the Prophets were as derivative as they were impassioned in their commitment to justice.

It was long a basic axiom of Bible scholarship (and modern secular thought) that prophets superseded the priesthood, emphasizing right over rite. But this tidy evolutionary progression, so supportive of the tenets of liberal Protestantism or Reform Judaism, simply cannot be sustained. Some of the Prophets, to be sure, spoke in what sound like strongly anticult overtones. Yet Israel expressed some of its deepest attachments to God through the mediation of the priestly cult. Israelite culture did not differentiate between covenantal obligation (law), cultic practice (ritual), and right conduct (morality). The cult (a collective term that includes the priestly caste and the rites of worship over which it presided) was a central institution of ancient Israelite society, rivaled only by the monarchy itself. In the holy sanctuaries, and at the public festivals, the people gained access to God and received their religious instruction. Individual piety and private prayer were not considered acceptable substitutes for public worship under priestly leadership. Through the cult, Israelite religion (like ancient religion elsewhere) "found its corporate expression, and a communication of religious ideals took place." When the Prophets began to proclaim their message of covenantal faithfulness, the priests were already respected leaders, the sanctuaries flourished, and the holy festivals were observed with ritualized elaboration.[31]

According to the Prophets, however, the cult had failed in its vital task of teaching "knowledge of God." A cult divorced from covenantal obligation, perhaps excessively influenced by local Canaanite practice, had lost its way, for "a religion without moral obedience, however elaborate its ceremonies and festivals, did not fulfill the demands of the holy God of Israel." And it was precisely those demands that the Prophets reiterated, understanding that the covenantal tradition itself depended upon "knowledge of God." According to Hosea's indictment, the priests had "forgotten the Torah." So God spoke through him, saying, "I desired loyal love, and not sacrifice; and the knowledge of God more than burnt offerings." Knowledge of God meant covenantal faithfulness, for it was through the covenant that God had instructed Israel. Hosea pleaded: "O Israel, return to the Lord thy God"; just as Amos had presented God's command, "Seek me, and you shall live." Prophetic intervention accompanied the perception that the cult, excessively devoted to ritual, had blunted the covenantal message. That is why Amos cried out, in God's behalf, "I hate, I despise your feasts, and I will not smell the sacrifices of your solemn assemblies. Though you offer me burnt offerings and your meal offerings, I will not accept them. . . . But let justice roll down like waters, and righteousness like a mighty stream."[32]

Prophets and priests did not disagree over the necessity of obedience to divine command; but the Prophets did question whether the shrines were the location "where the authentic word of Yahweh's covenant was to be heard." A people "laden with iniquity" (in Isaiah's description) had forsaken God by rebelling against the Torah. Therefore, "to what purpose is the multitude of your sacrifices," Isaiah asked. God was "sated with the burnt offerings of rams," and He could no longer "bear iniquity along with solemn meeting." Jeremiah, locating covenantal fidelity securely within historical tradition, delivered the divine reminder: "I did not speak to your fathers, nor command them in the day that I brought them out of the land of Egypt, concerning burnt offerings or sacrifices: but this thing I commanded them, saying, Obey my voice, and I will be your God, and you shall be my people: and walk in all the ways that I have commanded you, that it may be well with you." The Prophets did not denigrate the priestly cult; rather, they criticized "the worth of a cult that is not morally informed." Nor did they question the centrality of the Temple in the national religious life of the people, nor propose (the distinctively modern notion) that some form of deritualized moral behavior replace sacrificial ritual and formal worship. They were too deeply "rooted in the Torah of Moses, in its concepts of God, history, and the covenantal relationship" for that. They fully understood the seamlessness of law, ritual, and morality. Indeed, prophecy proclaimed it at a time when most others had forgotten it.[33]

One can go even further to note the close relationship that several prophets maintained to the priestly caste (a hereditary office), to cultic ritual, and to cultic institutions, especially the Temple. Nor should this attachment be surprising. How could they hope to communicate to Israel if they repudiated the very tradition (and the institutions that sustained it) on which their plea for covenantal fidelity depended? Several of the early Prophets, sparse evidence suggests, had important cultic connections. Although Amos, for example, identified himself solely as a shepherd (*noged*) and even disavowed any hereditary relationship to the prophetic guild, a quite similar Akhadian word (*naqidu*) referred to a supervisor of flocks who belonged to a temple. References in other ancient texts suggest that the high priest also supervised the *nqdm*. The term "shepherd," as Amos used it, may well have implied a relationship to the temple priesthood no less than to his flock of sheep.

Isaiah's prophetic call can be located even more explicitly in a cultic context. Isaiah recalled both his vision of God and his own instant apprehension, for he was "a man of unclean lips . . . in the midst of a people of unclean lips." But one of the holy seraphim came to him with a live coal from the divine altar, "and he laid it upon my mouth, and said, Lo, this has touched thy lips; and thy iniquity is taken away, and thy sin is purged." Only then, when God asked for a messenger to the people, could Isaiah answer (precisely echoing Abraham's reply to God's call), "Here am I." The ritual cleansing of Isaiah's lips, in anticipation of the divine call, was a vivid cultic symbol of Isaiah's readiness for his divine mission.[34]

The Prophet Ezekiel was himself a priest, whose categories of judgment resonated with references to defilement, cleansing, and purification. His revulsion with life in exile was evident. Ezekiel addressed the "rebellious house" of Israel, whose people "have eyes to see, and see not; they have ears to hear, and hear not." "Estranged" from God by their idolatry (not by an insufficient commitment to justice), they acted "faithlessly." Deutero-Isaiah, too, saw only "deaf" and "blind" people, unable to respond to divine command. But both prophets, insisting that exile was temporary, held out the divine reassurance of national redemption in the land of Israel (an irony that modern dispersed Jews, who revere the Prophets as the spokesmen of universal, ethical norms, might still ponder). Jerusalem would be rebuilt, Isaiah promised, and the Temple would rise from its own ashes. Ezekiel's vision of restoration was suffused with cultic and covenantal imagery. He relayed God's assurance: "Then will I sprinkle clean water upon you, and you shall be clean. . . . And I will put my spirit within you, and cause you to follow my statutes. . . . And you shall be my people, and I will be your God." Redeemed from exile, purified, with the Temple rebuilt, the covenant once again would bind Israel and God to each other.[35]

Once national restoration actually occurred, under the benevolent aegis of the Persian King Cyrus, the later Prophets of Israel— Haggai and Zechariah especially—were vigorous advocates of cultic renewal within a rebuilt Temple. Measured solely by tangible achievement, their prophecy represented "the zenith of prophetic activity," when word and deed were fused most successfully. From Haggai we learn that the people, still precariously reestablished in their homeland, remained reluctant to undertake the task of rebuilding "the Lord's house." God instructed His Prophet to encourage them with the assurance that "I will take pleasure in it, and I will be glorified." The people and the high priest responded immediately to that vision of renewed national glory centered upon the holy sanctuary, and they worked speedily to rebuild it. Similarly, Zechariah's prophecy overflowed with cultic symbols clustered around national restoration, and the day when all nations would display "holiness to the Lord" and worship the God of Israel at the Temple in Jerusalem.[36]

It was hardly coincidental that the prophetic era closed with the rebuilding of the Temple. Indeed, that tangible architectural symbol of national religious renewal may be taken as the crowning triumph of prophecy. None of the earlier prophets had elicited such an immediate and favorable public response to their message, nor does the prophetic literature suggest that any of them succeeded as conspicuously as Haggai and Zachariah in translating their message into enduring institutional form. However powerfully prophecy may be interpreted as a call for an independent spiritual, ethical religion, the Prophets—especially Haggai and

Zechariah—understood the relationship in the national religion of Israel between private morality and public worship; between personal striving toward holiness and the ritualized forms of its expression. With the rebuilding of the Temple, it has been said, prophecy returned "to the security of its original home in the sanctuary."[37]

It is, therefore, a gross distortion to separate prophecy from the institutional forms of religious observance in biblical Israel. Isaiah protested only against a "vain" cult, associated with "iniquity"; Hosea criticized only a cult comprised of thieving and murderous priests. The innovation so frequently attributed to the Prophets—an ethical, spiritual relationship to God unmediated by ritualized observance—is "a modern anachronism." Just as lawlessness was understood by the Prophets as a manifestation of disobedience to God, so their social criticism was indistinguishable from loyalty to God. It was not the novelty of their message but their "tremendous personal experience of God," their "sense of obligation to surrender heart and will completely to the command of God," that distinguished classical prophecy. Nothing was more characteristic of prophecy than its theocentricity, the self-perception of the Prophets as "champions of the original religion of Yahweh in its pure form." The ultimate failure of Israelite society, they knew, was "a deranged relationship to God." As Amos proclaimed: "Seek the Lord, and live." The God of Israel, by the very nature of His deliverance of His people from Egyptian slavery, was a God of justice and moral concern. So the prophetic demand for morality and justice could not be independent of divine will, but only an affirmation of divine command.[38]

The task of the prophet, as Amos (the prophet and shepherd) knew, was to return wayward stragglers, to prod the entire flock along the right-(eous) way defined by the sacred law. Righteous law, commanded by God, defined the boundaries of Hebrew prophecy. "The 'immorality' of the people was in reality their 'illegal' behavior," as the Prophets so relentlessly insisted. Their message would have been altogether meaningless, and surely not incorporated in the biblical canon, had their demands for "righteousness" and "justice" not been formulated well within the sacred-law tradition.[39] The historic unity of law and prophecy, which the Bible itself expresses, retains its centrality in Jewish worship to this day. The "associative link" between these texts, which are read in conjunction with each other, is now two thousand years old. This can hardly be construed as the attraction of polar opposites, with the stern rigor of law moderated by prophetic morality. Rather, it demonstrates what one scholar has called "the unity of the divine message inherent in Scripture as a whole. . . . Torah and Prophets speak the same language, although emerging from different times and backgrounds."[40]

There is no need to look to the eighth-century Prophets for a novel infusion of morality into Jewish law; law and morality were inextricably bound from the beginning of Israel's national existence. In Torah as in prophecy, the ultimate source of morality was divine will. In the explicit Deuteronomic warning to Israel about false prophecy, Moses insisted that a prophet, to be heeded, must be "like me." For God had assured him, "I . . . will put my words in his mouth; and he shall speak . . . all that I shall command him." Moses, appropriately, was lawgiver *and* Prophet. Inherent in his role duality was the unity of law and prophecy, inseparable parts of a single revelation. Obedience to divine command, as Moses and every prophet who came after him understood, marked the true prophet.[41]

Prophecy and law, as different expressions of a unitary message, have been taken to reveal a dialectical tension within the sacred-law tradition itself. There was the need in ancient Israel (as in any culture) for a balance between "institution and charisma, the claims of the past and those of the future." Torah provided the "norm of faith"; prophecy contributed millennial hope. But prophecy detached from law could only be a source of confusion and disunity. The inclusion of prophecy in the sacred canon, Joseph Blenkinsopp has suggested, may well have been the expression of "an unresolved tension, an unstable equilibrium" between order and disruption. Without the sacred-law tradition, there could be "no shared memory and therefore no community." Prophecy may have enabled that tradition to "breathe," amid the new and fearsome circumstances of internal disruption, external threat, invasion, defeat, and dispersion. The prophet was "a renovator of the tradition," enabling it to live and endure until Israel had once again rearranged its national life in accord with the terms of its covenant with God.[42]

The unity of the sacred-law tradition, with prophecy securely embedded in Torah, was shattered in 70 C.E., with the destruction of the Second Temple. At that critical juncture in Jewish history the rabbis, as the self-appointed defenders of that tradition, shaped it in their image. Locating themselves in the direct line of succession to Moses, they confined prophecy to a subservient position. The Prophets became mere rabbinical precursors, dedicated exclusively to the task of expounding the Sinai revelation and demanding obedience to it. This was reiterated in the opening sentence of the Mishnah tractate *Aboth* ("Fathers"), which linked the Prophets securely within the transmission of the sacred-law tradition: from Moses to Joshua to the Elders to the Prophets to the Men of the Great Synagogue—and, ultimately, to the rabbis. The Prophets were custodians of the Torah, passing intact to their successors what they had received from their forbears. Each, in turn, was engaged in the task of explicating the Torah and demanding obedience to its precepts.[43]

As the rabbis confronted the Christian claim that the Prophets had preached a new faith that reached its full and final expression in Christianity, it became all the more imperative to contain prophecy. While the early church maximized prophetic originality, the rabbis minimized it, insisting that the prophetic mission was to proclaim and interpret the Sinai revelation, not in any way to modify or expand it. Quite apart from Christian theology, however, the rabbis had their own reasons to locate prophecy securely within the revealed tradition. The prophetic potential for menacing rabbinical authority was considerable: anyone who claimed to bear a special message from God posed a serious challenge to the newly established rabbinical order.[44] So the rabbis, while affirming the validity of prophecy, effectively silenced it. Many centuries later, Christians and Jews found new reasons to hear and to heed the prophetic message.

Hebrew prophecy was rediscovered in the nineteenth century. The disintegration of Jewish legal authority after emancipation encouraged the search for alternative sources of Jewish legitimation. The Prophets, liberated from the constraints of tribe, cult, and sacred law, were hailed as the founders of a universal religion of moral idealism and ethical monotheism (which bore a remarkable resemblance to liberal Protestantism and Reform Judaism). Wrenched from historical context and stripped of legal content, prophecy appealed to a wide variety of Jews who had broken with traditional Judaism but still wanted to justify themselves in Jewish terms. More or less consciously, they internalized the Christian disjunction between law and prophecy, elevating prophecy to a position of independent morality that it had never claimed, or enjoyed, within normative Judaism.

But the characteristic attentiveness of modern Jews to the prophetic message may only suggest that they hear in prophecy what they want to hear. The prophetic "tradition" with which they identify (universal social justice divorced from divine command) is, in fact, little more than a century old. It can best be understood as part of the Jewish response to emancipation. As Jews conformed to Christian standards of dress, diet, decorum, calendar observance, and religious ritual, so they also absorbed the Christian conception of Hebrew prophecy, entirely detached from law. Prophecy provided a bridge, built in large measure by Christian exegetes, that Jews crossed in their modern exodus from historical Judaism to enlightened liberalism in the Christian West.

Severed from the Jewish covenantal tradition and grafted to Christian theology (and then to liberal politics), prophecy came to define enlightened Judaism. To Reform rabbis, the Prophets represented reason, progress, morality, and American democratic virtues. To radical socialists the Prophets were nascent Marxists, denouncing class exploitation and proclaiming universal brotherhood. To political liberals, they became (and remain) social-justice advocates who anticipated the correct liberal response to current political issues. Jews who were uncomfortable with Jewish law or ritual were free to cite the prophetic "alternative" of justice and righteousness. Prophecy, in its time a desperate cry to return to the ancient faith of covenantal obligation, became in the modern era an exit from that faith. The Prophets, who spoke to almost no one in ancient Israel, now spoke to almost everyone, even the faithless. The prophetic tradition had become the antithesis of tradition.

Prophecy served as a passport to modernity for American Jews— but not only for American Jews. Secular Zionists in Israel associated their act of statebuilding with Hebrew prophecy, not as a measure of their fidelity to the word of God but to justify their decisive break with religious Judaism. When Prime Minister David Ben-Gurion presented his first government to the Knesset, he echoed Israel's Declaration of Independence, declaring, "Our activities and policy are guided . . . by a political and social vision that we have inherited from our Prophets." He hardly meant to imply that Israel was to be dedicated to the word of God, to the covenant, or to the sacred law. His identification with prophecy was intended to repudiate, not fulfill, any notions of fidelity to divine command. But secular Zionists, like their liberal counterparts in the United States, created prophets in their own image. They have reflexively cited the Prophets as political allies in their struggles against the very conception of covenantal obligation that the ancient prophets so passionately defended.[45]

It is a measure of their powerful eloquence that the Prophets ultimately became so accessible to all faiths in every political season. As Robert Alter has written, they had "urgent ideas— indictments, warnings, words of consolation—to convey to their audience . . . and the imaginative authority with which history was turned into a theatre of timeless hopes and fears explains why these poems still address us so powerfully today."[46] But irrespective of the varied uses to which prophecy has been put, history also has its claims. Modern liberals may make of prophecy what they will; and their imaginative transmutations provide fascinating insights into the changing sources of legitimation, both political and religious, for modern Jews. But the temptation to trim prophecy to current political fashion may only reflect the anxieties of Jews who are eager to reformulate Jewish tradition in order to elude its historical distinctiveness and its sacred-law obligations.

In a time of supreme crisis for ancient Israel, prophecy reiterated those connections that defined the national religion of Judaism: between God and Israel, between law and justice, between morality and ritual. Only within the last century have Jews, responding to the imperatives of acculturation, transformed prophecy into a repudiation of the very sacred-law tradition that is at its core. Wrenched from sacred text and historical context, prophetic justice lost its intimate biblical association with covenantal obligation. Instead, it became a thoroughly secular, extralegal standard, the repudiation of the sacred law rather than an impassioned cry for fidelity to it.

To recapture the vitality of prophecy requires attentiveness to a delicate balance within Jewish tradition: between faith and hope, order and change, divine command and human choice. The unity of law and prophecy in the Hebrew Bible preserved that balance, leaving both prophecy and law to affirm, in different ways, divine authority, covenantal obligation, and the imperative of a restored national life in the land of Israel. The shattering of that unity, as Jews submitted to the authority of modernity, has made it all but impossible even to comprehend the message of the Hebrew Prophets, no less actually to abide by it.

CONVERGENCE: RABBIS & LAWYERS

Emancipation: The Disintegration of Jewish Legal Authority

P lausible arguments have been advanced for locating the moment when Judaism crystallized into a normative way of life, defined by the terms of the sacred law, at Sinai; or with the discovery of the Deuteronomic book during Josiah's reign; or with Ezra's leadership in Babylonian exile; or at Yohanan ben Zakkai's academy in Yavneh; or with the Talmudic sages who, as Salo Baron has written, welded "the enormous discrepancies in Jewish life . . . into a common basic pattern" that endured into the modern era. But there is little dispute over the tradition itself or the texts that defined and sustained it. It comprised the written Torah of divine revelation, the Oral Law of human interpretation, codified in the Talmud and administered by the exercise of rabbinical legal authority. It depended upon shared fundamental assumptions about God, the covenantal relationship with Israel, and redemption in the promised land.

The bonds of covenantal obligation, connecting Jews from Sinai to eternity, enabled Judaism to survive virtually every encounter with rival political or religious systems, from Persian and Roman imperial rule to Hellenistic polytheism, from monotheistic Christianity and Islam to medieval feudalism. Jews always responded to the dominant external culture, and Judaism always absorbed from it. Yet Judaism retained the internal resources to preserve its own autonomy within the various gentile societies that welcomed, tolerated, or resisted its presence. The sacred law, self-evident and self-contained, defined a religious nation in exile in which a Jew was "always a Jew" and "*only* a Jew."[1]

At the end of the eighteenth century that definition of Judaism, and the way of life that expressed and reinforced it, was irreparably shattered. The Enlightenment, with its sanctification of reason, undermined faith in religious authority. Separating religion from politics, it emphasized liberty, equality, and the rights of free citizens, simultaneously relegating religion to the realm of private conscience. The assertion of state power, and the obligation to obey it, undermined competing claims of religious authority. The benefits of citizenship demanded identification with the state and loyalty to its institutions. The Enlightenment instigated nothing less than "a radical rupture not only with traditional habits and beliefs but with the fundamental vision according to which Jews had long understood the world." For the first time in eighteen centuries, since their loss of national independence, Jews were free to define themselves.[2]

As the promise beckoned of political equality, and even social integration, Jews transformed their ghetto walls into the gates of freedom. But freedom was not an unrestricted gift. For Jews the price of their prized new status as enlightened citizens, in France and Germany, was the repudiation of Jewish sacred law, which had come to symbolize an irrational religious particularism that was intolerable within an "enlightened" society. Jews who wished to enter that society must be "emancipated," liberated from the constraints of religious authority. Emancipation, in its essence, was a process of legal divestment as Jews moved toward political and civic equality—the replacement of Jewish legal authority with the authority of the state. Judaism had become a religion only, devoid of national content and lacking communal autonomy. As Count Stanislas de Chermont-Tonnerre, a prominent advocate of emancipation, insisted during the debate over the eligibility of Jews for citizenship, "The Jews should be denied everything as a nation, but granted everything as individuals." It was "intolerable," he continued, "that the Jews should become a separate political formation or class in the country." Jews understood what was expected of them. "How absolutely necessary it is," implored a Jewish merchant from Nancy, "for us to divest ourselves entirely of that narrow spirit, of Corporation and Congregation, in all civil and political matters . . . we must absolutely appear simply as individuals, as Frenchmen guided only by a true patriotism."[3]

No one grasped the implications of Jewish emancipation more astutely than Napoleon, who carefully orchestrated ceremonies of renunciation and allegiance for French Jews. In 1806 he convened an Assembly of Jewish Notables to ratify the new status of emancipated Jews. Napoleon, one of his commissioners explained, genuinely wished Jews to become French citizens; whether they would accept the honor bestowed by "a Christian Prince" was a decision that turned, ultimately, upon their true legal allegiance. With hardly an exception, each of Napoleon's questions to the Assembly required Jews to choose between rival legal systems, deciding whether to retain or repudiate rabbinical legal authority. Whether the subject was polygamy, divorce, intermarriage, or usury, whether it concerned obedience to the French civil code or submission to rabbinical jurisdiction, the issue was the same. What did Jewish law prescribe? Were Jews still bound to obey it? Or, "Do the Jews born in France, and treated by the law as French citizens, consider France as their country? . . . Are they bound to obey [its] laws?"[4]

The Jewish Notables answered unequivocally. Jews "must, above all, acknowledge and obey the laws of the prince. . . . In the eyes of every Israelite, without exception, submission to the prince is the first of duties." The Notables conceded that "Jews no longer form a separate people." They pledged their undivided allegiance, as French citizens, to "the laws of the State." Accordingly, rabbinical authority was now confined "to preaching morality in the temples, blessing marriages, and pronouncing divorces."[5]

The climactic moment in this drama of legal transformation occurred when Napoleon, with his characteristic flair for the grand gesture, convened a great Sanhedrin in Paris to ratify the Assembly's decision. Such majestic irony: the Sanhedrin, the supreme judicial institution of the Jewish community during five centuries of Roman rule in Palestine, now was summoned to abrogate Jewish legal authority. Its task was defined as Jewish enlightenment, to "bring back the Jews to the true meaning of the law," by teaching them "to love and to defend the country they inhabit." The French Sanhedrin was delighted to accommodate. Blessing God for Napoleon as "the instrument of His compassion," and seizing the opportunity "to be one with the great family of the State," it split Jewish sacred law into political and religious components, repudiated the former ("since Israel no longer forms a nation"), and invoked "our sacred laws" as the authority to "religiously enjoin on all [Jews] obedience to the State in all matters civil and political." Its "holy enterprise" concluded, it vanished along with the legal authority that it had so eagerly relinquished.[6]

Emancipation provided the assurance to Jews that the boundaries and distinctions that had so long separated them from Christian society were no longer justified, or even permissible. It was nothing less than an invitation to assimilation. The promise of civil rights and legal equality was inseparable from the demand that Jews conform to the norms of Christian society. Emancipated Jews would eat the same food as Christians, wear the same clothes, and work the same days of the week. They would understand themselves within Christian categories: Judaism (like Christianity) was a religion only; as a religion, it no longer demanded legal obedience but was solely a matter of spiritual faith. Any attributes of Judaism that impeded full social and political integration must be eliminated, for emancipation instilled "the manifold need to diminish Jewish otherness." This assured a momentous crisis of Jewish legal authority. With fidelity to Jewish law disavowed, the juridical role of the rabbinate all but disappeared. The enlightened rabbi of a congregation of emancipated Jews no longer derived his authority from "a tangible, sacred and comprehensive legal tradition." Indeed, that very tradition had ceased to exist.[7]

Emancipation imposed new constraints upon Jewish life in the guise of freedom. "Suddenly extricated from the traditional bonds of autonomy," Jews experienced the altogether novel "compulsion to become a part of the modern state." Without the cohesion of a community, history, calendar, language, ritual, and law—without, that is, all the attributes of their national religious culture— "the Christianization of Judaism" was inevitable and irresistible. As the ghetto walls crumbled and Jews began their scramble toward freedom, they trampled the hedge surrounding the Torah, so carefully cultivated and intricately pruned during many centuries of rabbinical legal authority. "A Jewish community so conceived," Baron has concluded, "was but a pale reflection of its former self."[8]

As traditional legal obligations became modern options, obedience to law ceased to define what it meant to be a Jew. Each Jew could choose; every choice contained presuppositions about Jewish law, or its negation. At the antinomian extreme, Reform Jews insisted upon the freedom to choose which laws to obey, or whether to obey any. Orthodox Jews still insisted upon the Torah as the word of God and remained committed to the written and oral law regardless of shifting social values among the gentiles—or among Jews. In time, Conservative Jews, perhaps conceding the divine origin of Jewish law, would insist upon its human development and application. Secular Jews, of course, rejected the authority of Jewish law altogether. The fragmentation of Jewish life is the distinctive legacy of two centuries of emancipation.[9]

At the time, few enlightened European thinkers imagined that Judaism was the spiritual equal of Christianity, capable of ridding itself of archaic legalism. Jews could hardly ignore such denigration, which reflected precisely the modern categories of reason and freedom that Judaism had to absorb to demonstrate its spiritual capacity and intellectual vitality. Jews internalized the Christian critique, ultimately reformulating it as the rejection of *halakhic* authority that came to characterize Reform Judaism. Reform was "predicated upon harmonizing Judaism with modernity." Despite its valiant effort "to legitimate its novelty in terms of venerated tradition," by locating itself within the historical process of *halakhic* development, the Reform response to modernity constituted a decisive repudiation of Jewish legal tradition. Although it began (in Germany as in the United States) as a reform of ritual and liturgy only, it soon became an explicit rejection of the sacred law itself. To the radical Reformer Samuel Holdheim, law no longer served as an appropriate religious category. The Talmud, he insisted, had "mistakenly and artificially" preserved the legal system of ancient Israel. But the dispersion of the Jews had "abrogated the law" (precisely as Christians claimed their New Testament had done). For Holdheim, as for other Reformers, there could be no significant distinction between a delegalized Judaism and "undogmatic Christianity."[10]

The fullest implications of Reform ideology only became evident in the United States. Long before there was Reform, American Jews were already reformed. Just a year after national independence, a German visitor to the United States was startled to observe that Jews could not be identified "by their beards and costume, but are dressed like all other citizens, shave regularly, and also eat pork." The reasons are well known: Jews constituted a tiny fragment of the American population; there was no nationally established church; denominational pluralism and religious voluntarism enabled Judaism to legitimate itself in the American setting; the prevailing cultural norm of individualism encouraged Jews, like everyone else, to define themselves as they pleased. A more congenial environment for radical Reform to flourish can hardly be imagined, and none existed outside the United States.[11]

American Reform was devised by Jews, primarily from Germany, who wanted nothing less than a version of Judaism compatible with full integration into American society. Reform fit comfortably into the American political culture, which had already formally absorbed—in the First Amendment—the "separated double authority structure" of religion and state that was distinctive to Western Christian culture. But Reform, always attentive to "the spirit of the age," immediately encountered the dilemma of postemancipation Judaism: the impossibility of becoming American without conforming to Christian norms and the difficulty of conforming to Christian norms while remaining, in any recognizable form, Jewish. The agility of Reform in performing its delicate balancing act has been subjected to a wide range of comment, both critical and complimentary. No one interested in the process of American Jewish acculturation can fail to be impressed with Reform dexterity, for the inner logic of its own flexibility required sensitive monitoring of shifting political and religious currents. As "the intellectual child of the Enlightenment," Reform—in the United States as elsewhere—had to rearrange the shattered fragments of the national religion into a new pattern, suitable for an age of reason and progress in the land of freedom.[12]

The pioneers of American Reform ventured into a barren Jewish landscape. The first ordained rabbi did not arrive in the United States until 1840; his frustrations in a country where "most people eat foul food and desecrate the Sabbath in public" led him to wonder "whether it is even permissible for a Jew to live in this land." Disheartened, he left the rabbinate to open a dry goods store. But other rabbis persisted; by the Civil War, the direction of Reform was unmistakable: to modify ritual observance in ways that would make Judaism dignified and American. English replaced Hebrew as the language of prayer; organ music was introduced; men and women began to sit together, the men often with their heads uncovered; calls for decorum were as frequent as calls to prayer; the rabbi was becoming more valued for his pulpit lectures than for his learning; and a new prayerbook eliminated references to exile and prayers for the return to the land of Israel. As Isaac Mayer Wise, the author of this new *Minhag America* (American custom), declared, "The Jew must be Americanized." If, in isolation, none of these liturgical or ritual changes was especially momentous, taken together they made the obvious and intended point: American Reform would express the inner logic of emancipation, which defined freedom in Western Christian terms.[13]

The Americanization of Judaism, under the aegis of Reform, was simultaneously its Protestantization. Throughout most of the nineteenth century, American culture was so suffused with evangelical Protestantism that it is difficult to determine where one ended and the other began. In fact, if not in law, Protestantism was the established American religion. The union of church and state might be invisible, but it was there nonetheless. (The very fact that American laws did not enforce Christianity was understood, by an Ohio judge, to demonstrate that "they *are* the laws of a Christian people," for "true Christianity asks no aid from the sword of civil authority.") National unity and purpose, from the education of schoolchildren to the formulation of foreign policy, were defined by the postulates of "a common Christianity." In this context, the "reform" of Judaism could hardly proceed independently of Protestant influence. If Reform "too readily resolved the tension between 'being Jewish' and 'being American,'" it hardly had a choice. How could it better demonstrate its virtues than by conforming to American values?[14]

The process of Reform is illuminated by the contributions of the two most influential American rabbis of the nineteenth century, Isaac Mayer Wise and Kaufmann Kohler. They molded Reform into the Judaism of German immigrants who, like themselves, fervently wished to become Americans. Wise was the institutional architect of the movement; Kohler its ideological craftsman. Between them, they made Reform into the dominant expression of American Judaism, a Judaism whose ultimate source of authority was American patriotism, not Jewish law.

Wise came to the United States in 1846, a young man in his mid-twenties but already a veteran of the internecine conflict that had polarized European Judaism into the warring camps of Reform and Orthodoxy. After some bruising encounters with the Orthodox rabbinate and exposure to the soothing currents of liberal Judaism, he caught "the American fever" and emigrated with his wife, young child, and two dollars. His first exposure to American Jewish life filled him with dismay. In one New York synagogue he found "antiquated and tedious ritual"; in another, "crass ignorance"; in still another, "Polish cabbalistical rabbinism and supernaturalism." Wise, never one to mince words, described "a Babel-like confusion" where "darkness ruled."[15]

"It was perfectly evident to me," Wise concluded, "that Judaism would have no future in America unless mighty upheavals, accompanied by constructive action," reconciled it with "the atmosphere of American freedom." For the next half century, that task defined Wise's agenda. First in Albany, and then in Cincinnati, Wise "struggled and strove like one possessed" to unify American Jewry behind the principles of Reform. At first, however, he provoked only contention and division. Whether he rearranged seating to integrate men and women, introduced music and a choir, deleted liturgical references to the Messiah, the land of Israel, and sacrifice, or demanded decorum, his innovations exacerbated conflict. But Wise persisted, impervious to criticism, even when it erupted into physical violence. Assaulted by an angry opponent as he went to remove the Torah from the ark during a Rosh Hashanah service, Wise shrugged aside what one local newspaper described as "great excitement in the Jewish church" to pursue his relentless struggle for a Judaism of reason, culture, and enlightenment.[16]

Wise insisted upon a Judaism that was in harmony with "the spirit of the age and the opinions prevalent in the new fatherland." His primary sources of inspiration, quite literally, were church and state. To improve his command of English (and perhaps to observe decorous religious observance), Wise, for a time, attended Sunday church services, and he cultivated the friendship of the Christian clergy. What the church provided in form, the state offered in substance. During his first visit to the South in 1849, he was awestruck by his encounters with national politicians and southern aristocrats. He described the Senate as the "great Sanhedrin" and emerged from a meeting with Daniel Webster "utterly changed and metamorphosed." He proudly claimed credit for being the first rabbi to visit an American president; Zachary Taylor conceded that Wise certainly was the first rabbi that the president had ever seen. Wise's Washington visit enabled him to feel "that I was one of the American people." His sojourn in Charleston reinforced those feelings. "I was domiciled in splendid rooms. A negro was placed at my disposal. I was the guest of American aristocrats for the first time in my life." At the Charleston temple (dedicated, just a few years earlier, with the ringing declaration: "this synagogue is our temple, this city our Jerusalem, this happy land our Palestine") Wise encountered "people of all culture and refinement," who were Americans to the core. He returned north determined that "antiquated" Judaism would yield to Reform.[17]

"I think it is my sacred mission to teach an enlightened and pure Judaism," Wise wrote, "free from the chains of superstition and the fetters of legalism." In the East, however, Wise was plagued by (Orthodox) "obscurantists and night-owls who obstructed the progress of humanity." So, in 1854, he accepted an invitation from a staunchly Reform congregation in Cincinnati, part of that "new world" where people were "not yet cast into a fixed mold." Wise anticipated "a glorious future" for Reform in the American heartland, fulfilling his ideal of an American Judaism "free, progressive, enlightened, united, and respected." This meant that any Jewish law, custom, ritual, or doctrine that was foreign to American practice— "whatever makes us ridiculous before the world"—must yield. The only remedy for the encrusted defects of Judaism was Americanization. In the United States, Wise believed, "the unsophisticated principles of democratic liberty and of stern justice," promulgated by Moses thirty-three centuries earlier, had come to fruition.[18]

Wise found a receptive audience away from the eastern centers of orthodoxy, especially among the tens of thousands of new immigrants from Germany who settled in the Midwest, South, and Southwest during the 1840s and 1850s. In an unending stream of sermons and articles and with his revised prayerbook (*Minhag America*), Wise prepared the foundation for his two great institutional innovations: a union of American Hebrew congregations (organized in 1873) and a Hebrew rabbinical college (which opened two years later). Only "ministers" who were thoroughly American could assure the proper education of Jews as "American citizens." When the first rabbinical class graduated from the Hebrew Union College in 1883, its achievement (and Wise's) was celebrated with a banquet of oysters, shrimp, and crabmeat, in flagrant violation of the laws of *kashrut*. Judaism, as Wise had proudly proclaimed a few years earlier, had truly been reformed "to correspond with the spirit and tastes of this age and this country."[19]

But almost precisely at the moment when Wise's institutional innovations were securely in place and Reform had established its ideological dominance over American Jewish life, the new equilibrium was upset. The beginning of a massive influx of Jews from Eastern Europe, the geographical and cultural stronghold of Orthodoxy, decisively shifted the demographic balance of American Jewry. The Reform Judaism of an assimilated German community was altogether foreign to the newcomers. No matter how far the Eastern Europeans had strayed from Orthodoxy (far enough, certainly, to emigrate to a land that their rabbis described as *trefe*—ritually unclean), the radical transformation of Judaism from a comprehensive way of life to an occasional and decorous affirmation of faith had little to offer them.

Wise found the newcomers primitive at best and, at worst, repulsive. They may have reminded him of his visit (in 1855) to a Polish synagogue in St. Louis, where "the people cried out, sang, shook themselves, jumped and hopped about." Wise's hostility toward Eastern European Jews never abated. American cities, he complained thirty years later, were filled with a "half-civilized orthodoxy," Jews who ignored the blessing of freedom to "gnaw the dead bones of past centuries." The distinction, to Wise, was self-evident: "We are Americans and they are not."[20]

The task of defining the principles of Reform, in response to the challenges of immigration and Orthodoxy, was left to a younger generation of rabbis, whose dominating theoretician was Kaufmann Kohler. Kohler, a man of considerable intellectual substance, had grown up in Furth, the center of Bavarian Orthodoxy. His family and his earliest teachers (especially Rabbi Samson Raphael Hirsch, the founder of neo-Orthodoxy) were deeply rooted in traditional Jewish culture. But Kohler's university study in Munich shattered its precepts. Tasting the "forbidden fruit from the tree of knowledge," Kohler found it irresistible: "My eyes opened and I was driven out of the paradise of my childhood." In his doctoral thesis, an analysis of the blessing of Jacob, he insisted that religion must "serve the struggle of the age towards truth, unity, and ethical freedom." Such radical ideas blocked a rabbinical appointment in Europe; so, in 1869, Kohler came to the United States. The rabbi who once had described Reform temples as "a perversion of a house of worship" now found them altogether congenial in Detroit, Chicago (where he introduced Sunday Sabbath services), and, after 1879, New York.[21]

Kohler's energies were engaged by the widening rift between the Judaism of tradition and modernity. In 1885, he was provoked into his most thoughtful analysis by Rabbi Alexander Kohut, an Orthodox Talmudic scholar from Hungary, who, in a series of weekly discourses entitled "the Ethics of the Fathers," delivered a stinging rebuke to Reform. Judaism, Kohut argued, was still linked by an unbreakable "chain of tradition" to the Torah that Moses received at Sinai. Anyone who denies "the binding nature of the Law," he insisted, "writes his own epitaph: 'I am no Jew.'" Reform, to Kohut, was nothing but a "deformity."[22]

Kohler avidly responded to the challenge. In a series of lectures to his congregation, entitled "Backward or Forward?" he confronted the pivotal issue of postemancipation Jewish life: the role of law in defining the Jewish community. To be "real Jews," Kohler asked in his first lecture, must we "keep all the *rites and ceremonies* prescribed by law and tradition?" Surely not. The Bible, he insisted, was "the revelation offered to an uncouth and uncivilized age." As appropriate as Mosaic law may have been for such a "childish and semi-barbarous nation," it was rendered deficient by the only standard that Kohler and Reform would acknowledge: "modern enlightenment and progress." Kohler demanded freedom from the "rust and mould" of the past—freedom, that is, "from the yoke of mere *legality*." En-

lightened Jews must not harken to Sinai, to the thunder and smoke of revelation, but to the universal truths of prophecy. While Orthodoxy "wails
over the ruins of the past," preserving "obsolete observances," Reform
staked its claim to the religion which "our prophets . . . proclaimed to be
as broad as man and as wide as the globe."[23]

Judaism, for Kohler, was "the law of life." ("The life of the law," Oliver
Wendell Holmes, Jr., had written just a few years earlier in *The Common
Law*, "has been experience"—those "felt necessities of the time" that mold
legal development.) To be "a *living faith*," not a religious dead letter, Judaism must divest itself of "ceremonial and prohibitory ritual statutes," preserving only "the moral statutes" that derived from prophecy. Just as the
Prophets had cut through Mosaic legalism to proclaim their univerasl
truths, so Reform had cut through the "thick, impenetrable forest of legal
statutes" of rabbinical Judaism.[24]

Once liberated from servitude to "the letter of the law," Judaism could
then adapt to "the free soil of America." In his concluding lecture, appropriately delivered on July 4th, Kohler defined the alternatives as "Palestinian" or "American" Judaism. The date had a dual calendrical significance.
Not only was it the anniversary of American independence, but it was also
the Sabbath in the Hebrew calendar following 17 Tammuz (when the Second Temple walls were breached by the Roman legions), three weeks before the day of lamentation and fasting on the 9th of Av that commemorated the destruction of the Temple. Kohler, fully aware of the duality,
used it to clinch his argument. Every Jew, he insisted, must decide whether
to mourn the loss of the Temple or to celebrate the American "Holy Land
of Freedom and Human Rights." Only in the United States, "the land
where milk and honey flow for all," could those human ideals "which form
the essence and soul of our religion" be realized. Jews, truly at home in
America, could no longer pray for a return to Jerusalem, for that was "blas-
phemy." Nor could they "remain Hebrews in garb and custom, in views
and language." Only if they disregarded the sacred law, and instead
heeded the prophetic message, could Judaism become "truly American."[25]

Soon afterward, at Kohler's invitation, Reform rabbis gathered in Pittsburgh to proclaim formally the principles of their faith. The Pittsburgh conference was a decisive moment in Reform history. The movement was
threatened on two flanks: by the Orthodox claim that *halakhic* Judaism, the
Judaism of the sacred law, was the only valid Judaism; and by the new
Ethical Culture movement, which threatened to siphon away liberal Jews
who were committed to its "nonsectarian universalism," detached from divine revelation and authority. Kohler's task was to steer Reform away from
biblical and rabbinical legal authority, while retaining (in the words chosen
by the Pittsburgh delegates) "the God-idea as taught in the Holy Scriptures."[26]

Although Kohler had acknowledged, after his debates with Kohut, "We cannot afford to stand condemned as *law-breakers*," he declared in Pittsburgh that "Mosaic-Rabbinical Judaism, as based upon the Law and tradition, has . . . . irrevocably lost its hold on the modern Jew." His colleagues concurred. Condensing his ideas, they constructed the platform on which Reform Judaism stood for the next half-century. Mosaic law, they conceded, might have been an appropriate "system of training" for the Jewish people during its national life in Palestine. But modern civilization had rendered obsolete all laws regulating diet, ritual purity, and dress, whose observance "is apt rather to obstruct than to further modern spiritual elevation." Jews now comprised "a religious community," not a nation; no longer wishing to return to Palestine, they would not retain any laws appropriate to their national life. Only the spirit of prophecy, not the letter of Mosaic law, endured. It obligated Jews to apply "justice and righteousness" to ameliorate the ills of modern industrial society.[27]

The Pittsburgh Platform, obliterating Jewish law as the normative framework of Jewish life, was the high-water mark of radical Reform. What had begun as a movement to reform the law, to retain its spirit while altering its forms (especially the nature and language of prayer), culminated in the repudiation of Jewish legal authority. By 1885 the Reformers had fully absorbed the Christian critique of Judaism as obsessively ritualistic, legalistic, and exclusivist, which dovetailed with an enlightened rational critique of religious belief and observance. Implicitly conceding these allegations, Reformers rejected all laws and ceremonies foreign to "the views and habits of modern civilization" while transforming Judaism into a religion, like Christianity, divested of national or ethnic content. American Jews, Kohler noted without embarrassment in his lectures, craved "untrammelled intercourse with the Gentile world." The Pittsburgh Platform eased their way by erecting Christianity as the standard for Judaism to emulate. Felix Adler (the son of a Reform rabbi and founder of the Ethical Culture movement) was prompted to inquire after the Pittsburgh conference, "Why did the gentlemen not go all the way and declare themselves to be Unitarians?"[28]

Having rejected Jewish law, Reform accommodated itself to the spirit of the age through the rhetoric of Hebrew prophecy. The Prophet, transformed into "the central hero-image in Jewish religious culture," emerged as an enlightened modern Jew, closely resembling the Reform rabbis who glorified the prophetic tradition for its repudiation of law and ritual. But the more that Reformers came to rely upon prophecy to define their Jewish commitments, the further they distanced themselves from the Judaism of covenantal obligation to which the Prophets themselves had demanded fidelity.[29]

The link between prophecy and social justice, a staple tenet of Reform ideology, was less self-evident in the nineteenth century than it became later. During the Civil War era, several Reform rabbis attributed their anti-slavery position to biblical sources, perhaps the earliest Jewish application of Hebrew texts to American circumstances. But Hebew prophecy was inconspicuous in the debate over slavery. Rabbi David Einhorn, an outspoken Baltimore abolitionist, rested his opposition to slavery upon "Mosaic principle" and "Mosaic teaching." His primary reliance upon the Prophets was to justify his claim that political preaching was an acceptable form of religious discourse (contrary to the insistence of his congregation that he abstain from pulpit comment on "the excitable issues of the time"). Even Isaac Mayer Wise, who was far more critical of abolitionists (referring to them as "wicked preachers" and "fanatics") than of slaveowners, rested his argument upon the correct analysis of biblical texts regarding slavery, not upon prophetic morality.[30]

Despite the Pittsburgh conference, Reform rabbis had little to say about the "evils of the present organization of society" their platform condemned. Bound to "the spirit of the age," Reform was necessarily responsive to external cues. Not until the Protestant Social Gospel movement began to discover solutions in prophecy for the problems spawned by industrial capitalism did Reform rabbis begin to apply prophetic morality to contemporary political issues. And only after the Progressive reform movement decisively shaped the American political agenda early in the twentieth century did Reform Judaism align itself with political liberalism. (Reform Jews who were most conspicuous in public affairs, including Jacob Schiff and Louis Marshall, were committed Republicans.) Led by a younger generation of rabbis, Reform then began to march to the distinctively evangelical cadences of the Progressive movement (whose most popular reform anthem was "Onward Christian Soldiers").[31]

What seems clear, in retrospect, is that Hebrew prophecy was less an inspiration to social justice than an affirmation of American patriotism. The references to prophecy that punctuated rabbinical addresses around the turn of the century rejected "rabbinical legalism" for "a religion of rationality" suitable to "the citizens of a free and just country" who shared "the mission, promises and hopes" of the Hebrew Prophets. Prophecy and American patriotism were stridently linked: the American war against Spain in 1898 was interpreted as an opportunity to realize "Israel's prophecies, dreams and mission." Rabbi David Philipson, recalling his pride when the Protestant chaplain of the Senate invited him to deliver a blessing, referred to the United States as "the new Canaan," where "modern prophets" preached their inspirational truths. And Rabbi Jacob Voorsanger, the most outspoken Reform rabbi on the West Coast, cheerfully acknowledged Reform as the "instrument of assimilation." While rabbinical legalism kept Jews in "darkness and seclusion," and Orthodox ritual

made Americans "uncomfortable amidst Jews," prophetic universalism offered American Jews the welcome opportunity to "assimilate with their
gentile neighbors."[32]

Just when Reform had proclaimed the principles of an Americanized
Judaism, the massive influx of Jewish immigrants from Eastern Europe
challenged the adequacy of its definition. The presence of so many newcomers, so Jewish and so foreign, suddenly raised urgent questions about
the compatibility of Judaism with American values. Rabbi Philipson
warned that Russian immigration posed "a great danger to Judaism in its
relation to the republic." In the United States, where "the particularism of
the *halacha*" had yielded to "prophetism," Judaism enjoyed "perfect harmony with the law of the land." As Americans and Jews, Philipson declared, "our aim is to see that the two shall never come in conflict." But
Russian Jews comprised "a foreign element," unsympathetic to republican
ideals and institutions. The newcomers, Reform rabbis complained, confined themselves to "seething and sickening" ghettos, where they practiced "meaningless, Oriental rites" and spoke a language (Yiddish) that expressed their "antagonism to American institutions." As a Chicago rabbi
lamented, "they insist on carrying on their old-world customs and ceremo-
nials, many of which are foreign and repugnant to the American spirit."
Reform Jews, he suggested, must "go bravely forth" into the ghetto, denouncing the "false prophets and preachers" of all foreign orthodoxies, for
Jews must recognize "but one country and one flag."[33]

The United States, after all, was the Zion of Reform. For more than
a half-century Reform rabbis had repudiated (on religious, not political,
grounds) the idea of Jewish national restoration, expunging references to
Jewish national history or its messianic resumption. Dispersion was understood as the expression of divine purpose, enabling Jews to fulfill their universalist mission—and, not incidentally, to feel comfortable in their
adopted homeland. Back in 1841, when Gustavus Poznanski announced
at the dedication of the Charleston Reform Temple that the United States
was "Palestine," he had expressed the fervent wish that Jews would be at
home in the United States. At a minimum, this required the abandonment
of a distinctive national life (and the repudiation of a distinctive sacred
law). Yet no sooner had the issue of Jewish national distinctiveness been
resolved ("We consider ourselves no longer a nation but a religious community," according to the Pittsburgh Platform) than immigration, especially in conjunction with the birth of the Zionist movement at the end of
the nineteenth century, revived it.

Reform rabbis responded with rage, occasionally bordering on hys-
teria, to the first stirrings of Jewish national revival. They found frightening
any implication that Jews, especially American Jews, owed allegiance elsewhere, for it raised precisely the issues of patriotic loyalty that Reform had

struggled to suppress. Rabbi Isaac Mayer Wise quickly dismissed Zionism as "a momentary inebriation of morbid minds." But the danger was great, for any commitment of American Jews to Zionism "compromised in the eyes of the public the whole of American Judaism." Jews, he insisted, are American citizens "who will never violate our allegiance to our country"; therefore he had no patience with "any man who wants something better for Jews than the United States offers." Following Wise's lead, the Central Conference of American Rabbis strongly disapproved of Jewish national aspirations, which would only confirm allegations that Jews "are foreigners in the countries in which they are at home." Rabbi Philipson, Wise's successor, thundered against the twin evils that had suddenly beset Reform: "neo-nationalism" and "neo-orthodoxy." He warned American Jews not to be "ghettoized or russianized." Instead, the immigrants "under the spell of the spirit of our free institutions will be Americanized."[34] Zionism, in a word, was un-American.

Beneath the invective swirled the most tormenting, and enduring, issue of American Jewish identity: Were American Jews Americans first, or did Judaism (in either its religious or national forms) impose a competing allegiance? As marginal a movement as Zionism initially was (and long remained) in the United States, Reform rabbis correctly grasped its implicit challenge to their terms of American acculturation. Reform and Zionism offered competing definitions of Judaism—and, it was feared, of Americanism as well. If Judaism was a religion only, then it was entirely compatible with the obligations of American citizenship, precisely as the Reformers insisted. But if Judaism retained its national content, as the Zionists affirmed, then American Jews still confronted, in even more acute form, precisely the wrenching dilemma of dual loyalty that emancipation and Reform were designed to obliterate. Zionism was nothing less than a frontal challenge to the assimilationist premises and promises of emancipation, on which Reform had staked its very claim to legitimacy. Zionism asserted that not only had emancipation failed to resolve the Jewish Question but, indeed, had exacerbated it.

Suddenly the principles of American Jewish life, so recently and confidently asserted by Reform rabbis in Pittsburgh, were in disarray. With Judaism divested of legal and national content, the terms of Americanization left Reform with little that was recognizably Jewish to offer the Eastern European immigrants. Arrogant demands for Americanization were more of a rebuff than an invitation to the newcomers, whose vibrant culture of *Yiddishkeit* could hardly be confined within the decorous limits of Reform temples or philanthropic generosity.

Most Reformers rejected the Zionist movement and spurned the immigrant culture that sustained it. Yet some of the most important leaders of American Zionism in its early years were Reform rabbis: among them Richard Gottheil, Stephen S. Wise, and Judah Magnes (one of the handful of American Zionists actually to settle in Palestine). If Reform and Zionism were antithetical (as so many Reform Jews and Zionists insisted), what explains the conspicuous presence of these Reform rabbis in American Zionism? The urgent need to reduce the threat of competing national identities may well have drawn Reformers to Zionism. It surely was not accidental that Gottheil's declaration of American Zionist principles in 1898, the first official statement of American Zionism, warned of the menace of continued Jewish immigration to the United States, while proclaiming the wisdom of deflecting it to Palestine. Perhaps Reform rabbis came to Zionism, in part, to eradicate any hint of foreign allegiance within the American Jewish community. Only by Americanizing Zionism could the Reformers remove its stigma of dual loyalty.

But by the end of the nineteenth century, just when Reform needed to muster its resources to confront its challengers, the Reform rabbinate confronted the problem of its own diminished authority. Its sweeping repudiation of Jewish law and nationalism had left it entirely dependent upon American sources for its definition of Judaism. Kohler, who could claim credit for that achievement, may have scored only a Pyrrhic victory in 1885. He had won his debate with Kohut: the Americanization of Judaism demanded the abandonment of Jewish law. The majority of American Jews, then and since, refused to concede Kohut's claim that this also meant the abandonment of Judaism. But when Reformers, in their triumphant Pittsburgh convention, asserted the supremacy of "modern spiritual elevation" over Jewish legal authority, they simultaneously diminished their own authority, as rabbis, to lead the American Jewish community. Indeed, the confrontation between Kohut and Kohler marked one of the last occasions when an issue of such profound significance in American Jewish life was debated exclusively by rabbis. Once Kohler carried the day for Reform, the Reform rabbinate—like Napoleon's Sanhedrin—relinquished authority at the very moment of asserting it. In the nineteenth century the important issues in American Jewish life concerning the content of Judaism and the identity of Jews were decided by rabbis; thereafter, rabbis would either share power or relinquish it altogether.

The problem of diminished authority quickly became evident. Just a few years later, a member of Reform's Central Conference of American Rabbis inquired of his colleagues ("in whom are vested the authority and the duty," he believed, to decide such issues) whether a non-Jewish male could be converted without circumcision. Reform rabbis, disregarding the legal intricacies, were evidently stunned by any inference that they possessed power to decide the matter at all. Rabbi Felsenthal of Chicago quickly disposed of the ritual question to reach the authority issue. "Have indeed the rabbis of this land been vested with the authority to decide finally and bindingly for the Jewish masses all such matters? Since when? By whom?" Felsenthal conceded only two sources of authority in Jewish communities comprised of "free men . . . [who] live in a free country and in free times": congregational autonomy and individual conscience. No community of American Jews, "deeply imbued with Jeffersonian democratic principles," could accept rabbinical legal authority. The only legal power that a rabbi possessed was stipulated in his contract with his congregation or by state law. Any other claims to legal authority, even in ritual or doctrinal matters, were "more than un-Jewish . . . they were anti- American."[35]

Once the authority of law vanished, however, the source of rabbinical authority was elusive, if it indeed existed. Felsenthal cited "the spirit of prophetic Judaism." A Milwaukee rabbi found authority in "common sense and reason." A Chicago colleague preferred "the strictly scientific method of criticism." The Kansas City rabbi whose inquiry about circumcision had provoked the debate was astonished by these responses to his question. He had assumed that rabbinical authority endured, if based only upon the mastery of Jewish learning that a rabbi possessed. To be sure, rabbis could no longer command others to submit to their knowledge or training. "We can *enforce* nothing," he conceded. But "by right of all our history and tradition," even American rabbis remained empowered to exercise the authority of their office.[36]

Reform rabbis disagreed; denying any legal source of authority, they could not locate it anywhere else. A Houston rabbi yearned for "some ecclesiastical authority" to guide Jewish spiritual development. "We need authority," he asserted. Having relinquished it in Pittsburgh, however, Reform rabbis were in a quandary, for they simply could not agree where, in the absence of law, authority reposed. As they searched for a new role commensurate with their diminished power, citations to the Hebrew Prophets began to multiply. With Jewish law possessing merely "historical and antiquarian interest," the modern rabbi was advised to devote himself to "the prophetical mission of instructing, cheering up, comforting and consoling all [the] depressed and afflicted." But a Kentucky rabbi, attempting to define the duties of his office (a favorite subject of Reform convention oratory at the time), complained that he was expected to be an academic instructor, lecturing on everything from the tariff to current fiction—everything, that is, except issues with explicit Jewish content. He preferred the model of Ezekiel, speaking the word of God. But even such a modern rabbinical prophet, he conceded, must concern himself with preaching a "liberal and universalistic Judaism" based upon "love and good will."[37]

The more that Reform rabbis redefined their role in universal prophetic terms, the more they sensed, and expressed, the deterioration of their own prestige and influence. Never before, observed a Detroit rabbi, had the rabbinical function been defined as "preaching, lecturing, and fine talking." There seemed to be no secure middle ground between hierarchical authority based on law, which Reform rabbis rejected, and individual or congregational autonomy, which left them feeling altogether powerless. Perhaps, a New York rabbi dared to imagine, the problem was emancipation itself. The United States, he knew, was "a Christian country in all but name," and Jews had readily adapted to its contours as the price of their civic equality. If that was bad enough, the alternative surely was worse: a return "to the confining boundaries of an isolated nationality, to the galling disabilities of the ghetto, to the cramping legislation of the Shulhan Aruch."[38] The choice was clear, if distressing: not Jewish law or nationality, but freedom—the freedom to become an acculturated Jew in a Christian country.

The enticements of freedom transformed the American rabbi into "a novel and unique phenomenon" in Jewish history. The void created by the loss of legal authority was filled by the array of social functions that a rabbi now was expected to perform. Like the Protestant minister whom he emulated, the rabbi served primarily as a preacher, often instructing his congregants in the compatibility of Judaism and Americanism. (After unsuccessful trial sermons at Temple Emanu-El, Rabbi Gustav Gottheil went to visit three churches "to hear in what manner the American preachers spoke to their flocks." Suitably instructed, he changed his approach and was hired.) With fewer Jews able to comprehend, or even read, a Hebrew prayer service, the centrality of the sermon was magnified even more. As a Jewish ambassador to the gentile community, a rabbi had to be attentive to what Christians thought about Jews and to whether distinctive Jewish ritual was compatible with cultural integration. Pastor to the varied personal needs of congregation members, the rabbi absorbed the prevailing mode of ministerial responsibility, which significantly diminished his own independent authority by increasing his dependence upon congregational favor. In the new era of "post-halakhic Judaism," the rabbi could not fulfill his traditional role as law man; his new task was to "uplift, edify, and ennoble." But the multiplication of functions only testified to the diminution of rabbinical authority.[39]

To the generation of American Reform rabbis who presided over these changes, and encouraged them, the consequences were wondrous to behold. American Israelites stood "on freedom's holy soil," Kaufmann Kohler proclaimed, "unshackled by blind belief in authority." The Reformers felt certain that they had saved Judaism from "stagnation and decay." Without their commitment to liberty and progress, American Jews could not hope to rise above "national and sectarian narrowness," nor approach "the lofty prophetical ideal of Judaism." Orthodox rabbis might lament the neglect of law, but Reform had breathed "new life into the dry bones of Israel," enabling it to escape its "prison-house of . . . legalism" and "the customs and practices . . . of the Orient" to become "perfectly at home in our Western civilization." A Jew must choose between "loyalty to all the laws and customs of his national past or . . . unreserved acceptance of the mandates of his newly acquired citizenship."[40]

While Reformers completed the terms of Jewish accommodation, a growing community of Orthodox immigrants, concentrated in New York, struggled to mend the shredded fabric of traditional rabbinical authority. Until the 1880s, there was no Orthodox community of any consequence in the United States. Thereafter, the devastating combination of czarist pogroms, economic privation, and constricted opportunities began to push and pull hundreds of thousands, and finally millions, of Jews from the Pale of Settlement to the United States. But as late as 1887, when as many as 120,000 Jewish families had crowded into Manhattan's Lower East Side, there was barely a handful of rabbis. (Indeed, one Orthodox immigrant told a newcomer, "God has been left on the other side of the ocean.") The hundred or so congregations, quarreling incessantly over *kashrut* supervision and *bet din* jurisdiction, could only agree upon the urgent need to restore Jewish unity under the aegis of rabbinical legal authority.[41]

Desperate "to raise the standard of Judaism" in the United States, the Orthodox congregations of New York solicited the assistance of prominent European rabbis. "There is no authority nor guide revered and accepted by the whole community," they complained. Instead, each rabbi had become "an authority unto himself." They wanted a chief rabbi, noted for his "scholarship and piety," who could reassert traditional leadership. Two rabbinical respondents, blissfully ignorant of American conditions, inquired whether the American government would recognize the position of the chief rabbi as "an official permanent position"—the necessary prerequisite, in their judgment, for the assertion of rabbinical rule. The negative reply considerably depleted the available talent pool; but after months of search and negotiation Rabbi Jacob Joseph of Vilna, in financial straits and therefore available for an American appointment, consented.[42]

Rabbi Joseph, by all accounts a wise and respected man, confronted an impossible task. He held the title of chief rabbi, but it conferred no authority. Instead, it provoked further discord. Orthodoxy, challenged externally by American secularism and Reform liberalism, was beset internally by transplanted rivalries from Eastern Europe. Although Rabbi Joseph was charged by the association of Orthodox congregations that hired him "to teach us and to judge us in all matters pertaining to the laws of our holy Torah," its members declined to defer to his leadership. Hassidic Jews from Galicia, refusing to serve on a *bet din* presided over by a rabbi from Vilna, established their own rabbinical court. Supervision of *kashrut* was too lucrative a source of profit (and corruption) to relinquish; Galician butchers, like their rabbis, refused to cooperate with the newcomer. Soon there were two chief rabbis (in 1893, a third claimant, from Moscow, pronounced himself "chief rabbi of America"). Rabbi Joseph's appointment only intensified the problems of fragmentation that it was intended to resolve.[43]

Once again, during a time of crisis, Jews had turned to the rule of Jewish law to preserve their communal autonomy. But the disintegration of Jewish legal authority, so evident by the end of the nineteenth century, shattered any dreams of communal unity within the framework of *halakha*. Eastern European orthodoxy could not be transplanted to the United States, at least not yet. Orthodox rabbis noted the irony: in the very nation where Jews enjoyed the maximum freedom "to study, teach, observe, perform and establish our law," Jewish law languished. Law, the rabbis insisted, "has been our watchword for centuries; it is our very life." But no matter how fervently a rabbi might assert that the test of Jewish identity was recognition of the binding authority of law, American Jews refused to accept that definition. Consequently, Orthodox rabbis continued to experience a sharp, lingering sense of loss. In Europe, a rabbi recalled, "his word was law," but in America "the authority has been broken." "Strength we don't have," another rabbi conceded, "strength that we should say, 'you must . . . !'"[44]

By the end of the nineteenth century, American Judaism had been decisively shaped by the repudiation of Jewish law and the erosion of rabbinical authority. If, for Orthodox rabbis, this was a devastating loss, for Reform rabbis it was one of the manifold blessings of freedom. Kohler boasted of the new rabbi, committed to "moral and spiritual welfare" rather than to "dry learning and dead formalism."[45] Despite such confident assertions, however, the problem of authority endured, as elusive during the twentieth century as it was at the end of the nineteenth. Wherever authority reposed—whether in prophecy, history, the spirit of the age, science, reason, or nationalism—the enduring legacy of emancipation meant that for all but a small minority of Jews it could no longer be located in the law of divine command.

For the first time in Jewish history, Jewish law had proven inadequate to its task of national regeneration. During every national crisis, from the Egyptian exodus through Babylonian exile to Roman conquest, the authority of the sacred law had been asserted and accepted. From Moses at Sinai to Yohanan ben Zakkai at Yavneh (and for eighteen centuries thereafter), priests, prophets, judges, and rabbis had interpreted the sacred law to the people, binding them to its command. Even though the law of Israel and the land of Israel were intimately connected (much of the law presupposed life in the promised land), legal authority managed to survive independently of geographical location. The land was lost, a devastating loss, but the legal obligations of the covenant endured. Indeed, many of the most creative episodes in the legal history of the Jewish people had occurred outside the land—in the wilderness, in exile, in the diaspora. That fact alone testified to the extraordinary power of law in defining Jewish life and guiding it through a succession of national disasters.

But once the French Sanhedrin accepted the Napoleonic terms of emancipation the chain of Jewish legal tradition, stretching back to Sinai, snapped. The old faith in covenantal distinctiveness, the foundation of Jewish communal autonomy, yielded to the new ideal of individual freedom. But the exercise of freedom assured the demise of Jewish legal authority. For a time, as Moses Mendelssohn so brilliantly demonstrated, old and new commitments might be balanced. Mendelssohn, the exemplary Jewish symbol of Enlightenment possibilities, was as comfortable with the tenets of philosophical rationalism as he was adept in Talmudic exegesis. But as the gates of freedom swung open, emancipated Jews began their entry into Western society—upon the terms set by the Christian majority. Four of Mendelssohn's enlightened children, accepting what Heine called the ticket of admission to European society, converted to Christianity.

No other crisis in Jewish history had so debilitated Jewish legal authority. What conquest, destruction of the Temple, national obliteration, and the perils of exile had not accomplished during two millennia, enlightenment and emancipation achieved within two generations. Law was powerless to repair the damage, for emancipation undercut the very foundation of Jewish legal authority: its source in divine revelation, its unity as sacred law, its preservation of communal autonomy, and its adaptability through rabbinical interpretation. Modernity divided Judaism into warring camps: secular Jews located authority outside Judaism; Reformers located authority outside Jewish law; Orthodoxy froze law to preserve it from further deterioration. A small minority still accepted the binding authority of law, while the vast majority welcomed the transformation of Judaism into a religion that was differentiated from Christianity by some vaguely distinctive (if increasingly attenuated) forms of ritual observance. For emancipated Jews, this was the very definition of progress, the highest term of praise that enlightenment could bestow.

In the United States, where emancipation was an established fact of American life, not the outcome of a prolonged process, Reform established itself with relative ease, without the need to struggle against entrenched ideas or institutions. By the end of the nineteenth century, however, it confronted the first substantial challenge to its prevailing definition of American Judaism—from the immigrant carriers of Orthodoxy and Zionism. The malleability of Reform as it responded to the spirit of the modern age assured its repudiation by the Eastern European immigrants who, by sheer numbers alone, undermined the Reform consensus. To the Orthodox, it represented the Christianization of Judaism. To Zionists, it preached universalism but substituted American patriotism for Jewish nationalism. The Reform synthesis, a creative adaptation of Judaism to American life, suddenly was itself in need of reform.

Emancipation had created a "crisis of religious authority" for Jews and a crisis of legal authority as well. Reform institutionalized the Jewish self-divestment of legal authority. It launched the search for alternative sources of inspiration and cohesion located in the "spirit of the age." By the end of the nineteenth century, the rhetoric of prophecy enabled Jews who rejected "the sterner metronome of the law" to continue to locate themselves within Jewish tradition, although within a distinctively modern and Christian rendition of it. In time, American rabbis across the denominational spectrum would even recast "chosenness," the fundamental metaphor of Jewish self-identification, as a distinctively American concept. Once the process of legal divestment had run its course, Judaism, as Arnold Eisen has perceptively observed, all but became "a faith transmitted to Jews by America."[46]

To expropriate a biblical metaphor, emancipation was a blessing and a curse. The promise of freedom and equality—and, in the United States, the fulfillment of that promise—was costly, as the endless debates over the nature of Jewish identity, and even "who is a Jew," continue to demonstrate. Indeed, the very term "emancipation," which implies the inexorable movement from servitude to freedom, distorts the meaning of modern Jewish history. "Beware of conceiving Emancipation," Robert Alter has warned, "as a simple triumphal march from the dank medieval prisons of the ghettos to a modern world of light and latitude." Such a reading—or misreading—imposes analytical categories that fail to take Judaism seriously on its own terms. Jews hardly lived in slavery prior to the nineteenth century. To the contrary: they enjoyed an ample measure of self-governing autonomy, sustained by rabbinical legal authority. Emancipation required "the surrender of this self- determination" and the imposition of "new orders of coercion." Demanding the renunciation of Jewish distinctiveness, and the legal order that sustained it, emancipation undercut Jewish autonomy and replaced it with a Christian frame of reference to which Jews were expected—even required—to conform. It was, therefore, a process of Jewish self-renunciation. From the perspective of Jewish history, the dubious freedom of the newly emancipated Jew could hardly compare with the "real inner freedom" of ghetto Jews.[47]

No one described this loss more poignantly than Asher Ginsberg (under the pseudonym Ahad Ha-'Am). His rejection of the terms of emancipation in 1891 anticipated his emergence, within the next decade, as the creative theoretician of cultural Zionism. In a withering description of the consequences of emancipation for Western (especially French) Jews, entitled "Slavery in Freedom," he analyzed the moral and intellectual servitude that the rights of citizenship could not conceal. In his native Russia, there certainly was Jewish ignorance, poverty, and degradation; but the privileges of Western Jews, he insisted, had been purchased with the sacrifice of their intellectual and spiritual freedom, the freedom to be Jews. "I may not be emancipated," he conceded, "but at least I have not sold my soul for emancipation." In the end, emancipation was nothing but "*spiritual slavery under the veil of outward freedom.*"[48]

The overwhelming majority of American Jews believed otherwise. The terms of Americanization devised by Reform accepted emancipation as an unequivocal blessing that assured the full integration of Jews into American society. But once Reform rabbis discarded law, and relinquished rabbinical legal authority, they empowered others to define the content of American Judaism. In the twentieth century, when the sacred-law tradition was rephrased as liberty, democracy, and constitutionalism, the very function of law in Judaism was decisively modified. Historically the source of Jewish autonomy, law now served to integrate Jews into American society. The most urgent issues of American Jewish identity would be resolved within the framework of American law—the ultimate source of authority for American Jews.

The Authority of Tradition: Solomon Schechter and Louis Marshall

T he nineteenth-century debate over the terms of Jewish acculturation was predominantly between rabbis. The Jewish community—small,
fragmented, and eager to Americanize—depended upon rabbinical leadership even if it declined to submit to rabbinical authority. The debate between Kohler and Kohut was exemplary: not only did rabbis articulate the
competing principles of innovation and tradition; they also channeled their
principles into enduring institutional forms. Kohler convened the Pittsburgh conference, which defined the principles of radical Reform, while
Kohut helped to build the Jewish Theological Seminary, designed to train
an Orthodox American rabbinate. As late as the mid-1880s, the voice of
American Judaism was the voice of its rabbis.

Within a single generation, however, a dramatic transformation occurred. The tidal wave of Jewish immigration raised profoundly disturbing
questions about the compatibility of Eastern European varieties of Judaism
with American values. Not only were such issues far too momentous to
be left to rabbinical decision; the triumph of Reform had substantially diminished the authority of rabbis to decide anything. By the turn of the century, rabbis were compelled to share communal power. Within another
decade, the very institutions that had served as a forum for rabbinical debate, and as instruments of rabbinical power, had been all but eclipsed by
a spreading network of philanthropic, educational, and defense organizations established in response to the urgent crisis of immigrant absorption.

The essence of the transformation that occurred between 1900 and
1915 was the transfer of Jewish legal authority from rabbis to lawyers. The

process of acculturation through law was, of course, implicit in emancipation, which required Jews to transfer their allegiance from the sacred law to the law of the secular state. But this did not become a salient issue for American Jews until the influx of Eastern European immigrants threatened the stability of the established Jewish community. With Americanization of the newcomers the overriding priority, the role of lawyers assumed special importance. Enjoying privileged access to the rhetoric and rituals of American patriotism (and, increasingly, to the levers of organizational power), they could define responsible Judaism as fidelity to the rule of American law. Law might remain at the center of American Jewish life, but the Constitution, not the Torah, would determine the faith of American Jews.

The transfer of allegiance from a sacred to a secular legal system, and the accompanying transfer of legal authority from rabbis to lawyers, was not a single event but a process. It defies precise dating; no Sanhedrin was ever convened to ratify it. But by 1915 it was acknowledged that American Jewry was all but governed by "Marshall law," a grudging tribute to the power exercised by Louis Marshall, one of the foremost corporate and constitutional lawyers of his era and the undisputed leader of Jewish communal affairs until his death in 1929. By then, also, the American Zionist movement, numerically small but ideologically significant, had been decisively molded by the accession to leadership of the nationally renowned liberal lawyer and progressive reformer, Louis D. Brandeis. By World War I, a new synthesis of Judaism and Americanism, forged by lawyers, testified to the unbounded loyalty of Jews to the United States.

Although this synthesis now seems inevitable, at the turn of the century its terms were hardly self-evident. To the contrary: the integration of foreign Jews into American society, indeed the worrisome "foreignness" of Judaism itself, was an urgent problem whose resolution was anything but a foregone conclusion. Any claim to leadership within the American Jewish community depended upon a persuasive formula that would remove dual loyalty as an issue from American Jewish life. Once it was apparent that the principles of radical Reform had nothing to offer the immigrant newcomers, reconciliation came to depend upon the conservation and modification of Jewish tradition, rather than its sweeping repudiation. That effort linked a lawyer and rabbi whose names and remarkable achievements have been all but forgotten. The collaboration of Louis Marshall and Solomon Schechter in an effort to transplant historical Judaism to the United States provides a fascinating glimpse of possibilities and, ultimately, of limits. For it was Marshall the lawyer, not Schechter the rabbi, whose vision of the rule of law was destined to prevail.

Louis Marshall, born in Syracuse in 1856, was the son of Orthodox German Jews whose travail and fortitude as immigrants remained vivid throughout his entire life. With strong feeling, Marshall subsequently referred to their bitter experiences in Germany ("little calculated to inspire love or tender recollections" for the old country), his mother's wretched ocean journey to the United States (filled with "indescribable experiences"), and their "sufferings" as aliens in a strange land. Young Marshall learned German as his first language and spoke only German to his mother during her lifetime. She exerted the "greatest influence," reading to him from the Bible, reciting Schiller's poetry, and inspiring his love of language and literature. He described his father as an "industrious, conscientious, law-abiding" immigrant with "deep religious feeling." Long after their deaths, Marshall remembered his parents, quite simply, as "worthy people who possess[ed] the pioneer spirit."[1]

Marshall retained abiding respect for the courage of immigrant pioneers, and he demonstrated enduring gratitude to the nation that admitted them. Like so many children of immigrants, he was enraptured with American history, at an early age "engrossed in the creation of this new nation." He avidly studied "how its laws had been drawn and its institutions founded," learning about the Constitution in a school debating club. One of his sons recalled July 4th as the annual occasion for family Bible reading, followed by a flag-waving parade, the perfect combination of Jewish and American symbols. "We have taken great pride in our American citizenship," Marshall recalled, "and . . . we have sought to perpetuate American ideals." Marshall fused the experience of immigration to the meaning of American nationality in a way that deepened his empathy for all newcomers and solidified his loyalty to the United States.[2]

Marshall's interests led him to law: he thought it "a natural transition from the debating club to the bar."[3] After an apprenticeship with a local attorney, he completed the two-year program at Columbia Law School within a single year and returned to Syracuse to practice. There he remained for fifteen years, until 1894, when a Columbia classmate, Samuel Untermyer, invited him to become a partner in his Manhattan firm. Marshall's relocation to the emerging center of professional activity, commercial development, and Jewish communal affairs came at a propitious moment. The Untermyer firm offered a unique springboard for a man of Marshall's talents and ambition. The older professional ideal of the versatile solo practitioner was yielding to the demands of consolidation, organization, and specialization. Business corporations required a range of legal services that only the size and diversity of a law firm could provide. Guggenheimer, Untermyer & Marshall, the foremost (and virtually the first) Jewish law firm, attracted a prospering clientele of German Jewish bankers, brokers, and businessmen whose financial activities required

legal intervention and protection. Marshall's inexhaustible energy, remarkable memory, and verbal felicity quickly earned him an esteemed
place at the pinnacle of the New York appellate bar. His new clientele
brought him into the inner circle of the German Jewish elite, just then con-
solidating its power and asserting its claim to lead the American Jewish
community.

Marshall capitalized upon his professional success to transform his
personal life and to secure his influence within the Jewish community.
Within a short time after his arrival in New York, he married a cousin of
Untermyer's, purchased an East Side brownstone, and became an active
participant in the affairs of Temple Emanu-El, the Reform congregation favored by the pillars of German Jewry. It would be deceptively easy to characterize Marshall according to his professional, political, and religious affil-
iations: corporate lawyer, staunch Republican, Reform Jew. But such a
conventional portrait of affluence and influence hardly begins to explain
how Marshall not only gained access to power but also transformed its exercise by finding, in the concepts of law and citizenship, the key terms for
the integration of Jews into American society.

The episode that illustrates Marshall's unique contribution, and the
larger ramifications of his emergence to leadership, involved the reorganization of the Jewish Theological Seminary and the invitation to Rabbi Solomon Schechter to become its leader. The effort to revitalize that languish-
ing institution was also an attempt to defuse the demographic time bomb
that threatened American Jewry at the turn of the century. Just when the
children of an earlier generation of immigrants, the generation of
Marshall's parents, had settled securely into American society, the arrival
of waves of newcomers from Eastern Europe—so foreign, so impoverished, so Jewish— disrupted the comfortable process of acculturation. The
Reform synthesis of Judaism and Americanism made little sense to uprooted Russian and Rumanian Jews. Their immersion in Yiddish culture,
with its distinctive blend of religious and secular exuberance, raised
acutely troubling questions about the place of Jews, all Jews, in American
society. Confronting the immigrants, the German Jews confronted their
own family origins, their identity as Americans, and, at the deepest level,
themselves.

The Jewish Theological Seminary became a repository of their fears
and hopes. Established in 1886 in response to the Pittsburgh Platform, it
was designed to defend traditional Judaism against further Reform incur-
sions. By then, in some Reform congregations, the Jewish Sabbath had
been shifted to Sunday; the dietary laws of kashrut were dismissed as
"kitchen Judaism"; and the Hebrew language was largely abandoned as
a vestige of "Orientalism." A handful of Orthodox rabbis, led by Sabato
Morais of Philadelphia, responded by establishing a seminary in which

"the authentic tenets of Judaism" could be preserved within the bounds of Mosaic law and the rabbincal tradition.[4]

But the Seminary, plagued by insufficient finances, attracted only a handful of students. Worse yet, its leaders were condescending, if not actively hostile, toward the immigrants, the very carriers of the traditions that the Seminary ostensibly wished to preserve. The task of Seminary graduates, declared its president in 1890, was to instill "culture, refinement and civilization" in the newcomers, thereby mitigating the dangers of anti-Semitism that the foreign Jews might "inadvertently" provoke. The Russian Jews, a prominent New York rabbi predicted in a Seminary address, "will either be the fame or the shame of American Judaism." More likely the latter, for they might, "by uncouthness or by infidelity, or by lax ideas of moral right in business or social life, feed the prejudice against us." It was imperative for "our own safety, our own good name," that they be rapidly Americanized. But by the turn of the century the Seminary, debilitated by financial and administrative problems, had lapsed into institutional paralysis.[5]

Seminary difficulties presented an opportunity to a small group of German Jews led by the banker Jacob H. Schiff. Although they were all affiliated with Reform, they knew that the tumult of the Lower East Side could not be confined within the austere decorum of their own Temple Emanu-El. How, then, were the immigrants to preserve their attachment to Judaism, while developing an identification as Americans? Could they be guided past the assorted hazards of assimilation, Orthodoxy, political radicalism, and Zionist nationalism? For Schiff, Marshall, and their collaborators (drawn primarily from banking, business, and legal circles in New York and Philadelphia), safe passage could only be assured by the guidance of rabbis who were solidly grounded in Jewish tradition and American values. The task of a revitalized Jewish Theological Seminary was to train them.

Meeting at Schiff's New York home in 1901, the "chief conspirators" (as Cyrus Adler, an active participant, characterized them) launched their project. Schiff contributed $100,000; Leonard Lewisohn pledged $50,000; Daniel Guggenheim and his brothers added $50,000; and Mayer Sulzberger donated his exceptional library. With the necessary trust fund secured, Schiff agreed to purchase land near Columbia University for the Seminary site and to subsidize the cost of its new building. His choice of the location was revealing. Columbia, dominating Morningside Heights, transmitted the cultural legacy of the Christian West. It was safely remote from the Lower East Side and Brooklyn, the homes of most Seminary students. Their journey uptown, to the Jewish seminary at the edge of the distinguished American university, was an important symbolic step toward acculturation, one that they were expected to encourage among their congregants once their own rabbinical careers were launched. For Schiff, "the solution of the Jewish question" in the United States depended upon the success of the Seminary in fulfilling that mission.[6]

Marshall possessed a more expansive sense of possibilities. His original hope was to consolidate the Seminary with the Hebrew Union College, the Reform rabbinical institute. In that way, he wrote, "the interests of all classes of Jews throughout the country would be concentrated" in a single institution, committed to the encouragement of Jewish scholarship. Such denominational unity would arrest the massive tilt in American Jewry toward radical Reform, which threatened to sever an attachment to historical Judaism that Marshall wished to preserve. Animated by the vision of a seminary that could unite American Jews, while binding them to a Judaism that carried "the sanction of thousands of years," Marshall assumed responsibility for translating the ideals of the founders into the charter of an institution that could promote them.[7]

Marshall worried that he lacked appropriate Jewish credentials for the task. "I am not a Shulchan Aruch Jew," bound to Jewish law, he acknowledged. But his lawyering skills proved even more vital. They converted a philanthropic commitment into an institutional reality. Schiff and the donors who supported his various projects found in Marshall's talents the means to combine generosity and control, the prerequisite for their continued involvement in (and dominance over) the spreading institutional network that was the major legacy of German Jewry to American Jewish life. As Marshall worked out the details of reorganization, drafted a charter of incorporation (which no "tribune of the people" could dislodge), and guided it through the state legislature, he assured a self- perpetuating Seminary directorate of "conservative and successful financiers." Although Americanization of the immigrants was their primary objective, Marshall remained insistent upon the preservation of traditional Judaism. Believing that "Judaism and Americanism can go hand in hand," that there must be "no life and death struggle of Judaism in America," he rejected assimilation as a goal. Marshall expected the Seminary to fuse Jewish tradition with American values, the reconciliation that was at the core of his own self-identity as an American Jew.[8]

Marshall believed that rabbis still held the key to the integration of Judaism with American culture. Preserving Jewish tradition was only part of their task, the part that Marshall took for granted. What most concerned him was their ability to represent Judaism in a way that assured respect for the entire Jewish community. Since the rabbinate constituted "the representatives of our people before the public," it was imperative to educate rabbis who would "reflect credit on us." The Jewish community needed rabbis "who shall stand for all that is best in morals, culture and scholarship." For Marshall, this meant a rabbinate "trained in American colleges" and "permeated by the American spirit." If Jews were not inspired by their religious leaders to become "good American citizens," they would submit to "the spread of socialistic and anarchistic ideas," a prospect that Marshall found "deplorable." It was essential, he insisted, that the rabbinate "command the respect of the country." From the Seminary, Marshall wanted nothing less than rabbis who were "filled with the spirit of God and of American patriotism."[9] Unable to imagine a Jewish community without rabbinical leadership, he did not yet appreciate that the authority to define the acceptable contours of American Judaism might repose elsewhere.

The reorganization of the Seminary was accompanied by the determination of its sponsors to secure the leadership of the foremost rabbinical scholar in the West, Solomon Schechter. The inevitable turn to Europe was itself revealing of the unstable foundation of American Jewish life. Just as the founding generation of American Reformers had looked to Germany for doctrinal inspiration, and as the Orthodox rabbinate of New York had recruited their chief rabbi from Vilna, so the traditionalists who invested their hopes in the Seminary found their leader abroad, in Cambridge University. For an American Jewish community that still had a precarious sense of its identity and direction, Europe symbolized Jewish authenticity. It was, however, an ambivalent symbol, for the very authenticity that European Judaism conferred also constituted the primary threat to Jewish acculturation in the United States.

The Seminary founders were acutely aware of this dilemma; indeed, their very identity as a group personified it. Born in the mid-nineteenth century—twenty years separated Sulzberger, the oldest, from Adler, the youngest—they were themselves immigrants from Germany or the sons of German immigrants. Adler and Sulzberger were closely related; Adler had grown up in the Sulzberger household after his father's death. They all came from observant, if not Orthodox, Jewish families. Sulzberger's father was a *chazan* (while Sulzberger himself would write several books about Jewish law); Schiff was descended from a distinguished rabbinic family; Adler devoted his life to Jewish scholarship. They never lost their attachment to an exclusively religious definition of Judaism—which helps to explain why none of them was attracted to Zionism. Supremely successful—Schiff in investment banking, Marshall and Sulzberger in law, Adler as a Semitic scholar—they devoted enormous energy to Jewish education and philanthropic activities. Their names recurred as founders and directors in the spreading network of organizations and institutions that were designed both to preserve Jewish culture and to integrate Jews into American society: among them, the American Jewish Historical Society, the Jewish Publication Society, the American Jewish Committee, the Jewish

Theological Seminary. With their institutional commitments, Schiff, Adler, Sulzberger, and Marshall stitched their religious and patriotic loyalties into the seamless fabric of American Judaism.

As early as 1890, Adler had envisioned Schechter in the Seminary. He had met Schechter during a London visit and was enormously impressed with the range of his learning and the passionate energy that infused it. In collaboration with Sulzberger, he secured an invitation for Schechter to deliver a series of lectures in Philadelphia that were designed to enhance his prospects for an American appointment. Schechter was eager, but it took six years of sporadic negotiations, and the virtual collapse of the Seminary, before Adler and Sulzberger could secure the necessary financial support. The participation of Schiff, "*the* Yehudi of New York" (according to Sulzberger's description), was essential. Without his financial backing, there was little hope of revitalizing the Seminary or persuading Schechter to leave Cambridge.[10]

By 1901, the terms of reorganization and the conditions of Schechter's appointment were finally set. Schiff made the venture financially feasible; Adler initiated and sustained contact with Schechter; Sulzberger negotiated with the Americans on Schechter's behalf; Marshall secured the Seminary charter and protected the interests of its founders. Marshall's active involvement and willingness to chair the board of trustees provided necessary reassurance to the donors that Seminary governance, until then under rabbinical control, would pass decisively into lay hands. "With him at the head of us," Sulzberger assured Schiff, "things would be perfectly safe." Schechter's appointment has aptly been described as "a pivotal incident" of American Jewish history. Not only did the Seminary become a distinguished center of Jewish learning and scholarship, training a rabbinate that was firmly grounded in Jewish tradition and American culture, but Conservative Judaism, in time the numerically predominant religious affiliation of twentieth-century American Jews, was "the lengthened shadow" of the institution.[11]

No one seemed better qualified to lead a movement to conserve traditional Judaism in America than Solomon Schechter. Rumanian born, raised in a Habad Hassidic family, he had left Eastern Europe as a young man on an odyssey that carried him progressively further—geographically if not culturally—toward the modern West. First to Vienna, where he received rabbinic ordination; then to Berlin, for further study; finally to England, where he analyzed ancient Hebrew texts in the British Museum and the Bodleian Library. He achieved international renown with his startling discovery, and painstaking interpretation, of the crumbling manuscripts (including fragments from the Jerusalem Talmud and the original text of Ecclesiasticus) buried for centuries in the Cairo *geniza*, the repository of discarded Jewish books and documents. Despite his scholarship, an appointment at Cambridge, his retainer as Claude Montefiore's private tutor, and an admiring circle of London friends, Schechter could not find spiritual comfort in England. Recalling the physical beatings he had suffered in Rumania as a youngster returning home from *heder*, he insisted that his "real suffering" only began with his emigration to the West, which "burns the soul though it leaves the body unhurt."[12]

No sooner had Schechter settled in England than his gaze shifted to the United States. Restless as Montefiore's tutor, and uncomfortable with his dependence upon the patronage of an assimilated Jew who preferred to observe a Sunday Sabbath and pray in English rather than Hebrew, Schechter complained, "there is no spiritual life here, and I feel myself dead." His university appointment in Talmudics still left him financially insecure; worse yet, Cambridge offered "no community and no synagogue." He wrote despairingly, "I lose my life among Christians." The only future for Judaism, he came to believe, was in the United States. He remained informed about the Seminary, and he made known his interest in a position there. His lecture trip to Philadelphia heightened his optimism about American possibilities. Returning to England, he told Adler of his "zeal for democratic institutions" and his belief that the United States was "the greatest and best of nations." He could even imagine the United States as "a place of Torah," despite "the little foxes who destroy the vineyard, orthodox or reform." There was no future for Jewish learning, he thought, "if America remains indifferent."[13]

As Schechter's despair in England deepened, his faith in American possibilities expanded. The more he complained about his spiritual malaise among the gentiles, the more vividly he imagined a life "among Jews" in the United States, "where the future of Judaism is." He was angered by the thrust of contemporary Bible scholarship, written in the shadow of Wellhausen's work, which found a receptive English audience. The higher Bible criticism, he subsequently complained, was merely a thinly disguised form of "higher anti-Semitism." In the United States, he believed, "a House of Learning for the Law of Israel" could rescue the Hebrew Bible from hostile hands. "The proper study of the Torah and real knowledge of our past will give *us* the future," he predicted. "To be able to shape this future in some way is what I have always prayed for." In New York, "I may become—if I am deemed worthy by God—the saving of conservative Judaism."[14]

As Schechter weighed his decision to leave England, he was reassured that there was "great need for you here. . . . America is Judaism's center of gravity and you can become the new Ezra"—the ancient scribe who led his people back to Jerusalem from Babylonian exile, there to implement "the law of God of heaven." Schechter believed that in the United States, "this great, glorious and free country," Jews "need not sacrifice a single iota of our Torah." Nothing in American citizenship, he insisted, was incompatible with any law essential to the preservation of Judaism. Indeed, Schechter found much in American history to sustain his optimism. He fondly recalled his childhood encounters with stories of the Pilgrims and biographies of the Founding Fathers. He was particularly drawn to Lincoln, whose religious mysticism tempered by legal training ennobled the Constitution as the "sacred writ" of the American people.[15]

Schechter saw himself (according to Norman Bentwich, his English friend and biographer) as a "Hassidic *Zaddik*," the wise man of religious faith who could preserve traditional Judaism in the modern West. The bedrock of Schechter's faith, of course, was Torah, "the underlying principle of Law" that distinguished Jews from gentiles—and traditional Judaism from Reform. In his inaugural address at the Seminary in 1902, Schechter insisted that the past was "an integral and inalienable part of ourselves." Judaism, he declared, "permeates the whole of your life. It demands control over all your actions, and interferes even with your menu. It sanctifies the seasons, and regulates your history." It was, in sum, "absolutely incompatible with the abandonment of the Torah." Schechter often returned to this theme, asserting "the binding authority of law" in Jewish life. In Judaism, he insisted, "everything must emanate from the Torah and culminate in it."[16]

Schechter's commitment to the sacred law of Judaism, in turn, shaped his conception of the role of the rabbi. The sole claim to rabbinical authority came from the Torah, which shaped the rabbi's "law-mindedness" or "law-conscience." Any attempt to locate rabbinical authority elsewhere, outside law, must fail. Ethics and spirituality were fine, Schechter conceded in a swipe at Reform, "but laws and commandments, bidden and commanded by God, are better." Without law, Schechter warned, Judaism was reduced to "platitudes . . . borrowed from Christian apologetics." The obligation of the rabbi was to represent "the principle of law and authority and obedience" that had defined the distinctiveness of Judaism and accounted for its survival through the eighteen centuries since the destruction of the Second Temple. Rejection of the authority of law, to Schechter, was nothing less than "betrayal of the Jewish nation."[17]

But it did not take long for Schechter's euphoric expectations about the future of Judaism in America to turn into bitter disillusionment and despair. In his own conception of Judaism, divine revelation was constantly mediated by the evolving claims of human history. The sacred law retained its undiminished authority, but its meaning came from human encounters with divine command. Molded by his own immersion in European Hassidism and Western culture, he personified the interplay of tradition and change that he defined as the essence of Judaism. "The real authorities," he wrote, "are those who, drawing their inspiration from the past, also understand how to reconcile us with the present and to prepare us for the future."[18]

In the United States, however, that dialectical tension between the Jewish past and the American present had been all but dissipated. Schechter felt besieged by "hostile influences," which he identified as "Cincinnati," "downtown," and "Columbia"—the homes, respectively, of Reform, Orthodoxy, and Western secularism. Reform had abandoned the authority of law altogether; Orthodoxy "hopelessly separated" law from life; the worship of reason undermined Judaism as a revealed religion. As a defender of "the living tradition" of Judaism, the Judaism of Torah, Schechter was most preoccupied with the dangers of Reform, still the preferred identification of American Jews and a continuing source of conflict over the direction of the Seminary itself. Schechter's Judaism meant "orderly and regular development in accordance with our laws and traditions." He was determined to resist, and if possible to reverse, the inroads of radical Reform.[19]

Insisting that Jews "be Jews and remain Jews," Schechter dismissed Reform as an unacceptable accommodation to Christianity. He condemned the full range of Reform innovations—Sunday Sabbath, English prayer, deletion of references to Zion and messianic redemption, dilution of synagogue ritual—as the abandonment of Torah. "Judaism may mean anything" in the United States, he complained to Marshall, where rabbis rejected the authority of the Bible and Talmud. Schechter dismissed the Reform identification with Hebrew prophecy ("playing off the prophets against the law") as a capitulation to Christian theology. He could only tolerate reform within the bounds of authority defined by Torah and Talmud. These, he insisted, "are elastic and wide enough for all reasonable purpose." But appeals to universalism, ethics, progress, and spiritual mission—the staples of Reform rhetoric—were "largely verbiage." Jews, Schechter warned, "cannot live on oxygen alone." The bedrock of Judaism, he reminded a Reform rabbi, was "God, Israel, and the Torah."[20]

Schechter's animosity toward "Cincinnati" was fed by, and in turn reinforced, divisions within the Seminary. The Seminary had come to resemble a political party at election time, uneasily balancing the competing claims of its rival factions. Founded by Orthodox rabbis to counter Reform, it had been revitalized by lay Reformers who, in turn, chose "a proper English gentleman" from an Eastern European Hassidic family to devise the appropriate reconciliation of tradition and modernity. The trustees were themselves divided: Adler, the most observant among them, hoped for an alternative to Reform; Schiff despaired about the growing strength of secularism; other donors were apprehensive about Lower East Side radicalism; Marshall wanted a traditional Judaism that was suitable to American conditions (perhaps a contradiction in terms). Although it is recounted, perhaps apocryphally, that even Schechter once conceded that "no one can be a rabbi in America who does not know how to play baseball as well as study Talmud," he did not normally treat the issue with such levity. He felt undermined by the Seminary directors, who seemed to be "more interested in questions of civics than in rabbinical Jewish learning."[21]

As Schechter's frustrations within the Seminary increased, his optimistic faith in the prospects for Judaism in the United States diminished. It did not take him long to discover the "peculiar individualism" that he described as "the bane of American life." He attributed the difficulties of preserving Jewish religious observance to the "worship of individualism" and "disregard of authority" that pervaded American society. He worried about the fate of Judaism in the American melting pot, which, he predicted presciently, "will devour Judaism ruthlessly as soon as the social prejudice on the part of our neighbors will sufficiently relax." As he moved closer toward an acknowledgement that even American Jews confronted the destructive dilemma of modernity—anti-Semitism at one extreme, or assimilation at the other—he began to sense some conflict between Jewish commitments and American values. His prediction that the future of Judaism was in the United States, made so confidently from England, yielded within five years of his arrival to the concession that "America is not the final destiny of Judaism." In 1906, after a prolonged period of soul searching, Schechter publicly identified with Zionism.[22]

Schechter's commitment to Zionism did not come easily. Even though he had long believed in the return to Zion as a fundamental axiom of Judaism, and his own twin brother had been among the first group of Hovevei Zion settlers in Zichron Yakov, he kept the Zionist movement at a distance. It was too secular, and too political, for his taste; the "nihilism" of the Russian Zionists, and the conspicuous absence of settlers with "religious zeal," distressed him. "We are 'Gerim' [strangers] in Europe," he had conceded in 1897, "and must look out for a home." But he declined to attend the Zionist conference at Basle convened by Herzl; he had no time nor, he confessed, "am I Zionist enough." Yet he could not reject the Zionist movement altogether, for he remained convinced that "you cannot sever Jewish nationality from Jewish religion."[23]

The reconciliation of religion and nationality was as integral to Schechter's Judaism as his synthesis of divine law with the living needs of the Jewish people. The longer he remained in the West, the stronger his impulse grew to restore those ancient Jewish unities that modern Western thought and culture had wrenched apart. It became increasingly difficult for Schechter to resist Zionism— although he tried. "I am not claiming to be a Zionist," he wrote, "but I mean to remain a Jew in religion and nationality," adding, "I abhor all universalism." By 1903, he was prepared to believe in Zionism if only the Zionists would "maintain Jewish institutions." A year later, he proclaimed his faith in Zionism without an open identification with the movement. "If Zionism means admiration of Israel's past, hope and faith in its future, devotion to the national literature and reverence for the national institutions," he wrote, "then I am trying in my humble way to be a Zionist." But he remained convinced that the greatest danger to Judaism came from the Jews of wealth, "with their indifference, with their rage for assimilation, with their aping the Christians." It was more important, therefore, to "convert their cosmopolitan homes into Jewish homes" than to "discover a new continent for Russian emigrants."[24]

It is not entirely clear what finally provoked Schechter's public affirmation of Zionism. He may have hoped to counter the rampant secularism of the Zionist movement. The willingness of territorialists, including his friend Israel Zangwill, to settle for a homeland outside the land of Israel infuriated him. He was angered by the incessant anti-Zionist criticism of Reformers. Wherever he looked, he saw the deleterious effect of assimilation, with Zionists tolerating "the assimilation of Judaism," while Reformers acquiesced in "the assimilation of the Jew." Determined to unify Jewish nationalism and religious Judaism, he announced in 1906 that, "after long hesitation and careful watching," he had turned to Zionism "as the great bulwark against assimilation."[25]

Schechter's statement of Zionist identification was simultaneously a poignant lament over the "loss of identity" that Jews had experienced in the modern West. Schechter described a "tragedy of despair and helplessness" (his own, surely) as a "process of disintegration" stripped "a great ancient people" of its devotion to the sacred law and its language, forcing it to borrow indiscriminately from the ideas and institutions of its religious enemies and secular critics. The temptations, Schechter acknowledged, were compelling: "the innate desire for comfort; . . . the natural desire not to appear peculiar; the accessibility of theological systems, possessing all the seductions of 'newness and modernity,' patronized by fashion and even by potentates, and taught in ever so many universities." But the conclusion was painfully clear: even in the United States "We are in Galut [exile]. This may not be the Galut of the Jews, but it is the Galut of Judaism, . . . the Galut of the Jewish soul, wasting away before our very eyes."[26]

Schechter did not quarrel with the prevailing terms of Americanization—mastery of the English language, familiarity with national history and literature, the yearning to become "a law-abiding citizen, thoroughly appreciating the privilege of being a member of this great commonwealth." Rather, he despaired over the tendency toward "absorption in the great majority," the inevitable fate of Western Jews. Emancipation, he conceded, must lead to "the extinction of Judaism." Unwilling to submit to "the tortures of a slow death," Schechter rejected the "terrible consequences" of assimilation for the promise of national and religious regeneration that he found in Zionism.[27]

Zionism, Schechter declared, was "the Declaration of Jewish Independence from all kinds of slavery, whether material or spiritual." He welcomed its varied expressions—national, religious, cultural—as long as they embraced "the great idea of Zion and Jerusalem," the restoration of an independent national life in the land of Israel. He credited the movement with significant successes, most conspicuously its appeal to Jews "who otherwise would have been lost to Judaism." National rebirth, Schechter insisted, was inseparable from "the revival of Judaism," for nationalism expressed (to Schechter) the most ancient precepts of the Jewish people: faith in God, covenantal chosenness, and redemption in the promised land. Zionism, with its "reassertion of the Jewish soul," gave Jews the opportunity to revive biblical faith in "the religious national idea, . . . under the discipline of the Law."[28]

Schechter's statement testified to his enduring attachment to the precepts of historic Judaism—and to his loss of confidence in American prospects for their fulfillment. Schechter bluntly stated that American Jews lived in *galut* and that only the revival of Jewish national life, within the framework of the sacred law, could save them from spiritual death. He gave scant attention to the issue that so preoccupied most American Zionists: how to reconcile Jewish nationalism with American patriotism. He never relinquished his belief that Jews were, by historic destiny, a people apart, needing—even in the United States—to be "invigorated by sacred memories and sacred environments" that could sustain their distinctive national life. His justification for Zionism, therefore, was entirely within Jewish terms and did not depend for its validity on any presumed compatibility with American values. He assumed the devotion of American Jews to American institutions, but his primary concern was assimilation, not patriotism. The Zionist goal, he insisted, must be "the Jewish historic ideal."[29]

Committed to the unities of Judaism, Schechter normally was tolerant of the varieties of Zionism. Drawn at first to the spiritual Zionism of Ahad Ha-'Am, he subsequently moved closer to the religious Zionism of Mizrachi. Least comfortable with the political Zionists for their rampant secularism, he labeled them "enemies of Judaism" and "traitors of their God." His statement of Zionist identification was remarkable for its synthesis of the fragmented components of modern Jewish consciousness: religion *and* nationality; law *and* prophecy; Zion *and galut*; national purpose *and* universal mission. "Mere nationalism," he believed, "is not worth striving for." Jewish nationality "without a sacred literature, without reverence for its ancient institutions, without love for its past, without devotion to its religion, . . . will be of very little promise." For Schechter, only a "religious-national consciousness" could preserve "everything Jewish." The "most sublime" expressions of Jewish nationalism, he told the last graduating class at the Seminary before his death, "are to be found in the Bible and the Prayer

Book." A national revival detached from religious faith would culminate in "spiritual disaster." For Schechter, the eternal core of Zionism was "God and His people, Israel."[30]

Schechter's Zionist credo expressed the weight of his accumulated frustrations with American Judaism. He came to the Seminary believing that Judaism could be reconciled with Americanism. By 1906, he had come to understand that the priorities of the directors (to say nothing of American values) sharply conflicted with his own. His affirmation of Zionism was an attempt to reassert the claims of Judaism against their desire for acculturation. Predictably, it only exacerbated relations. "Speaking as an American," Schiff wrote to him, "I cannot for a moment concede that one can be at the same time a true American and an honest adherent of the Zionist movement." Zionism placed "a prior lien" on the citizenship of American Jews, retarding "perfect Americanization." To Schechter, however, Americanization was the problem, not the solution. At the Seminary he tried to navigate a course for Judaism between Reform and Orthodoxy; as a Zionist, he tried to harmonize religion and nationality. Wherever he turned, however, he was caught in the crossfire between tradition and modernity. As synthesis became more elusive, Schechter grew more disillusioned and embittered.[31]

The Seminary only fed his frustration. The trustees seemed to be more interested in issues of patriotism and loyalty than in traditional Jewish learning. "I must take it out of their minds," he wrote, "that I come into this country for the purpose of converting the downtown [immigrant] Jew to a more refined species of religion." He had relinquished his "ideal life" as a Cambridge scholar, he reminded Marshall, because he was convinced that "the future of Israel was in America" and that the Seminary, combining the "best in modern thought" with "traditional Judaism," would become a "great centre of Jewish learning" that would compare favorably with Eastern European *yeshivot*. Instead, he realized that the Seminary had been designed by its founders to tame "the most unruly element in Jewry," to give the immigrants some "religious refinement" to ease their journey to Americanization. His hopes, he conceded finally, were "shattered to pieces."[32]

"I hoped to find in Zionism repose and rest," Schechter wrote, "and I can see my hopes shattered with every day." Invited to lead the American Zionist movement, he declined; his statement of faith defined the limits of his active participation. The rampant secularism of the Russian Zionists, leaders of the movement in Europe and the most committed settlers in Palestine, kept him at a distance. He chastized the secular Zionists as "outspoken enemies of Judaism," without "a spark of religion," whose influence was "polluting the Holy Land." Between the "assimilation of the Jew" in the West, which had turned him toward Zionism, and "the assimilation of Judaism" that he blamed on Zionism, Schechter found little room to maneuver. Yearning for Zionist leadership "from the West" (as always, the repository of Schechter's hopes), he was dismayed once Louis Brandeis provided it. "I was a Jew and even a Zionist long before Brandeis was a Zionist," he complained, "whilst he probably will never be a Jew."[33]

Zionism failed to revive Schechter's hopes for the future of Judaism in the United States. He was convinced that "the very framework" of Judaism was being destroyed by the relentless pressures of assimilation. "I feel the humiliation so deeply sometimes that I wish I had never lived to see it," he wrote. "It is terrible." He hoped for "a remnant" of Jews "to bear witness against the majority," but he despaired of finding it. The "real problem," he insisted, "was not the Americanization of the immigrants," as assimilated Jews claimed, but "whether we are able to keep the immigrant within Judaism after he has become Americanized."[34] Schechter's anxiety and despair seem to have contributed to a serious breakdown in 1913; he never fully recovered his health and died two years later.

Schechter's entire adult life had been a struggle to salvage a viable modern Judaism from the fragments of an ancient tradition. A rebel from Eastern European Orthodoxy, he always journeyed westward, believing that the future of Judaism was in Berlin, or London, or New York. Only near the end of his life did he turn back to the East, to Zionism; characteristically, once he made the commitment he drew back from it because it excluded more of Judaism than he could comfortably relinquish. He could no more readily embrace the rampant secularism of the Jewish national revival than he could tolerate the unyielding orthodoxy that defended the revealed tradition—or, for that matter, the yearnings for assimilation that coaxed western Jews from the historic national religion.

Schechter yearned for a Judaism that could reconcile ancient and modern, religious and secular, Eastern and Western, Orthodox and Reform—but it was a fusion that enlightenment and emancipation did not permit. The more inclusive his reach, the more difficult his task and the greater his frustration. He was, his biographer wrote, "too liberal for orthodox Jews, too conservative for the reform leaders; he antagonized the Zionists because he demanded a religious life in Palestine; he antagonized the anti-Zionists because he was passionate for the cause of Zion." Marshall, who deeply admired and respected Schechter, conceded that his sensitivity to criticism, his impatience, his intensity made him difficult to work with. Yet the depth of his learning and the passion of his Jewish faith were compelling. Marshall despaired of finding anyone else like Schechter, who combined scholarly ability and "religious authority."[35]

Religious authority was precisely the problem for which modernity offered no solution, not even to Schechter. The pieces of the ancient religious national synthesis were too finely shattered, and too widely scattered, even for a rabbinical scholar of Schechter's considerable talents to restore them to their original unity. Schechter tried to gather them all into some coherent pattern: he affirmed divine revelation, and the authority of *halakha*, but he insisted also upon the vitality of Jewish history, and he recognized the power of Jewish national yearnings. He tried to reconcile divine revelation with the claims of what he called "Catholic Israel," the changing needs of a living people. But he never lost his appreciation for "institutions, ceremonies and symbols" that bound a people to its history, nor could he accept any diminution in the authority of Torah, least of all for some conception of "prophetic Judaism" that encouraged Jews to escape their own historical distinctiveness.[36]

Schechter confronted an American Jewish community, swollen by immigration, that faced the dilemma of American Jewish life in the twentieth century: How were Jews to live within Jewish history, yet become Americans? How were they to reconcile Jewish claims with American commitments? His answer came from Jewish tradition: from the historic unity of religion and nationality. But the meaning of his American years, between 1902 and 1915, was the impossibility of reconstructing the ancient synthesis in the modern era, at least in the United States. Neither the Seminary nor the Zionist movement could sustain the burden of Schechter's expectations—although, in time, the Conservative Judaism nurtured at the Seminary developed a synthesis of religious tradition and modern critical thought, along with Zionism and Americanism, that second- and third-generation American Jews found persuasive. Surely this was Schechter's great and enduring ideological achievement, even though it was not yet evident during his lifetime. In that way, Conservatism confronted "the urgent problem of alienation" for Jews who, as Jacob Neusner has suggested, have wanted the impossible: to retain their attachment "to a past that, they knew, they had lost."[37] Solomon Schechter never conceded the loss. Refusing to submit to any authority external to the Jewish historical tradition, he struggled to preserve it at a most inopportune time in a most unlikely place.

Louis Marshall once compared the Jewish Theological Seminary to the academy at Yavneh, where "a saving remnant," led by Rabbi Yohanan ben Zakkai, had "preserved Judiasm" after the destruction of the Second Temple and termination of the national life of Israel. The comparison is instructive. Ben Zakkai had demonstrated that Judaism could transcend its own worst historical tragedies through fidelity to the sacred law—and accommodation to the Roman Empire. To Marshall, who frequently drew analogies from Jewish history, American Jewry confronted as momentous a challenge of reconstruction as had the Jews of Palestine two thousand years earlier.[38]

Marshall's commitment to the Seminary expressed his yearning for compatibility between ancient Jewish precepts and the obligations of American citizenship. The Seminary, he wrote, "is intended to create a bridge by means of which, while adhering to the principles of Judaism as they have been handed down to us by our forefathers, the foreign-born Jews may nevertheless become imbued with the spirit of American institutions." For Marshall, as for Schechter, the task was to define a viable American Judaism amid the demographic upheaval that resulted from the arrival of two million Eastern European Jews in the United States between 1881 and 1915, creating (despite Marshall's denials) a "Jewish question" of massive proportions. Schechter always insisted that immigrants must remain "within Judaism"; Marshall, however, wanted to coax them toward a new identity as *American* Jews. He looked to a new generation of rabbis, "thoroughly American in manner, thought and speech . . . and exponents of everything that is fine in Judaism," to lead the way.[39]

Marshall's role in the reorganization of the Seminary brought him into the circle of self-appointed Jewish leaders who gathered around Jacob Schiff, whose philanthropic generosity shaped Jewish life at the turn of the century. Schiff, accompanied by members of the Sulzberger, Warburg, and Straus families, often joined by Adler, Schechter, and now Marshall, met monthly to discuss issues of Jewish significance. Beginning in 1903, a series of devastating pogroms in Russia stirred the concern of American Jews, many of whom knew from personal experience the brutalities of the czarist regime. Despite the distance between Kishinev and New York, it was impossible to deny the intensity of the bond between American and European Jews, as Jews; yet, for Marshall and the others, it was dangerous to affirm it. Any such assertion might be taken to demonstrate Jewish political unity, a prospect fraught with "serious perils" for Marshall. But the Schiff circle, prodded by apprehension lest more impetuous Jewish spokesmen (especially Judah Magnes, who became Marshall's brother-in-law) take charge of the protest movement, authorized Marshall to explore the idea of a "general Jewish committee to consider matters of general interest." Wary of any Jewish organization based on nonreligious grounds, Marshall insisted upon a committee "free from all objectionable tendencies" that would "meet the approval of the general public." The American Jewish Committee was organized in 1906 "to aid in securing the civil and religious rights of the Jews in all countries where such rights are denied or endangered."[40]

The cautious language conveyed Marshall's characteristic concerns. Its restricted focus, to countries where the rights of Jews were jeopardized, automatically excluded the United States. None of the Committee founders believed that the rights of American Jews were endangered (and Mayer Sulzberger, the first president, confined its jurisdiction to foreign issues). Only the rights of Jews as individuals (not as members of a religion, a peo-

ple, or, least of all, a nation) were addressed; protection would come from
a "committee" of "leading" Jews, not from a representative "congress,"
which several founders (although not Marshall) considered "un-American." The "leading" Jews were carefully selected, largely from the ranks
of lawyers, bankers, and the Reform rabbinate. (One lawyer complained,
after scrutinizing the list of prospective members, "the selection of Rabbis,
indiscriminately, is . . . a serious error.") What Marshall was "trying to
avoid more than anything else," he confided, was "the creation of a political organization." That would suggest that Jews "have interests different
from those of other American citizens."[41]

Despite his apprehensions, the American Jewish Committee provided
Marshall with his primary institutional base of power and influence. Between 1906 and Marshall's death in 1929 (and especially after he assumed
the presidency in 1912), hardly an issue of consequence in American Jewish
life was resolved independently of his contribution. Because Marshall was
determined to lead circumspectly, it is not easy to recreate his style of firm
persuasion. Often described as imperious (he was known to some as Louis
XIX), he was, more than anything else, extremely cautious. "The greatest
wisdom," he once observed, "consists in knowing when to remain silent."
He usually preferred "dilatory tactics" to immediate action. His restraint—
the insistence upon "tact, patience and perseverance"—was dictated by his
perception of the American Jewish community. Not only did it comprise
a tiny fraction of the American population, but, in Marshall's unyielding
judgment (expressed on a wide range of issues), it had no right to get involved in issues "as a nation." Any form of "political"—as opposed to religious or philanthropic—activity would inevitably isolate Jews from the
American majority, precisely what Marshall most wished to avoid. He rig-
orously restricted his public statements and interviews and expended
enormous effort to deflect publicity from Jewish affairs, especially from the
rambunctious disagreements that erupted periodically within the efferves-
cent, but fragmented, New York Jewish community.[42]

Although Marshall never formally articulated an ideology of American
Judaism, his reiteration of certain fundamental precepts defined it. "I am
not one who believes in distinctions of race, creed or nationality," he asserted. "We are all American citizens who know no allegiance except that
which we owe to the Flag." That stated Marshall's bedrock faith, and he
never deviated from the vision of national unity that it expressed. Reality,
however, was less comforting: "In view of the oft-repeated slander that the
Jew is not a patriot, our people have become actuated by an intense desire
to convince their fellow citizens of the falsity of such a charge, and that
they are ready to serve their country whenever it calls." That expressed
Marshall's deepest concern, which inspired his sustained effort to define
American Judaism in ways that would decisively put to rest any claim that

Jews were not loyal and patriotic Americans. He dismissed all "metaphysics" and "ecclesiastical refinements," insisting only that Jews "observe the laws of the state and the rule of decency and morality." "Of all people in the world," he insisted, Jews "owe to the United States the utmost gratitude and the duty of permitting nothing to intervene between us and the obligation which we owe to our country."[43]

Marshall missed few opportunities to assert his credo: "the American Jew is an integral part of the American people." During the celebration in 1905 of the two hundred and fiftieth anniversary of the arrival of the first Jews in New Amsterdam, he developed his enduring theme of Jewish patriotism. He referred to those early settlers as "the Jewish Pilgrim Fathers," who had arrived in the New World with "the same capital as the Pilgrim Fathers—a yearning for liberty, an abiding trust in God, the Bible—no more, no less." The purpose of the celebration, he explained, was "to point out to the people of this country, that the Jews are here as of right; that they are not interlopers; that they were among the earliest of the Colonists." At a time when it was widely asserted that immigrants could no longer be safely absorbed into American society, Marshall insisted upon the compatibility of immigrant aspirations with American values. Immigrants "love our country and its institutions," Marshall wrote; they wanted nothing more than "the privileges of citizenship."[44]

Marshall's intense—even consuming—concern with the patriotism and loyalty of American Jews resonated with deeply personal meaning. He never forgot, and frequently cited, the struggle of his own immigrant parents to become law-abiding citizens. Their "sufferings" lingered with him; because of their travail, he once explained, he had "probably given as much thought to the subject of immigration as any man in the country." Marshall lobbied and corresponded incessantly to combat efforts to restrict immigration, impose national origin quotas and literacy tests (his father had never learned to read English, nor could his mother speak it), and tighten deportation procedures.[45]

Like so many other American Jews who were the children of immigrant parents, Marshall was extremely sensitive to the duality of his own heritage. No theme of American Jewish history is more poignant (or persistent) than the familiar dilemma of immigrant acculturation: how much of the old culture to retain? how much of the new culture to absorb? The children of immigrants inherited the dilemma, for the more Americanized they became, the further they distanced themselves from their own family origins. In journeys abroad, or to the Lower East Side, they often experienced a shock of self-discovery as they encountered the culture that their families had left behind. To acculturated American Jews, Eastern European Jewry was a powerful symbol of Jewish authenticity, which evoked strong, and often conflicting, feelings of identification and uneasiness.

Among Marshall's contemporaries, several vividly recalled— sometimes after many decades—their first encounters with Old World Jews. Judah Magnes studied in Germany after his ordination at the Hebrew Union College. There he was transformed by his contact with the Eastern Europeans. They were, he wrote, "complete" Jews, sustained by "Talmud Judaism" with "tremendous spiritual power." ("God help them if . . . our cracked-up ideas of 'progress', etc. ever reach them.") Spiritually reborn, Magnes changed his name (from Julian Leon to Judah Laban) and announced to his parents his determination "to live more like a Jew"—at the same time that he worried lest Jewish immigration pose "a danger to the Jews of America." Similarly, Bernard Drachman, who grew up in a nonobservant family in New Jersey, discovered in European Jews "a demonstration of genuine, living Judaism such as I had not witnessed in America." He contrasted their "compellingly real and vital faith" with the "divided souls" of American Jews. Stephen Wise, raised in the enclosed German Jewish community of New York, experienced personal liberation in Basle, where he attended the second Zionist Congress. Among Eastern European Jews, Wise wrote in his autobiography, "I found my brothers . . . I found myself."[46]

Marshall had no such dramatic encounter—only the enduring memories of his parents' struggle to become Americans. But those sufficed. More than any other member of the German Jewish elite, whom Marshall referred to scornfully as "Lords and Ladies bountiful," he retained deep respect for the Lower East Side and for immigrant attachments to Jewish traditions. He learned to read Yiddish; he defended the "great intellectual treasures" of Yiddish literature against allegations that it was un-American to speak a foreign language; and he praised the "admirable . . . loyalty" of Orthodox Jews to their ritual observances. He could, in exasperation (and always in private to another Jew), condemn the "downtown rabbi" and his "superstitious followers" for "digging a grave" for Judaism, but he was equally quick to chastise a critic of Orthodoxy for "vulgar bickering." To Christian outsiders he was unyielding in his defense of Orthodoxy as legitimately American, for it displayed "the very spirit which made the Puritan so powerful an instrument in the shaping of the American Commonwealth." Marshall had no patience for disagreements between "rival theologians," nor for the incessant wrangling between native American Jews and the Eastern European newcomers. "We are all immigrant Jews," he noted on one occasion; on another, he wrote, "Here we are all American Jews." For Marshall, there was no contradiction. "Nothing Jewish is alien to me," he insisted.[47]

Marshall, whose personal inclinations were reinforced by professional training, abhorred conflict. Just as Schechter had used the term "Catholic Israel" to refer to the collective historical experience of the Jewish people,

Marshall insisted upon a united Judaism of religious faith, characterized by "harmony, union, and concord." He could not tolerate distinctions or divisions between Orthodoxy and Reform, native American and immigrant, "uptown" German Jew and "downtown" East European Jew, or Zionist and anti-Zionist. He was not, as he acknowledged, a "Shulhan Arukh Jew" committed to the sacred law and its observance. But he was profoundly traditional, and he believed that all Jews were "essentially conservative," still bound, after thirty centuries, to the Ten Commandments and to the Hebrew Prophets.[48]

Yet Marshall's confident assertions of immigrant patriotism could not entirely conceal underlying anxieties. His persistent concern about allegations of disloyalty suggests that he probably shared those anxieties. Explaining to Schechter why the rabbi had to be excluded from the executive committee of the New York *kehilla*, Marshall referred to the "great peril" that would confront American Jews if noncitizens (even those, like Schechter, who were "saturated with the spirit of American institutions") participated in such activities. "We should be charged with disloyalty to this country," predicted Marshall, who insisted that most immigrants did not "adequately understand the relations of the Jews in this country to the state," which required their uncontested loyalty to American institutions. Especially during World War I, Marshall worried lest American Jews be accused of sympathy for Germany. Learning that the *Forward*, the widely read Yiddish newspaper, might lose its mailing privileges, he secured a pledge of American loyalty from its editor, which he submitted to the postmaster general with his own promise to read the *Forward* carefully and report anything that was unpatriotic. To prevent government censorship, and to protect Jews against claims of disloyalty, Marshall volunteered to serve as a private censor.[49]

Marshall never eluded the tension between American nationality and Jewish particularity, between the allegiance of Jews to the United States and their simultaneous attachment to an ancient tradition with religious and national components. He seldom missed an opportunity to defend Jewish interests, but he always insisted that Jews had no interests that differentiated them from other Americans. Proclaiming their rights as equal citizens, he was apprehensive lest others deny them—or lest Jews act in concert to assert them. "I have never shrunk from the assertion of Jewish rights," he once declared, but he preferred to rest his claims, wherever possible, upon "general principles applicable to every American citizen." Whether the issue was a criminal defense case, resistance to the Ku Klux Klan, or opposition to immigration restriction, Marshall counseled Jews not to become involved as Jews. Any such issue, he advised, "should be approached, not from the standpoint of a religious body or of a race, but from that of citizenship." Jews should "keep in the background," especially on issues with latent Jewish content, for any assertion of a specifically Jewish interest was "apt to irritate" the majority of Americans.[50]

Marshall was especially leery of distinctions that implied Jewish social separation or political distinctiveness. He sharply rebuked publisher Adolph S. Ochs for a *New York Times* description of the Lower East Side as a "ghetto." "There is no such thing as a Ghetto in this country," Marshall protested, expressing his concern lest the term imply that Jews were "pariahs." The ghetto was a European memory, not an American reality. "It has been a long journey for us to emerge from the Ghetto and to acquire equal political rights," Marshall once reminded the organizers of a Jewish political club. Therefore, any identification of Judaism with politics was suspect. "When a man once becomes a citizen," Marshall declared, he ceases to be "a Hebrew," and his religious or racial identity "becomes merged in his Americanism."[51]

Yet Marshall resisted all efforts at assimilation as "mischievous"—the term he used to denigrate Israel Zangwill's romantic drama, *The Melting Pot*. The rabbinate, he cautioned a Seminary graduate in 1911, should no longer be "speeding the process of assimilation." Rather, it must "appeal to Jewish consciousness," becoming "a conservator of Jewish institutions." Such conservatism might indeed preserve Jews as a "peculiar people," but Marshall preferred such religious (not political) distinctiveness to "the dead level of agnostic uniformity." Although he was a trustee of Temple Emanu-El, he lamented its extreme modifications of the traditional liturgy. Ancient melodies had been replaced by an excess of "sermons" and "Wagnerian music," prompting Marshall to compose his own translation of *L'cha Dodi* (which Schechter praised as "beautiful"). He valued anything that sustained Judaism as "a living religion"—but *only* as a religion.[52]

Marshall's blend of religion and patriotism expressed his determination to reconcile Judaism with Americanism. He knew that Reform Judaism had too readily absorbed the assimilationist thrust of emancipation to command the allegiance of Eastern European immigrants; and he feared that Zionism menaced the successful integration of Jews into American society. His definition of American Judaism, drawing heavily upon the language of American law, was calculated to avoid the hazards of both extremes.

As a lawyer, Marshall enjoyed privileged access to the special language and symbols of law that had come to define American identity, cohesion, and purpose. Although "Marshall law" referred to the autocratic leadership for which Marshall was renowned (and occasionally resented), the phrase had a deeper significance for which Marshall has yet to receive his full measure of recognition. "Marshall law," in practice, meant the power to define American Judaism in legal terms, emphasizing concepts of constitutionality, citizenship, equality, and rights. It elevated the rule of American law as the ultimate authority for American Jews and the locus of their deepest veneration as American citizens. Marshall, more than anyone else, expounded the principles that linked Jews to the American constitutional and legal tradition, enabling them to identify their struggle for full integration into American society with the rule of law and the assertion of rights.

For Marshall, there always was an implicit compatibility between his political conservatism, his faith in American law, and his respect for Jewish tradition. Marshall's legal faith bound Jews to American society. "It is the glory of our country that before the law all men are equal"; therefore, "every member of the state owes unqualified loyalty to it." Respect for law, Marshall insisted, was consistent with the "ancient virtues" of the Jewish people. In a revealing infusion of Jewish symbolism into American legal terms, he once described the Constitution as the "holy of holies, an instrument of sacred import."[53]

"Life, liberty and property," Marshall reminded Jacob Schiff, "owe their protection in this country to the Constitution." And all American Jews must learn, he insisted to Magnes, "that while we must insist on equal rights, we have no right to ask for . . . special privileges. We must not be made exceptions to the law." Fearing "a Babel-like confusion of laws" if any part of Jewish religious law was granted legitimacy, Marshall demanded unequivocal Jewish submission to the "law of the state."[54]

Marshall applied these principles in varied contexts. In the Leo Frank murder case, in which he served as counsel on appeal, he insisted that Frank be considered not as a Jew, but only as "a respected, industrious, law-abiding citizen," whose rights must be honored "as a matter of justice." (The refusal of the Supreme Court to reverse Frank's conviction elicited from Marshall the bitter response that "I shall never again be able to feel that reliance upon the courts in respect to the accomplishment of the ends of justice, that I have hitherto entertained.") When Harvard imposed a Jewish quota, Marshall opposed it with the demand of "one rule for all." Defending the minorities treaties drafted at the peace conference after World War I, Marshall extended his consitutional principles internationally, insisting that the American constitutional guarantees of equal rights now applied to the "fundamental law" of all nations. Consequently, Jews everywhere had become "part and parcel of the citizenry, . . . each individual having the guarantee of constitutional rights."[55]

These formulations of the promise of American law, and loyalty to it as an American Jewish obligation, are by now so deeply ingrained that it is difficult to imagine that they once emerged as original propositions. Few would attribute them to Louis Marshall, whose name is now all but unknown even within the American Jewish community that is still guided by his principles. But Marshall, as a Seminary faculty member once wrote appreciatively, was "the great constitution maker of American Jewry." His talent was evident, drafting the Seminary charter, participating in the work of two New York State constitutional conventions, engaging in constitutional advocacy before the Supreme Court (as fervently defending the rights of black and Asian citizens as those of Jews), or holding Congress, Harvard, and Henry Ford to constitutional standards that discrimination against American Jews surely violated. "My great desire," he once stated, "is to bring about the emancipation of the Jews, to help them attain their civil, religious and political rights."[56] To a considerable extent, his wish defined his achievement. Encouraging Jews to pledge their allegiance to the American legal system, and demanding that it protect their rights (as citizens, not as Jews), Marshall devised the legal *quid pro quo* that enabled immigrant Jews to become Americans.

But Marshall's terms of reconciliation between Judaism and Americanism overlooked one vital ingredient of Jewish immigrant consciousness: the passionate yearning for a strong Jewish identification that Zionism expressed. For religious and political reasons, he could not feel comfortable with the Jewish national revival; and the limits of his identification with Zionism, in conjunction with his political conservatism, ultimately curtailed his influence as a leader—and his reputation among historians. Marshall never understood that even Zionism could be reconciled with Americanism. It took another lawyer, Louis D. Brandeis, to articulate their compatibility, thereby securing the allegiance of the immigrant Jewish masses, through American Zionism, to the United States.

Zionism was, and long remained, the paramount issue in American Jewish affairs. Unlike any other, it possessed the power, for good or ill, to define the place of Jews within American society—or to place them beyond its limits of pluralistic tolerance and legitimacy. Consequently, no one who claimed a position of leadership in Jewish public affairs after the turn of the century could fail to grapple with it, either by opposing it in the name of patriotic loyalty or by shaping it to conform to American patriotism.[57]

From the beginning of the Zionist movement, Marshall kept his distance. "The racial aspect of Judaism does not appeal to me as strongly as does the religious side," he explained, although he early confessed to some admiration for the passionate commitment of Herzl and his followers. Marshall defined himself as "a Jew from conviction and sentiment," but "certainly not a Nationalist." Yet, characteristically, he kept informed about Zionist literature and demonstrated familiarity with its content. His contact with Schechter deepened his appreciation for the cultural Zionism of Ahad Ha-'Am, to the point where he could even express, in public, his commitment to "a Jewish spiritual centre in Palestine." But he had no patience with Zionist political activists. He conceded their enthusiasm, but he chastised them for lacking "good judgment, common sense and cash." Their cause, he believed, was "inadvisable and . . . dangerous." Judaism, to Marshall, must remain a religious faith, not a national movement.[58]

But he remained receptive to Zionist needs as long as they satisfied his criteria of apolitical activity. When the Palestinian Zionist, Aaron Aaronsohn, came to the United States to seek financial support for his agricultural experiment station near Haifa, Marshall acted with alacrity on his behalf. Aaronsohn, who had settled in Palestine as a youngster, had discovered a strain of winter wheat that could survive the Middle Eastern climate. His work as an agronomist, and his evident personal charm, deeply impressed Marshall (and, subsequently, Brandeis), who directed him to potential donors. Once again, as he had done for the Seminary, he drafted the articles of incorporation that legally secured the field station charter. But the task was more onerous and complex than Marshall had anticipated. Aaronsohn relied heavily upon Marshall to tap his network of fundraisers and to handle the legal paperwork, prompting Marshall to express exasperation at being asked to assume "not only the labor but also the expense" of establishing still another Jewish institution. He complained of the waste of his time on "clerical work," which subjected him to "the moods and humors and foibles of the millionaires" whose contributions Marshall was expected to secure. He also had to persuade Jacob Schiff, as always a major benefactor, that Aaronsohn's field station had scientific and educational, but not political, purposes. "With the precautions that we have taken in framing our by-laws," he reassured Schiff, there was "no possibility" that their commitment could be construed as "Zionistic." Marshall once again used the fine arts of lawyering to translate philanthropy and ideology into acceptable institutional form.[59]

Philanthropic generosity to Palestine was encouraged; but Zionist "political" activity was impermissible. Marshall, like other members of the German Jewish elite, drew the line precisely and firmly at the point where Jewish nationality might threaten the allegiance of American citizens. Clearly influenced by Schechter, Marshall contemptuously criticized Zionist leaders as "atheists or agnostics"; and he dismissed the notion "that nationalism can take the place of religion." Jews comprised an "ethnic family" or "a people," who could enjoy "free scope for development on the sacred soil of Palestine." But that opportunity need not—must not—imply "a nation in the political sense of the term." Bluntly, Marshall rejected "the idea of a Jewish State," for Jewish nationalism was "political," the striving for "a political society in its sovereign capacity."[60]

The underlying issue, of course, was divided allegiance; the fear that Jewish national sovereignty would jeopardize the status of Jews as loyal citizens of the United States. When the Balfour Declaration was issued in 1917, favoring a national home for the Jewish people in Palestine, Marshall reiterated his insistence that there be "no political allegiance whatsoever, save that flowing from our American citizenship." He could tolerate "*a* home in Palestine," but not "*the* home of the Jewish people." Such an idea was "an historical and a practical absurdity." As always, Marshall gave priority "to those controlling principles which we look upon as essential to the preservation of our status as American citizens." Ironically, Marshall's opposition to political Zionism was quickly moderated by American government endorsement of the British declaration. With *opposition* to Zionism suddenly in conflict with American foreign policy objectives, Marshall (in consultation with the secretary of state) steered the American Jewish Committee toward a delicate acknowledgement of Zionist legitimacy within the affirmation of American patriotism. It was "axiomatic," declared Marshall's statement on behalf of the Committee, that American Jews "recognize their unqualified allegiance to this country, which they love and cherish and of whose people they constitute an integral part." Simultaneously, however, they expressed their "whole-hearted sympathy" with the hope of Jews who, "moved by traditional sentiment, yearn for a home in the Holy Land for the Jewish people." Inspired by "religious or historic associations," some Jews could establish "a center for Judaism" in Palestine, while the majority remained "loyal and patriotic citizens" of their own nations.[61]

Marshall assured the anti-Zionists that "I am not in favor of a Jewish State and never have been." But, as always, he favored anything that "tended to stimulate interest in Judaism among Jews who otherwise have been entirely indifferent to Jewish history, Jewish life and Jewish tradition." Zionism could be understood as "a pious wish" that "every true Jew who loves the traditions of his faith" might respect. Conceding that Zionist references to statehood had raised disturbing questions about "the attitude of the Jews toward the States to which they owe allegiance," Marshall found nothing objectionable in the idea of a Palestinian "centre (not the centre) for Jewish learning and Jewish culture." Indeed, opposition to Zionism might now be "resented," for it could place Jews "in serious jeopardy" (just as earlier support for Zionism had done) by raising questions about their patriotism. Anti-Zionism might isolate American Jews from "our government"—as always, Marshall's deepest concern.[62]

By 1917, there was no substantial disagreement between Marshall and the American Zionist leadership. This was, in part, because Marshall, prodded by the American government, had edged toward acceptance of at least a limited statement of Zionist purpose, but also because the American Zionist leadership, caught in the same loyalty dilemma as Marshall, drew back from endorsements of Jewish national sovereignty. Marshall, Brandeis, and Julian Mack (the nominal leader of the American Zionist movement after Brandeis's appointment to the Supreme Court in 1916) were bound by a fundamental unity of outlook, demanding allegiance to the United States as the fundamental obligation of American Jews, Zionist or not.[63]

Marshall never doubted that Brandeis and Mack shared his appreciation of "the dangers" of a Jewish state and his opposition to "the principle of independent sovereignty." He trusted Mack to bridge the "artificial chasm" between the Zionist organization and the American Jewish Committee. By the spring of 1919, Marshall reported, "the idea of Jewish statehood is dead," and even the Brandeis-Mack leadership (if not the more militant Eastern Europeans in the Zionist movement) had "given up" on the idea. After several conversations with Brandeis later that year, Marshall was even more convinced that he and Brandeis agreed upon the fundamentals. Brandeis, Marshall wrote, "practically admits that Zionism as a political organization has performed its purposes"—by 1919! Both men preferred the eradication of malaria and industrial development in Palestine as Zionist priorities instead of massive immigration, to say nothing of eventual statehood. The American Zionist organization, Marshall learned, "is anxious to let the people know that it is premature to contemplate a large Jewish settlement in Palestine." It was willing to deemphasize immigration lest Eastern European Jews especially, and even Jews elsewhere, actually come to believe in the possibility of their relocation to a Jewish state. Given the extreme caution of American Zionist leaders, it was unnecessary for Marshall to actively oppose Zionism.[64]

Marshall always felt more comfortable with the Jewish question as a struggle "to secure equal rights" than as an expression of national identity. Yet as far back as 1914 he had confided that "the star of hope points to the land of our fathers." As he aged, he told a friend, "the feelings of love and reverence for the cradle of our race increase in intensity." Despite Marshall's hesitant commitment to the Zionist cause, his strong identification with Judaism was easy to discern and never in doubt. Thirty years after the Paris Peace Conference, Chaim Weizmann, by then the first president of the new Jewish state that Marshall (and Brandeis) had never wanted, still recalled Marshall's "deep sense of sympathy" for the aspirations of Eastern European Jews. He was "much nearer to Jews and Judaism" than his assimilated associates, Weizmann recalled; "nearer, in fact, than Brandeis, an ardent Zionist, ever was."[65]

Ever attentive to opportunities for integrating Judaism and Americanism, Marshall overlooked one of the most potent instruments of Jewish acculturation: the political process itself. He had little patience for the rallies, congresses, and publicity that enabled less affluent and influential Jews to participate in the political rough-and-tumble and, with increasing frequency, to influence its outcome. So, quite often, Marshall was a leader without many followers, except among the small circle of German Jewish philanthropists whose generosity built the institutional foundations of American Jewish life before the First World War. Marshall found his appropriate synthesis of Judaism and Americanism in Jewish tradition and American constitutionalism: or, as he succinctly phrased it in his letter to a Seminary student, in "the spirit of God, and of American patriotism." Religion and the rule of law would protect Jews from the perils of assimilation and separatism, nourishing their Judaism while dispelling allegations that they were not, or could not become, loyal American citizens.

By World War I, Jewish lawyers were defining both sides of the major issues that divided the American Jewish community. By then, power was concentrated in the hands of Marshall and Brandeis (reinforced by the coterie of lawyers whom Brandeis had recruited for the Zionist movement). Communication between Zionists and their opponents often resembled legal negotiations between corporate clients. Their respective attorneys were preoccupied with precise definitions (were Jews a "race," "religion," or "nationality"). They relentlessly scrutinized the language of documents (like the Basle Platform and the Balfour Declaration) as though the words came from legal contracts; and, like the good lawyers they were, they vigorously insisted upon the importance of procedural steps at the expense of substantive results (should Jacob Schiff join the Zionist organization and then try to re-orient it, or should the organization recast itself in Schiff's image before he joined).[66] The debate over the terms of American Jewish acculturation, begun by nineteenth-century rabbis, came to be dominated by twentieth-century lawyers.

Schechter and Marshall were the key transitional figures in this process. They defined the possibilities—and limits—of locating American Judaism within a framework of Jewish tradition. In one sense, they succeeded brilliantly: Conservative Judaism, still the dominant religious identification among American Jews, testifies to the power of Schechter's vision; and his synthesis of religion and nationality at least offered the reassurance that Zionism, despite the denials of Reform and Orthodox Jews, was compatible with Judaism (leaving it to others to demonstrate its compatibility with American traditions). Marshall's contribution, allegiance to the rule of constitutional law, still defines the secular faith of American Jews, whose passionate commitment to American legalism is now far stronger than it ever was in Marshall's lifetime.

But despite Schechter's synthesis, so finely attentive to the nuances of Jewish history and American possibilities, Americanization could not depend exclusively upon rabbinical leadership. That belonged to the traditional culture that American Jews were determined to leave behind. The circumstances of Schechter's appointment to the Seminary indicate that the power to lead American Jewry had already passed into other hands. The invitation to Schechter, the handiwork of Marshall and Mayer Sulzberger, marked the decisive moment of transition, when legal authority passed from European rabbis to American lawyers.

For all but a tiny minority of American Jews, Schechter's concept of "the binding authority of law"—Torah—was overwhelmed by Louis Marshall's faith in American constitutionalism. Once the ultimate source of legal authority was relocated in the Constitution, the way was open for Jewish immigrants to become American Jews. The authority of the sacred law, and with it rabbinical authority, was all but obliterated. (Marshall bluntly affirmed the point in 1905, when he rejected Stephen Wise's demand for pulpit freedom at Temple Emanu-El. "Congregational law," Marshall wrote, required that if the trustees and rabbi were in conflict over the content of a sermon, one must yield; "naturally it must be the rabbi."[67]) From sacred to secular law, from Torah to Constitution, from rabbis to lawyers, from Solomon Schechter to Louis Marshall—that transition defined the essence of American Jewish acculturation. Despite Marshall's wish, yet because of his influence, there could be no Yavneh in America. Lawyers and judges were the new law men of American Judaism.

Louis D. Brandeis:
Zionism as Americanism

The legend remains compelling: Louis D. Brandeis, the esteemed "people's attorney" and renowned Progressive reformer, who would become the first Jew to sit on the Supreme Court, shed his identity as an assimilated Jew and proclaimed himself a Zionist. His personal conversion, when he was past the age of fifty, triggered the momentous transformation of the American Zionist movement that followed his ascension to leadership. A moribund organization without members, leaders, resources, or ideas became the powerful, respected voice of American, even world, Zionism. The movement was the extended shadow of the man, still revered half a century after his death as the American Isaiah.

Like most legends, this one mixes fact and fiction. It implies that Brandeis experienced a deep personal conversion, leading to his strong self-affirmation as a Jew, and that his persuasive synthesis of Zionism and Americanism uncovered some deep truth about the movement for Jewish national restoration. His reconciliation of Zionism with American tradition continues to satisfy the strong need of American Jews to merge two national movements, each of which might legitimately claim their loyalty. But the mythical Brandeis is much less interesting than the real man, whose Zionist identification was not only belated but also spasmodic, hesitant, and constricted. The popular Brandeisian synthesis of Zionism and Americanism expressed the yearnings of American Jews, not Zionist ideology. Indeed, it suggests why Brandeis still retains his secure position in the pantheon of American Jewish heroes, the eminent American jurist whose Jewish leadership was largely symbolic. He made it possible for American Jews to be better Americans by becoming Zionists. Zion was still the promised land, but Brandeis located Zion in the United States, securely within the contours of American history.

Brandeis grew up in a Jewish family whose primary ethnic identification was German, as it long remained for Brandeis himself. Until shortly before his fiftieth birthday in 1906, the limit of his participation in Jewish affairs was defined by an occasional charitable donation. He evaded entreaties for deeper involvement, whether to attend a meeting with Israel Zangwill, the Jewish territorialist leader, or to speak on behalf of the victims of the terrible Kishinev pogroms. Not until 1905, when he accepted an invitation to commemorate the two hundred and fiftieth anniversary of Jewish settlement in the United States, did he deliver his first address to a Jewish audience. In a remarkable preview of his consuming concerns as a Zionist leader, he demanded loyalty "to American institutions and ideals." The eradication of class and ethnic distinctions was imperative; there was no place in the United States, he warned, for "hyphenated Americans." To be a good Jew required precisely the traits that distinguished loyal Americans: energy, perserverance, self-restraint, intelligence, and austerity. The description, more revealing of Brandeis than of Judaism, enabled him to celebrate the loyalty of Jews to the United States. With these words of warning and reassurance, Brandeis lapsed into public silence on Jewish issues. The limits of his Jewish identification were apparent: considered for nomination to the executive committee of the new American Jewish Committee, he was shunned because (in the judgment of its secretary) "he has not identified himself with Jewish Affairs and is rather inclined to side with the Ethical Culturists."[1]

Five years later, in 1910, Brandeis was called to New York to mediate a garment workers' strike in an industry that was almost entirely Jewish. He was evidently intrigued by the struggle between socialist workers and capitalist employers, who not only argued vehemently about wages and unions but also denounced each other in Yiddish, citing biblical authorities to justify their demands. Like other German Jews of his time—including Judah Magnes, Stephen Wise, and even Herzl—Brandeis was attracted to the rambunctious *yiddishkeit* of the new immigrants, whose roots in Eastern Europe tapped centuries of vibrant Jewish tradition. Once again, however, he rearranged the ingredients of Jewish identity to fit his American mold. Brandeis discovered within the garment workers "the qualities which, to my mind, make for the best American citizenship, . . . a true democratic feeling and a deep appreciation of the elements of social justice," a compatibility attributable "to the fact that twentieth century ideals of America had been the age-old ideals of the Jews."[2]

Shortly after the strike Brandeis, who devised the protocol that established new terms of industrial self-government, was the subject of an interview in which he significantly expanded his identification as a Jew. He commended the enduring mission of the Jewish people "to struggle for truth and righteousness to-day just as the ancient prophets did." He reiterated his concern that Jews should demonstrate "above all things loyalty to American institutions," warning once again that "habits of living, of thought which tend to keep alive difference of origin or to classify men according to their religious beliefs are inconsistent with the American idea of brotherhood and are disloyal." Brandeis commended the Zionists, who "are entitled to the respect and appreciation of the entire Jewish people." But, he asserted firmly, "I believe that the opportunitites for members of my race are greater here than in any other country."[3]

Brandeis's ambivalent pattern of identification and retreat persisted. It was heightened by political circumstance in 1913, when he was considered for an appointment in Woodrow Wilson's cabinet. Business and banking interests resented his advocacy of corporate regulation; their hostility, especially in Boston financial circles, was tinged with anti-Semitism. Prominent Jewish leaders, most of whom were conservative Republicans, were diffident to his appointment. Jacob Schiff, declaring that Brandeis was, "without doubt, a representative American," could only provide "a qualified reply" to the question whether Brandeis was a representative Jew. So Brandeis, too Jewish for the Brahmin bankers and insufficiently Jewish for Schiff, lost the support of both—and the cabinet position. Stung by anti-Semitism and rebuffed by Jews, he remained at the periphery of American Jewish life.

Two chance encounters with committed Zionists, during the spring of that year, seem to have affected Brandeis deeply. At a dinner to honor Nahum Sokolow, the European Zionist leader, Brandeis was stirred by his appeal to American Jews to participate in the effort to "recreate Zion." Brandeis confided to Sokolow, "You have brought me back to my people." Some weeks later, Brandeis met Aaron Aaronsohn, the Palestinian Zionist who was on one of his frequent fundraising tours for his agricultural field station near Haifa. Brandeis, who knew of Aaronsohn's work (which had excited Brandeis's interest in "the possibilities of scientific agriculture"), was fascinated by the man. During a discussion about the recent "unpleasant" implication of New York Jews in prostitution and assorted gangster activities, Aaronsohn contrasted "the little communities" of law-abiding, industrious Jews that flourished in Palestine. Brandeis was inspired by the example. In a public address, some weeks later, he cited it as "a lesson which must apply to Jews all over the world." American Jews, he urged, must identify with the "noble traditions" that inspired the Palestinian pioneers.[4]

Once again, however, Brandeisian rhetoric was unsupported by activity. Preoccupied with his Boston law practice and his advisory role to President Wilson, Brandeis continued to demonstrate slight interest in Jewish affairs. But for the outbreak of the war in Europe during the summer of 1914, there is every reason to believe that his inattention would have persisted, punctuated by an occasional public address that demonstrated the intellectual and emotional distance that separated Brandeis from Jewish history, tradition, and faith. The war, however, crippled the Zionist organization in Europe, endangered Jewish communities in Palestine, shifted the center of Zionist activity to the United States, and propelled Brandeis to the forefront of the American Zionist movement.

The initiative did not come from Brandeis, nor was there a personal conversion to account for his deepened involvement in Zionism. With the European Zionist organization, whose headquarters were in Berlin, all but incapacitated by the war, the movement desperately needed a safe geographical haven, which only the United States could provide. But why Brandeis? A far more intriguing question than why Brandeis became a Zionist is why Zionists should have wanted Brandeis as their leader. It was not a random selection; there are some hints of a "very careful analysis of his career which was made before we presumed to ask him to lead us." But surely that search would not have disclosed a significantly stronger identification with Judasim than the American Jewish Committee had discovered a decade earlier. Only Brandeis's national prominence in American public affairs could have accounted for his appeal. American Zionists, among them the philosopher Horace Kallen who played an important role in recruiting Brandeis to the movement, had their own American agenda to promote. They were surely attracted to a Jew who was respected, above all, for his American credentials, who could dilute the Jewish national zeal of Zionism. World War I provided the opportunity; Brandeis was the perfect choice.[5]

When Brandeis assumed the mantle of Zionist leadership he confessed, candidly and accurately, "I have been to a great extent separated from Jews. I am very ignorant in things Jewish." He had given but passing attention to Zionism, "far as it was from me."[6] Yet precisely these deficiencies, in conjunction with Brandeis's towering stature as a liberal reformer, qualified him to lead the American Zionist movement from obscurity to respectability, from its preoccupation with urgent issues of Jewish identity to a far more secure identification with American history and liberal policies.

Biographers have long been fascinated by Brandeis's Zionist conversion. Why should this very prototype of an assimilated German Jew, who emulated the Boston Brahmins in all but his political preferences, suddenly identify with the most nationalistic expression of Judaism? Sharing Brandeis's secular liberal political orientation, they posit the natural affinity of Zionism with progressivism. Once Brandeis understood that Zionism was the Jewish expression of democracy and social justice, and that fundamental Jewish and American values were indistinguishable, he turned to Zionism as the Jewish expression of his progressive commitments. It has even been suggested that Brandeis, who deeply admired the Athenian *polis* as the institutionalized ideal of political virtue, found in Zionism the appropriate link to ancient Greek democracy, the very source of Western humanism. Inspired by Alfred Zimmern's *The Greek Commonwealth* (Zimmern, a half-Jew, scattered references to the Bible, the Hebrew Prophets, and ancient Palestine in his 1912 book), Brandeis embraced Zionism, not only as a progressive reform, but as the modern recreation of the values of Periclean Athens.[7]

It has occasionally been recognized (usually by less reverential Israeli scholars) that even Brandeis did not function exclusively at such abstract levels of intellect and principle. His austere exterior, reinforced by a thick veil of privacy, was (and remains) a barrier to access. But there is no reason to believe that Brandeis, more than anyone else, was impervious to ambition, immune to criticism, or indifferent to the implications of mass Jewish immigration for his own place in American society. His identification with Zionism (after years of apathy, moderated only by vacillation) and his willingness to lead the American movement (after resisting repeated efforts to enlist his participation) had to do with more than an ideal, a book, or a reform, as compelling as these surely were to Brandeis. By 1914, Brandeis had been twice spurned: by the Brahmins for his liberalism (to say nothing of the fact that he was a Jew); and by the German Jews for his tepid identification as a Jew (to say nothing of his liberalism). Zionism may have offered Brandeis an escape from his impasse. Rebuffed for a cabinet appointment in 1913, he almost immediately thereafter made known his commitment to Zionism. Within two years, by the time Wilson nominated him to the Supreme Court, Brandeis had displayed his own credentials as an American Jew—so impeccably that even Schiff could acknowledge him as "one of our most eminent co-religionists."[8]

But political opportunism is no more satisfactory an explanation of Brandeis's Zionist conversion than the assumption of a natural affinity between Zionism and progressivism. In 1914, an identification with Zionism was hardly the passport to expanded career opportunities, which Brandeis, as a political figure of national prominence, surely did not need. Furthermore, if Zionism, progressivism, and Americanism were as compatible as many Brandeis biographers (echoing Brandeis) suggest, then one is left wondering why Brandeis did not become a Zionist a decade earlier, when he first became the champion of progressive causes. In the end, neither "explanation" truly explains, because both focus on the wrong issue. The fundamental issue is not why Brandeis became a Zionist, but what kind of a Zionist Brandeis became. He was neither the clever opportunist that cynics decry, nor the pure idealist that hero-worshippers cherish. He made a calculated choice, based upon assumptions about the compatibility of Zionism and Americanism. It proved to be persuasive, indeed decisive, because Brandeis, sharing the abiding anxieties of his generation about Jewish identity and American loyalty, personified the terms of reconciliation between them.

The years between 1912 and 1914 were especially crucial to this formulation. There was a decisive relationship between Brandeis's public career and his Jewish concerns. It seems paradoxical that the more conspicuous a national figure that Brandeis became, the more clearly he articulated the content of his Zionist identification. Given the times and context, one would anticipate that the higher Brandeis rose in American government circles the more he would wish to distance himself from Jewish nationalism. Yet as he reached his apogee as a nationally active progressive—the proponent of Wilson's New Freedom, a prospective cabinet member, and a presidential adviser—he strongly identified with Zionism. But—and this is the critical point—he defined it in a way that left no doubt that American Jews, even Zionists, were patriotic Americans. As he explained, in the single sentence that became the motto of Brandeisian Zionism: "To be good Americans, we must be better Jews, and to be better Jews, we must become Zionists."[9] With that astonishing *non sequitur* Brandeis became the leader of the American Zionist movement. Indeed, it qualified him for leadership because no other prominent American Jew so unerringly identified, and immediately resolved, the implicit conflict between Jewish and American loyalties that defined the nagging dilemma of American Jewish life. Zionism as Americanism was the Brandeisian resolution of that dilemma.

The Zionist movement that Brandeis inherited in 1914 was, by most accounts, in disarray, without purpose, leaders, members, or financial resources. Although American Zionism could trace its origins as far back as the early 1880s, it still was precarious three decades later. The first Hovevei Zion societies had been organized less to encourage settlement in Palestine than to deter assimilation. As one Hebrew writer complained, "every spark of love and holy feeling for the land of our fathers, for God and his Torah, has been extinguished" in the United States, where Jews preferred to "worship the Golden Calf."[10] Herzl's dramatic call for a Jewish national home barely aroused an American response; only one delegate from the United States attended the first Basle conference. By 1898, however, the Federation of American Zionists had begun to stitch together a national movement, small though it was. More significantly, its most articulate spokesmen had begun to wrestle with the implications for American Jews of the rebirth of Jewish nationalism.

There were two sides to the problem. First, Zionist theory posited the restoration of national sovereignty as the end of *galut*; with a Jewish national home the Jewish diaspora must wither away. But few American Jews (then or since), no matter how fervent their Zionist attachments, applied that principle to themselves. From the beginning, therefore, American Zionism insisted upon its own exceptionalism. What was good for the Jews of Russia and Rumania, and later of Poland and Germany, had no relevance for American Jews. (As Evytar Friesel has noted, "Any attempt in America to proclaim the hopelessness of life in the diaspora was a contradiction in terms and an exercise in futility.") Second, Zionism as a movement of national regeneration implicitly challenged the loyalty of American Jews to the United States—if not in the minds of Christians, then surely among Jews themselves.[11] Enormous energy was expended dispelling allegations of dual loyalty. These may have been all the more potent because they expressed a latent internal fear rather than an active external threat.

For all of its organizational fragility, however, the Federation of American Zionists, from its inception, had confronted and explored these implications of Zionism for American Judaism. Its leaders—at first disciples of Herzl and, after his death, adherents of the cultural Zionism of Ahad Ha-'Am—worked out a reasoned set of responses to the issues of political loyalty, and religious and cultural identity, that Zionism provoked. This would not be especially noteworthy but for the fact that Brandeis, largely ignorant of the content of the debate, all but ignored it. Recasting Zionism exclusively in American terms, he deflected its original concern with Jewish national identity to its prolonged preoccupation with American loyalty.

The earliest official statement of American Zionist policy was drafted by Richard Gottheil, professor of Semitics at Columbia University and the first president of the Federation. Gottheil, the son of a prominent Reform rabbi, brought considerable Jewish learning, and some characteristic American anxieties, to his defense of Zionism. He embraced a definition of Judaism that combined religion and nationality; indeed, he clearly favored national revival as an instrument of religious regeneration. The overwhelming justification for Zionism, he insisted, was the need to rescue fully three-quarters of world Jewry from "places in which it has become impossible for them to live." (Gottheil thereby excluded American Jews, who enjoyed unprecedented security and abundant opportunity.) The history of the Jews, he wrote, was "the log of a storm-tossed ship which can find no rest until it gets back again into the haven from which it started . . . the land of their fathers—Palestine." Only with "a home of his own" could the Jew cease to be "a pariah among the nations."[12]

Jewish national revival, for Gottheil, was also bound up with the security of American Jewry. Mass Jewish immigration to the United States, one possibility for the rescue of Russian Jewry, was unacceptable. "It is more than an open secret that we cannot cope" with the 400,000 Jews already in New York City; any significant increase would be intolerable. Gottheil suggested that anxieties about Jewish immigration be converted into support for Zionism. By diverting European Jews from the United States, Zionism would facilitate the absorption of the existing Jewish community into American society. Jews should "greet with joy" the deflection of Jewish immigration to "some place other than the land in which they dwell."[13]

With Herzl's death in 1904, the emphasis upon political Zionism receded. Neither the hope of Jewish national revival nor the fear of Eastern European immigration sufficed for the Zionist intellectuals, mostly rabbis and scholars, who gathered around Solomon Schechter at the Jewish Theological Seminary. They wanted to restore the spiritual content of Jewish culture, not merely rebuild its political structure. Conceding the centrality of the land of Israel to the spiritual life of the Jewish people, they simultaneously insisted upon the development of a vigorous Jewish culture in the United States, a diaspora center of Judaism in tandem with the national center in Palestine.

Schechter's Zionist credo, which affirmed "everything Jewish" as part of the regeneration of Judaism, pointed in new directions. It was less a political blueprint than an attempt to inspire "the reassertion of the Jewish soul." It drew upon the writings of Ahad Ha-'Am, whose English translator, Israel Friedlaender, joined Schechter at the Seminary and presented cultural Zionism as his own alternative to "the decomposition of Judaism . . . under the influence of freedom." Friedlaender (like Schechter) understood what few native American Jews could imagine, that "the more emancipated, the more prosperous, the more successful the Jews become, the more impoverished, the more defenseless and the more threatened becomes Judaism."[14]

If, as Friedlaender conceded, a return to the ghetto was impossible but assimilation was intolerable, the only healthy resolution of the dilemma was the cultivation, beyond politics and religious ceremony, of "the Jewish spirit and the whole life of the Jews." Friedlaender envisioned two centers of Judaism, the restored national home in Palestine and "the center . . . of the Jewish people in the Dispersion": "Zionism plus Diaspora, Palestine plus America." Zionism, for Friedlaender as for Schechter, would keep American Jews "deeply rooted in the soil of Judaism." If this was a rather loose translation of Ahad Ha-'Am, designed in part to dilute its Palestinian focus, it nonetheless expressed a deep commitment to the range of the Jewish historical experience, an inclusive blend of politics, religion, and culture.[15]

The American cultural Zionists were committed, above all, to the preservation of Judaism against the inroads of assimilation. As rabbis and Judaic scholars, they were comfortable with Jewish tradition, knowledgeable about Jewish history, and tolerant of most varieties of the Jewish experience. But they rejected the Reform separation of religion and nationality;

and they refused to strip Zionism of Jewish content (which would become Brandeis's singular contribution). Zionism, for them, was not some wild Jewish beast from Eastern Europe to be tamed into a domestic American pet, but a legitimate—indeed necessary—expression of Judaism, every bit as vital to the sustenance of American Jews as to the Eastern Europeans, if for different reasons. They did not expect American Jews to emigrate to Palestine; all the more reason, therefore, for the Jewish national revival to reaffirm the distinctive cultural identity of the Jewish people, wherever they resided.

Consistent with their expansive sense of Judaism, the cultural Zionists at the Seminary forged links to other primary centers of Jewish activity. Rabbi Judah Magnes, drawn to their circle, expanded its reach. Few Jewish causes failed to elicit his enthusiastic commitment. The associate rabbi of Temple Emanu-El, a founding member of the American Jewish Committee, the guiding spirit of the New York *kehilla*, and the secretary of the Federation of American Zionists, he enjoyed unique access to the varied, often contentious, institutional centers of American Judaism. With Magnes as the conduit, the Seminary faculty (especially Schechter, Friedlaender, and Mordecai Kaplan) contributed "a rabbinical variant of cultural Zionism" to the work of the Federation. Americanized though it surely was, the Federation grappled with the perplexing but exhilarating issues of modern Jewish identity that dominated the Zionist agenda.[16]

All that changed after 1914, when Brandeis became the leader of American Zionism. A movement of resistance to Jewish assimilation quickly became an instrument of Americanization. In the terms that mattered most to Brandeis—"men, money, and discipline"—he was astonishingly successful. The Federation always was beset by the organizational problems that characterized the Zionist movement itself; furthermore, it never fully overcame the divisions that accounted for its origins as a federation, combining secular Western Jews with religious Eastern Europeans. But ideas, passionately debated, always were taken seriously, far more so than accounting procedures and managerial principles.

Brandeis reversed these priorities. He was dedicated, above all, to organizational efficiency. His correspondence testifies to his passion for precision, order, and accuracy, for managerial effectiveness and financial solvency. His letters overflow with the minutiae of organizational detail: instructions for pledge campaigns; insistence upon monthly, even daily, reports of activities; consuming concern with accurate recordkeeping. It is virtually impossible to locate in the Brandeis correspondence any sustained consideration of Zionist, rather than organizational, issues. Perhaps Brandeis's most characteristic gesture was the installation of a time clock in the Zionist office. The Zionist organization, once a debating society for issues of Jewish consequence, came to resemble a business corporation whose success was measured by the willingness of investors to purchase its stock. Even Horace Kallen, who had done so much to recruit Brandeis to the movement, was dismayed. Brandeis, he wrote, believed that political activity was "rather futile" and must yield to organizational imperatives. Kallen attributed this preference to Brandeis's "training and interests" (as a lawyer). With mild exasperation, he counseled Stephen Wise to disregard these deficiencies and "to stand loyally behind" their new leader.[17]

The Brandeis emphasis upon men, money, and discipline galvanized the American Zionist movement during the wartime emergency. Membership swelled; men of affairs (mostly lawyers) assumed executive responsibility; and they cultivated links to government centers of power in Washington. For these achievements, deeply rooted in the American value system of practical work and material success, the Brandeis era has been portrayed in glowing terms. It surely was a time (however short-lived) when the financial difficulties, chaos, and internecine conflict of the Federation years yielded to organizational efficiency, growth, and influence.

But the cost was high: Brandeis's priorities all but depleted American Zionism of Jewish content. Even conceding the urgent tasks that world war presented, he cared little for the issues that continued to agitate political and cultural Zionists, in Europe or America. To Brandeis, all ideologies were suspect, except the amalgam of Jeffersonian liberalism and Wilsonian progressivism which defined his natural order of things. He was equally impatient with the orthodoxy of the Mizrachi Zionists and the socialism of Poale Zion, both of which he consigned to fringes of the American movement. Under his leadership, the issues that had been relentlessly probed and debated—by Gottheil, Schechter, Friedlaender, and others in the Federation—retreated from the American Zionist agenda.

With Brandeis, the Jewish Question (whether Jews could escape anti-Semitism anywhere but in their own homeland) became the American Question (the place of Jews in American society). Zionist answers, which had been debated "in *Jewish*" terms" among Jews, were superseded by a Brandeisian formula, stated "in general American terms," which he addressed as much to the American majority as to the Jewish minority. Political Zionism, Herzl's argument for a Jewish state, had no appeal to Brandeis, who wanted no such outcome. Cultural Zionism, which linked the problem of Jews (arguably confined to Eastern Europe) to the spiritual problem of Judaism (conspicuously evident in the emancipated communities of the West), raised substantive Jewish issues that Brandeis lacked the comprehension, concern, or commitment to grasp. While Schechter's Zionist credo had reverberated with echoes of Herzl, Ahad Ha-'Am, even Rabbi Kook (the creative theoretician of the fusion of Orthodoxy and Zionism), Brandeis punctuated his discussions of Zionist issues with references to colonial New England and classical Greece. He remains the most revered of American Zionists, but his leadership represented the empowerment of thoroughly assimilated Americans, whose Jewish roots were "thin and feeble." He could, therefore, transfer Zionism from a movement of Jewish national restoration into an expression of American patriotism and liberal reform. Perhaps that, more than anything else, explains his enduring appeal.[18]

Only one issue of Jewish consequence deeply engaged Brandeis (and helps to account for his "conversion" to Zionism). That was the reconciliation of Judaism with Americanism. Brandeis, like other successful assimilated Jews of his generation, was determined to mold foreign immigrants into loyal Americans. His first public address on a Jewish subject in 1905 had expressed his concern about immigrant loyalty to the United States. His apprehension about divided loyalties, expressed in his attempt to conflate "Jewish" and "American" attributes, was a recurrent theme in his public addresses thereafter. It is difficult to exaggerate the dimensions of this concern among assimilated Jews of Brandeis's generation. When Brandeis insisted that differences of origin or belief were "inconsistent with the American ideal of brotherhood, and are disloyal," he was merely voicing the conventional wisdom of those Jews who wanted to eradicate any vestiges of Jewish distinctiveness in American society, lest their own security be jeopardized. So Jacob Schiff, claiming to be "an American pure and simple" who "cannot belong to two nations," declined even to meet with Herzl lest he be contaminated by contact with a living Zionist. When Julian Mack (who later joined the Zionist inner circle under Brandeis's leadership) testified before a congressional committee on immigration, he requested that Jewish immigrants be classified according to their country of origin, not as Jews. Jewish nationalism, to Mack, was the misguided notion of new immigrants "who are not yet American citizens."[19] For Brandeis, too, demonstrating the unimpeachable loyalty of American Jews to the United States was, for both public and private reasons, an urgent task.

Brandeis's law partner once described him as "more Brahmin than the Brahmins," a characterization that has too often been accepted at face value. For a provincial outsider to Boston like Brandeis, becoming a Brahmin could not have been easy and may not even have been possible. His academic distinction and legal brilliance aside, Brandeis still had to depend upon the social and financial connections of his Brahmin classmate, Samuel D. Warren, for his entry to Boston law practice. He quickly adopted the manners and mores of the Boston elite: with his Beacon Hill residence, summers in Dedham and Chatham, riding-club memberships, household servants, and proper private schooling for his daughters, he lived in the style of the Brahmin aristocracy that he so admired. "Of all the prominent Jews of the early twentieth century," one of his biographers has written, "none had so little identification with Jewish life as he did, nor did any have so wide a network of Gentile friends and colleagues." Some of them it seems, did not even know that he was a Jew, which surely reveals as much about him as about them.[20]

No matter how successfully Brandeis surmounted the social barriers in Boston society, and the bar, he could never (by the very definitions of geography and genealogy that defined the Brahmin elite) truly become an insider. Brandeis yearned for acceptance, and he may truly have believed that he enjoyed it, but the virulent hostility, laced with anti-Semitism, from Boston businessmen, bankers, and lawyers at the time of his Supreme Court nomination in 1916 certainly suggests that Brandeis had always remained an outsider. His lingering concern with loyalty, and his eagerness to transpose Jewish values and traditions to an American setting, reveal someone who strongly felt the need to justify himself as a Jew who was indisputably a good American.

His occasional encounters with foreign Jews—especially Aaron Aaronsohn—were formative. They provided Brandeis with a new, quite positive, Jewish image, suggesting that Jews might actually be more than immigrants with suspect loyalties. He repeatedly inserted the lessons he learned from the New York garment workers, and from Aaronsohn, in his public addresses. But characteristically, he always translated their attributes into idealized American virtues: democracy, social justice, law-abiding citizenship, the pioneering spirit. In this way, Brandeis managed to construct an image of the modern Jew that bore a striking resemblance to two of his favorite American prototypes, the seventeenth-century Pilgrim and the contemporary Progressive.

Aaronsohn, more than anyone, provided Brandeis with an important missing link between Zionism and Americanism. After their initial meeting, an enraptured Brandeis decided that "the values of the Massachusetts founders were being carried on in far-off Palestine." A recurrent theme in his Zionist addresses thereafter was the identification of Zionists with the earliest settlers in New England. In one 1914 speech he referred to Zionists as the "new Pilgrim fathers"; in another, he compared the rebirth of the Jewish nation to "the birth of New England." Zionism, he had decided by 1915, was "the Pilgrim inspiration and impulse all over again." Therefore, he told a journalist, "the descendants of the Pilgrim Fathers" (a reference, surely, to the Boston Brahmins) "should not find it hard to understand and sympathize with it." They certainly should not accuse Zionists, among all Jews, of disloyalty. The interview, appropriately, was published on July 4th.[21]

Brandeis was not the first American Jew to invest Judaism with such patriotic content. Oscar Straus had preceded him by thirty years; and the linkage had been a staple of late nineteenth-century Reform. But the Brandeis formula came at a time of heightened anxiety about loyalty, the product of a decade of unprecedented immigration exacerbated by the outbreak of war in Europe, a war that, long before American intervention, pulled at the loyalties of Americans of British, Irish, and German descent. The context, far more than the content, helps to explain why Brandeis's assertion that Zionism was Americanism reached such a receptive Jewish audience. For no one better symbolized the integration—indeed the submersion—of Judaism in American culture than Brandeis himself.

There is compelling evidence that the Brandeis formula—to be good Americans, Jews must become Zionists—was decisively influenced by Horace Kallen, the philosopher of cultural pluralism. Kallen had struggled to work out for himself the secular terms of compatibility between Zionism and Americanism. The son of an Orthodox rabbi, young Kallen had come to Harvard after the turn of the century determined, as he subsequently wrote, to shed "the outmoded burden" of his religious identity for the universal ideals of "'humanity' and social justice." In a literature course, however, he was astonished to learn from Professor Barrett Wendell, a venerable Yankee patrician, that the Hebrew prophetic tradition had inspired the founders of the American nation. With that insight Kallen found the way to legitimate Judaism in American terms. With his new understanding of the Bible as the source of American freedom and equality, he was reborn as a secular Jew—and a patriotic American. From there it was an easy leap to Zionism, which Kallen invested with the very biblical ideals that had inspired seventeenth-century New Englanders. By 1910, Kallen had fit Zionism into his emerging conception of cultural pluralism, a definition of American nationality that encouraged ethnic distinctiveness and solidarity as a legitimate contribution to "the harmony of civilization." Kallen had found a way to convert dual loyalty into a national virtue, a way to be Jewish, yet become a better American.[22]

In 1913, Kallen approached Brandeis, whom he had known slightly and admired greatly from his Harvard days; but Brandeis, with a typical plea for the urgency of other commitments, had little time for "the Zionist question" in the months preceding Wilson's inauguration. They evidently talked at some length the following year during Brandeis's journey to attend the Zionist Conference in New York that selected him as its leader. Kallen presented Brandeis with a memorandum, drawn from one of his articles, that fit Zionism into his theory of cultural pluralism. Brandeis was evidently impressed, for echoes of Kallen resounded in his early Zionist addresses. No longer did he warn against "hyphenated" Americans. Instead, he identified Judaism as an important source of American ideals and advocated Zionism as their fullest expression. For Brandeis, as for Kallen, Zionism was most valued for its identification with American patriotism. To Kallen, it added a "Hebraic note" to the "American Symphony." For

Brandeis, "the Jewish spirit" had become "essentially American." Not in two thousand years had Jewish values been "so fully in harmony with the noblest aspirations of the country in which they lived."[23]

In a series of addresses during his first months as a national Zionist leader, between August and November 1914, Brandeis candidly explored his new identification with Zionism and defined its meaning. He confessed to "slight" prior contact with Jews (or Judaism). "I gave little thought to their problems," he conceded, except to wonder whether American Jews were sufficiently appreciative of "the opportunities which this hospitable country affords." It was evident, however, that Brandeis had been troubled by the problem of Jewish "demoralization." The immigrant generation, uprooted from the traditional structures of religion and law, lacked the "moral and spiritual" resources to resist the lure of crime and vice. This distressed Brandeis, for among a "distinctive and minority people," he noted, the "dishonorable conduct" of a single Jew affected the security of all Jews—including, by implication, his own. "Large as this country is, no Jew can behave badly without injuring each of us." Therefore, Brandeis concluded, American Jews needed "a center from which the Jewish spirit may radiate"—to inspire them with worthy ideals and to remove the stigma of their distinctiveness.

Zionism offered Brandeis an answer, for Jews were "by reason of their traditions and their character peculiarly fitted in the attainment of American ideals." The Jewish spirit was "essentially American." The American commitment to universal brotherhood, social justice, and democracy expressed values for which "religion and life have peculiarly fitted the Jew." Brandeis had discovered (during the garment workers strike) that "the twentieth century ideals of America have been the ideals of the Jew for more than twenty centuries." Even his own goals, which he had always understood to be "essentially American," were, in fact, "the Jewish ideals of thousands of years." These ideals, expressed in the new Zionist communities of Palestine, could provide a model for American Jews. Indeed, by demonstrating the compatibility between Judaism and Americanism, "this new Jewish Palestine will make it possible" for American Jews to be "loyal Americans."

In a quite remarkable projection, Brandeis transformed modern Zionists into seventeenth-century New Englanders, referring to them as "our Pilgrim Jewish fathers." The little Zionist communities in Palestine became his romanticized recreation of the earliest American communities; Zionism replicated the process of national regeneration in New England three centuries earlier. The following year, referring again to "the Jewish Pilgrim Fathers" in Palestine, Brandeis compared the Bedouin to the Indians. Zionism, after all, was "the Pilgrim inspiration and impulse all over again." With Palestine as a replica of colonial New England, and simultaneously a modern laboratory of democratic values, the American Jew surely would be "a better American" by supporting Zionism.[24] Brandeis identified with Zionism, and urged American Jews to do likewise, so that they might become "good Americans." His yearning for acceptance as an American transformed him, paradoxically, into a Zionist. For, as he explained a year later, "the Zionist ideals representing the highest Jewish ideals are essentially American in every important particular." Zionists were nothing but "Jews carrying out the American ideals." If "we must become Zionists" to be "good Americans" (the ultimate goal), Brandeis was prepared to make the commitment—and to justify it entirely in American terms. The compatibility of American and Jewish ideals meant that "our loyalty to America cannot be questioned; because conflict between American interests and Jewish aims is not conceivable."[25]

The Brandeis "conversion" to Zionism was not, therefore, a conversion at all. It was the culmination of his persistent effort, for nearly a decade, to define loyal Americanism. Between 1905 and 1915—from his warning to "hyphenated" Jews to his formulation of Zionism as Americanism—Brandeis intermittently searched for the terms of Jewish acculturation in the United States. It is instructive that he rejected the most readily available, and persuasive, reconciliation of Judaism and Americanism: Reform. Everything about Brandeis—his German heritage, his integration into Boston society, his professional success and affluence, his liberalism, and his apprehensions about loyalty—perfectly qualified him for quiet affiliation with a Reform temple and comfortable identification with Reform tenets. One can only surmise that Reform may have been too Jewish for Brandeis; certainly it expressed a religious side of Judaism that Brandeis never embraced. Zionism better served Brandeis's purpose: once converted from an expression of Jewish nationalism into a manifestation of loyal Americanism, it could serve as an instrument of Jewish acculturation. That it surely did for Brandeis: equating Zionists with Pilgrims, he could extend his own roots back to seventeenth-century New England, the very source of American civilization. Brahmin vilification, as Ben Halpern has written, "was a blow that took its toll" on Brandeis, who needed the assurance that only Brahmin approval could provide. Rejected by the modern descendants of the Pilgrims and Puritans, Brandeis found in Zionism the way to identify with Puritan New England; the way, that is, to become as impeccably American as the Brahmins themselves.[26]

In a 1915 address to Reform rabbis, Brandeis gathered the strands of his Zionist commitment into a succinct statement of his abiding American identification. "Let no American imagine that Zionism is inconsistent with Patriotism," he admonished. For "multiple loyalties are objectionable only if they are inconsistent." It was, he claimed, inconceivable that Zionism conflicted with American patriotism. Indeed, "the Jewish spirit . . . is essentially modern and essentially American." Never since the destruction of the Second Temple "have the Jews in spirit and in ideals been so fully in harmony with the noblest aspirations of the country in which they lived." Those aspirations, Brandeis continued, were expressed in the compatibility of Jewish and American strivings for social justice under the rule of law—the essence of democracy. Therefore, he insisted, "conflict between American interests or ambitions and Jewish aims is not conceivable. Our loyalty to America can never be questioned." Despite the claim of compatibility, however, Brandeis's American loyalty left him far short of an identification with Zionism. Throughout his address, Brandeis, the world Zionist leader, invariably referred to the Zionists as "they."[27] He carefully withheld himself from them.

After 1914, with the outbreak of war and Brandeis's accession to leadership, American Jews flocked to the Zionist movement in unprecedented numbers. Brandeis, after all, had demonstrated that there was "no inconsistency between loyalty to America and loyalty to Jewry." How could a Jew be a suspect American if even such a distinguished Jew as Brandeis was a Zionist? Brandeis drew the identical conclusion in 1916, when he interpreted his nomination to the Supreme Court as proof, which he welcomed and needed, that "in the opinion of the President there is no conflict between Zionism and loyalty to America."[28]

The men recruited by Brandeis to the inner circle of Zionist leadership were quite distinguishable from the rabbis and scholars who had dominated the Federation. Brandeis wanted "men of leadership"; the men he attracted, with the conspicuous exception of Stephen Wise, all were lawyers: Julian Mack and Felix Frankfurter especially, along with Robert Szold, Bernard Flexner, and Benjamin Cohen in subsidiary positions. They affiliated with the Zionist movement once Brandeis became its leader; their primary allegiance was to the man, not the cause. Entering after 1914, most of them left by 1921, when the Brandeis leadership was defeated.

These Zionist lawyers, like Brandeis, came from German Jewish families; their religious orientation, if any, was Reform; their professional identification was shaped by the Harvard Law School; their politics were progressive. Their primary qualification for Zionist leadership was their devotion to Brandeis. He conceded the "anomaly" of his power and theirs—the movement he linked so directly to American democratic values was ruled by an increasingly remote leader and his coterie of followers, all of whom were distant, culturally and ideologically, from their Eastern European constituency. But that was precisely the point of their Zionist involvement. Brandeisian Zionism did not express the strength of their Jewish commitment, which (in Halpern's apt term) was "peripheral." Rather, it provided assurance that even the most nationalistic expression of Judaism was entirely compatible with American values; even the most "foreign" of Jews were loyal Americans.[29]

The Balfour Declaration of 1917, with its promise of a Jewish national home, exposed the fragility of the Brandeis synthesis. It elicited a euphoric response among European Zionists who had struggled, since Herzl's day, to secure international recognition. But the Declaration starkly posed issues of Jewish loyalty that left Brandeis distinctly uncomfortable. It was one thing to proclaim the compatibility of Zionism and Americanism in the abstract. But it was a far more urgent and formidable task once there was the actual prospect of a Jewish national home. On the day the Declaration was issued, Brandeis (who had been consulted during its drafting) wrote to Jacob Schiff; "I am but expressing the views of my colleagues, of all Zionists with whom I have personal relations, when I state that they and I neither advise nor desire an independent state." For statehood, Brandeis asserted, was "a most serious menace."[30]

Brandeis's greatest achievement—his translation of Zionism into Americanism—had become, by 1917, the debilitating weakness of American Zionism. While Brandeis depicted Zionism as a mixture of seventeenth-century pioneering and twentieth-century progressivism, he had become increasingly aloof from the aspirations of Zionists in Europe and Palestine. Brandeis understood this. When Frankfurter passed along a letter from Alfred Zimmern suggesting that Brandeis was "too remote" from "the strange emotional world" of Eastern European Jewry, the Justice circled the passage and scribbled in the margin "Of course Z[immern] is right in this." Zionist definitions of the national unity of the Jewish people, their sense of the diaspora as *galut* (exile), and their commitment to settle in the land of Israel were contradicted by the tenets of Brandeisian Zionism.[31]

"Our crying need," Brandeis declared, "is businessmen—financial and managerial ability. . . . We also need some good practical legal ability." But the more emphasis that Brandeis placed upon efficient management, and the more lawyers he recruited, the more the American movement disengaged from issues of Zionist concern, resembling a corporate law firm rather than a movement of national revival. Robert Szold, one of Brandeis's ablest lieutenants, was preoccupied with organizational efficiency. He insisted that the Zionist movement absorb "a large number of capable, efficient, American *permanent* administrators" to rescue it from financial chaos. "Good management," for Szold, was paramount; "the objective mind," he insisted, understood the importance of budgets and the danger of deficits. But the European Zionists, he complained, lived in "a world of dreams and unreality." When Walter Meyers, a young graduate of Harvard Law School, was sent to Palestine on a fact-finding mission, he discovered that the greatest need was for men who "have absorbed American methods and principles," who would bring "their ability and their money" and dedicate themselves to business growth and industrial development. Ben Cohen, for all his impressive legal skills, was cautioned by Mack to be more tolerant of "other people's unsound methods." Before Cohen went to Palestine, Brandeis urged him to prepare for his trip by visiting Massachusetts—to study credit unions.[32]

As Brandeis prepared for his own (and only) visit to Palestine in the summer of 1919, the subjects of his requests for information defined his priorities: the accounting procedures of the international Zionist organization and the economic structure of the *yishuv*. "Strengthening the organization," as always, was his primary task. (So, in response to a telegram cabling news of the British conquest of Jerusalem, he had responded: "Is it creating big 'Money & Members'?") He was confident that solutions for Palestinian problems depended upon "our American experience." On his way, he stopped in Egypt long enough to confirm his belief in the superiority of Anglo-Saxon civilization, contrasting the "dreariness" of the East with Western "superiority in moral, mental and physical cleanliness."[33]

Once Brandeis arrived in Palestine, however, he was deeply moved, especially in Jerusalem where he was thrilled by "a wonderful city." He remained for two weeks, sufficient time to visit the major cities and many of the smaller Jewish settlements. It was one of the rare moments when emotion superseded practical details in his correspondence. "The ages-long longing, the love is all explicable now," he confessed to his wife. The Zionist struggle is "worthwhile," he continued, for "it is indeed a Holy Land." Palestine, "a wonderful country," "has won our hearts," he told Chaim Weizmann, the leader of the European Zionists; "It is no wonder that the Jews love her so."[34]

Brandeis left Palestine confident that "we really know all the main problems and the difficulties and the possibilities." But by the time he reached England to address the Zionist General Council, all the emotion had evaporated and he was prepared to reassert his faith in efficiency, self-reliance, scientific expertise, and cleanliness. To the stunned surprise of his Zionist audience, he dismissed mass immigration to Palestine (the overriding Zionist commitment) as chimerical; the transcendent issue, he announced, was sanitation. The primary task was not to build a national home, or even to settle the land, but to eradicate malaria. Brandeis (according to one European Zionist) "looked like a Puritan minister"; but he sounded like a Progressive reformer determined to clean up an urban slum. He was prepared to postpone Zionist objectives, Shmaryahu Levin complained, "until the last mosquito is wiped out."[35]

By then Brandeis had all but lost touch with Zionist passion and Palestinian reality. As he berated Zionist leaders for their organizational mismanagement and financial carelessness and threatened to withhold American financial contributions unless the Europeans improved their bookkeeping procedures, he stirred deep antagonism among the European Zionists and within his American following. While the Eastern Europeans were determined to secure a Jewish homeland, Brandeis drew the line of American participation at economic development. Palestine, for Brandeis, had become an attractive investment prospect for American Jews. (There were "opportunities for inspired millionaires" he told Mack: a library, a museum, a university, a department of agriculture.) He proposed that American Jews form "investment companies" to channel funds to Palestine; but American Zionists, he cautioned, were to assume "no moral responsibility" for what transpired there.[36]

That was precisely the problem: Zionism was something more than philanthropy and double-entry bookkeeping. As Brandeis and his associates concentrated upon philanthropic and economic matters to the exclusion of other issues, they isolated themselves from the world Zionist movement. Financially generous, but frightened of responsibility, the Brandeisian Zionists were maximally committed to protecting their emotional investment in the United States. They would give their money to Palestine, but not themselves. At every critical juncture, American priorities prevailed over Zionist commitments.

The paradigmatic example of withholding was Brandeis's refusal in 1920 to resign from the Supreme Court to assume the presidency of the World Zionist Organization. Citing "judiciary limitations," he declined the invitation. (That repeated an earlier episode: just two years before, when Chaim Weizmann had resigned his university position in Manchester to represent Zionist interests in Palestine, he had invited Brandeis to do likewise and join him; Brandeis declined and appointed Wise; Wise declined; so did Mack.) As Brandeis explained, he represented "the Liberal, Progressives . . . hope in American life." If the first Jewish Justice chose Zionism over the Supreme Court, or even over the cause of liberal reform, he would undermine the very principle that he had so vigorously asserted: the compatibility of Zionism and Americanism. They were compatible, of course, only if Zionism yielded. As Mack observed, the European Zionists "are giving their lives to their work and are ready to give them in Palestine. Ours are not yet prepared for this."[37] The withholding of commitment was the fatal flaw of the Brandeis leadership.

All of these conflicts and disagreements, between the American and European Zionists and within the American movement itself, erupted in the spring of 1921. Weizmann had long imagined (as "part of my Zionist creed") that American Jews "cannot be so very fundamentally different from other Jews." But the thrust of American Zionism, he had finally concluded, required "the complete suppression of our political, social and cultural aspirations." Zionism, he insisted, "cannot be converted merely into a development company." The only alternative to suppression was schism. "There is no bridge between Pinsk and Washington," Weizmann reluctantly concluded (and loudly proclaimed).[38]

When the Weizmann group arrived at the Zionist convention in Cleveland, delegates spontaneously sang "Hatikvah," the Zionist anthem of hope. But the substantive disagreements could not be eradicated. After the Americans lost the crucial convention vote on the issue of financial autonomy, the entire Brandeis circle resigned from the Zionist organization: Brandeis, Mack, Frankfurter, Szold, Cohen, and Bernard Flexner, along with rabbis Stephen Wise and Abba Hillel Silver, and two men who had done so much to coax Brandeis into the Zionist movement, Horace Kallen and Jacob deHaas. With money once again serving as the symbol of power and control, the Americans declared their independence from the world Zionist movement. Brandeis could not share authority with Jews whose nationalistic ideals and emotional passion he mistrusted. In the future, the crucial decisions about the fate of the Jewish homeland would be made by those who were prepared to invest their lives, not only their dollars, in the land of Israel. The Americans, Brandeis declared, were "humble workers in the ranks." Weizmann was hailed as "the political leader of the Jewish nation." The formative era of American Zionism had ended.[39]

Weizmann once confessed, "To be a Zionist it is not perhaps absolutely necessary to be slightly mad, but it helps." American Zionist leaders were eminently sane; their approach to Zionist issues was sober and sensible, befitting a group of professional men who worried most lest their Jewish attachments cost them dearly. Zionism was safe as long as it was securely grounded in the American experience. One searches in vain through their letters and addresses for evidence that they were passionately committed to Jewish issues that were unrelated to their own status as Jews in American society. Insinuations of divided loyalty provoked angry denials, coupled with ringing patriotic affirmations. The lure of Bolshevism to Eastern European Jews stirred deep apprehension. Diversion of immigration from American shores to Palestine evoked enthusiastic approval. ("Is it desirable," Brandeis had inquired, "that America should be practically the only country to which the Jews of eastern Europe may emigrate?") Excited by philanthropic possibililties in Palestine, stirred by the idea of a university dedicated to Western liberal values, and captivated by the "new" Jews of Palestine, like Aaron Aaronsohn, who seemed to resemble seventeenth-century Pilgrims, the American leaders recast Zionism in their own constricted image. Zionism, an ideology of Jewish national liberation, became a strategy of American accommodation.[40]

The Cleveland convention episode helps to explain why Brandeis and the other lawyers who followed his leadership—Mack, Frankfurter,

Cohen, Szold—were drawn to Zionism and why they departed so precipi-
tously. It was not, for them, the revival of Jewish national life, but the identification of Zionism with American liberalism and patriotism that was so
compelling. Only the assurance that their Zionist commitment expressed
"good" Americanism made Zionism palatable. They came to it belatedly,
lingered briefly, and left hastily once they could no longer confine it within
ideological boundaries that made them feel comfortable as Americans. Reconciled with progressivism and patriotism, Zionism appealed to them only
as long as it could demonstrate their attachment as Jews to the United
States. Once it intensified their uneasiness, as by definition it had to do,
they quickly relinquished it.

Brandeis remained faithful to his vision of lawyers as the natural leaders of American Zionism, even though it had cost him his own leadership
and theirs. "I begin to believe again," he wrote just a few years later, "that
no man without legal training is to be trusted in American public affairs."
Zionism was no exception to his rule. When Brandeis was momentarily
drawn back into Zionist affairs, after rioting Arabs in Palestine murdered
and wounded several hundred Jews within a single week in 1929, he once
again relied upon lawyers and resorted to legalisms. "Our group of able
lawyers," he proposed, should make a careful study of Great Britain's
mandatory record. Brandeis seemed far more offended by British procedural improprieties—the failure to submit copies of evidence to the League
of Nations Mandate Commission and efforts to shield their own officials
from cross-examination—than by their abject failure to protect Jewish lives.
As he had done twice before, he declined to relinquish his Supreme Court
seat to provide Zionist leadership during a critical moment for the nascent
Jewish homeland. Indeed, Brandeis virtually declined to speak about the
riots, and advised his coterie of admiring lawyers to maintain their public
silence.[41]

Linking Zionists to Pilgrims, the Hebrew Prophets to progressivism,
and Zionism to Americanism, Brandeis developed a rationale for Zionism
that expanded its appeal by contracting, indeed all but eliminating, its Jewish content. If Zionism was nothing more than the struggle for social justice and democracy, it was, as Brandeis insisted, indistinguishable from the
American liberal tradition—and a safe commitment for American Jews.
That may help to explain the tremendous surge in Zionist membership
after 1914. But the argument from numbers can be deceiving; for it not only
credits Brandeis with achievements that were independent of his efforts
but also accepts his quantitative framework ("men and money") as the sole
measure of Zionist strength. To be sure, the American movement enjoyed
a spectacular spurt, from 7,500 enrolled members just before Brandeis became its leader to 149,000 five years later. But, as Evytar Friesel has suggested, Brandeis can neither be solely credited with Zionist growth, nor

blamed for its collapse (to 24,000 members immediately preceding his res-
ignation). The American Zionist movement periodically spurted: in
1903–1904, after the Kishinev pogroms; again during World War I; finally,
1943–1947, culminating in statehood. In each instance, the impetus came
from Europe, and the American movement responded to international
events, quickly subsiding once the immediate crisis had passed.[42]

Brandeis certainly must be credited with making Zionism attractive to
unprecedented numbers of American Jews. His formula was persuasive;
and his personal example was an inspiring symbol that confirmed its truth.
But while Brandeis located American Zionism at the periphery of the world
movement, he all but isolated it from the main currents of American Judaism. Disconnected from any form of Jewish institutional life, he set American Zionism on an independent course that severed the relationships
developed by the Federation of American Zionists with the Jewish
Theological Seminary, the American Jewish Committee, and with sympathetic Reformers. Brandeis wanted nothing to do with radical socialist Zionists nor with Orthodox religious Zionists, nor even with Seminary intellectuals. Seminary leaders reciprocated: Adler complained that Brandeis's
professions of ignorance about Jewish matters were "no doubt truthful,"
while Schechter dismissed Brandeis as a "demagogue," who "probably will
never be a Jew."[43] It is not difficult to understand why Brandeisian Zionism,
so isolated from primary sources of Jewish nourishment in Europe and the
United States, had run its course after barely five years.

In the end, it was the committed Eastern European Zionists within the
American organization who rebelled against Brandeis's leadership. By 1919
they knew that their leader would not lead; as a Supreme Court Justice who
had coupled Zionism with patriotism, he could not. Worse yet, Louis
Lipsky complained, "We were not in harmony with the trend of Zionist
events. We felt ourselves strangers to it, unable to influence it." Lipsky,
a Zionist activist since the turn of the century, believed in Zionism as an
expression of the faith that "all Jews are embraced in the Jewish destiny."
He had long felt that Zionism and Americanism were potentially incompatible: "The nearer Palestine is brought, the more devoted the American Zionist must become not to the Stars and Stripes, . . . but to the blue and
white flag and that land, which rises out of the dim past." The true Zionist,
"caught up by a different current," must declare himself "either an American or a Zionist." Despite the Brandeis formula, the fundamental issue remained: was Zionism Americanism or, as an actively competing loyalty,
might it ultimately be un-American?[44]

For the Eastern Europeans (even those, like Lipsky, who never made
aliyah), Brandeisian Zionism was a pallid expression of their Zionist faith.
Weizmann heard, in Zionism, "the echo of our innermost feelings" as Jews.
"Our Jewishness and our Zionism," he insisted, "were interchangeable."

But for Brandeis and his followers, who were remote from Jewish history, religion, and culture, Zionism offered the least common denominator of Jewish attachment compatible with American patriotism. Zionism expressed their minimalist commitment as Jews, not, as it did for the Eastern Europeans, the burning intensity of a pervasive Jewish self-identification. In Eastern Europe, Zionism flourished among the most fervently committed Jews. The American movement, however, was led by Jews for whom Judaism was, at best, marginal, and, indeed, an obstacle to their full integration into American society. For them, Zionism expressed their deepest longings as Americans.[45]

Brandeis understood, better than his reverential biographers, that loyalty *was* a problem—not merely *a* problem for American Jews, but *the* nagging dilemma of American Jewish life. If his preoccupation with the subject is an accurate indicator, it was even a nagging problem for him, and there is ample evidence that those within his inner circle shared his concern. Indeed, it qualified them for membership. It has been argued that Brandeis's greatest achievement as a Zionist was to have "calmed the fears of those worried about dual allegiance" and "legitimized the movement in non-Jewish eyes." To the contrary: his reconciliation represented, in Jewish terms, his greatest failure. For as he transformed Zionism into progressive Americanism, he all but severed its roots in Jewish history and disconnected it from the Jewish national revival of his own time. Zionism as Americanism came perilously close to becoming Americanism without Judaism. It did not solve the problem of dual loyalty for American Jews, a problem that has surfaced periodically to demonstrate the fragility—if not futility—of the Brandeis "solution."[46]

American Zionism, in its formative phase, was caught in the eddies of a larger Zionist dilemma: whether the Jewish national revival should aspire to normalization or distinctiveness; whether the Jewish nation should be part of, or apart from, the community of nations. The answers varied. Many Zionists anticipated that once Jews finally obliterated the debilities and anomalies of statelessness and became a nation like other nations they might truly be a normal people. To that extent, Zionism represented a giant stride toward fulfillment of the Enlightenment promise of universal freedom, equality, and justice (which, to many secular Zionists, was the modern expression of the ancient vision of the Hebrew prophets). By the end of the nineteenth century, however—when Herzl comprehended the meaning of the Dreyfus trial—the dangers of emancipation were as evident as its rewards. Freedom had encouraged assimilation; enlightenment (even in the country that had sounded the revolutionary call for liberty, equality, and fraternity) had not eradicated anti-Semitism. Jewish sovereignty was imperative, therefore, not merely to fulfill Enlightenment values but to save Jews and Judaism from Enlightenment perils.

Led by Brandeis, American Zionists sought normalization as Americans, not distinctiveness as Jews. Were Jews like other Americans, or were they different? Brandeis answered unequivocally: Jews were good Americans with progressive commitments. His answer enabled American Jews to become organizational or philanthropic Zionists, while remaining loyal American citizens. It also explains why non-Zionists like Schiff, Marshall, and Felix Warburg (who feared that Palestine would become "a trash basket" filled with a "Hebrew-talking mob") made common cause with the Brandeis Zionists—for philanthropic purposes only. They believed that an infusion of funds, tightly controlled by American donors, might save the land of Israel, and Jews everywhere, from the Zionists. If, for Warburg, collaboration with the Zionists was (as Weizmann claimed) "just one among the fifty-seven varieties of his philanthropic activities," Brandeis's Zionism was one progressive reform among many—a movement for efficiency, order, and control in American Jewish life.[47]

At most, Brandeis temporarily suppressed the latent conflict between Judaism and Americanism. He certainly did not eradicate it. Nor could he, for they are quite distinctive historical traditions, with far more substantial differences than a selective reading of Jewish history and texts through American lenses might suggest. No matter how fervently, or frequently, American Jews intoned "Zionism as Americanism," the conflict always was there. That is why the significance of Brandeis's Zionist leadership was its contribution to American Jewish acculturation—and the pivotal role of Jewish lawyers in defining its terms. By 1915, with Marshall as president of the American Jewish Committee and Brandeis as leader of American Zionism, lawyers controlled the major organizational expressions of American Judaism.

Rabbinical influence upon Jewish public affairs, so evident before the turn of the century, had sharply receded by World War I. Not only did the rabbis abdicate; lawyers stepped in to provide a secular legal frame of reference for Jewish acculturation. For Marshall, it was citizenship and equal rights; for Brandeis, it was the American liberal tradition, which he traced back to seventeenth-century New England. For both men, the allegiance of American Jews could be only to the Constitution and to the rule of law that it symbolized. Their fervent attachments to the American legal system defined a new identification for American Jews.

Marshall and Brandeis shared important attributes. Each was the American-born child of German immigrants. Molded within the strongly German cultural milieu of their families, they were sensitive to issues of national identity and were especially eager to identify with their American homeland, its history, traditions, and symbols. As German Jews, they were virtually defined by competing loyalties. (Bernard Felsenthal, another German Jew and a Reform rabbi, once confessed: "Racially I am a Jew. . . .

Politically I am an American. . . . Spiritually I am a German."[48]) Given such internal divisions, it is not difficult to understand how German Jews like Marshall and Brandeis decisively defined themselves as Americans by their choice of profession. Successful corporate lawyers in major metropolitan centers, with wide-ranging public commitments, they left behind all forms of cultural provincialism and enclosed themselves in the most protective and transcendent of American symbols: the rule of law.

Marshall and Brandeis went to considerable lengths to proclaim their identity as Americans and their attachment to American traditions. Their worst apprehension was that Jews might be considered insufficiently American. Although the focus of their concern invariably settled upon Eastern European immigrants, there can hardly be any doubt of their unease about the place of all Jews, surely their own place, in American society. When Brandeis stated the significance of his nomination, as a Zionist, to the Supreme Court (in President Wilson's opinion, there was "no conflict between Zionism and loyalty to America"), he vividly expressed one of his abiding concerns—whether he would be accepted (by genuine Americans like Boston Brahmins and the President of the United States) as a loyal American.

Marshall and Brandeis were the new American prototypes of the *shtadlan*, the wealthy European Jew who interceded with Christian rulers to protect the Jewish community and his own privileged place within it. As American lawyers, they redefined the role. Their power did not depend upon wealth, although both were wealthy men. Rather, it came from their ability to formulate the terms of Jewish acculturation within the framework of American patriotism. Marshall, the traditionalist, utilized the language of legalism— citizenship, equality, rights; Brandeis, the progressive, preferred the language of liberalism, emphasizing social justice. As Marshall reminded American Jews of their overriding legal obligation to the Constitution, Brandeis redefined Zionism to emphasize its compatibility with American nationalism. Law and land, the historic pillars of Judaism, now defined the loyalty of American Jews to the United States. A good Jew, Brandeis and Marshall concurred, was a patriotic American whose deepest loyalty, to the United States, must never be compromised. No American Jews were better positioned to define and defend that proposition than lawyers, which explains why, in the twentieth century, legal authority within the Jewish community passed inexorably into their hands.

Marshall and Brandeis shared the same anxiety about Zionism because they shared the same preoccupation with loyalty. Indeed, the more carefully that one examines their substantive positions, the more evident is the irony that Marshall's distrust of Zionism was far more deeply rooted in Judaism than Brandeis's support for it. That may help to explain why Brandeis, not Marshall, still enjoys such a towering reputation among American

Jews as the enduring symbol of reconciliation between Hebrew prophecy and American democracy. It says something significant about the terms of American Jewish acculturation that Marshall is all but forgotten, though his active leadership in Jewish communal affairs long predated (and outlasted) Brandeis's relatively brief service as Zionist leader. Marshall was too much a political conservative (and, perhaps, a committed Jew) to command the enduring adulation that Brandeis has enjoyed. American Jews still fervently believe that Brandeisian liberalism binds them to Jewish tradition—when, precisely as it did for Brandeis, it emphasizes their remoteness from it.[49]

Brandeis closely resembled another assimilated, successful Jew who, from the periphery of Jewish life, inspired the Jewish masses to identify Zionism with the values of enlightened liberalism. In the United States, as in Europe, "the urbane assimilationist . . . became the savior of the suffering chosen people." Just as Brandeisian Zionism was largely devoid of Jewish content, so Theodor Herzl's model state was "not a Jewish utopia," as Carl Schorske has noted, "but a liberal one. The dreams of assimilation which could not be realized in Europe would be realized in Zion." The state that Herzl envisioned was a state inhabited by Jews ("just another modern secular state," Ahad Ha-'Am compained), not a Jewish state. Yet Herzl, like Brandeis, won a passionate following among the Jewish masses who found in that definition of Zionism the satisfactory reconciliation of Jewish distinctiveness *and* normalization. Herzl, the Jew as Viennese aristocrat, favored a state for the Jews, a Jewish Switzerland with cricket and tennis, where "we shall keep our priests within the confines of their temples." Brandeis, the Jew as Boston Brahmin, envisioned a Jewish Denmark, populated by modern Pilgrims and Puritans. Herzl was the charismatic leader, propelled by the sheer force of his vision into the company of sultans and kings who might assist him in realizing his dream. Brandeis was the American Isaiah, who prophesied the reconciliation of Zionism and Americanism through liberal reform.[50]

Their achievement also measured their failure. As Ahad Ha-'Am wrote sorrowfully, just before the turn of the century: "Almost all of our great men, those, that is, whose education and social position fit them to be at the head of a Jewish State, are spiritually far removed from Judaism." It was a poignant reminder that even Zionism had not resolved the fundamental dilemmas of modernity for Jews and Judaism. That criticism of Herzl still serves aptly as an epitaph for Louis Brandeis, the Zionist as American. Not long before Brandeis died, he reminisced about Sabbath observance in the home of his beloved uncle Louis Dembitz, a distinguished lawyer whose Jewish legal erudition Brandeis never cared to emulate. "I recall vividly the joy and awe" with which he welcomed it, and "the piety with which he observed it," Brandeis recalled, comparing that "Sabbath peace" with the "elusive something" that "prevailed in many a home in Boston on a Sunday." He expressed some yearning for "the Jewish-Puritan Sabbath," but without its "oppressive restrictions."[51] As remote from Judaism as ever, Brandeis, virtually until his death, looked to Brahmin Boston and Puritan New England to define his Jewish frame of reference.

Isaiah's Disciples:
Julian Mack and Felix Frankfurter

As lawyers bound to the American Constitution, Marshall and Brandeis infused ancient Jewish concepts of law and justice with American content. Under their leadership, the rule of law that governed American Jewish life came to depend upon the Constitution, not the Torah. The meaning of justice, stripped of the covenantal fidelity demanded by the Hebrew Prophets, was defined within the American political tradition. The two lawyers complemented each other: Marshall's constitutionalism affirmed the allegiance of Jews to American legal institutions; Brandeisian Zionism made it clear that the United States, not a Jewish national home in Palestine, was the true homeland of American Jews. The synthesis of Judaism with Americanism was completed, and the authority of lawyers to define the loyalty of American Jews was secured.

Marshall and Brandeis, however, were among the tiny handful of prominent Jewish lawyers before World War I. The entry of Jews into the legal profession was prolonged and painful, strewn with obstacles of exclusion and discrimination set by law schools and law firms. Law, like other professions, attracted Jews who were struggling to escape from immigrant poverty. But a legal career offered a special reward: only law afforded Jews (as officers of the court sworn to defend the Constitution) the opportunity to demonstrate their patriotic allegiance to the United States. In retrospect, their remarkable journey from rags to robes, from "shyster" to a "Jewish seat" on the Supreme Court, testified to their perseverance and success. But it took decades to accomplish and, until the New Deal provided its stamp of legitimacy, the stigma of professional inferiority lingered.

During the early years of the century, Jews encountered deeply entrenched anti-Semitism at the bar. "The doors of most New York law offices were closed, with rare exceptions, to a young Jewish lawyer," recalled Joseph Proskauer, who subsequently became an appellate judge in New York. Felix Frankfurter, amply supplied with glowing recommendations handwritten by the dean of the Harvard Law School, finally was hired by a New York firm that had never before employed a Jew (after the hiring partner strongly advised Frankfurter to change his name). Marshall had learned, to his surprise, that few Jews were admitted to the New York City bar association, and "it was only in exceptional cases that men of my faith were appointed to committees of the organization." By World War I, the older generation of German Jews had begun to establish their own corporate law firms—both Marshall and Proskauer were partners in distinguished firms that served a predominantly Jewish corporate and financial clientele. For Eastern European Jews, however, opportunities were narrowly constricted by rampant professional anti-Semitism, which long consigned them to the lowest strata of professional life.[1]

After Brandeis's accession to power in the Zionist movement in 1914, lawyers were conspicuously present as his assistants. Like their leader, they wanted to Americanize Zionism while simultaneously defining themselves as good Americans. Chaim Weizmann, who grasped the significance of their presence, was dismayed by the predominance of lawyers in the American movement. He once enumerated them all (calculating Benjamin Cohen as "ten lawyers" in one) and deplored their prominence and influence.[2] For millennia, Jews had repeated Isaiah's prophecy that the law would go forth from Zion; but for American Jews after 1916, the law went forth from the Supreme Court, where the words of the American Isaiah were spoken. Two of Brandeis's handpicked disciples, Julian W. Mack and Felix Frankfurter, carried his precepts far beyond the Zionist movement, ultimately—in Frankfurter's case—to demonstrate the fateful consequences of Zionism as Americanism for constitutional law and for the American Jewish community.

The issues of loyalty that led Brandeis to his synthesis were also salient for Mack, who assumed many of the administrative and diplomatic tasks that Brandeis yielded once his appointment to the Supreme Court insulated him from daily involvement in Zionist affairs. Mack had grown up in Cincinnati, the geographical stronghold of Reform, where Rabbi Isaac Mayer Wise had urged his congregants to cultivate Judaism as a religion only and become good Americans. Mack complied; by the time he graduated from the Harvard Law School in 1887 he was, according to his biographer, a "fully Americanized Jew." In Chicago, where Mack practiced law, his rabbi, a radical Reformer, denounced Zionism as a contradiction of American patriotism. During the 1890s, Mack was drawn to Jewish affairs by his apprehension about the impact of mass Jewish immigration upon American life. So, for a time, he worked with a new committee organized to disperse Russian immigrants to the rural hinterlands, where they would be less conspicuous than if they clustered in urban ghettos. During the early years of the new century, he developed his own synthesis of Reform Judaism and Progressive reform. A crusader for juvenile justice, a respected federal judge, active in philanthropic circles, and a founding member of the American Jewish Committee, he moved easily within the comfortable uptown New York circles of emancipated, successful, assimilated German Jews.[3]

Mack's most urgent Jewish concerns were expressed in his testimony before the United States Immigration Commission in 1909. Mack vigorously resisted any distinctive identification of Jews; Judaism was a religion, nothing more. Not only would a racial or national classification convert Jews into a group of unwelcome foreigners, but the Jew would become "a stranger to our land. That is the thing we resent." While Henry Cabot Lodge, the Brahmin senator from Boston, insisted upon the distinctiveness of the Jewish people, Mack, the assimilated Jew, denied it. (Mack was sharply rebuked by the *Jewish Advocate* in Boston for his "cowardly and disgraceful" position.) Over time, however, his position softened. His encounter with Aaron Aaronsohn led him (as it did Brandeis) to a positive vision of the new Jew, shaped by the land of Israel rather than an Eastern Europe *shtetl*. But not until 1915, when Mack (again like Brandeis) was persuaded by Horace Kallen that Jewish distinctiveness could be a legitimate contribution to American nationality, did he respond to Brandeis's invitation to become a Zionist. For Mack, as for Brandeis, it was less a dramatic wrench than a gentle transition—once he was persuaded that Zionism expressed, rather than repudiated, American values.[4]

Mack's participation in the work of the American Jewish Committee made him an especially valuable recruit to the Brandeis circle. Committee opposition to Zionism was no secret; its insistence upon the exclusive loyalty of American Jews to the United States was unyielding. Mack served as a bridge between two groups of assimilated German Jews, dedicated to the common cause of American patriotism and opposed to Jewish nationalism. Under his stewardship as *de facto* Zionist leader, any significant differences between the Committee and the Zionist leadership on matters of Zionist substance were all but obliterated. Mack enjoyed the confidence of both Marshall and Brandeis, to the point where it became difficult to determine where the anti-Zionism of the Committee ended and the Zionism of the American Zionist organization began. The ascendancy of assimilated Jews in the American Zionist movement, initiated by Brandeis, was consolidated by Mack. At one of the critical moments in modern Jewish history,

American Zionists were led by men with little sympathy for Jewish national aspirations.

The Balfour Declaration was as distressing to Mack as to Brandeis. He surely was among the colleagues whom Brandeis identified as neither advising nor desiring statehood. Mack added his own firm disclaimer a few weeks later. Jews, he wrote, were a people with a "common tradition and history," bound "culturally and ethnically." But they must not become "a political community." Repeating verbatim Brandeis's rejection of statehood, he limited his endorsement to "a common religion, the renaissance of a common language, and the revival of the social spirit of the prophets."

Mack developed his position more fully in a pamphlet entitled *Americanism and Zionism*, published by the Zionist organization. Whether inspired by wartime xenophobia, which had placed all Americans of German origin in a vulnerable position, or by the Balfour Declaration, it revealed the depth of Mack's concern—less with Zionism than with American patriotism. Asserting the compatibility of Americanism and Zionism, Mack nonetheless felt impelled to focus upon "the dangerous doctrine of dual nationality." Jews, he noted, were "rather peculiar; we want to be more loyal than the King himself, holier than the pope. We want every possible cloud dispelled, every conceivable doubt removed." Conceding that Jews comprised "a people," he insisted that no Jew "owes any political allegiance to that Jewish people." At most, there might be "a kinship" based upon a "common inheritance and a common religion." Sympathy for Jewish ideals, Mack continued, must be understood as an expression of "the devotion of the American Jew to American ideals"—because "there is essential agreement between them." The political loyalty of American Jews to the United States, he affirmed, "will remain single and undivided." It was "unthinkable," Mack insisted, "for Jews scattered all over the world . . . to present a united political front." Mack confided his "lurking fear" of "the public danger" of such a commitment: it constituted an open invitation to allegations of dual loyalty, which the Brandeisian Zionists had entered the movement to suppress.[5]

American Zionists could not accept the European commitment to "diaspora nationalism," the theory of the national unity of the Jewish people cutting across geographical boundaries. That difference defined the fundamental ideological cleavage between the American and European Zionists. Diaspora nationalism was anathema to the Brandeisians, for it underminded their claims of exclusively American loyalties. American Zionists had to protect themselves, at all costs, from the political implications of Zionism. It was imperative, therefore, to concentrate upon philanthropy, economic development, managerial efficiency, financial solvency, organizational structure, and legal proprieties—anything but political sovereignty. At the Cleveland convention in 1921, when the Zionist movement fractured, Mack—speaking for the Brandeisians as president of the American organization—eloquently stated the preferred American approach: "method, procedure, order, propriety, right, correctness, following all agreements and orders and mandates." His ritualistic recital of legalisms was designed to obliterate the very issues of Jewish identity and loyalty that the European Zionist movement was determined to confront and resolve. Defeated overwhelmingly, the Brandeisians departed from the Zionist organization, all the while proclaiming "the intensity of their Zionism." Mack called the roster of the departing Americans, lawyers conspicuous among them. All but functionless in the Zionist movement once legal procedure yielded to Jewish substance, he had little to contribute thereafter.[6]

Unlike Mack, Felix Frankfurter was anything but an Americanized Jew when he followed Brandeis into the Zionist movement. Emigrating to the United States as a young boy, he grew up in a ritually observant family. His father was descended from a long line of rabbis; Frankfurter once mentioned, with evident feeling, that he recalled "Next year in Jerusalem" from his earliest childhood memories (adding that he admired the "vitality" of its "courageous optimism"). But during his adolescent years Frankfurter felt a growing "disharmony" between self and synagogue. The decisive break came at City College, during a Yom Kippur service, when Frankfurter acknowledged that religious observance no longer had meaning for him. He left the synagogue, never to return. Although he claimed never to have lost his concern for "whatever affects the fate of Jews," in time he redirected his deepest loyalties, even his feelings of piety and worship, to the Harvard Law School, which elicited his "quasi-religious" feelings; to the American rule of law; and to the United States, the adopted country of his childhood.[7]

Frankfurter left the synagogue behind as a young man, but he never comfortably resolved the issues that his Judaism raised. "You'll encounter a great deal of anti-Semitism in your life," an uncle had predicted, before warning him not to "go around sniffing anti-Semitism." Frankfurter seems to have internalized the fundamental ambiguity of that message. At times he demonstrated a heightened sensitivity to Jewish issues, but he could also demonstrate a startling indifference to their persistent intrusion in his own life and to his own efforts to disguise or suppress them. He recalled in his published reminiscences that "I was very early infused with . . . a very profoundly wise attitude toward the whole fact that I was a Jew, the essence of which is that you should be a biped and walk on the two legs that man has." But his Judaism was never something that he could take so comfortably for granted, as inconsequential a mark of identity as the color of his eyes. The more that Frankfurter struggled to elude the particularities of his Judaism, the more evidently he became enmeshed in them.[8]

As a graduate of the Harvard Law School, he was drawn to a firm that was known never to have hired a Jew. "I thought it would be interesting to go there and have them realize that this was just an artifact of theirs, that a Jew was something different"—as though Frankfurter had nothing to prove to himself. Similarly, as a Harvard faculty member (the only tenured Jew on the faculty for twenty-five years), he insisted, "I was not a Jewish professor at the Harvard Law School, but I was a Harvard Law School professor who happened to be a Jew." Yet that happenstance did not, Frankfurter conceded, deter him from exacting "higher standards from Jews" than from other students—although he passionately proclaimed Harvard to be a pure democratic meritocracy, pervaded by "objectivity and disinterestedness," where academic achievement was independent of "who you were." In his relationships with his Brahmin mentors—Henry L. Stimson, Oliver Wendell Holmes, Jr., and Franklin D. Roosevelt— as in his courtship of Marian Denman, the daughter of a Congregationalist minister ("You know how deeply rooted the feeling against intermarriage is in us Jews," he told Holmes), Frankfurter "happened to be a Jew" who was irresistibly drawn to exemplars of Brahmin culture, in law and politics as in love. His life was a continuing struggle to overcome what he referred to in his autobiographical reminiscences as the legacy of his "father" and his "face"—his origins as an immigrant Jew.[9]

The death of Frankfurter's father in 1916 coincided with the bitter struggle, laced with anti-Semitism, over Brandeis's nomination to the Supreme Court as its first Jew. (Suggestively, Frankfurter insisted that there must be "no boisterous Jewish celebration" of the Brandeis confirmation, preferring that Jews "carry our pride with humility and mostly in silence.") As he struggled with his personal loss and with a loneliness that remained "with me deeply," Brandeis drew him into Zionist activities. Frankfurter had resisted earlier entreaties. "He needs jogging," Kallen advised Brandeis; "the issue is not yet alive and momentous to him." The Balfour Declaration helped; to Frankfurter it meant that "allied statesmen" regarded Zionists with "respect." Brandeis eased Frankfurter into Zionist activities, beginning with a request for information about the status of European Jews (which Brandeis had earlier imagined that Frankfurter's Harvard colleague, Roscoe Pound, might provide). Then Frankfurter was delegated diplomatic responsibilities, first on the Morgenthau mission to Turkey in 1917 and then, two years later, as a member of the Zionist delegation to the Paris Peace Conference. Frankfurter's lack of knowledge of Zionism or the Middle East was no impediment (to him or to Brandeis). "As is the way of lawyers," Frankfurter recalled, "I began to study up this case." Describing himself as "a disciplined lawyer," he absorbed information, dispensed advice, and negotiated with T. E. Lawrence (of Arabia) and the

Emir Feisal to secure a statement of Arab support for Jewish settlement in Palestine. Frankfurter was dazzled by the experience, which propelled him into the vortex of international affairs.[10]

There is little evidence, however, that Frankfurter went to Paris, or left, with any significant understanding of, or appreciation for, the Jewish national revival. Like Brandeis, he filtered Zionism through American lenses that magnified the importance of money and management and diminished its Jewish content. The "most effective way" to assert American influence upon the Zionist movement, he insisted, was "through money." With "money, money, money . . . all the other things will come to us." He vigorously supported fundraising efforts for a new university in Jerusalem, an institution that could demonstrate the attachment of Zionism to modern Western values. A university, moreover, would impress the British and help to dispel "the rankling feeling about American Jewry." When, on rare occasions, Frankfurter attempted to define Zionism, his prose was stilted, abstract, and detached: the movement, he wrote in 1918, was "a concrete application of the proper respect for small nationalities, of the safeguarding and encouragement of the rich contributions of a persistent civilization which for the world's sake must endure." His support strengthened only when he realized that "the Zionist cause is part of the Allied cause." Once the Balfour Declaration was endorsed by the American government, Zionism was an ingredient of American foreign policy and, therefore, an obligation dictated by American loyalty. But Frankfurter understood that "dual allegiance in a juristic sense is not permissible. Zionism can exist as a philanthropy but not as a political motive." The American people had "a right to demand of Jews complete allegiance."[11]

In Paris, Frankfurter proudly defined Zionism as "an interest which has behind it the formal sanction of the Allies and of our government." He rejected the claims of the European Zionists that the proposed British mandate for Palestine did not sufficiently protect Jewish interests. Frankfurter's "fundamental conviction" was "a deep faith in Great Britain," a faith that conveniently permitted American Jews to maintain their distance from Palestinian affairs. For Frankfurter, it was an "incontrovertible principle" that financial contributions must define the limit of the political participation of American Jews in Palestine. Americans, however, should remain active in the Zionist movement; not only were they "better workers," with "a stronger sense of reality," than the Eastern Europeans, but also their active presence served "the added purpose of allaying fears of Bolshevism" in Zionist affairs.[12]

Frankfurter's commitment to Zionism, as he once explained to President Wilson, expressed his feelings as "a passionate American." He fervently wanted Jews to be "a reconstructive and not a disruptive force in the new world order." But Jewish "moderation" and "restraint," especially in Palestine, depended upon continued American support for the principles of the Balfour Declaration. "On our side"—the Zionist side—"the task is to keep literally millions of Jews in check," millions who might otherwise permit their Zionist enthusiasm to overflow permissible limits. The fear of Zionist radicalism, and its harmful consequences to American Jews, nagged deeply at Frankfurter, as it did at Brandeis. When Lord Balfour reminded Brandeis that Jews were actively engaged in postwar revolutionary movements, Brandeis (according to Frankfurter who attended their meeting as Brandeis's aide) reiterated his determination to channel Zionist zeal. Brandeis, speaking as an American, expressed his concern with "the vast number of Jews, particularly Russian Jews," who were emigrating to the United States. Zionism, he hoped, would deflect their revolutionary fervor into "constructive" activities.[13]

Lawyers were particularly adept in restraining Zionist fervor; hence their conspicuous place in the American Zionist movement during the Brandeis era. Brandeis insisted upon "men of standing and influence," to exert influence not only within the movement but also upon those outside it. Frankfurter (like Mack) was an ideal recruit. As he explained, describing his work drafting the British mandate for Palestine, "A mandate is a constitution . . . a legal document and called for lawyers of experience and understanding." He complained about the "tenacious adherence to abstractions" displayed by European Zionists, but he could never imagine that his own legal craftsmanship was far more tenaciously abstract than any Zionist theory. Describing his draft, he wrote: "Having limited the mandatory by the general terms of the trust, it was deemed important to leave the mandatory flexibility of government and administrative means by which to carry out the defined aims." As Horace Kallen observed, years later, Frankfurter functioned as an attorney for Zionism, "for the movement, but neither in nor of it."[14]

That surely was why Weizmann complained bitterly to Frankfurter: "Brandeis could have been a prophet in Israel, you have in you the making of a Lassalle. Instead you are choosing to be only a professor in Harvard and Brandeis only a Judge in the Supreme Court." "Only" a Harvard professor; "only" a Supreme Court Justice! How contemptuously Weizmann dismissed the stunning achievements of the first Jews to enter those sacred portals of American law. But to Frankfurter (perhaps proving Weizmann's point), the differences between them were not "spiritual conflicts," but only "issues of management, of politics in the professional sense." Neither Weizmann nor Frankfurter could understand, nor empathize with, a true believer of a different faith. Surely Frankfurter might have said, as Weizmann said to him: "Your Zionism is not my Zionism. Your Jewishness is not my Jewishness. . . . I shall not be led by you."[15]

Zionism, for Frankfurter, served a variety of purposes far removed from Jewish nationalism. Through Zionism, Frankfurter found a way to leave the insecurities of his "father" and his "face" behind him. It assured access to Brandeis and, through him, to the president of the United States. It enabled him to identify, as a Jew, with American foreign policy—and to demand the allegiance of Jews to the American government. The Balfour Declaration, endorsed by the American president, affirmed Zionism as an expression of Anglo-American ideals. Frankfurter, like Brandeis, had found a way to stand the issue of dual loyalty on its head: only if American Jews became Zionists could they demonstrate their American loyalties.

Frankfurter left the Zionist movement when Brandeis lost his show-down with Weizmann in 1921. He remained attentive to Jewish issues at Harvard during the postwar decade, especially efforts to impose a quota on Jewish students at the college and the law school's resistance to the appointment of other Jews to the faculty. But despite his professions of "devotion," he remained aloof from Zionist issues. Perhaps his passionate Anglophilism persuaded him that the British mandate for Palestine had placed the Zionist cause in good hands.

The Arab riots of 1929, which prompted the first in a series of British efforts to undercut the Balfour Declaration by restricting Jewish immigration and land purchase in Palestine, momentarily rekindled Frankfurter's interest. But his action was carefully circumscribed by caution. He declined to make a public defense of Zionism (although he contributed to the *New Republic* on a wide range of public issues), despite a week of bloody carnage in which Jews, killed and wounded by the hundreds, were blamed for insti-gating the Arab uprising. He counseled Brandeis to remain silent and to meet privately with the British prime minister. "I do not believe that the tone of truculence, of public demand, of exactions, of assurances, is the tone to take. . . . Our line is wisdom," he insisted to Mack, "and style forms no mean portion of wisdom." (Frankfurter had ignored precisely that counsel of wisdom just two years earlier, in his truculent public advo-cacy on behalf of Sacco and Vanzetti.) Frankfurter largely confined his ef-forts to defending the disputed authenticity of the Emir Feisal's letter to him (which Lawrence and Frankfurter had drafted in 1919), welcoming the Zionists to Palestine. Oblivious to Palestinian reality, he was content to in-sist that, legally, "No Colonial Minister can change the obligations of the Balfour Declaration, incorporated into the public law of the world by the Palestine Mandate." He was carefully attuned to the policy of the Ameri-can government, especially the State Department, which was distin-guished by its deference to British appeasement of Arab demands. Frank-furter's public silence, Naomi Cohen has concluded, was "a clear abdication of responsibility."[16]

With characteristic ambivalence, Frankfurter claimed that "there is nothing I would rather do" than travel to London to negotiate for the Jewish Agency with British officials about immigration policy. Impelled to go by "every impulse to be of some help in a cause to which I am so deeply committed," he nonetheless cited "intricate problems" and "insuperable difficulties" which confined him to Massachusetts: passions were high in Palestine; an agreement satisfactory to the Zionists would only irritate the Arabs; there was British opinion to consider; Jewish opinion was divided. Since the issues could not be resolved in a "quiet scientific way," Frankfurter preferred not to participate. Long after the uprising had subsided and the British had issued the first of several White Papers limiting Jewish immigration, Frankfurter finally contributed an article to *Foreign Affairs* in which he confined Zionist objectives to "a recognized legal position" in which a people can enjoy territorial access "without receiving the rights of political sovereignty." A Jewish state, he reminded Mack, "implies political control of the government. Now we are not for that."[17]

Several years later, during a sabbatical year at Oxford, Frankfurter visited Palestine for the first and only time. After a quarter of a century, he still recalled his trip as one of his "most vivid and cherished of experiences." It was (he wrote to Roosevelt) "a most exciting land—its beauty is magical and the achievements of the Jewish renaissance almost incredible." But the only recorded subject of his conversations there was the New Deal's National Recovery Administration. Jacob deHaas, the veteran Zionist, noted perceptively after Frankfurter's return that "his findings are based on what he prefers and approves in American life." Frankfurter might not have disagreed. He described himself, somewhat distantly, as "a Jew who didn't want anything," except to place Zionism in "the perspective of general considerations of statesmanship and from the point of view of an Anglophile." By 1937, he had all but disengaged from Zionist objectives. "All this talk about 'state' and 'sovereignty' is romanticism—chasing a mirage," he complained at the time the Peel partition plan was debated. Frankfurter actively assisted in the publication of a resounding critique of Jewish statehood.[18]

During the 1930s, of course, Frankfurter's extracurricular energies were directed primarily toward New Deal Washington. He derived enormous satisfaction from the "great state service" that lawyers performed in the Roosevelt administration. Indeed, there the problem was not too few Jews, but too many. Some New Deal lawyers, Jews included, were troubled by the abundant supply of qualified Jews and by the political liabilities inherent in placing too many of them on their staffs. As Adlai Stevenson, a young lawyer on Jerome Frank's staff, observed: "There is a little feeling that the Jews are getting too prominent." Stevenson distinguished between the "autocratic" (or "pushy") Jews and those, like Frank, who lacked such invidious "racial characteristics." Frank, an assimilated German Jew from Chicago, was exceedingly sensitive to the issue and indeed "embarrassed" to be surrounded by Jewish lawyers. "One of my problems," he wrote Frankfurter, "is the possibility of having too many Jews on the legal staff." Frank repeatedly referred to the Jewish origin of staff attorneys, citing it as an unfortunate "disability." He was sufficiently concerned, once the number of Jews had reached five (out of thirty), to impose his own unofficial quota. "I have taken such care to discourage Jewish applicants," he reported to the secretary of agriculture, "that I have gained the reputation . . . of being anti-Semitic. At least half a dozen very able lawyers have been rejected by me on this ground." He explicitly advised his assistants "if possible to recommend lawyers who are not Jews."[19]

Although Frankfurter gained public notoriety as "the Jew, the 'red', the 'alien'" within New Deal councils, nothing was more revealing of his deepest patriotic yearnings than his adoration of Franklin D. Roosevelt. He was, as the annotator of the Roosevelt-Frankfurter correspondence aptly concluded, "an artist in adulation" who "laid on flattery with a trowel." Frankfurter's relationship with Roosevelt elicited the same sycophancy he had already bestowed upon the other towering Brahmin figure in his life, Justice Holmes, whose "awing majesty and wonder" had captivated Frankfurter years earlier. The justice and the president provided "a Jew of alien origin" with appropriate symbols of legal majesty and national authority.[20]

When Roosevelt appointed Frankfurter to the Supreme Court, it meant everything to him; and not only for all the obvious reasons. Frankfurter had not managed to elude the burden of his immigrant Jewish origins—not in his early job interviews, nor at Harvard Law School, nor as presidential adviser. He knew that he was perceived as the alien Jew, and he accurately detected anti-Semitism in some political opposition to New Deal policies—and to his own prominent, if unofficial, role in the Roosevelt administration. With two Jews (Brandeis and Cardozo) already on the Court, Frankfurter realized that his own chance for an appointment, which he desperately wanted and eagerly sought, was slim. Even after Cardozo's death there was still strong opposition to another Jew on the Court—especially from prominent conservative Jews, including Arthur Hays Sulzberger of the *New York Times*, who feared that Frankfurter's nomination would further provoke anti-Semitism. Frankfurter sharply rebuked Sulzberger, insisting that "Jews should take themselves for granted as Americans who were born Jews." Remarkably, Frankfurter cited himself as a Jew "without any of the usual 'Jewish' conflicts or difficulties." Yet the presidential appointment of a Jew to the Supreme Court "had such significance for me," Frankfurter recalled (demonstrating the nearly identical response to presidential recognition that Brandeis had evinced at the time of his own nomination two decades earlier). "Of all earthly institutions," he conceded, "this Court comes nearest to having, for me, sacred aspects."[21] There could be no more explicit statement of his American legal piety.

Frankfurter's unresolved ambivalence about himself as a Jew and an American found dramatic expression within one year of his appointment to the Court. The challenge of Jehovah's Witnesses to a compulsory flag-salute law pitted a tiny religious minority, claiming the protection of the First Amendment for the free exercise of religious beliefs, against the cherished symbol of the United States. Frankfurter well understood that a "conception of religious duty" might conflict with secular interests that defined "the general good." But he insisted that "the binding tie of cohesive sentiment" must prevail. "'We live by symbols,'" Frankfurter wrote, quoting Holmes, for the Court. "The flag is the symbol of our national unity, transcending all internal differences, however large, within the framework of the Constitution." He demanded of the Jehovah's Witnesses that they elevate American patriotism over religious conviction, precisely the choice that Frankfurter had made for himself. To an immigrant Jew serving on the Supreme Court, no claim was more exalted than that symbolized by flag and Constitution.[22]

The issue would not rest. In two cases decided during the 1943 term (including reconsideration and reversal of the flag-salute decision), Frankfurter vividly displayed his determination to resolve any conflict, political or religious, as a patriotic American. The first of these cases involved revocation of the naturalized citizenship of a Communist Party leader, who was deemed insufficiently attached to the Constitution for his oath of allegiance to be valid. Frankfurter argued passionately to sustain the revocation decision. "Perhaps this case arouses in me feelings that could not be entertained by anyone else around this table," he insisted during conference discussion. For Frankfurter, who had served thirty years earlier as a government attorney in naturalization proceedings, the case vividly recalled "hundreds of men and women . . . who had to shed old loyalties and take on the loyalty of American citizenship."

That was not only a professional memory; it precisely described Frankfurter's most intimate personal and family experience. "None of you has had the experience that I have had with reference to American citizenship," Frankfurter declared, recalling his father's naturalization and the "great solemnity" and family pride that accompanied it. "As one who has no ties with any formal religion," Frankfurter continued, "perhaps the feelings that underlie religious forms for me run into intensification of my feelings about American citizenship." He conceded "that a convert is more zealous than one born to the faith." His own conversion zeal, channeled into American patriotism, shaped his insistence that the Constitution must be "the binding force of our political fellowship." Frankfurter conveyed his meaning, and the intensity of feeling behind it, by reading to the other Justices from a letter written to him by an Italian immigrant, a naturalized American citizen (and a Harvard professor): "When I took my oath [of citizenship] . . . I was throwing away not my intellectual and moral but my juristic past. I threw it away without any regret." Having proclaimed "allegiance to the Constitution of [his] adopted country," an immigrant could feel "at home" in the United States. Professor Salvemini thereby affirmed Frankfurter's own experience: the renunciation of a "juristic past" to feel "at home" as an American.[23]

Conflicts over patriotism continued to torment Frankfurter. The flag-salute issue returned to the Court, and Frankfurter, suddenly in the minority as the Court reversed itself, displayed his discomfort in a highly emotional, intensely personal, opinion. "One who belongs to the most vilified and persecuted minority in history is not likely to be insensible to the freedoms guaranteed by our Constitution," he wrote. Were his "purely personal attitude relevant," Frankfurter continued, he would align himself with the claims of religious freedom. But, he insisted, in a characteristic disavowal of personal involvement at the very moment that he asserted it, "as judges we are neither Jew nor Gentile. . . . We owe equal attachment to the Constitution . . . whether we derive our citizenship from the earliest or the latest immigrants to these shores." With "promotion of good citizenship" as a legitimate end of state policy, a compulsory flag salute (even when it violated the religious conscience of those for whom it represented worship of a graven image) must be constitutional.[24] Legal obligation must override religious identity; the Constitution was the instrument of American acculturation. Frankfurter, claiming to assert "judicial obligations" over "private notions of policy," persisted in injecting his own most deeply held personal feelings about himself as an immigrant Jew into his judicial opinions. Identifying as a Jew, he enclosed himself in the Constitution to deny the claims of that identification.

When Frankfurter came to the Court, the plight of European Jews had become desperate, and the unwillingness of the American government to admit refugees fleeing from Nazi terror was evident. By then, however, his involvement in Jewish affairs, sporadic at best, had all but evaporated. During his first decade on the bench, coinciding with the Holocaust and the birth of Israel, there is little evidence that Frankfurter was active in, or especially concerned with, Jewish issues. He might, on occasion, talk about Palestine, meet with Chaim Weizmann, or request an audience for Weizmann with a government official. But despite what he described (with characteristic exaggeration) as his "long and deep connection . . . with problems of Palestine," he remained detached from Jewish issues during the most destructive and creative years in modern Jewish history. As David Ben-Gurion observed, at the time of Frankfurter's appointment to the

Court, Zionism was "only a desultory, secondary undertaking, not his heart's core." Ben-Gurion quickly realized, during his struggle to secure the support of American Jews for a Jewish army and, ultimately, a Jewish state, that his objective must be "not to try to convert the non-Zionists to Zionism, but rather to make Zionists out of the Zionists." It was a hopeless task, for he found few exceptions to "the all-pervasive timidity" of the Americans.

Frankfurter was not among them. When Ben-Gurion, desperate for a meeting with Roosevelt to press Jewish concerns, turned to Frankfurter for assistance, he was disappointed. Frankfurter invited Ben-Gurion to lunch with David Niles and Benjamin Cohen, whom Frankfurter considered among the more sympathetic administration members. But Frankfurter said little, while Cohen bluntly asked, "Why fight as Jews?" In Ben-Gurion's judgment, Frankfurter lacked "any serious and consistent attitude to our cause." It is possible to attribute his silence, as Frankfurter did, to his "absurd fastidiousness" as a sitting Justice regarding the impropriety of extrajudicial activities. As Frankfurter subsequently noted concerning his reticence about the partition of Palestine, "I did not even exercise the rights of citizenship to do what I legitimately could to further the Presidential policy regarding Palestine." But since his fastidiousness did not keep Frankfurter from a wide range of political activities during the war years and after, its confinement to Jewish issues is especially revealing.[25]

By World War II, no prominent American Jew (with the exception of Rabbi Stephen S. Wise) had as prolonged a relationship to the Zionist movement as Frankfurter; no lawyer had struggled with such determination against professional anti-Semitism; few New Dealers enjoyed the relationship with Roosevelt that he had cultivated; and none held as high a position in national life. It might be argued (as Frankfurter himself claimed) that his sense of propriety about extrajudicial activity decisively inhibited his participation in Jewish affairs. Yet the range of Frankfurter's political activism during his early years on the bench, even measured by the tolerant standards of that era, was extraordinary. It went far beyond his diligent efforts to place friends and former students in influential government positions. He worked actively on behalf of Roosevelt's reelection in 1940; he campaigned vigorously for American aid to Great Britain, in effect presenting Roosevelt with a legal brief for rescinding the neutrality laws; and he was intimately involved in the drafting of the critical Lend-Lease legislation to rescue that beleaguered ally. His hand was evident in the program for wartime industrial mobilization. He concerned himself with affairs in India, Australia, and Vichy France. Yet Frankfurter would not utilize his position and contacts, or his irrepressible energy, in the service of Jewish needs during the most desperate years of Jewish history.

Among the varied causes that engaged his extrajudicial efforts, the rescue of Jews from the Holocaust was not among them.[26]

Perhaps the explanation, as one writer has suggested, lies in the fact that, "as a Jew and a foreign-born one, Frankfurter felt he has to move circumspectly" while he was on the Court. Or, as one of his more reflective biographers has observed, it may be attributable to Frankfurter's "fundamental ambiguity about his place in the world— whether he was an insider in the Brahmin establishment, or an outsider because he was a Jew." There was, however, an even deeper ambivalence that may have inhibited Frankfurter, an ambivalence about the very meaning of his own Jewishness and its compatibility (or incompatibility) with his yearnings to be an American. He never resolved the acute tension between the claims of his Jewish heritage and his denial of its influence. The conflict remained with him as long as he lived. Characteristically, he left firm instructions that he did not wish a rabbi to speak at his funeral; instead, he chose his "only close personal friend who is also a practicing, Orthodox Jew," a former law clerk, to conclude the service. As he explained: "I came into this world a Jew and although I did not live my life entirely as a Jew, I think it is fitting that I should leave as a Jew." But his final instruction to his biographer just before he died suggested even more evocatively the meaning of Frankfurter's silence on Jewish issues: "Let people see how much I loved Roosevelt," he insisted, "how much I loved my country."[27]

Frankfurter was *sui generis*; no other Jew in American public life engaged in such a prolonged, tormenting, and conspicuous struggle over Jewish identity. He resolved his ambivalence to the extent that he could, by locating his surrogate religion in law and patriotism. With those consummate patricians, Holmes and Roosevelt, as his patriarchal authorities, he found in the Constitution and the American flag the most meaningful symbols of his quest, as an immigrant Jew, for American identity. He always remained sensitive to the tension inherent in immigrant origins; and he always compensated for his "father" and his "face" with his fervent patriotism. His struggle to reconcile the claims of old country and new—his "juristic past" with his constitutional passion—poignantly revealed the dilemma of immigrant acculturation.

Frankfurter, the only Jew on the Supreme Court (after Brandeis's retirement in 1939), was also a court Jew—indeed, the most conspicuous example of the phenomenon in American history. The court Jew, historically, was a transitional figure between the medieval and modern worlds, uneasily combining in himself "the Jew of the Ghetto with the Jew of the emancipation." Consequently, he always displayed deeply ambivalent relationships with the Jewish community, whose representative he was, and with the prince, whose power he respected and protection he craved. Needing the support of the Jewish community, he also needed to escape from it.

So in speech, dress, and manners he emulated his Christian protectors, to whom he was subservient. These ambiguities of role and identity shaped a distinctive personality: the court Jew, filled with "tensions and inhibitions," was creative yet constrained, defenseless yet arrogant, successful yet apprehensive, privileged yet eager for the trappings of privilege to conceal his precarious status. Eager to assimilate, he could never forget that, as exceptional as he was, he was still a Jew. Because the instability of governments made any commitment to a particular prince risky, the court Jew invested his ultimate loyalty in the authority of government itself.[28]

Frankfurter was not, in any formal sense, a representative of the Jewish community; rather, by 1941 (after Brandeis's death), he surely was its most conspicuous exemplar of success in American public life. He was not bound—as the court Jew once was—to the community; by then, Frankfurter had completely enclosed his Jewish self in the trappings of patriotism. Indeed, his appointment to the Court had provided Frankfurter with his ultimate justification for withdrawal from participation in Jewish affairs, although he permitted Weizmann and Ben-Gurion, among others, to approach him as if he was a prominent American Jewish leader. But for Frankfurter, as for the court Jew, the tension of competing identities never was fully resolved; as his flag-salute opinions so evocatively demonstrated, Frankfurter invariably asserted the continuing relevance of his "face" precisely at the moment that he denied its significance. He displayed all the ambivalence that historically had characterized the court Jew, whose deference to the authority of the state could never entirely compensate for—rather so vividly expressed—his fundamental insecurities as a Jew.

Although Frankfurter's loyalty torments were deeply personal, they had larger significance as a paradigm of American Jewish acculturation. Precisely when Frankfurter and, indeed, the entire American Jewish community entered the American political mainstream, the horrors of Nazism confronted them with a conflict between competing Jewish and American commitments. Roosevelt's overwhelming electoral triumph of 1936 assured Jewish voters a secure place in the new national political majority forged by the New Deal coalition. Simultaneously, Jewish lawyers—among them Jerome Frank, Samuel Rosenman, Abe Fortas, Simon Rifkind, and Charles E. Wyzanski, Jr.— achieved prominence in New Deal circles (which, in time, certified them for federal judgeships, private practice, and personal success). With Frankfurter's appointment to the Court as the crowning symbol, immigrant Jews had finally become Americans. Yet nothing was more characteristic of American Jews than their acquiescence in Roosevelt's "abandonment of the Jews" of Europe. Proximity to power, which they had struggled so long to attain, all but silenced them to Jewish tragedy.[29]

Frankfurter was not the only New Deal lawyer who was extremely circumspect in confronting issues of Jewish consequence. Jerome Frank, already worried lest too many Jews join his legal staff, had imposed hiring quotas to "blunt political attacks." Being a Jew, he confided to Frankfurter, was a "disability." He read anti-Semitism into Roosevelt's decision not to appoint him to the Court of Appeals; and he went out of his way to assert (in the *Saturday Evening Post*) that most American Jews "regard as their significant heroes Jefferson and Lincoln, not Moses and David." Samuel Rosenman, a trusted presidential adviser, carefully steered sensitive issues of Jewish content, like the rescue of refugees, away from Roosevelt's desk. Persuaded that any American assistance to Jews would arouse anti-Semitism, he declined to expose the president to political risk.[30]

It was not merely a lawyer's problem, however, but a problem for American Jewry. The Roosevelt years culminated their struggle for American recognition. The New Deal converted outsiders to insiders; the "common man," not the businessman, was an American hero; Roosevelt was everyman's president. There were benefit programs for the needy; and presidential compassion for forgotten Americans. Jews, along with millions of other Americans, were grateful beneficiaries. For Jews especially, Roosevelt was an inspiring symbol of the democratic alternative to Nazi tyranny. Their "blind adoration" of Roosevelt can surely be attributed to their perception that the president of the United States, for the first time, cared about *them*. Indeed, so strong was their identification with Roosevelt that no demonstration, however blatant, that the president was indifferent to the plight of European Jewry, and to the Holocaust itself, could diminish it. "In the end," David Wyman has written, Roosevelt, "the era's most prominent symbol of humanitarianism turned away from one of history's most compelling moral challenges."[31] Yet American Jews, steadfastly loyal to the president, dissipated their political influence at the very moment they achieved it.

What can possibly explain such an outpouring of Jewish gratitude, undiminished by the passage of time, to such an unresponsive political leader? Did it suffice that the New Deal, to Roosevelt's political enemies, was known as the "Jew deal"? Or that Frankfurter and Rosenman, like Bernard Baruch and Henry Morgenthau, Jr., had access to the president? It surely went deeper than that. American Jews gave so much to Roosevelt; but he gave so little to them as Jews. Why, then, did they love him so? Because, perhaps, he gave them so little. By giving them nothing as Jews, he was confirming their status as Americans. Recognition as *Americans* was what American Jews craved more than anything else; it was all Roosevelt ever gave them, but it was more than enough.

Roosevelt responded to Americans, and to the Allied nations, but not to Jews; and least of all to the desperate plight of foreign Jews. American

Jews internalized presidential priorities as their own. They would assert no interest as Jews independent of presidential definitions of the national interest. By their silence as Jews they could demonstrate what good Americans they were. For, as Frankfurter wrote from the bench, Jews, belonging to "the most vilified and persecuted minority in history," must pledge their allegiance to "the binding force of our political fellowship" as Americans. If there was a contrary admonition—"Put not your trust in princes"—American Jews had forgotten it. The loss of Jewish memory, and their American voice, was the price of acculturation.

Whether American Jews paid an exorbitant price, or received fair value, has been vigorously disputed. The journey of Jews from their sacred-law tradition, from Torah to Constitution, invariably is taken as testimony to Western enlightenment, American freedom, and Jewish achievement. But the experience of American Jews, the custodians of two legal cultures, suggests that acculturation, whatever benefits it surely provided, ultimately was a process of renunciation and divestment. Undeniably, American loyalties enabled Jewish immigrants to acquire the abundant privileges of a new identity—and spared them the worst horrors of retaining their old one. But with their old identity stripped away, they were all but paralyzed, as Jews, when their response was most desperately needed.

Rabbi & Lawyer:
Stephen S. Wise, Joseph M. Proskauer,
and the Dilemmas of Patriotism

During a visit to the United States in the spring of 1921, Chaim Weizmann listened while a prominent rabbi, long an active Zionist, praised Judge Julian Mack for his judicious leadership of the American Zionist movement. Weizmann, with some impatience, turned to the speaker, and remarked, "You have too many lawyers; nothing but lawyers." The conspicuous exception, to whom Weizmann addressed his pointed aside, was Rabbi Stephen S. Wise, after Brandeis the most revered American Jew in the twentieth century. Between Herzl and the Holocaust, there was no more impassioned advocate of the fusion of prophetic Judaism, Zionism, and American liberalism than Wise; nor did any American Jew so exemplify the perils of that alluring identification.[1]

Wise, the irrepressible rabbi among lawyers, was himself the son and grandson of rabbis. His father had emigrated from Hungary when Stephen was a young boy; his mother's financial security (from the family porcelain business) enabled Stephen to live comfortably among the German Jewish elite of Manhattan. Aaron Wise provided the compassionate understanding that his son, tormented during his youth by "a withering sense of inferiority," desperately craved. A prominent New York rabbi and one of the founders of the Jewish Theological Seminary, he arranged for Stephen to study Bible, Talmud, and Hebrew with his friends on the Seminary faculty. Stephen studied Semitics at Columbia College with Professor Richard Gottheil, the son of a rabbinical friend of his father; after graduation, he prepared for the rabbinate in Vienna. Before his twentieth birthday, Stephen Wise was the rabbi of Congregation B'nai Jeshrun, a prestigious Madison Avenue synagogue.[2]

In 1896, Aaron Wise, barely past fifty, suddenly died. It was a devastating loss for Stephen, so deeply dependent on his father for emotional support and intellectual guidance. Its enduring impact can be measured by his successive attachments to older Jewish mentors— first Theodore Herzl and then Louis Brandeis—who were the heroic "fathers," respectively, of European and American Zionism. Young Wise invested enormous emotional energy in these relationships; he was invariably frustrated when his adulation was not reciprocated, for he may never have overcome his need for the caring father of his childhood. The pattern climaxed during World War II: Wise (by then in his sixties) lavished such deference upon Franklin D. Roosevelt, the presidential "father" of the nation, that his own effectiveness as the leading spokesman of American Jewry was seriously compromised. Wise's personal dilemma, the dilemma of his dependence upon external authority, precisely reflected the dilemma of the American Jewish community, so deeply enmeshed in American self-definitions that it was virtually powerless to assert competing Jewish concerns.

Wise's autobiography, written during the last year of his life, offers a revealing glimpse (in an otherwise unreflective account) of his formative experience: "Among the most fateful occasions in my life," Wise recalled, was his attendance at the Second Zionist Congress in Basle in 1898, two years after his father's death. There he met Herzl, "a king among men," who resembled "some ancient monarch of the Near East." Instantly, Wise "felt a bond with him, apart from my unreserved acceptance of his leadership." The intensity of the bond can be attributed to filial attachment, for, as Wise wrote (in the paragraph preceding his description of Herzl), "my Zionism I owed chiefly to my father," whose Zionist commitment was "one of the earliest and sweetest memories of my life."[3]

The experience resonated with family significance for Wise. In Basle, his autobiography suggests, he experienced the intense emotions of a family reunion and a personal conversion. Not only did Herzl elicit his filial attachment; among the Eastern European Jews who gathered there, Wise wrote, "I found my brothers." (Wise's relationship with his own brother had been strained by his mother's evident adoration of the older boy.) Living exclusively among German Jews, he had never encountered the intellectual energy or spiritual vitality of the Eastern Europeans, "who were not victims or refugees or beggars, but proud and educated men." It was "a revelation" to Wise. "Not only did I find my brothers, but . . . I found myself." At that moment, "the Jewish people became my own." Wise's recollections, fifty years later, preserved the intensity of that experience; nothing was "more deep and challenging" than his "rebirth" in Basle.[4]

The depth of Wise's commitment to Zionism, before his tranforming encounter with Herzl, is difficult to gauge. His earliest known statement of support, a year before Basle, expressed the sympathetic detachment that characterized even the most committed of Reform Zionists. Zion must be rebuilt for European Jews, he had insisted; but "the American Jew longs for no Palestine. He gives his individual allegiance to this land which alone can satisfy his very passion for liberty in conviction and freedom of soul." Yet at a time when the Zionist movement was struggling to be born in the United States ("we have a hard, up-hill fight for Zionism in this country," he conceded), Wise participated in the founding convention of the Federation of American Zionists. He was elected secretary and selected as one of three delegates to Basle, perhaps at the instigation of Federation president Richard Gottheil, his Columbia professor. But there is no question that Herzl inspired Wise to deepen his dedication to the Zionist cause. Within a year, Wise proudly reported to Herzl, his "commander-in-chief," that "the movement is progressing very favorably . . . despite the sharp opposition of the anti-Zionists, and the lethargy and indifference of the well-to-do American Jews."[5]

In the flush of his early enthusiasm, Wise was an active speaker and writer on behalf of the Zionist cause. His rhetorical powers were evident; his was "a voice that . . . stirred the emotions." But the durability of his commitment was less certain; within little more than a year, perhaps in exasperation with the intramural squabbling that was one of the distinguishing features of the movement, he had resigned his secretarial post. His relocation to Portland, Oregon, removed him from the center of Zionist activities in New York; once Wise discoverd how little his opinions mattered to the European Zionists, he was furious and withdrew even further. "I cannot and will not work with men who refuse to place in me their fullest confidence," he thundered. The refusal of Herzl and his associates to consult with him about American issues was "an indignity to which no gentleman can submit with honor."[6]

Just weeks after Wise's final meeting with his "chief" in Vienna, Herzl died suddenly at the age of forty-four. The news of his death "almost prostrated me," Wise confessed, for it was "so swift, so tragic, so catastrophic"—and so clearly reminiscent of the death of his father eight years earlier. Wise, "sick at heart," could not bring himself to attend Herzl's funeral. Nor did he sustain his Zionist commitment, which lapsed until Brandeis rekindled it a decade later. Caught up in progressive causes in Oregon, determined to emulate the leading Social Gospel ministers of his time by applying the principles of liberal Judaism to public issues, Wise dedicated himself to social justice and interfaith harmony.[7]

Wise's commitments, and the new rabbinical role that they defined, flowed inexorably from the abrogation of Jewish legal authority. Once the structure of Jewish law collapsed, the rabbi— especially the Reform rabbi— was responsive to cues from the larger society. The generation of Reform rabbis who came of age around the turn of the century, led by Wise and Judah Magnes, comprised the first rabbinical cohort whose lives and Jewish values were fully defined within an exclusively American setting. Virtually all of their American predecessors—whether Reform, Conservative, or Orthodox—had been profoundly molded by European Judaism. From Isaac Mayer Wise and Kaufmann Kohler, through Solomon Schechter, to Alexander Kohut and Jacob Joseph, the American rabbinate—whether it rejected, modified, or reformulated traditional Judaism—bore its distinctive imprint.

By the turn of the century, however, the young Reformers had begun to redefine rabbinical commitments in conformity with prevailing American patterns. The rabbi, traditionally the *dayan* (judge) and repository of legal knowledge, now adopted the preaching function of the Christian minister. His leadership authority was bestowed by secular organizations (like the Zionist movement), not the rabbinate. Just as liberal Protestant ministers applied Christian teachings to contemporary social problems. Reform rabbis emulated their model of social activism. Wise and Magnes, who launched their rabbinical careers during the early years of the Progressive era, exemplified the pattern. Both men merged the roles of preacher and reformer, committing themselves to the public issues and liberal causes of their time. Progressive politics, infused with the Social Gospel, defined the public agenda of Reform rabbis.[8]

Wise, for whom a pulpit sermon or a public address defined normal discourse, was perfectly suited to articulate the new rabbinical role. The "rabbi as Progressive" (according to his biographer) fused liberalism and Judaism. Wise attributed that linkage to the contribution of the Hebrew Prophets, with whom he strongly identified. Grateful for a gift of an edition of the Prophets, Wise wrote of his admiration for Micah, who "had laid broad and deep and enduring the ethical foundations of the Jewish church" with his admonition to do justice, love mercy, and walk humbly with God. In prophecy, not in the law code of Maimonides or in the affirmation of the *Sh'ma*, Wise found the "fundamentals" of Judaism.[9]

Wise's rendition of prophecy enabled him to locate his Judaism securely within the dominant secular and religious trends of the era. Wise implicitly accepted the Christian linkage of the Prophets to Jesus; the preaching of Jesus, he wrote, could only be understood as the fulfillment of Micah's prophecy. Wise (strongly attracted to Jesus as a subject of personal study) linked Judaism, through Christianity, to the struggle for social justice in modern America.[10] At his Free Synagogue, established after a sharp disagreement with Louis Marshall over freedom of the pulpit at Temple Emanu-El deprived him of that position, Wise institutionalized his vision. Wise's sermon was always the highlight of the service, held on Sunday mornings before overflow audiences at Carnegie Hall. Preaching gave him "the only means of uttering my soul on great causes in the spirit and freedom of truth." Except for Wise's oratorical passion, as he cited prophetic authority for the resolution of some current social issue, the service was decorous, even sonorous, with little identifiable Jewish content. Cyrus Adler once complained to Schechter that "the services consist of saying Kaddish. The rest of the time was occupied by Wise's speech and a quartet."[11]

The most conspicuous omission was the Torah, which Wise relegated to secondary status, literally and symbolically. Often it was not even visible, which prompted a prominent New York rabbi to rebuke Wise for the striking omission. "That is our flag," Rabbi H. Pereira Mendes wrote; it enabled everyone to see "what it is that has held us together all these centuries." "An American meeting should have the American flag," he concluded; "but a Jewish service should surely have the Sefer [Torah]." But the authority of Torah, the distinctive symbol of Jewish sacred law and history, interfered with what critics complained was Wise's "ministry to the gentiles." So he abandoned it, preferring always to preach to the largest, most inclusive, audience. Appropriately, Wise's most cogent statement of his Judaism came in an article that he published in *Christian Century*. That surely helps to explain why Wise enjoyed such enormous popularity, within and outside the Jewish community. He did far more than any rabbi of his time to stake out common ground between Judaism, Christianity, and American liberalism.[12]

That might make Wise's commitment to Zionism seem all the more anomalous, since the potential conflict between Jewish nationalism and American patriotism left so many American Jews uneasy. But it was no accident that Reform rabbis—Gustav Gottheil among the older generation and Wise and Magnes among the younger—were conspicuous in the American Zionist movement. As Reform Jews, they were determined to dilute the particularistic national content of Zionism with an infusion of American liberalism that would enhance its appeal to Jews and Gentiles alike.

Between Herzl's death in 1904 and Brandeis's assumption of Zionist leadership a decade later, Wise was distant from Zionist activities. His first visit to Palestine, in 1913, rekindled his interest. He found Jerusalem "glorious beyond words" (no small concession for someone with Wise's verbal proclivities); and he subsequently conceded that "no man can truly be said to have looked on Jewish life steadily nor to have seen it whole until after having been in the Holy Land." Even at the end of his life, Wise recalled from that Jerusalem visit how "the Jew gave form and color to his environment instead of being formed and colored by it." But Wise, so thoroughly "formed and colored" by his American environment, did not find his way back into the Zionist movement until another charismatic leader pulled him in, precisely as Herzl had done just before the turn of the century.[13]

Brandeis, Wise wrote rhapsodically, was "our leader and inspiration . . . our guiding spirit and our constant unfailing counselor." He was "an American prophet"—after Herzl "indisputably and incomparably our greatest Jew"—who inspired in Wise the feeling of being drawn "nearer to the sources of truth and justice." Like Herzl (who resembled an "ancient monarch"), Brandeis (who possessed "the genius of prophecy") tapped deeply personal (and surely filial) sources of identification in Wise. Its depth even troubled Wise, who characterized his loyalty to Brandeis as "the loyalty of self-forgetting friendship," in which Wise asked nothing yet gave everything. Wise made the sacrifice willingly, for Brandeis, the symbol of liberal rectitude, tapped his yearning to identify Judaism with American values. As Wise frequently observed, "there is nothing incompatible between liberal Judaism and Zionism." Once Brandeis added that "Zionism was Americanism," the circle was complete.[14]

Inspired by Brandeis, Wise worked tirelessly for the Zionist cause. The rabbi among lawyers, he was the only member of the inner circle with extensive contacts, and a national reputation, within American Jewry. Wise became the public voice of American Zionism, serving as a dedicated lobbyist for its program in Washington and at the Paris Peace Conference. But American Zionism always was defined by its insistence that Zionism was a solution for other Jews, not for Americans. Wise, like Brandeis, carved out time for Zionism among the plethora of other public activities that engaged his attention, but it never could be an exclusive commitment. Wise shared Brandeis's constricted vision of Zionist objectives. "We are all agreed that the desire is not an independent Jewish state," Wise wrote shortly before the Balfour Declaration was issued. For Wise, a British Protectorate—"a Jewish commonwealth in Palestine under the British flag"—defined "the ideal solution of the Zionist question." As he subsequently explained: "Certainly the recreation of a Jewish nationality (even if it were possible) is not carrying out the ideas of prophetic Judaism."[15]

Wise's preference for a "non-political" Zionism was consistent with his overriding commitment to American liberalism. Writing from Paris in 1919, he declared his support for Zionist claims "because the things that we want are things that America wants and things that are dictated by the spirit of democracy." He invested considerable energy refuting the claims of anti-Zionists, especially among wealthy German Jews and at the Hebrew Union College, that Zionism and Americanism were incompatible. That could hardly be true if, as Wise so passionately believed, Zionism was merely the Jewish expression of American democratic values, a modern restatement of the prophetic striving for social justice.[16]

Perhaps the nature of Wise's definition of Zionism accounts for the tenuousness of his early attachment to it. If Zionism merely was progressivism with a Jewish accent, then competing liberal causes must invariably exert their claims. American liberalism, not Jewish nationalism, ultimately defined the American Zionist commitment. For Wise, there always was an additional destabilizing factor in his Zionist allegiance: his intense personal attachments to Herzl and Brandeis. They both were assimilated Jews, precisely the sort of leaders (as Ahad Ha-'Am had written about Herzl) who were "spiritually far removed from Judaism." Wise's highly personalized commitments to them left him vulnerable. Once his "chief" was removed from Zionist affairs, Wise himself drifted away. Furthermore, he was inordinately susceptible to feelings of personal betrayal, which twice led to his estrangement from the Zionist movement.

In 1920 (as in 1904) Wise, frustrated by personal slights, resigned from the Zionist organization—reconsidering his decision only at Brandeis's personal urging. But the widening schism between the Weizmann and Brandeis wings of the Zionist movement, and the defeat of the Americans in 1921, led once again to Wise's departure. Along with the entire Brandeis circle, he resigned from a movement that demanded far more of the American leadership than it could ever give. For more than a decade he channeled his efforts elsewhere. Although Wise never completely cut himself off from Zionist affairs, he was unwilling (or unable) to deepen his involvement without committing himself to a magnetic leader. When the reins of leadership were offered to him in 1928, he declined to accept them. He was not "a free man," he explained, "able to put everything aside and to give all to the battle."[17]

Five years later, however, Wise decisively asserted himself in the desperate struggle to save Jews from Nazism. No American Jew was quicker to perceive the menace of Adolph Hitler; none did more to publicize it, decry it, and rally Americans to protest against it. For his unceasing efforts, especially during the period of Hitler's accession to power in Germany, Wise amply deserves the accolade bestowed by his biographer: "a solitary voice crying out in the wilderness against the madness which otherwise sane and sensitive people chose to ignore or dismiss."[18]

But the pattern of Wise's responses, which shaped his role as the preeminent leader of American Jewry until the end of World War II, is far more complex than that. Wise's early boldness and courage ultimately was severely constrained—indeed tragically undercut—by his own persistent deference to powerful leaders. The arc of Wise's personal attachments, from 1898 until World War II, bent unerringly toward heroic public figures—and to men whose ascent to power made them progressively less committed to Jewish concerns. From Herzl to Brandeis and then, most fatefully, to Franklin D. Roosevelt, Wise was drawn into the orbit of priorities set by his heroic models. The president, of course, was the ultimate "chief"; and Wise's faithful allegiance, long after Roosevelt's indifference to the plight of the Jews had become tragically evident, was the fatal flaw in his Zionist leadership.

Wise's strong attraction to Roosevelt, by the war years, is even more intriguing when it is contrasted with his earlier sharp personal criticism, not only before Roosevelt was elected president but also throughout his first term. Wise complained to Frankfurter, after Roosevelt's 1932 nomination, "There is no basic stuff in the man. There are no deep-seated convictions. . . . He is all clay and no granite." Nothing in Wise's early encounters with the new president led him to revise his judgment. Indeed, the more alertly that Wise detected the menace of fascism, and the more energetically he committed himself to oppose it, the more understandably frustrated he became with Roosevelt's aloofness and indifference.[19]

Wise's initial attempts to engage Roosevelt's concern for the plight of German Jewry were thwarted by the president's circle of legal advisors—especially by Brandeis and Frankfurter. The situation in Germany, Wise knew as early as March 1933, was "rotten"; but it was unclear whether Roosevelt, beset by the problems of a devastated economy at home, should be troubled by such remote events. Wise hesitated to "add to his terrible cares," especially once Brandeis indicated that "it would make a bad impression on Roosevelt, in the midst of his overwhelming responsibilities, Felix [Frankfurter] assenting, . . . to trouble him with our, in a sense, lesser problems." For some weeks, Wise followed Brandeis's advice "in not trying to gain access to F.D.R."; when he finally telephoned the White House, Louis Howe, Roosevelt's faithful assistant, told Wise that it would be a "mistake" to schedule an appointment with the president.[20] So the fateful pattern was set in the first month of Roosevelt's presidency; the Jewish problem, defined as a "lesser problem," could not be permitted—even by Jews—to intrude upon the presidential agenda.

But Wise, suffering through "days and nights of hell" as he contemplated "our awful responsibility," could not remain silent. Responding to the German announcement of a boycott of Jewish business, Wise demanded retaliation and organized a massive protest meeting in Madison Square Garden to rally support for a reciprocal American boycott of German products. Despite "hideous" pressure to desist from the assimilated German Jewish leaders of the American Jewish Committee who were terrified of calling attention to themselves as Jews, Wise would not relent. "Silence is acquiescence," he explained to Mack; "We must speak out," he insisted. "If that is unavailing, at least we shall have spoken."[21] Wise, more than anyone, knew the power of speech—especially his own.

The Madison Square Garden protest attracted more than fifty thousand people and a national radio audience. Wise delivered the keynote speech, which he tried to make "as prudent and cautious" as possible lest

Nazi wrath fall even more harshly upon the Jews of Germany. To read it now, from the brutal benefit of hindsight, is to sense the enormity of Wise's dilemma: he was determined to activate the silent Jews, while preserving "the high and classic tradition of Jewish forbearance." It was, of course, impossible to do both. Wise strongly condemned those Jewish leaders in Germany (and, perhaps, by implication, their American counterparts) whose "uncomplaining assent and . . . super-cautious silence has borne evil fruit." But his commitment to "Jewish forbearance" left him with no choice but to appeal to "the conscience of Christendom to save civilization from the shame that may be imminent."[22]

As boldly as Wise acted, his words—public and private— revealed his apprehension and his underlying caution. Until virtually the eve of the Garden rally (with Brandeis's concurrence), Wise was willing to permit Hitler to "determine the tone of the meeting provided we could get from him an authoritatively reassuring message." The initial decision of NBC to carry only an hour of the proceedings prompted Wise to schedule two Catholic bishops, along with prominent Catholic politicians, Senator Robert Wagner and former Governor Alfred E. Smith, for the national broadcast time. "We put only Christian speakers on the air," he noted (although NBC, deciding to expand its coverage, had also broadcast Wise's address). He wrote with evident pride, a week later, that "the self-restraint of American Jews has been extraordinary and indeed most admirable."[23]

Yet what is most striking about the Madison Square Garden rally was its dramatic impact: within a week, the Nazi government, clearly concerned about American economic retaliation, cancelled its boycott of Jewish products. Hitler had indeed capitulated, at least momentarily, to external pressure. For Wise, who had condemned the "evil fruit" of silence, insisting that "we must speak out," the consequence of vigorous protest must have been immensely gratifying.

Wise fully grasped the enormity of the horror that was welling up in Germany. With terrifying prescience he understood, as early as April 1933, that "it is a war of extermination that Hitler is waging." Learning of Nazi restrictive quotas and the exclusion of Jews from professional positions, Wise knew that he was "looking into the deeps of hell." He was infuriated by the "timid and fearful German-Jews both in Germany and America at my heels to desist." He anticipated that the Nazi pattern might well become "a world-wide undertaking against the Jews," which ultimately might even tap the "deep and strong" sources of American anti-Semitism. And he knew that President Roosevelt "has not by a single word or act intimated the faintest interest in what is going on."[24]

Yet within a month of the Madison Square Garden protest, at the very pinnacle of his influence, Wise lapsed into his familiar pattern of deferential caution. Once he learned (from Frankfurter) that Roosevelt "had spoken in the friendliest terms of me and had understood how hard I had worked in order to prevent his being unduly rushed," Wise became exceedingly compliant. He complained about being in the "terrible position of seeming to do nothing about Washington," but he accepted the constraints of inactivity "on what, from the American point of view, is a lesser matter." Wise reflected, "Perhaps at the head of this job . . . there should be one who feels that nothing else matters and who is ready to smash through all barriers. I wonder." But he continued to defer to Brandeis. He imagined that half an hour of conversation between the justice, the president, and the secretary of state, could "bring the impact of [Brandeis's] mighty understanding and that mighty conscience upon their souls," and "something could be done." Wise truly believed that Brandeis should leave the bench, "to give himself to the leadership of his people who need him as they have never needed him before." But there is no evidence that Brandeis seriously considered the possibility: indeed, he declined even to accede to Wise's "mild request" that he speak out publicly. Wise, as always, acquiesced; "at every step," he conceded, "I am guided by his counsel which is wisdom itself."[25]

Increasingly, Wise felt "guilty" acting to restrain public pressure on the president. But he found it impossible to penetrate the coterie of lawyers surrounding Roosevelt who counseled delay. After a meeting in Washington, when Brandeis, Ben Cohen, and Frankfurter acquiesced in the advice of caution from Joseph M. Proskauer (a New York corporate lawyer who was a rising star within the American Jewish Committee), Wise commented bitterly on "the legal jargon which apparently is so impressive even to great legists." He remained unsparing in his criticism of Roosevelt, for being "immovable, incurable and even inaccessible excepting to those of his Jewish friends whom he can safely trust not to trouble him with any Jewish problems." (Wise had in mind Treasury Secretary Morgenthau and Bernard Baruch, perennial counselor to presidents.) Roosevelt, he knew, "has not lifted a finger on behalf of the Jews of Germany." But as Wise clearly understood, Roosevelt was not the problem. "I wonder how much we have gained," he asked plaintively, "by walking warily, by being afraid to be ourselves, by constantly looking over our shoulders to see what impression we make upon others." He predicted that "if we are done in the end, it will not merely be because of the effectiveness of our foes but because of the timidity and cowardice of ourselves."[26]

Through Roosevelt's first presidential term, Wise retained his independence and his effectiveness. After the outbreak of the Arab riots in Palestine in 1936, Wise repeated the success of his earlier protest. Disregarding Frankfurter's (predictable) counsel of silence, Wise—by then the president of the Zionist Organization of America—appealed directly to Roosevelt to exert pressure on the British government, not only to protect

Jewish lives during the emergency but also to sustain existing levels of Jewish immigration. Roosevelt acceded to Wise's request. Whether or not the president's intervention was decisive (there was also considerable opposition to immigration restriction within the British Parliament), Great Britain agreed to retain current immigration levels—a policy decision that permitted tens of thousands of Jewish refugees to enter Palestine before draconian restrictions were imposed three years later. By then, Wise surely "stood as the pre-eminent Jew in America, and his contacts with those in power had wrought great things."[27]

But the attraction to power, especially to the power of the president of the United States, began to undermine Wise's effectiveness precisely when he had attained his maximum influence. Roosevelt's overwhelming electoral triumph in 1936 was the decisive turning point. Very soon thereafter, Wise reported that the two men had resolved their long-standing political disagreements; Roosevelt, he proclaimed, was "a warm and understanding friend." Within a year, Wise referred to the president as "the All Highest." By 1939, in a vain effort to secure presidential opposition to the forthcoming British White Paper, Wise informed Roosevelt that "it had been rare indeed throughout the forty centuries of Jewish history that we have turned to the head of a great Government with the confidence with which you have given us fullest reason to turn to you." Wise's confidence was dangerously misplaced, for Roosevelt did nothing. By the presidential campaign of 1940, Wise's judgment had seriously faltered. Noting State Department obstruction of efforts to admit political refugees, Wise insisted that Roosevelt's reelection was far more important "than the admission of a few people, however imminent be their peril." Inexorably drawn to what he had earlier defined as the "American point of view," which required that Jewish concerns be treated as a "lesser matter," Wise sacrificed his independence and soon would lose his influence.[28]

Wise's deepening deference to Roosevelt was accompanied by his increased dependence upon Brandeis. The Justice's insulated detachment from Jewish affairs in no way impeded Wise's attentiveness to his wishes. Despite their lingering differences, and Wise's frustration with his own posture of supplication, the pattern persisted. Wise always overcame his disappointment with Brandeis's judgment concerning issues of critical import to European and Palestinian Jewry. "I did his will, whatever it was," he confessed to Frankfurter—opposing the Peel partition plan, fighting Chaim Weizmann (toward whom Brandeis harbored deep feelings of personal distrust)—because Wise was "under the spell of L.D.B.'s utter integrity." By 1936, Wise was referring reverentially to Brandeis in his correspondence as "Him"; the man of "sanity, soundness, clarity, nobleness," who (with Mack) had become Wise's "Zionist conscience." The original Brandeis coterie—Mack, Frankfurter, Szold, Cohen, and Wise—still retained its influence as the shadow government in American Zionist affairs. Wise acknowledged, in a letter to Szold, "I am willing to defer to your judgment and that of L.D.B. And Felix." At the apex of his leadership, Wise had become the deferential follower of those who would not lead.[29]

For Wise, as for so many American Jews of his era, Brandeis and Roosevelt symbolized, in complementary ways, the extraordinary blessings of American citizenship. Brandeis, Wise believed, "is what an American Jew ought to be—a Democrat, a liberal, with his life integrated into, as it is dominated by, the spirit of American democracy." As for Roosevelt, Jews "rightly look up to him, revere him and love him as an exemplar of that truly just and American spirit which abhors intolerance and feels that Jews have their rightful place of service and honor within the American polity." Wise likened that attachment to a "feeling of Jewish homage before a sovereign and liberating spirit."[30]

Brandeis and Roosevelt gratified Wise's consuming need for a Jewish identity that was fully compatible with American patriotism. Brandeis symbolized the attachment of democratic liberalism to Jewish tradition—with the Hebrew Prophets, of course, as the connecting link. Roosevelt was the caring national father, the sovereign leader, whose benevolence enveloped his Jewish subjects. Together, they enabled Wise to experience "the most perfect concord" between Judaism and Americanism. "My Jewishness strengthens my Americanism," he declared in a paraphrase of the familiar Brandeis formula; "my Americanism deepens my Jewishness." For Wise, as for so many Jewish immigrants and their children, that integration was fundamental. "I could not speak of myself as an American who is a Jew," Wise wrote in 1939. "I am an American Jew . . . I am of the American nation, and an American citizen; and there is no conflict between my Jewish race and faith and my American citizenship, of which I am most proud."[31]

Had the reconciliation between Judaism and Americanism been as comfortable as Wise asserted, he would hardly have needed to proclaim it so fervently or frequently (even as he neared the age of seventy). "I am doubly an American, because I am foreign-born," Wise declared in the summer of 1942, adding, "I thank God that my parents brought me to this country." The timing of his pronouncements suggests that Wise was less persuaded by the "perfect concord" between Jewishness and Americanism than he claimed. To the contrary: World War II, and the alarming chasm between the policy of the Roosevelt administration and the desperate needs of European Jewry, placed Wise in a situation of tormenting conflict. The more acutely he experienced it, the more desperately he tried to submerge it. Wise claimed to be "doubly an American" precisely when his government was doing nothing for his people. Perhaps the assertion enabled him to combat the overwhelming, and irreconcilable, demands that being an American and a Jew placed upon him.[32]

Wise's behavior during World War II is likely to remain the most vigorously debated issue of his life, because of his role "at the very heart of the bitter controversy concerning American Jewry during the Holocaust." The haunting question remains: Could American Jews (with Wise as their acknowledged spokesman) have done more—more to save European Jewry or, at the very least, more to protest their annihilation? Hitler's Final Solution, Haskell Lookstein has written, "may have been *unstoppable* by American Jewry, but it should have been *unbearable* for them. And it wasn't."[33]

The single most critical episode for Wise occurred in 1942. In August, Dr. Gerhard Riegner of the American Jewish Congress in Switzerland gave to the American vice-consul in Geneva a memorandum for the American government documenting the Nazi plan to exterminate the Jews of Europe. State Department officials in Washington dismissed Riegner's information as "wild rumor inspired by Jewish fears" and spurned Riegner's request to forward it to Wise. Three weeks later, however, Wise received the Riegner information from an English source. After consultation with other Jewish leaders, Wise chose to contact the American government—specifically Under Secretary of State Sumner Welles. In early September Welles informed him that it was the understanding of the State Department that Jews who were being deported would be put to work, not death. He asked Wise not to publicize the Riegner information until the State Department could verify it. Wise complied.[34]

One week later, Wise met in Washington with State Department officials and Vice President Wallace, sharing his information with them. Welles promised to press the American chief of mission in Switzerland for corroboration. Finally, on November 23rd, three months after receipt of the Riegner telegram, Welles called Wise to Washington to confirm its contents. The next day Wise summoned the press and publicized the evidence that four million Jews were "on the verge of complete annihilation." On December 8th, Wise and other Jewish leaders met with Roosevelt, just a few days after Wise had reminded the president, "I have had cables and underground advices for some months, telling of these things. I succeeded, together with the heads of other Jewish organizations, in keeping these out of the press." Wise pleaded with the president to "speak a word" to give solace to the Jews. At the meeting, Roosevelt assured them that "every step" would be taken by the Allied nations to end the slaughter of Jews. But Roosevelt neither spoke nor acted—other than to join the British government in a statement condemning the Nazi killings. For more than another year the Roosevelt administration did nothing to assist refugees from Nazism. "By that time," as Walter Laqueur noted, "most of the Jews in Europe were dead."[35]

Wise's defenders have vigorously exonerated him, insisting that the political weakness of American Jews (like Jews everywhere) rendered effective action impossible. Conceding that Wise and his followers achieved little, they claim that little could have been done to deflect administration priorities from winning the war to saving Jewish lives. "American Jewry was far from silent and passive," Melvyn Urofsky, Wise's biographer maintains, "but it was powerless." Nothing it could have done would have helped the Jews of Europe; even protest "would have accomplished little." With so little to show for their efforts, "we have no reason to assume that doing more would have been any more efficacious." The blunt fact was that "Wise and his fellow Jewish leaders . . . did not have the power to change Roosevelt's policy."[36]

The central issue, as Henry Feingold has insisted, was "what was realistically possible." Given the fanatical Nazi determination to exterminate Jews, and the Allied priority on winning the war, there was little that American Jewry could do. At worst, it naively believed in "a spirit of civilization whose moral concern could be mobilized to save the Jews"; but it can hardly be castigated for its "failure to arouse and mobilize" a nonexistent moral concern. Therefore, any indictment of Wise specifically, or American Jewry generally, must be dismissed for it "cannot produce authentic history."[37]

But authentic history must ask the right questions. The issue is not whether it was "realistically possible" to expect that Wise, or the American Jewish community, could reverse the Roosevelt administration's refugee exclusion policy, alter its wartime priorities, commit it to bombing the railroad lines to the Auschwitz death camps, or even prod it to issue a press release on any or all of these matters. Of course it was not "realistic" to expect the Roosevelt administration to do anything to save Jews. The issue is whether it was "realistically possible" to expect Wise, as the preeminent leader of American Jewry, with his unrivaled eloquence and passion, to speak out—to shatter the American wall of silence. Jews can hardly be blamed for their failure to arouse the "conscience" of civilization, which did not exist. But Wise cannot so easily be exonerated for his silence in deference to State Department wishes; nor, as he reminded Roosevelt, for his successful suppression of the information about the Holocaust. It was not, in the end, an issue of power, but of courage—and the lingering question is why Wise could not lead, and why his followers were so docile? American Jews were indeed powerless to save European Jewry, but they surely were *not* powerless to protest the Final Solution, or the silent acquiescence of the Roosevelt administration in the Holocaust.

No fair assessment can be extracted from the superior wisdom of hindsight. It must be located in the values that Wise himself embraced and defended. In 1942 the issue was hardly new to him. He had confronted it, directly and courageously, nine years earlier at the time of the Madison

Square Garden rally against the Nazi boycott. It had not been an easy decision; it had given Wise "days and nights of hell for I am mindful of our awful responsibility." But he had correctly identified the choice: silence or protest; and he had then understood that "silence is acquiescence." Wise agonized over "the very, very lamentable thing of crying out against the President"— but he had cried out, and his cries were heard, even in Germany.[38] Those who justifiably praise Wise for his uncommon prescience in 1933, and for the prophetic power and courageous utterance of his public jeremiads, do not contribute to the writing of authentic history when they exonerate Wise for his deferential silence nine years later.

How, then, can Wise's fateful shift be explained? To be sure, Wise was nearing seventy, beset by serious health problems. But there is no evidence of his diminished vigor during the war years; only of his diminished independence. And that was not attributable to any physical malady. Rather it was the recurrence, in its most acute form, of Wise's persistent deference to powerful leaders at the expense of his own deeply cherished principles. His determined pacifism during the early years of World War I had quickly dissipated after Woodrow Wilson's reelection in 1916 (a "turnabout," his biographer concedes, that "was not one of Stephen Wise's finer moments"). So, too, his Zionist priorities had been overwhelmed by his awe of Brandeis. Not only did the pattern hold with Roosevelt; it intensified. The president's electoral triumphs in 1936 and 1940 exerted a magnetic attraction upon Wise, pulling him from critical independence to sycophancy.[39]

There could have been no doubt in Wise's mind, by June 1941, that Roosevelt would not act. Responding to Wise's flattering assurance that "we rely upon you as upon no one else to lend us your saving help in this time of crisis" (over the defense of Palestinian Jewry), Roosevelt—in a letter quite rare for its length and substantive content—palpably distanced himself from Jewish concerns. Palestine was a "British" problem, the president replied; furthermore, given "a far larger number of Arabs" there, the British must attend to Arab needs (disregarding Arab flirtations with Hitler); therefore, the administration could only advise England of its "deep interest . . . and our concern" for the plight of Jews.[40]

Wise did not misread the message. In September 1942, while maintaining his silence about Hitler's Final Solution, he confided to Frankfurter, "I don't know whether I am getting to be a *Hofjude* [court Jew], but I find that a good part of my work is to explain to my fellow Jews why our government cannot do all the things asked or expected of it." Even three months later, when news of what Wise called "the most overwhelming disaster of Jewish history," the extermination of at least two million Jews, was public knowledge (and surely known to Roosevelt), Wise assured the president, "I do not wish to add an atom to the awful burden which you are bearing."

But would it be possible, Wise implored, for Roosevelt to provide a word of solace to Jews in their time of mourning? In February 1943 he finally exploded (to his son): "If only [Roosevelt] would do something for my people!" By then it was too late for Roosevelt to act, or for Wise to speak out effectively.[41]

It is important that the psychological dimension of Wise's deference, like Frankfurter's, be securely located within the larger framework of American Jewish acculturation. For nearly a century, by World War II, the fundamental component of American Jewish identity, articulated by rabbis and lawyers alike, was the inherent compatibility of Judaism with Americanism. During World War II, the inconceivable occurred: what was good for the United States was not good for the Jews; what was urgent for the Jews was a matter of insignificance to the American government and to the president.

Once the inconceivable happened, American Jews who had accepted the acculturation bargain were paralyzed. "Forceful and public assertions of special Jewish requirements in the midst of a world war," as one historian has observed, "might have made Jewish loyalty to America suspect." Wise and Frankfurter, the two most prominent and powerful American Jews during the war years, succumbed to the loyalty dilemma: Frankfurter in his flag-salute opinions and in his restrained communications with Roosevelt about Jewish issues; Wise with his silence during 1942 and his lingering inability to criticize Roosevelt's indifference to Jewish concerns. (They were not the only ones: Samuel Rosenman, Roosevelt's adviser, and Henry Morgenthau, Jr., the secretary of the treasury, also did not press the issue. And Ben Cohen, long active in the Zionist movement and a member of the inner circle of Roosevelt advisers, could only offer this retrospective observation about American refugee policy: in war, "some will suffer more than others. . . . We live in an imperfect world.") The only role left to them, as Wise painfully understood, was the role of court Jew. The president's iron grip upon their allegiance demanded complicity through silence in the abandonment of European Jewry.[42]

Wise's faith in Roosevelt never wavered. His identification of Judaism with American liberal values left him with no alternative but to acquiesce in presidential indifference. But Wise's unrequited loyalty substantially weakened his leadership; even within the Zionist movement, he confronted serious challenges. In desperation, Zionists who were impeded by his paralyzing attachment to Roosevelt, and all that it symbolized, abandoned moderation for militancy. Perhaps the most remarkable feature of that challenge was the bitter criticism that it elicited from the established Jewish leadership, echoed in recent years by historians who have restated the familiar platitudes about the unity of Judaism and Americanism.

During 1939–40, a small group of Palestinian Jews, Revisionist Zionists who belonged to the Irgun (the underground movement soon to be led by Menachem Begin), arrived in the United States. Led by Hillel Kook, nephew of the Chief Rabbi of Palestine during the mandatory period, they demanded action. Their agenda, which gave priority to Jewish issues, frightened and angered the established American leadership. The Bergsonites, as they were called (Kook, in the United States, was known as Peter Bergson), demanded anti-Nazi protests, vigorous rescue efforts, the establishment of a Jewish army, and the creation of a Jewish state.

American Jewish leaders were outraged. Their opposition usually was stated in procedural terms: the Bergsonites were irresponsible interlopers, without any mandate from American Jewry, who were disrupting Zionist unity in pursuit of their own misguided objectives. Wise rejected their program, his biographer maintains, because their "pyrotechnics" demonstrated a "frantic and self-serving search for attention" that "did much to weaken the unity necessary for the American Jewish community to exert any leverage on the government or on public opinion." Quite properly, nothing was more important to Wise than American Jewish "solidarity."[43]

The real issue posed by the Bergsonites, however, was not solidarity, but substance. Their persistence, even flamboyance, and consequent divisiveness can hardly be disputed. And it is undeniably true that they achieved "scant success"—in part, of course, because the American government (as Wise himself knew so well) was indifferent; and in part, surely, because Jewish leaders were so hostile. But Wise's preference for solidarity at any price assured the perpetuation of the existing leadership and its policies, which the Bergsonites understood to be part of the problem, not a solution. Wise criticized the Bergsonites for working outside the American Zionist consensus. By 1942, however, they understood that the Zionist consensus was an altogether inadequate response to a horrific Jewish calamity. To be sure, their only tangible achievement was noisy publicity. Nothing else was possible. But that was not insignificant (as even Wise had once conceded), given the realities of American Jewish politics at the time. It was an accomplishment for which they incurred the enduring enmity of those who could not deliver an outspoken rebuke to power, or break their own silence.[44]

The more consequential challenge to Wise's leadership erupted within the mainstream Zionist movement. It came from Abba Hillel Silver, like Wise a Reform rabbi and a brilliant orator, who had been an active Zionist since the Brandeis era. As early as 1920, Wise had hailed Silver as "the ablest rabbi in America . . . [who] will do great things for Israel." Like Wise, Silver had left the American Zionist movement when Brandeis's leadership was rejected. Again like Wise, he had returned to wrest purpose and commitment from the diluted Zionism that was the enduring legacy of the partnership between lawyers and philanthropists who dominated Zionist councils. Indeed, the ascendancy of Wise and Silver in the American Zionist movement, from the outbreak of World War II to the birth of Israel, can be understood as an effort by rabbis to reclaim a measure of the communal leadership that had been willingly yielded to Marshall and Brandeis after the turn of the century. Marshall had died in 1929; Brandeis in 1941; Mack, elderly and ailing, did not live out the war years; Frankfurter, without Brandeis to inspire him, had drifted away. The most prominent lawyers who remained actively involved in Jewish politics (Jerome Frank and Joseph M. Proskauer) were militantly anti-Zionist. As lawyers abdicated leadership, Wise and Silver reasserted a measure of rabbinical authority in American Jewish affairs.[45]

Wise's deferential moderation and insistence upon Jewish unity assured Silver's triumph. In 1943, Wise, eager to secure the participation of the anti-Zionist American Jewish Committee (led by Proskauer) in a major Jewish conference, agreed to postpone consideration of Jewish statehood, which in any case was not yet the policy of the American government. "We are Americans," Wise insisted. "Nothing else that we are, whether by faith or race or fate, qualifies our Americanism." Silver rejected Wise's compromise (or surrender). With an impassioned plea for Jewish "national restoration" in Palestine (a subject ignored by Wise in his own address), he wrested the mantle of Zionist leadership from Wise. In a hotel corridor, Silver lashed out at Wise for his silence: "We finally have . . . a battle cry for a Jewish State, and you, who claim to be a Zionist leader, refuse to talk about it."[46]

The breach widened irreparably the following year. Both men worked to secure political support for unrestricted immigration to Palestine and for Jewish statehood. Their efforts climaxed with endorsements from both political parties. After Roosevelt's reelection, Senators Taft (an Ohio Republican with whom Silver, the Cleveland rabbi, maintained close relations) and Wagner (a New York Democrat who cooperated with Wise on Jewish issues) introduced a congressional resolution favoring Jewish statehood. At Roosevelt's urging, however, the State Department persuaded the Senate Foreign Relations Committee to defer action. Silver, who rejected personal entreaties to presidents, argued the issue in public, loudly condemning the failure of the Roosevelt administration to deliver on its campaign promises. Wise, as always, deferred to the president, assuring him that "we would not press for such [a] Resolution unless it had your approval." He condemned Silver's "continued defiance of and attacks upon the President." Roosevelt, after all, had requested "that we have confidence in him and leave our problem in his hands for a little while longer." Silver, Wise believed, had used "extremely bad judgement," which ended his usefulness as a Zionist spokesman.[47]

In fact, it was Wise's usefulness that had ended. Silver had become the acknowledged leader and spokesman of American Zionism. For Wise (and his defenders), the issue was a conflict between Silver's "authoritarian attitudes and dictatorial demands" and Wise's "democratic" priorities. But it was hardly that. Rather, the Zionist split and reorganization under Silver's leadership marked the recognition that misguided faith in princes (and presidents) had frozen the movement in the paralyzing mold of Wise's supplications. Wise, Felix Frankfurter had written in tribute for his seventieth birthday (in 1944), "has shown that a Jew can be as passionate an American as any descendant of those who first landed at Plymouth or at Jamestown."[48] That was indeed the source of Wise's great strength as an American Zionist leader. It was, simultaneously, his fatal weakness.

Loyalty to the United States, Wise's biographer concluded, "constituted the bedrock upon which he built his ministry and his life." Believing fervently that "the ethical teachings of the ancient Hebrew prophets merged with the Jeffersonian ideals of an egalitarian society," Wise insisted that "the destinies of the Jewish people and of the United States were inextricably intertwined." Indeed, there was "perfect concord" between Judaism and Americanism; they were, Wise believed, mutually strengthening.[49] There can be no question that Wise exemplified this faith; but nor can it be denied that in the end it destroyed his effectiveness as a leader.

Wise, the most devoted of Brandeis's disciples, had channeled his Zionism into good Americanism with such fervent patriotism that he undermined his own ability to represent Zionist interests. For half a century, the leaders of American Jewry, whether or not they were Zionists, had wagered everything on the proposition that Judaism and Americanism were fully compatible. Indeed, their insistence upon it accounts for their elevation to leadership. American-Jewish compatibility was the only formulation of Judaism that American Jews could tolerate. As long as the historical incongruities between the Jewish and American traditions—whether expressed in religious, legal, or nationalistic forms—could be suppressed, the formula was persuasive.

But by 1938, at the latest, the compatibility synthesis was shattered by events in Europe. The murderous Nazi ferocity toward Jews, and the policy of "American appeasement" toward Nazi Germany, forced American Jews into the very quandary that the Brandeis formula had been designed to obliterate. It is to Wise's enduring credit that he foresaw the terrifying danger that Hitler posed for world Jewry and that he issued impassioned warnings and denunciations while so many other prominent American Jews cowered in silence. But in the end Wise, too, had to be a "good American"—even as Americanism contradicted what it meant to be a "good Jew." The president of the United States, as Roosevelt demonstrated so frequently, protected American, not Jewish, interests—which might be not only incompatible but also contradictory.[50]

The formula that Wise inherited from Brandeis posited the fulfillment of Judaism in Americanism. It assured the paralysis of American Jews once American and Jewish interests diverged. While the Holocaust raged, American Jews were little more than passive spectators. The terms of acculturation, which Wise synthesized from Reform Judaism, the Christian Social Gospel, political liberalism, and Brandeisian Zionism, required nothing less.

The concluding episode in the prolonged struggle of rabbis and lawyers to define the normative values of American Judaism was the struggle over Jewish statehood. What was, in Palestine, a Jewish war for independence, became in the United States an internecine conflict between Jews. The Zionist movement, between 1942 and 1948, conducted an intramural debate over strategy, with Silver's militancy finally overriding Wise's hesitancy. But both men were well within the American Zionist consensus which, by 1943, had come to accept the necessity of a Jewish state.

The more fundamental disagreement was between Zionists and anti-Zionists. It was, in its essence, a disagreement over the political identity of American Jews—precisely the disagreement that every Jewish leader since Rabbi Isaac Mayer Wise had tried to suppress. Zionists and their opponents waged a prolonged struggle to capture the allegiance of American Jewry and to define a position on Jewish statehood that would not compromise the loyalty of Jews to the United States. (At the outer extremes of the debate the Bergsonites, led by the Palestinian Revisionists, and the American Council for Judaism, a rejectionist coalition of Reform rabbis and wealthy businessmen, refused to recognize any competing claims to their exclusively Jewish or American identifications.) But the actual prospect of Jewish statehood created its own imperatives, rendering obsolete the older compromises. As in Ezekiel's vision of the dry bones, depicting the miraculous resurrection of Israel ("I will take the children of Israel from among the nations, . . . and bring them into their own land"), the promise of Jewish national redemption had a transforming power of its own.

Just as Wise and Silver were the last Brandeisians to preside over the Zionist movement, Joseph M. Proskauer was the last disciple of Louis Marshall to lead the opposition to Zionism. Proskauer grew up in a German Jewish family in Mobile, Alabama. He had felt doubly an outsider: as a Jew, he was familiar with the "bloodied noses, both physical and metaphorical," that the Christian majority was empowered to deliver; as a southerner, especially in New York where he attended college and law school, he felt "alien." A Columbia student, around the turn of the century, he was pulled in two directions: to the turbulence of the Lower East Side, where he did volunteer work in the Educational Alliance to assure that Eastern European Jews "were trained in the traditions and ideals of our country"; and to the more refined precincts of the Columbia English department ("as crowded with three-barreled Anglican names," another Jewish youngster recalled some years later, "as the House of Bishops"), where Proskauer absorbed the norms of Anglo-Saxon civility.[51]

Proskauer was drawn to Professor George Edward Woodberry, who taught him English Romantic poetry and guided him through those rites of passage into polite company that so many unpolished but promising Jewish students navigated with the assistance of their cultured Christian instructors. As fervently as Proskauer studied Shelley and Wordsworth, he cherished even more the invitations to Woodberry's home for evenings of civilized conversation, punctuated by sips of brandy, before a log fire. They completed Proskauer's metamorphosis to civility; the provincial Jewish boy from Mobile became, in his mature adulthood, "an elegant Edwardian in style": gourmet, club member, horseback rider, and world traveler in the fashion of "an English milord."[52]

Proskauer paid the standard price for acculturation. With his closest friend, he suffered the ignominy of rejection, as a Jew, from a literary club that Woodberry helped to establish. (Years later, after the invitation was renewed, his friend declined unless the earlier humiliation was expunged; Proskauer unconditionally accepted.) His yearning for acceptance, and apprehension about rejection, was a continuing theme throughout his life. Anglo-Saxon civility offered too much to decline, but never enough for comfort.

Years later, during Al Smith's presidential campaign of 1928, all of Proskauer's apprehensions about "belonging" were reactivated. As a close Smith adviser, he was shocked by widespread allegations that Smith's Catholicism compromised his fidelity to American constitutional principles. Smith, more puzzled than angry, dismissed the claim, insisting that a legalistic debate over the jurisdiction of Papal bulls and encyclicals had nothing to do with his religious faith. Proskauer, however, was deeply disturbed: if a Catholic could not be a loyal American, then neither could a Jew. Not only did he insist that Smith respond; but Proskauer, who drafted the reply, was uncomfortable until both a priest and a cardinal had approved it. Smith never doubted that he could be a "Catholic and Patriot" (the title of his rejoinder); it was Proskauer who most needed the reassurance.

By then, Proskauer was approaching the apex of his distinguished legal career. From a young associate in a successful German Jewish firm (whose senior partner, Abram I. Elkus, parlayed his extensive Tammany Hall connections into a lucrative law practice and an ambassadorship to Turkey), Proskauer had quickly risen to the New York Supreme Court, and then to the Appellate Division. Hitching his star to Smith's political fortunes, he had every expectation of national prominence, surely as solicitor general in a Smith administration, with appointment to the Supreme Court a likely prospect. But it was not to be. Smith's defeat in 1928 closed off those possibilities. In 1929 Proskauer resigned from the bench to resume private practice in an office that quickly established itself as one of the preeminent Jewish Wall Street firms. Professionally fulfilled but politically frustrated, Proskauer increasingly channeled his abundant energy into Jewish communal and philanthropic activities. Not long after Marshall's death, Proskauer began his ascent within the American Jewish Committee. Immersed in American Jewish politics between 1933 and 1948, he was determined to demonstrate (as he later expressed it) that "the Jews of America suffer from no political schizophrenia. . . . We are bone of the bone and flesh of the flesh of America."[53]

On every major issue of Jewish content during those years— public protest against Nazism, a Jewish boycott of German products, Jewish statehood— Proskauer cautiously counseled accommodation to American government policy. Rejecting public Jewish demonstrations against Nazism, he wanted nothing to do with the Madison Square Garden rally of 1933. Proskauer preferred that a prominent Christian, not a Jew, mobilize American opposition. The passion of Al Smith's public denunciation at the rally underscored the irony of Proskauer's silence. Just five years earlier, Proskauer had applauded Smith's condemnation of Ku Klux Klan bigotry; now, while Smith protested the Nazi treatment of Jews, Proskauer remained mute. Encouraged by State Department officials to resist the boycott as an intrusion upon its own policy initiatives, Proskauer condemned it as an "emotional product of a noisy minority." "Our primary obligations as American citizens," Proskauer insisted, left Jews with "no moral right to bind ourselves as a separate group inside the United States," disturbing diplomatic relations between nations. "For Jews in America, *qua* Jews, to demand any kind of political action," he wrote, "is a negation of the fundamentals of American liberty and equality."[54] The tortured logic reflected his inner turmoil: Proskauer asked Jews to accept the status of second-class citizens to earn approbation as first-class Americans.

In the *shtadlan* tradition of quiet intercession with government officials, Proskauer made his views known in Washington. Using his extensive government contacts, he met with Secretary of State Cordell Hull to urge that immigration restrictions be eased; he asked sympathetic senators to speak out against Nazism; he counseled the American ambassador to Germany to protest the persecution of Jews. His political connections made him "especially useful" to the American Jewish Committee, bereft of a substantial Jewish following or significant public influence since Marshall's death.[55]

If public protest had its perils for Proskauer, they were nothing compared to the torments elicited by mounting pressure for Jewish statehood. That issue, more than any other, propelled Proskauer into a leadership position, yet forced him to walk a hazardous emotional tightrope. An assimilated Jew threatened by Zionism, he never lost his need for approval from priests and princes. His role as mediator between the State Department and the wealthy Jewish elite expressed his deeper struggle to forge an integrated personal identity as a Jew who was a loyal American. There is no doubt that Proskauer was shocked by the virulence of Nazi anti-Semitism into the fuller development and deeper appreciation of his own Jewishness. But as fervently as he insisted that American Jews did not suffer from "political schizophrenia," his attitudes toward Jewish statehood revealed the depth of his own inner conflict.

By the outbreak of World War II, Proskauer was the acknowledged leader of the anti-Zionist faction within the American Jewish Committee. "From every point of view of safety for Jews in America," he insisted, "there has got to be an open, vocal Jewish dissent from nationalism and political Zionism." The American public must understand that "the Jew is not a political unit, either nationally or internationally, in Palestine or out of Palestine." A Jewish state, Proskauer firmly believed, would be "a Jewish catastrophe." His ardent anti-Zionism paved the way for his selection as Committee president in 1943.[56]

For the next five years, Proskauer functioned as one of the important American Jewish obstructionists to the creation of a Jewish state. Ever attentive to the attitudes of "right thinking Christians," and to the position of the American government, he assured Under Secretary Welles that the Committee would never act "even remotely at variance with any policy of our government." So, when Abba Hillel Silver made his eloquent demand for statehood at the American Jewish Conference ("There is but one solution for national homelessness. That is a national home"), Proskauer quickly consulted with the State Department and relayed its warning that "it would be a tragedy to put forth this maximal demand." After Proskauer withdrew the Committee from the Conference, his alliance with the State Department was solidified. Both Hull and Welles reassured Proskauer of their appreciation for his loyalty to government policy. Proskauer also enjoyed access to Roosevelt through Samuel Rosenman, who had resigned from the American Jewish Committee when he became a presidential adviser but remained attentive to Proskauer's entreaties.[57]

By 1944, however, there was no longer a unitary government policy. The State Department, responsive to British interests and Arab oil, vigorously opposed Zionist objectives; but Congress and the president were affected by mounting public pressure for a Jewish state. Roosevelt's verbal commitment to the Zionist goal during the presidential campaign, reinforced by strong congressional resolutions of support, activated precisely the conflict that Proskauer was determined to suppress. While Zionists spoke to a growing Jewish majority, Proskauer spoke to the State Department, which was only too happy to retain Jewish allies for its anti-Zionist policy.

Proskauer was caught in the whipsaw between the White House and the State Department (to say nothing of Roosevelt's palpably contradictory statements to Arabs and Jews, and to Zionists and anti-Zionists). He tried desperately to focus attention on the humanitarian issue of Jewish immigration to Palestine rather than the political goal of statehood. In the end, however, Jewish actions in Palestine overrode policy decisions in Washington and Jewish vacillation in New York. When the State Department finally acquiesced in the partition of Palestine, which meant the creation of a Jewish state, Proskauer dropped his opposition. Indeed, he responded with such alacrity to a request for support from Secretary of State Acheson that he embarrassed other Committee leaders with the suddenness of his conversion. A Jewish state might be intolerable to Proskauer, but disagreement with the American government was inconceivable.[58]

When American policy wavered during the waning months of the British mandate, Proskauer echoed its equivocation. Despite his statements of public support for partition, he conceded that his preference still remained "strongly against a Jewish state." As State Department officials struggled to find an alternative to statehood, they found in Proskauer a sympathetic ally. He urged Moshe Shertok, the *de facto* foreign minister of the nascent state, to act in ways that would retain the goodwill of the American government. As late as April 30th, 1948, with a declaration of statehood impending, he pleaded with David Ben-Gurion for "strengthen[ed] public relations" with the State Department, warning him that "you cannot fight the whole world." It was a forlorn, futile last gasp of opposition. Just two weeks later, the State of Israel proclaimed its independence. With immediate American recognition of the new nation, Proskauer's long struggle to reconcile his Judaism and Americanism finally ended. Just as his fear of isolation from American policy had sustained his anti-Zionism, the identical fear now eased his acceptance of a Jewish state. American foreign policy transformed Proskauer into a Zionist. In 1948, for the first time, he could be an American, a Zionist, and a Jew without inner torment.[59]

Zionism had always raised the frightening prospect that Proskauer's Edwardian facade of manners and style, so carefully in place since Columbia College days, might be stripped away to reveal nothing more than—a Jew. He compensated for his vulnerability by identifying with the authority of government and by seeking the approval of Christians for his actions as a Jew. (The dust jacket of his autobiography bore Cardinal Spellman's revealing encomium of Proskauer as "An Apostle of Americanism.") His cozy relationship with the State Department, traditionally the most Anglo-Saxon (and anti-Semitic) enclave in the American government, enabled him to justify his anti-Zionism in patriotic terms. But when even that trusted government ally abandoned its anti-Zionism in 1948, Proskauer no longer had a cause to lead. Yielding to the inevitable, he cultivated praise as a Jewish statesman, returning to his law firm and social clubs (there, ironically, to claim credit for his contributions to the establishment of Israel).[60]

The creation of the State of Israel decisively closed the formative chapter of American Jewish leadership, opened a century earlier with the determined efforts of Isaac Mayer Wise to define a Judaism that was compatible with Americanism. Ever since, leadership in the American Jewish community had depended upon fidelity to that overriding principle. There were, of course, various shadings of emphasis and nuance; but the task never could be evaded. The rabbis, nearly all of whom (both Wises, Kohler, Schechter, and Silver) were born in Europe, were (except for Schechter) drawn to Reform as the denominational expression of that desired compatibility. It is hardly coincidental that Reform rabbis dominated the national leadership positions in American Jewish life, for it was they who most avidly demanded an Americanized Judaism. Strangers to America, they were determined to be at home in the United States.

If the rabbis were stamped by Europe, the lawyers who contested with them for leadership were a generation further along in the process of Americanization. Marshall, Brandeis, and Mack were the children (and Proskauer the grandchild) of German immigrants. They grew up in the American hinterland: Syracuse, Louisville, Cincinnati, Mobile. They all came to Jewish communal affairs (as did Frankfurter, the only immigrant among them) as successful lawyers, who had earned professional distinction long before they turned their attention to Jewish issues. Indeed, it was precisely their success outside the Jewish community that made them so attractive within it, as the Zionist invitation to Brandeis, and the American Jewish Committee welcome to Marshall and Proskauer, demonstrated. As successful Americans, and especially as distinguished lawyers, they had patriotic credentials for leadership that even wealthy bankers (like Jacob Schiff) or Judaic scholars (like Cyrus Adler) did not possess. Just as nineteenth-century lawyers (Daniel Webster and Abraham Lincoln among them) had inherited the political authority that New England ministers (John Winthrop and Cotton Mather) once wielded, so Jewish lawyers took over from rabbis the power to govern Jewish communal affairs and to define the obligations of American Jews to the United States.

Despite their active competition for power, rabbis and lawyers had collaborated in defining a Judaism, whether religious or secular, that was comfortably American. By 1948, that process had run its course. Stephen Wise, Abba Hillel Silver, and Joseph Proskauer participated in the concluding episode, the reconciliation of American Judaism with Zionism and the new Jewish state of Israel. As sharp as their disagreements surely were (exacerbated by the personality clashes of strong-willed individuals), they orbited around shared concerns. Wise and Proskauer battled for Jewish support and avidly pursued Roosevelt's favor, but their disagreements often were moderated by visits to each other's summer homes on opposite sides of their Lake Placid island retreat.[61] Similarly, the bitter contest between Wise and Silver for leadership of the Zionist movement can easily obliterate what those two Reform rabbis shared in common. Their major disagreements, usually more tactical than substantive, more personal than ideological, were located securely within the American Zionist consensus.

But Silver understood, far better than Wise or Proskauer, the imperatives of a militant response to the plight of European Jewry during and after the Holocaust. Jewish national homelessness was the problem; statehood, for Silver, provided the only solution. He had never been unduly troubled by the issue of dual loyalty, which set such clear limits to the advocacy of Wise and Proskauer. Rejecting the "counsel of fear," based upon apprehensions over disloyalty, he demanded a "counsel of faith" derived from the imperatives of Jewish history. The real tragedy of Jews, he had insisted just after World War I, was not the ghetto, or anti-Semitism, or even pogroms, but "the yellow streak which [Jewish] children are compelled to carry within their souls." He had no patience with "timid, cowardly" Jews, or with their counsel of moderation. Silver exerted considerable political leverage because, unlike nearly every other major Jewish leader since the Brandeis era, he retained his independence as a staunch Republican. Unconstrained by allegiance (or subservience) to Roosevelt, he capitalized upon his close relationship to Senator Robert Taft of Ohio, which provided access to Republican leaders and enabled Zionists to exert pressure on both parties for enactment of their program. Depending more upon public opinion than presidential favor, he dismissed "personal intercession" as anachronistic, contemptuously declaring (in 1945), "It is too late for court Jews."[62]

The democratic nations, Silver admonished, had "wagged their heads in sympathy" over the desperate plight of Jews, but they had spoken with "barren legalism . . . of their inability to intervene," while defending their own restrictive immigration laws. American Jews must, therefore, relinquish their "pleasant sense of almost complete identification" as Americans, instead "consciously orienting themselves as Jews in a non-Jewish environment." Sharply rejecting the repeated claims of American Jewish distinctiveness, based upon the exceptional freedom and opportunity that the United States afforded, Silver insisted that "our lives as American Jews have now fallen into the well-known pattern of Israel's millennial experience in Diaspora."[63]

The imminent birth of Israel restored a measure of confident moderation to Silver's public addresses. "The nations of the world" had, after all, validated the Jewish claims to national independence. The new nation surely would blend "social justice and the modern scientific methods" with "prophetic idealism." Life in Israel, Silver predicted, "will be characterized . . . by that same energy, initiative, and inventiveness which have characterized American life." Israel would embody "those same great Biblical ideals of justice, brotherhood and peace which inspired the founding fathers of this Republic." With Israel cast as a replica in miniature of the United States, Silver could confidently assert that the attachment of diaspora Jews to the new Jewish state "will in no way interfere with their duties and obligations as citizens of their respective countries."[64] For Silver, American and Jewish history had finally converged in 1948. American Jews could comfortably embrace the reality of Israel, for it had absorbed the ideals of the Biblical Prophets, relayed through the American Founding Fathers. They could, that is, admire Israel within their own mirror image of themselves.

Whether the new Jewish state would fulfill, or frustrate, the expectations of American Jews lay in the future. The euphoric reconciliation of 1948 was more precarious than it seemed (although an American Jew, paraphrasing Jefferson's words from 1800, might have proclaimed, "We are all Americans, we are all Zionists"). Israel could hardly fail to confront American Jews with their perennially nagging dilemmas of identity and loyalty. Furthermore, the very existence of a Jewish state, however small and vulnerable, decisively tipped the balance of power in world Jewish affairs. After 1948, the crucial decisions, on a wide range of Jewish political, cultural, and religious issues, would be made in Israel, not in the United States. Consequently, American Jewish leaders would pale into insignificance against Israeli prime ministers, generals, and even rabbis. The stature of lawyers like Marshall, Brandeis, and Proskauer—or rabbis like Schechter, Wise, and Silver—could not be replicated once there was a Jewish state. American Jews, for the most part, were fated to respond to Jewish initiatives elsewhere. As attentive spectators as they might be, the privilege of active participation was reserved for Jews who lived in Israel.

The overriding imperative of American Jewish history, the reconciliation of Judaism with Americanism, had assured that outcome. During the formative century of American Jewish life, no one could aspire to, or attain, a national leadership position who did not offer an American definition of what was permissibly Jewish. An American Jewish leader was someone who accommodated Jewish interests to American priorities. The inexorable realities of Jewish life in the diaspora, even in the American promised land, demanded of Jewish leaders (rabbis and lawyers alike) that they be loyal American patriots. After 1948, the remnants of their independent authority, which had been steadily eroded under the pressures of American acculturation, all but vanished.

Epilogue: Since 1948

The creation of the State of Israel marked a miraculous moment in Jewish history. Its Declaration of Independence, proclaimed on 5 Iyar 5708/14 May 1948, recalled that "The Land of Israel was the birthplace of the Jewish people. Here their spiritual, religious and national identity was formed." And here, after nearly two thousand years of exile, and the Holocaust that annihilated one-third of the Jewish people, it was renewed. But amid the affirmations of historical continuity were some unresolved ambiguities: now there were two calendars, Jewish and Christian; the boundaries for "the soil of the homeland" were undefined; and the pledge of trust in "the Rock of Israel" (perhaps God, perhaps not) was ambiguous. But the significance of the moment, a national renewal without historical precedent, was indisputable.[1]

It was a moment that American Jews joyously celebrated. Yet the birth of Israel also complicated their lives as American Jews. Israel posed the choice: American home or Jewish homeland. It was not a choice, then or since, that many American Jews would explicitly confront. (Some forty thousand Jews from the United States have made *aliyah*.) But ideologically, at least, Israel could hardly avoid activating some of the deepest anxieties of American Jews about loyalty: the fear that if their allegiance as Americans and as Jews conflicted, their loyalty to the United States would be suspect. Although myth would have it that American Jews have been impassioned and faithful in their support of Israel, the historical record of forty years suggests a significantly more ambivalent relationship than that. Despite repeated, even euphoric, proclamations of unity (reiterated in the formula "We are One"), it might more accurately be said that the overriding task for American Jews has been to assert their attachment to Israel in ways that would not jeopardize their oneness with the United States.

With their imaginative transformations of Jewish tradition, American Jews had long since found (or placed) in American history and institutions the modern expression of their ancient Jewish heritage. Israel, too, would be quickly absorbed within an American framework—or deemed undeserving of American Jewish support. "We American Zionists know that Zionism is good Americanism," declared the *New Palestine* two weeks after Israeli independence. The new Jewish state, it predicted, would promote "the American ideals of freedom, peace, and prosperity."[2] But, Prime Minister David Ben-Gurion noted at the end of that year, American Zionists still had not adjusted to "the revolutionary fact" of the State of Israel. Perhaps Ben-Gurion was correct: reflexive repetition of the Brandeis formula hardly confronted the new Zionist reality. Yet he may have missed something. ("Possibly . . . I lack a full comprehension of the feelings of an American Jew," he would concede.) American Jews had already adjusted to the reality of Israel by instantly confining it within their American priorities.[3]

Israel, however, had its own overriding imperatives, defined by the urgent need to resist unremitting Arab hostility and absorb hundreds of thousands of Jewish immigrants. Ben-Gurion looked desperately, if forlornly, to the United States for an infusion of Jewish settlers whose youthful energy, scientific training, and managerial experience would aid Israel with its enormous tasks of resettlement and development. In September 1949, according to press reports, he appealed to American parents to send their children to settle in the Jewish state. Even if the parents refused, Ben-Gurion told a *Histadrut* delegation, "we will bring the youth to Israel."

A storm of protest erupted in the American Jewish community, aghast at the prospect that a Jewish pied piper in Tel Aviv would lure their children with the melodic strands of "Hatikvah." American Jewish Committee leaders were especially outraged. With Joseph Proskauer's guidance, they had belatedly made their peace with the idea of a Jewish state. But their accommodation to Zionism was, at best, a marriage of convenience. Ben-Gurion's appeal reawakened old anxieties; any insinuation that American Jews belonged in Israel, or that Israel would encourage American *aliyah*, raised the spectre of dual loyalty that had defined their uneasiness with Zionism since Marshall's day. Ben-Gurion, advised that Proskauer was "fuming," wrote a long, soothing letter in which he tactfully tried to reconcile Zionist principles with American Jewish sensibilities. Not every Jew, he conceded, possessed the "inner moral need" to "live a full Jewish life . . . in the Jewish homeland." Lacking it, a Jew should be permitted "to remain a Jew and live on terms of equality with all others, wherever he may be." A Jew living outside Israel owed "no political or legal allegiance" to the Jewish state. Therefore, "there can be no contradiction between an American Jew's duty to his country and his relation as a Jew to the State of Israel."[4]

The Committee was not mollified. In the summer of 1950 Jacob Blaustein, Proskauer's successor, visited Israel as a guest of the government. After protracted negotiations, befitting the leaders of two sovereign communities, a luncheon was carefully orchestrated in his honor at the King David Hotel in Jerusalem. Ben-Gurion, in a speech expressing his understanding of the proper relationship between American Jews and Israel, said exactly what Blaustein wanted to hear. "As a community and as individuals," Ben-Gurion declared, American Jews were exclusively attached to the United States. The Jewish state respected their right "to develop their own mode of life and their indigenous social, economic and cultural institutions in accordance with their own needs and aspirations." Israel, dependent upon American Jews for financial assistance, was "anxious that nothing should be said or done which would in the slightest degree undermine the sense of security and stability of American Jewry." The decision to emigrate to Israel, Ben-Gurion conceded, "rests with the free discretion of each American Jew."[5]

Blaustein, satisfied with Ben-Gurion's concessions, firmly reminded Israel of its responsibility for "not affecting adversely the sensibilities of Jews who are citizens of other states by what it says or does." American Jews, he noted, "vigorously repudiate any suggestion or implication that they are in exile. . . . To American Jews, America is home." He concluded with a pointed demand for "unmistakable evidence" that in the future Israeli leaders would respect "the feelings and needs" of American Jews. It was an astonishing exchange. Blaustein, representing a private organization with a long history of anti-Zionism, demanded that Israeli policy be constrained by the apprehensions of American Jews. In turn, Ben-Gurion, the Zionist prime minister of a sovereign Jewish state, accepted the American limitations. He relinquished basic Zionist tenets, diaspora nationalism (the national unity of the Jewish people) and *aliyah* (the ingathering of exiles), to conform to the security needs of American Jews—as Americans. The prime minister's concessions, as Blaustein subsequently acknowledged, were necessary to free American Jews "in the minds of other Americans from the serious charge of dual-nationality."[6]

The issue subsided, but never disappeared. Blaustein continued to demand reassurance that Israel would say or do nothing that would "give the impression of creating any dual loyalty on the part of American Jews." Any references to *aliyah* must, therefore, specifically exempt American Jews, "who certainly are not in exile." Ben-Gurion continued to reassure Blaustein that his "apprehensions about dual loyalty are . . . unfounded." By 1951, however, the prime minister's irritation was evident. "As a Zionist," he wrote, "I believe that there is one Jewish People in the world." He wished for the continued prosperity of American Jews, but he remained skeptical of their unbounded optimism regarding their future in the United States. Their protestations of security, amid such abundant evidence of their feelings of insecurity, reminded Ben-Gurion (although he tried to minimize the comparison) of German Jews during the 1930s. He feared that still another Jewish community would follow its own self-delusions to destruction.[7]

The Blaustein–Ben-Gurion accord, actually an American *dictat*, imposed the terms of an acceptable relationship between American Jews and Israel. Ben-Gurion had been forced to concede the fundamental American precept of individual choice, which no conception of Jewish obligation formulated in Israel could be permitted to overcome. American Jews preferred their autonomy, which secured their distance from the Jewish state. For most, during nearly two decades after 1948, Israel flickered only occasionally, and dimly, in their consciousness. If they thought about Israel at all, it was only to reiterate what Israel must do to calm their anxieties in the diaspora. In his classic survey of American Judaism (published in 1957), sociologist Nathan Glazer observed that "the two greatest events in modern Jewish history, the murder of six million Jews by Hitler and the creation of the Jewish State in Palestine, have had remarkably slight effects on the inner life of American Jewry."[8]

Judaism itself, to say nothing of Israel, barely impinged on their inner life. No one subjected the insular suburban affluence of American Jews to more scathing scrutiny than the novelist Philip Roth, who was all too readily taken as an enemy of Judaism when his poisoned fictional darts were directed at assimilated Jews, an altogether different target. In "Eli, the Fanatic," he explored the schizophrenic turmoil of an enlightened Jewish suburbanite (a lawyer, appropriately) who was suddenly forced to confront himself as a Jew. Eli Peck was retained by his enraged Jewish neighbors to enforce zoning regulations against a new yeshiva, whose teachers and pupils (eighteen, the number signifying "life") were Holocaust survivors and Orthodox Jews. It was a simple legal issue: the zoning code, Eli patiently explained to the bemused yeshiva director, prohibited boarding schools in residential areas. "The law is the law," the director conceded, before asking Eli, with a disarming flash of Talmudic logic, "When is the law that is the law not the law?"[9]

The presence of the yeshiva, at the outskirts of town, was distressing enough to the suburban liberals of Woodenton. Even more offensive to their standards of decorum was the bearded instructor with the hat, always clothed in black, whose public appearances evoked alarming childhood memories of Bronx peddlers. Judaism, after all, was something to outgrow; religious fanaticism must yield to "common sense" and "modera-

tion." To resolve the impasse, Eli gave the man his own respectable cloth-
ing to wear, only to receive, in return, that "lousy black suit." Eli, unable
to resist the temptation to try it on, suddenly encountered himself as a Jew.
Astonished and emboldened by the transformation, he even displayed his
new identity in public. But to be a Jew on the street breached the unwritten
rules of decorum; indeed, it convinced friends that Eli had suffered a nerv-
ous breakdown. At the hospital to see his new baby, he was addressed
as "rabbi"—who else would dare to be a Jew in public?— and forceably
sedated. Who, then, were the real fanatics: Orthodox Jews, or assimilated
suburban zealots?[10]

The comfortable insulation of American Jewry was abruptly shattered
in the spring of 1967. With Arab armies from Egypt, Jordan, Iraq, and Syria
massed at its borders, Israel faced the possibility of annihilation. For the
second time in a generation, Jews confronted extinction amid the silent indifference of the West. The United States, since 1957 a coguarantor of
Israel's right to navigate the Straits of Tiran, capitulated to the Egyptian
blockade. President Lyndon Johnson insisted that the United States would
not act unilaterally, and no other nation cared to respond. The United Nations, where Ambassador Arthur Goldberg issued a futile plea for international diplomatic intervention, was impotent. American Jews, financially
generous as always, watched apprehensively.

The Israeli military victory—swift, stunning, spectacular—was a
transforming moment. Anguish gave way to wonder, wrote the theologian
Abraham J. Heschel; "*terror* and *dread*" became "exultation." Even battle-
hardened Israeli soldiers suddenly realized, with startling pride, that they
were Jews. The weeping paratrooper photographed at the Western Wall
provided an intimate glimpse of the intensity of that discovery, which instantly connected him—and Jews everywhere—to their common history
and destiny. For he was not merely touching ancient stones, another sol-
dier explained, but "facing two thousand years of exile, the whole history
of the Jewish people." American Jews shared Heschel's profound realization: "I had not known how deeply Jewish I was."[11]

After June 1967, Charles Silberman has written, "concern for Israel"
defined the identity of American Jews (although it is revealing that he devoted far more space to fundraising than to all other expressions of concern
combined).[12] Certainly for the next decade American Jews basked in the
glow of their new identification with Israel and the vicarious strength that
it provided. For Jews whose only experience was powerlessness, as far back
as they could remember, Israel had become a tangible symbol of Jewish
power. Yet what is remarkable, in retrospect, was the brevity of the identification. The nagging loyalty conflicts still lingered; and a victorious Israel
was likely to intensify them.

Two important books, published in 1973, explored the problem. Sociologist Charles S. Liebman identified "the ambivalent American Jew," still "torn between two sets of values—those of integration and acceptance into American society and those of Jewish group survivial." American Jews yearned for "full acceptance as Americans, yet they still want to be Jews." Since these were competing, not complementary, impulses, ambivalence was an entirely appropriate, if perpetually enervating, response. In Liebman's reading of the plight of American Jews, Israel had only compounded their difficulties. American Jews fervently wanted to believe that American and Israeli values were entirely compatible, but they were doomed to disappointment.[13]

Rabbi Eugene Borowitz, observing the same problem from a different perspective, asserted in *The Mask Jews Wear* that American Jews, like their Marrano forebears (who posed as Spaniards after the Inquisition), wanted to be "just like everyone else." Ever since emancipation, Borowitz wrote, Jewishness had been "a special burden," assuring "the divided Jewish self" that was the Jewish hallmark of modernity. In the United States, where emancipation had reached its outer limits of freedom, the burden was heaviest and the need for masks that much greater. Eager to pass as Americans, Jews wore the mask of their heightened ethical sensitivity, which "justified what the Jews really wanted—membership in the society . . . and a low profile of Jewish existence."[14]

If Liebman and Borowitz were correct, the identification of American Jews with Israel after 1967 had failed to resolve their deepest identity conflict and even exacerbated it. Within a decade there was substantial confirmation for their analysis. In 1977 a disgruntled Israeli electorate chose Menachem Begin as their new prime minister. For the first time in the thirty-year history of the state, the party of the founders had been rejected. Begin, the perennial political outsider, the defiant disciple of Jabotinsky and militant Irgun leader, had been implicated in some of the most controversial episodes in the history of Israel—including the bombing of the King David Hotel, the massacre at Deir Yassin, and the *Altalena* affair. He was the irascible *shtetl* Jew, haunted by Holocaust memories, who grafted traditional Jewish symbols to the secular political culture of Israel. That did not make it easy for American Jews to like him. They had idolized Ben-Gurion, embraced Golda Meir as a Jewish grandmother, and admired Moshe Dayan as a modern Maccabee. But Begin demolished their liberal fantasies about Israel; for that, above all else, American Jews could never forgive him.

The Jewish state, for the first time, had a prime minister who wore a *kipa* and prayed comfortably at the Western Wall. His strident commitment to the land of Israel, including Judea and Samaria (usually known by their Jordanian name as the "West Bank"), was disturbing. The evident seriousness with which he took the divine covenant with the biblical patriarchs was alarming (although even the resolutely secular Ben-Gurion had insisted, before the Peel Commission thirty years earlier, "the Bible is our mandate"). Begin's first official visit to the United States, several months after the election, set him on a collision course with the American government. His sharp disagreements with President Jimmy Carter, especially over the issue of Jewish settlements in the territories, confronted American Jews with the clash they had always dreaded, between the United States and the Jewish state.

Jewish settlement in the land of Israel was precisely what Zionism had always been about. The Labor government, since 1967, had permitted Jews to settle in Judea and Samaria; prominent Labor leaders, including Yigal Allon, Yitzhak Rabin, and Shimon Peres, had encouraged settlement, or acquiesced in it. But Jewish settlement, the venerable Zionist tactic to secure the Jewish homeland, had become an embarrassment to American Jews. The religious-nationalist fervor of the new settlers merged Zionist theory and Jewish theology in profoundly unsettling ways for American Jews (and for many Israelis). The notion that state policy might flow from religious sources was fundamentally incompatible with Western liberal values. Furthermore, by 1977 Zionism (according to the United Nations) was "racism," and Israel was routinely denounced in political, intellectual, and liberal forums. Identification with the Jewish state had become a riskier commitment for American Jews than it had been a decade earlier. The more distinctively Jewish and the more independent of the United States that Israel became, the more it antagonized American Jews and the more frequently they found reason to distance themselves from it.

The Lebanon War rapidly accelerated the distancing process. International vilification transformed Israel into a pariah state: at best, David had become Goliath; at its obscene worst, it was Nazi Germany reincarnated. Respectable American newspapers, especially those renowned for their silence during the Holocaust, suddenly discovered Nazi brutality when they could impute it to the Jewish state. An unrelenting barrage of media criticism, reinforced by the contextual distortions for which television became notorious, made Israel an embarrassing commitment, and a convenient target for American Jewish critics.

But the underlying issue, the inherently unstable relationship between American Jews and Israel, was hardly novel. Neither Menachem Begin nor the Lebanon War created it, although both surely exacerbated it. When Israeli President Yitzhak Navon (a long-time Labor party leader who began his career as Ben-Gurion's political secretary) visited the United States early in 1983, while the war raged and Begin was still prime minister, he encountered Jewish audiences seething with anger at Israel for its conduct of the war and for its settlement policy. Navon responded by venturing boldly into hazardous ideological terrain: the relationship of American

Jews to the Jewish state. He bluntly told members of a Boston academic gathering that if they wished to criticize Israel on national security matters they should, as a prerequisite, come there to live. In New York he extended an invitation, phrased as a moral obligation: it was the duty of (six million) American Jews "to do what the six million Jews exterminated in the Holocaust would have done—come on *aliyah*." Insisting that the diaspora was "exile," he urged American Jews to trade their "shallow comfortable life" as Americans for "a challenging life" as Jews in Israel.[15] Navon's audiences, accustomed to Israeli appeals for financial donations, were palpably distressed at the suggestion that they donate themselves instead.

The distancing of American Jews from Israel, already evident during the Lebanon War, accelerated during the Arab uprising (*intifada*) that erupted in December 1987. Once again, Israel was pilloried in the media for a vast array of political, military, and especially moral transgressions (endlessly recited in the *New York Times*, in what was described as the "Anthony Lewis conjugation": "Israel will lose its soul; Israel is losing its soul; Israel has lost its soul"). American Jews joined (and often led) the chorus of denunciation, with pointed contrasts to their own refined ethical sensitivities. The "profound impact" of the uprising on American Jewry was vividly described by Reform spokesman Albert Vorspan in a remarkable *Times* confession. American Jews, he wrote, were "traumatized" by the events in Israel. Suffering "shame and stress," they wanted "to crawl into a hole," where they might escape guilt by association with "the political and moral bankruptcy of Israeli policy." After all, American Jews were "implicated" in the actions of the Jewish state. "It's about us."[16]

Once American Jews confronted the terrifying specter that their own security might be jeopardized by the behavior of Jews in Israel, they responded as they had since the very beginning of the Zionist movement: by taking flight. The fervent identification of American Jews with Israel during 1967–77, when it was a source of empowerment, had become a debilitating liability once Israel was under assault. Jews who had proudly proclaimed their "oneness" with Israel could no longer even bring themselves to visit there; and by 1988 they were outnumbered by Christian tourists in the Jewish state.

The momentum of events in Israel generated its own literature of disenchantment among American Jews. The old Zionist slogan, "the negation of *galut*," was all but inverted to become "the negation of *Eretz Israel*." Criticism of Israel—and, by extension, the "tragedy" of Zionism—resounded as a popular refrain among American Jews whose political liberalism was betrayed by the varieties of religious and nationalistic Judaism that flourished in Israel. Profoundly disillusioned with the Jewish state, they preferred to believe that the sources of Jewish regeneration and vitality were in the United States. Zion, just as the first Reform rabbis had declared, was in America. The most popular of these accounts was Charles E. Silberman's *A Certain People* (1985). Silberman, a self-described product of "acculturated middle-class Orthodox[y]," wrote an elegy to the United States, and to the mobility, success, and prosperity of American Jews. They lived, he proudly observed, "in a freer, more open society than that of any Diaspora community in which Jews have ever lived before," a reassuring demonstration that the United States "really *is* different." Indeed, reserving the crowning compliment for his concluding sentence, "for American Jews, the United States is now home as well as haven."[17]

Silberman revealed his priorities when he wrote that the overriding challenge for American Jews was "to express their Jewishness without inhibiting their full participation in American life." But with "full participation" as the goal, the kind of Jewishness—or Judaism—that American Jews could express was tightly constrained. For Silberman, nothing mattered more than "individual autonomy." In the United States, Jews "choose their own approach to Judaism"; any approach was valid as long as it had "meaning for oneself." There was, Silberman conceded (and applauded), "a heavy emphasis on the subjective self"; every Jewish option is measured "by how it looks, or feels, to *them*." In this "self-centered" Judaism, reflecting the most narcissistic varieties of American individualism, Silberman managed to detect "the early stages of a major revitalization of Jewish religious, intellectual, and cultural life." It was, he thought, a welcome antidote to a different form of Jewish self-centeredness, which he brusquely dismissed: "exclusive preoccupation with Israel, or with a narrowly defined Jewish agenda," a dangerous expression of "parochialism" that encouraged "self-ghettoization."[18]

A far stronger argument might be made, however, that Silberman had not located the early stages of a revitalized Judaism, but the late stages of a process of disintegration that had begun two centuries earlier with emancipation. Two of his favorite examples, drawn from the world of American law, suggested that the success of Jews and the revitalization of Judaism were far less compatible than he imagined. First, he cited the proliferation of Jews among deans of elite law schools as evidence of the "new climate of acceptance" that enabled Jews to "make it" within the enclaves of the old Protestant elite. But any correlation with Jewish revitalization, which Silberman chose to illustrate with Professor X of the Harvard Law School, was murky. Professor X described how "pale and inadequate" Judaism once seemed, in contrast to "the world of universal, cosmopolitan culture" that Harvard had symbolized for him. But fortuitous invitations to a bar mitzvah and to Israel had inspired "an increasingly intense and meaningful involvement with Judaism." Professor X, filled with Jewish pride, had "turned to the Jewish tradition" and now felt confident that "the core" of his Jewish identity had been "secured." Yet (although neither he nor Silberman noted the incongruity) prayer remained "a difficult issue" for him; he still considered Jewish ritual "hollow and empty"; Jewish law was "fundamentally alien to [his] sensibilities"; God was missing altogether; and Israel soon became one of his favorite targets of denunciation. The secure core was unattached to any fundamental precepts of historical Judaism. Nonetheless, Silberman concluded, Professor X had securely located religious observance within the "more elaborate whole" of his revitalized Judaism.[19]

A similar message of reassurance, within a more serious analysis, was offered by Jonathan S. Woocher in *Sacred Survival* (1986), his study of the "civil religion" of American Jews. It combined the familiar ingredients: "a positive Jewish identity" that was, simultaneously, "distinctively and wholeheartedly American." In the United States, where Jews enjoyed "unprecedented opportunities for both integration and Jewish self-expression," there was little reason to fear assimilation, for "Jewishness and Americanness are mutually reinforcing." The civil religion, as "a faith for 'the ambivalent American Jew,'" taught Jews "how to live in two civilizations," pursuing their "dual destiny" as "members of the American family." But that civil religion, Woocher noted, had elevated philanthropy above all other expressions of Judaism; it rearranged the Jewish calendar according to the timing of federation fund-raising efforts; and it legitimated a Judaism without synagogues or rabbis—or any religious content. The slogan "We are One" had even become "a more immediate and compelling watchword of the faith" than the affirmation of the *Sh'ma* (the central prayer in the Jewish liturgy) that "the Lord is One." Nonetheless, Woocher concluded that "civil Judaism," in reality little more than philanthropic generosity, was somehow a "reaffirmation of Jewish destiny and faith."[20]

The self-congratulatory cadences of American Judaism resounded in Leonard Fine's *Where Are We?* (1988). Fine was captivated by the American Jewish experience, among "the most intriguing" and "exhilarating" chapters "in all the chronicles of Jewish wandering." It had produced the "American Jewish Way," a residue of "the intersection of two complementary traditions that have been immeasurably enriched each by the other." For Fine (as for Silberman) Judaism was whatever American Jews decided to do: "We want to be free to be Jewish or not to be Jewish, and if to be Jewish, to define for ourselves what being Jewish shall mean." Precisely that expansive freedom of choice, so characteristically American, provided the geographical and spiritual answer to the question posed in Fine's title: "We are, at last, at home in America."[21]

Although Fine tried to adorn his American home with some Jewish furnishings, he could only locate the threadbare "compatibility between classic Jewish conceptions and historic American conceptions." As richly textured as this tapestry may have once been, it had become tattered with age. Its warp and woof, for Fine as for the Reform rabbis whose identical claim preceded his by a century, was prophetic justice: "We are here invited to take the Hebrew prophets seriously," Fine asserted. But his claim that the liberal pluralism favored by American Jews was a composite of "both the Jewish rabbinic and the Jewish prophetic traditions" hardly reflected a careful reading of rabbinic Judaism, Hebrew prophecy, or, for that matter, liberal pluralism. Although Fine vigorously rejected the notion that "the real American Jewish synthesis is the abandonment of Jewish values," his book persuasively refuted his claim.[22]

Such celebrations of Jewish vitality, invariably within American terms (success, philanthropy, liberalism), provided rhetorical camouflage for the flight from Israel and the sacred law. For all but a tiny percentage of (largely Orthodox) American Jews, Judaism had come to mean little but personal taste, which usually excluded anything that differentiated them from other Americans. (As one disillusioned rabbi wrote, it was as though Jewish tradition had become "a gigantic menu from which each might choose *à la carte*, and any dish might be substituted for any other."[23]) Any notion of normative Judaism, shaped by historical attachments to land and law (to say nothing of God), was summarily rejected—as it must be if Jews were to preserve their comfortable status in the United States.

The distance American Jews had traveled became evident in 1988, when Orthodox religious parties in Israel suddenly disrupted their comfortable accommodation to American values. For a time, it seemed that a coalition government would depend upon new legislation stipulating that any Jewish convert claiming the right to immigrate to Israel under its Law of Return must be converted according to *halakha*, as interpreted by the Orthodox rabbinate. Although the number of American Jews, let alone converts, who made *aliyah* was infinitesimal, the American Jewish community was incensed. The very fact of rabbinical political activity was outrageous; few American Jews cared that the separation of religion and state, an American constitutional principle, was not enjoined by Torah nor by Israeli law. American Jews were hardly prepared to concede to *any* Israeli source, no less the rabbinate, power to define "Who is a Jew?"

The crux of the issue was intermarriage, already endemic to American Jewish life. By most accounts, as many as one-third of Jewish marriages were intermarriages. Even if there were conversions, few were halakhically valid. Consequently, in any family where the mother had been a gentile the children would not be considered Jewish—because according to Jewish law, descent is matrilineal. Suddenly, American Jews confronted the prospect that the Jewish credentials of their own children might be suspect (at least for the purpose of *aliyah*). At a deeper level, they were shocked to discover that the fundamental premise of American Jewry, that Judaism could mean whatever they wanted it to mean, made little sense in Israel.

A more pointed symbolic rebuke to American Jews, who defined themselves as autonomous individuals free (as Americans) to choose their own Jewish identity, could hardly be imagined. If the Orthodox rabbinate in Israel could decide "Who is a Jew," American freedom of choice would find no sanction in the law of the Jewish state.

For the vast majority of American Jews, American Judaism had all but fulfilled Isaac Mayer Wise's wish, expressed in the title of his 1857 prayerbook, *Minhag America*: the final arbiter of Judaism was American custom. Yet even the flexibility of custom had not resolved the inherent dilemma of American Jews, struggling to reconcile two disparate traditions and conceal the contradictions between them. The conversion of Judaism into Americanism provided some protection against allegations of dual loyalty. But it required each generation of American Jews to prove that the more American they became the more Jewish they remained. That helps to explain their recurrent need, expressed in endlessly repetitive books, sermons, speeches, and editorials, to explore, define, and justify their own identity. Their relentless quest is not only a reflection of the postemancipation disintegration of Jewish legal authority but also a measure of the distance that American Jews have imposed between their own Judaism and the historical sources of Jewish religion and nationality. For in the United States, as Arnold Eisen has written, "all but the immigrant Orthodox ran to embrace America . . . not yet aware how fatefully the battle for the American Jewish soul had been joined."[24]

Fervent identification with American values only assures that the struggle for "the American Jewish soul" will persist. American Jews long ago came to believe that Torah and Constitution, Hebrew prophecy and political liberalism, merged to form a single unified tradition. Rabbis and lawyers devised the fundamental principles of reconciliation, which still define the content of American Judaism nearly a century later. Their translation of the Jewish sacred law, and then Zionism, into American patriotism expressed the deepest yearning of American Jews for a secure American identity. But it also created the lingering paradox of American Judaism: the very freedom of choice that Jews cherish as their American birthright requires perpetual efforts of self-definition. Once American Jews rejected the Jewish imperatives of land and law, they forever obligated themselves to justify their own proliferating varieties of Judaism, to other Americans, to Israelis, and especially to each other.

Afterword

The night before Jacob returned to the biblical promised land, he wrestled in lonely solitude—whether with another man, an angel, or his own conscience is left ambiguous. As day broke, he was blessed with a new name, which acknowledged his struggle with God. No longer was he Jacob, who supplanted Esau in a struggle that had begun in Rebekah's womb. Now he was Israel, father to sons who would become the twelve tribes of the nation that would bear his name. Finally, legitimacy was conferred. His elusive blessing and birthright were secured for posterity.[1]

In Jewish worship, a reading from the Prophets accompanies the biblical narrative, in some way expressing thematic unity with it. The story of Jacob's identity transformation is linked to the prophecy Hosea. Israel, the Prophet laments, "has forgotten his Maker, and builds palaces." Hosea warns: "My God will cast them away, because they did not harken to him: and they shall be wanderers among the nations." But in time, he consoles, "they shall walk after the Lord, who shall roar like a lion." And when God roars, Hosea prophesies, "the children shall come trembling from the west," to reclaim their historic birthright as Jacob did.[2]

Perhaps.

Notes

INTRODUCTION

1. Milton M. Gordon, *Assimilation in American Life* (New York, 1964), 185.
2. *Genesis* 12:7; *Exodus* 34:11.
3. Robert A. Burt, *Two Jewish Justices* (Berkeley, 1988), 2, 5.
4. Cynthia Ozick, *Bloodshed and Three Novellas* (New York, 1976), 9.
5. Deborah Dash Moore, "Response to Schiffman and Cohen," in American Jewish Committee, *Conflict or Cooperation?* (New York, 1989), 47–48.

1. AMERICAN ZION

1. Harry S. Stout, *The New England Soul* (New York, 1986), 300.
2. *Ibid.*, 74; Conrad Cherry, ed., *God's New Israel* (Englewood Cliffs, N.J. 1971), vii, 27, 41–43; Harry S. Stout, "Word and Order in Colonial New England," in Nathan O. Hatch and Mark A. Noll, eds., *The Bible in America* (New York, 1982), 27–29; William A. Clebsch, *From Sacred to Profane America* (New York, 1968), 47.
3. John F. Berens, *Providence and Patriotism in Early America* (Charlottesville, 1978), 14–23; Moshe Davis, "The Holy Land Idea in American Spiritual History," in Davis, ed., *With Eyes Toward Zion* (New York, 1977), 4–7; Sacvan Bercovitch, *The American Jeremiad* (Madison, 1978), 78, 80; Richard B. Morris, "Civil Liberties and the Jewish Tradition in Early America," 46 *PAJHS* (1956), 23–24.
4. Mason I. Lowance, Jr., *The Language of Canaan* (Cambridge, 1980), vii–viii, 28–32; Sacvan Bercovitch, *The Puritan Origins of the American Self* (New Haven, 1975), 61–62, 121–22; Stout, "Word and Order," 27–29; Berens, *Providence and Patriotism,* 17.
5. Stout, *New England Soul,* 54, 138; Lowance, *Language of Canaan,* 128–30, 162; Bercovitch, *Puritan Origins,* 39, 189–91.
6. Peter Grose, *Israel in the Mind of America* (New York, 1984), 316; Davis, "Holy Land Idea," 4–7.
7. Bercovitch, *American Jeremiad,* 72; Bercovitch, *Puritan Origins,* 106; Ursula Brumm, *American Thought and Religious Typology* (New Brunswick, N.J., 1970), 46–47.
8. Brumm, *American Thought,* 22–28; Lowance, *Language of Canaan,* 4, 22; Lowance, "Cotton Mather's *Magnalia* and the Metaphors of Biblical History," in Sacvan Bercovitch, ed., *Typology and Early American Literature* (Amherst, 1972), 140; Stout, *New England Soul,* 45.
9. David S. Katz, *Philo-Semitism and the Readmission of the Jews to England, 1603–1655* (Oxford, 1982), 6–9, 11, 167, 216–17, 232–33. The same was true of New England: religious tolerance of "Turke, Jew, Papist" struck one Plymouth governor as absurd; Cotton Mather referred to Newport, Rhode Island (soon to become the largest American Jewish community), as "the common receptacle of the convicts of Jerusalem." John Adams, approving the idea of restored Jewish sovereignty in "Judea," hoped that Jews "would soon wear away some of the asperities and peculiarities of their character and possibly in time become liberal Unitarian Christians." Jacob R. Marcus, *The Colonial American Jew, 1492–1776* (3 vols., Detroit, 1970), I,

297–304, 412–16; Salo W. Baron, *The Jewish Community* (3 vols., Philadelphia, 1942). I, 261; Grose, *Israel in the Mind of America*, 7–8.

10. Perry Miller, *The New England Mind: The Seventeenth Century* (Cambridge, 1954), 475, 477; Bercovitch, *Puritan Origins*, 35–36; Lowance, *Language of Canaan*, 79; Brumm, *American Thought*, 41.

11. Daniel J. Boorstin, *The Americans: The Colonial Experience* (New York, 1958), 19; Peter Gay, *A Loss of Mastery* (Berkeley, 1966), 9, 31–33; Stout, *New England Soul*, 7–8, 54.

12. Lowance, *Language of Canaan*, 35–37; Bercovitch, *American Jeremiad*, 69–72, 166; and especially David M. Scobey, "Revising the Errand: New England's Ways and the Puritan Sense of the Past," *Wm. & Mary Q.* 41 (1984), 3, 12–16.

13. Eugene R. Fingerhut, "Were the Massachusetts Puritans Hebraic?" *New England Q.* 40 (1967), 521–31; Jesper Rosenmeier, "'With My Owne Eyes': William Bradford's *Of Plymouth Plantation*," in Bercovitch, ed., *Typology*, 69; Richard Reinitz, "The Separatist Background of Roger Williams' Argument for Religious Toleration," in ibid., 111, 124; Bercovitch, *Puritan Origins*, 106.

14. Stout, *New England Soul*, 173; Lowance, *Language of Canaan*, 294–5.

15. Stout, *New England Soul*, 253, 288, 307; Bercovitch, *Puritan Origins*, 146, 150.

16. Nathan O. Hatch, *The Sacred Cause of Liberty* (New Haven, 1977), 3, 16, 53, 60; Berens, *Providence and Patriotism*, 73–80, 83, 89–90, 107, 109–10; Bercovitch, *American Jeremiad*, 129n; Cherry, ed., *God's New Israel*, 65, 68–81.

17. Mark A. Noll, "The Image of the United States as a Biblical Nation, 1776–1865," in Hatch and Noll, eds., *Bible in America*, 44; Cherry, ed., *God's New Israel*, 13, 93–97; Hatch, *Sacred Cause*, 85, 159.

18. Morris U. Schappes, ed., *A Documentary History of the Jews in the United States* (New York, 1971), 78; Hatch and Noll, eds., *Bible in America*, 4–10; Berens, *Providence and Patriotism*, 4–6, 71–72, 115, 127, 169–70; Bercovitch, *American Jeremiad*, 145–47.

19. Davis, "Holy Land Idea," 19; Cherry, ed., *God's New Israel*, 93–94, 98–99; Berens, *Providence and Patriotism*, 119, 123–24; Bercovitch, *American Jeremiad*, 129; Hatch, *Sacred Cause*, 88, 138.

20. Hatch, *Sacred Cause*, 138–41, 145, 157; Jefferson's and Madison's contributions, and a perceptive essay by Robert T. Handy interpreting their significance, appear in John F. Wilson and Donald L. Drakeman, eds., *Church and State in American History* (Boston, 1987), 75–77, 79–80, 85–89.

21. Lowance, *Language of Canaan*, 209–210; Herman Melville, *White-Jacket* (New York, 1959), 189; Joseph Story, *Commentaries on the Constitution of the United States* (Boston, 1833), III, 722–23; *Vidal v. Girard's Executors* 2 How. 127 (1843). Nearly a century later, in 1931, the Court reiterated: "We are a Christian people." *U.S. v. Macintosh* 283 U.S. 605 (1931).

22. For examples, see Lloyd Lewis, *Myths after Lincoln* (New York, 1929), 92–97.

23. Naomi W. Cohen, *A Dual Heritage* (Philadelphia, 1969), 3–6, 10, 71–72; Naomi W. Cohen, *Encounter with Emancipation* (Philadelphia, 1984), 168–69.

24. Oscar S. Straus, *The Origin of Republican Form of Government in the United States of America* (New York, 1885), 70–71, 76–80, 86, 100–101, 104, 108, 118, 131, 141–42.

25. Cohen, *Dual Heritage*, ix, 72, 295–96, 298; Oscar S. Straus, *The American Spirit* (New York, 1913), 279–80, 288, 292.

26. Kaufmann Kohler, "Palestinian or American Judaism?" *Studies, Addresses and Personal Papers* (New York, 1931), 229–32. Isaac Mayer Wise had made the identical point, thirty years earlier, with his claim that Moses promulgated the princi-

ples of democratic liberty that culminated in the American revolution. Wise, *History of the Israelitish Nation from Abraham to the Present Time* (Albany, 1854), iv.

27. David Philipson, *My Life as an American Jew* (Cincinnati, 1941), 63, 126–28, 289.

28. Jonathan Sarna, *et al.*, eds., *Jews and the Founding of the Republic* (New York, 1985), 108.

29. Moses Rischin, *The Promised City* (Cambridge, 1962), 166; Louis Harap, *The Image of the Jew in American Literature* (Philadelphia, 1974), 292–93; Gerald Sorin, *The Prophetic Minority* (Bloomington, 1985), ix, 3, 89, 91–92.

30. Sorin, *Prophetic Minority*, 3, 92–93, 110, 114, 163–64, 168; Jonathan Frankel, *Prophecy and Politics: Socialism, Nationalism, and the Russian Jews, 1862–1917* (Cambridge, 1981), 481.

31. Robert Wistrich, *Revolutionary Jews from Marx to Trotsky* (London, 1976), preface, 7–8, chaps. 1–2.

32. Naomi W. Cohen, *Not Free to Desist* (Philadelphia, 1972), 3–4, 10–11, 13, 25–29; Charles Reznikoff, *Louis Marshall: Champion of Liberty* (2 vols., Philadelphia, 1957), I, 274–75.

33. Allon Gal, *Brandeis of Boston* (Cambridge, 1980), 72–77, 92–94, 124–26, 131–36, 181; Jacob DeHass, *Louis D. Brandeis: A Biographical Sketch* (New York, 1929), 52, 151–52, 162–63, 168–69, 179, 184–85, 194–95, 202–203.

34. For "social memory" and the Puritans, see Scobey, "Revising the Errand," 30–31.

35. Kaufmann Kohler, "The Tocsin Call of Liberty and Democracy," *A Living Faith* (Cincinnati, 1948), 113–14.

36. Abraham A. Neuman, "Relation of the Hebrew Scriptures to American Institutions" (Jewish Theological Seminary, 1939), 4, 6–8, 11, 17, 22–3; Abraham I. Katsh, *Hebraic Contributions to American Life* (New York, 1941), 2, 10, 26, 38; Isidore S. Meyer, "A Fount of American Democracy," *Menorah J.* 27 (Oct.-Dec. 1939), 251, 258.

37. Levi A. Olan, *Interpreting the Prophetic Tradition* (Cincinnati, 1960), 132–35; Rabbi Samuel Belkin quoted in Stuart E. Rosenberg, *The New Jewish Identity in America* (New York, 1985), 35; Milton R. Konvitz, "Judaism and the Democratic Ideal," in Louis Finkelstein, ed., *The Jews* (3 vols., Philadelphia, 1949), III, 110–11; Daniel J. Elazar, "American Political Theory and the Political Notions of American Jews," in Peter Rose, ed., *The Ghetto and Beyond* (New York, 1969), 204–205, 218, 223.

38. Robert Gordis, "Judaism and the Democratic Ideal," *Congress Monthly* 43 (May 1976), 12–15; Daniel J. Elazar, *Community and Polity* (Philadelphia, 1976), 23–24; Davis, "Holy Land Idea," 3–33; Simon Greenberg, *The Ethical in the Jewish and American Heritage* (New York, 1977), xiv–xv, 220–23; Abraham I. Katsh, *The Biblical Heritage of American Democracy* (New York, 1977); Jeffrey B. Morris, "The American Jewish Judge: An Appraisal on the Occasion of the Bicentennial," *Jewish Social Studies* 38 (1976), 195–223.

39. Simon Greenberg, *Foundations of a Faith* (New York, 1967), 307, 309; Milton R. Konvitz, *Judaism and the American Idea* (Ithaca, 1978), preface, 16, 30, 51, 90, 140. Konvitz had earlier concluded that the Bible, like the Constitution, affirms "the significance of law and a legal order." Milton Konvitz, *Judaism and Human Rights* (New York, 1972), 88, 139.

40. Konvitz, *Judaism and Human Rights*, 87; Konvitz, "The Confluence of Torah and Constitution," in *Jews, Judaism and the American Constitution* (Cincinnati, 1982), 10–17; Daniel J. Elazar and Stuart Cohen, *The Jewish Polity* (Bloomington, 1985), 4, 10–12, 21–22; Theodore R. Mann, "The Jewish Roots of the Constitution," *Congress*

Monthly 54 (Nov.-Dec. 1987), 22; Anthony Lewis, "An Ingenious Structure," *New York Times Magazine*, Sept. 13, 1987, p. 39. For assertions of the compatibility of "bedrock American ideals" with "traditional Jewish ones," combined with criticism of the State of Israel for its departures from American constitutional norms, see "The Evolving American Civilization" and "Liberties in Israel," *The Reconstructionist* (Sept. 1987), 5–7.

41. Benjamin E. Scolnic and Elliot S. Schoenberg, eds. Study Guide, "Covenant: People of the Living Law" (New York, 1988), 1, 5, 11–13, 22, 24, 72.

42. The preceding paragraphs are a composite of views expressed in Robert St. John, *Jews, Justice, and Judaism* (New York, 1969), xv; Robert Gordis, *The Root and the Branch* (Chicago, 1962), 14–15, 81–82; Lawrence H. Fuchs, *The Political Behavior of American Jews* (Glencoe, Ill., 1956), 197–200; Fuchs, "Introduction," *AJHQ* 66 (Dec. 1976), 186; Donna E. Arzt, "The People's Lawyers: The Predominance of Jews in Public Interest Law," *Judaism* 35 (1986), 52, 55, 59, 61–62; E. L. Doctorow, *The Book of Daniel* (New York, 1971), 132–33; Robert A. Burt, *Two Jewish Justices* (Berkeley, 1988), 2, 65–67. Morris, "The American Jewish Judge," sees the "pursuit of social justice through law," a legacy of Hebrew prophecy, as the connecting link. Yet he notes, without further comment, that the only "common bond" between American Jewish judges was "the degree of apparent assimilation" that they shared! (Pp. 217–20).

43. The biblical framework of American constitutional interpretation has recently become a favorite subject among legal scholars. For the possibilities and limits, see Thomas C. Grey, "The Constitution as Scripture," *Stanford Law Review* 37 (1984), 1– 25. For a demonstration of how strained the analogy can become, by someone confessing to how "little I know about my own Jewish tradition," see Sanford Levinson, *Constitutional Faith* (Princeton, 1988), x. Leonard W. Levy, whose earlier constitutional scholarship showed no penchant for citations to Jewish sources, suddenly was captivated by those that supported his preference for textual interpretation over original intent. See *Original Intent and the Framers' Constitution* (New York, 1988), xiv, 397. In a delightful example of infinite scholarly regression, Levy constructed a lawyer's brief against original intent—based largely, of course, on the Framers' "original intent" to have their own original intent disregarded!

44. Jessie Bernard, "Biculturality: A Study in Social Schizophrenia," in Isacque Graeber and Stuart Henderson Britt, eds., *Jews in a Gentile World* (New York, 1942), 265; Jacob B. Agus, "Assimilation, Integration, Segregation—The Road to the Future," *Judaism* 3 (1954), 503.

45. Steven M. Cohen, *American Modernity and Jewish Identity* (New York, 1983), 34–35, 134–37, 174; Charles S. Liebman, "American Jewry: Identity and Affiliation," in David Sidorsky, ed., *The Future of the Jewish Community in America* (New York, 1973), 128–30, 133–34; Charles S. Liebman, *The Ambivalent American Jew* (Philadelphia, 1973), 135, 152–56, 157– 58; Werner Cohn, "The Politics of American Jews," in Marshall Sklare, ed., *The Jews: Social Patterns of an American Group* (New York, 1958), 626; Joel Carmichael, Werner J. Dannhauser, Leon Wieseltier, "Symposium: Liberalism & the Jews," *Commentary* 69 (Jan. 1980), 26, 30, 79.

46. Arnold Eisen has perceptively observed, in his fine study of American Jewish conceptions of chosenness, how extensively American rabbis borrowed from Puritan, rather than Jewish, sources to define their subject. As with law and justice, chosenness was "a faith transmitted to Jews by America," not by Judaism. Eisen, *The Chosen People in America* (Bloomington, 1983), 169–70. On a related point, Shlomo Avineri has dismissed as "utter nonsense" the parallel claim that Jewish tradition planted the seeds of democracy in modern Israel. The ancient Hebrew

commonwealth of King David, he observed, "was more like contemporary Saudi Arabia than like contemporary Israel." Avineri, "The Historical Roots of Israeli Democracy," Address delivered at the University of Cape Town (1985), 3. Jews, constantly admonished to remember their past, everywhere in the modern era seem determined to invent it.

2. THE RULE OF SACRED LAW

1. Max Rheinstein, ed., *Max Weber on Law in Economy and Society* (Cambridge, 1954), 229, 247–50, 303–304, 336–37, 351. Weber's sociology of law was entwined with his sociology of religion. For the place of ancient Israel in both categories of Weber's thought, see ibid., 244–50; and Max Weber, *Ancient Judaism* (Glencoe, Ill. 1952). For Weber, it was a relatively short conceptual step from his discovery of a "rational religious ethic" to a rational legal order.

2. Weber, *Ancient Judaism*, 4–5.

3. Exod. 19:5–6, 8, 17; 21:2–23; 24:3, 7–8. All citations, unless otherwise indicated, are to *The Jerusalem Bible* (Jerusalem, 1984), whose English text is revised and edited by Harold Fisch.

4. Exod. 19:17; Deut. 5:22–23, 26.

5. Num. 16:3ff; Ze'ev W. Falk, *Law and Religion: The Jewish Experience* (Jerusalem, 1981), 52–53.

6. Deut. 31:12–13.

7. For Joshua's covenantal renewal, see Josh. 8:32; 23:6; 24:15, 24–25.

8. Yehezkel Kaufmann, *The Religion of Israel* (New York, 1972), 174–75, 211; Michael Fishbane, *Biblical Interpretation in Ancient Israel* (Oxford, 1985), 6–7, 163. I am hardly qualified to resolve the debate over the Bible as "really" a single text, or a compilation from different times by various authors. For my purposes, the text as it presents itself is determinative. Its message about the covenantal relationship stands independent of any conclusions about authorship or dating. For a parallel conclusion, see Harold Fisch, *Poetry with a Purpose* (Bloomington, 1988), 23.

9. 2 Chron. 34:14, 19, 21–22. See also 2 Kings 23.

10. 2 Chron. 34:30–32; E. W. Nicholson, *Deuteronomy and Tradition* (Oxford, 1967), 94–101, 120–23; Joseph Blenkinsopp, *Wisdom and Law in the Old Testament* (Oxford, 1983), 101; Delbert R. Hillers, *Covenant: The History of a Biblical Idea* (Baltimore, 1969), 149; J. Weingreen, *From Bible to Mishna* (Manchester, 1976), 151; Kaufmann, *Religion of Israel*, 210, 290; Deut. 13:1–5; 18:15–22.

11. Hillers, *Covenant*, 149–54; Gerhard von Rad, *Deuteronomy* (London, 1966), 23–25; Peter C. Craigie, *The Book of Deuteronomy* (Grand Rapids, 1976), 19–37; Blenkinsopp, *Wisdom*, 98; Moshe Weinfeld, *Deuteronomy and the Deuteronomic School* (Oxford, 1972), 288–94; Deut. 16:20–21; 17:11.

12. Craigie, *Book of Deuteronomy*, 42–43; Gerhard von Rad, *Old Testament Theology* (2 vols., London, 1975), I, 222–25; Calum M. Carmichael, *The Laws of Deuteronomy* (Ithaca, 1974), 7, 53–54; Kaufmann, *Religion of Israel*, 290; Helmer Ringgren, *Israelite Religion* (London, 1966), 302; Deut. 6:18; 17:20. "The study of Deuteronomy is therefore a study in the history of tradition," as covenantal ideas were adapted and transmitted under new circumstances. Nicholson, *Deuteronomy and Tradition*, 121–23. See also Fishbane, *Biblical Interpretation*, 18–19.

13. Roland de Vaux, *Ancient Israel* (2 vols., New York, 1965), II, 343–44; von Rad, *Old Testament Theology*, I, 81–89; Ps. 137:4–5.

14. Fishbane, *Biblical Interpretation*, 265; Richard Elliott Friedman, *Who Wrote the Bible?* (New York, 1987), 159, 223–25; Ezra 7:10–11, 14, 21; 9:1, 10; 10:3; Neh. 2:3.

15. Ezra 10:11–13; Neh. 8:5–9, 18; 10:30.

16. Kaufmann, *Religion of Israel*, 448; J. Newman, *Halakhic Sources* (Leiden, 1969), 6–8; Fishbane, *Biblical Interpretation*, 18–19, 113–14, 168; Blenkinsopp, *Wisdom*, 117–20.

17. I Macc. 1:11, 14, 37–40, 43–44; 2:20–21, 23–27; Elias Bickerman, *From Ezra to the Last of the Maccabees* (New York, 1962), 100-101.

18. Deut. 16:18; 17:9. For examples of divine dispute settlement, see Num. 9:8–14; 15:32–26; 27:1–11; Lev. 24:10–16.

19. Jacob Neusner, *A Life of Rabban Yohanan ben Zakkai* (Leiden, 1962), 114–21, 141, 147–50, 155, 163; Jacob Neusner, *From Politics to Piety* (Englewood Cliffs, N.J., 1973), 97–98, 150–51, 153.

20. Gedaliah Alon, *The Jews in Their Land in the Talmudic Age*, trans. Gershon Levi (2 vols., Jerusalem, 1980), I, 96–98.

21. Ibid., 86, 108, 119–20; W. D. Davies, *The Territorial Dimension of Judaism* (Berkeley, 1982), 107–108, 112: Jon D. Levenson, *Sinai and Zion* (San Francisco, 1987), 181.

22. Ben Zion Bokser, *Pharisaic Judaism in Transition* (New York, 1935), 1–4,; Neusner, *From Politics to Piety*, 2–3.

23. Neusner, *From Politics to Piety*, 50, 54, 146, 151– 153; Neusner, *Yohanan ben Zakkai*, 64–65, 68, 103, 141; Neusner, *There We Sat Down* (Nashville, 1972), 39–41.

24. Joel Roth, *The Halakhic Process* (New York, 1986), 123–25; Joseph Blenkinsopp, *Prophecy and Canon* (Notre Dame, 1977), 116–19; Ephraim E. Urbach, *The Sages*, trans. Israel Abrahams (Cambridge, 1987), 306; *Pirke Aboth* I:1.

25. *Bava Metzia* 59a–59b.

26. Eliezer Berkovits, *Not in Heaven* (New York, 1983), 1, 48; Elliot N. Dorff and Arthur Rosett, *A Living Tree* (Albany, 1988), 14; Roth, *Halakhic Process*, 1, 83–85, 150.

27. *Menahot* 29b; Mendell Lewittes, *The Nature and History of Jewish Law* (New York, 1966), 21–22; Berkovits, *Not in Heaven*, 19, 22, 32, 50–51, 65–70.

28. Alon, *Jews in Their Land*, 220, 254; Menachem Elon, ed., *The Principles of Jewish Law* (Jerusalem, 1976), 19–22; David Biale, *Power and Powerlessness in Jewish History* (New York, 1986), 11–26; Weingreen, *From Bible to Mishna*, ix–x, 22.

29. Neusner, *From Politics to Piety*, 50, 54; Ellis Rivkin, *A Hidden Revolution* (Nashville, 1978), 185–87, 232–35, 251; Urbach, *The Sages*, 305–306.

30. Elon, ed., *Principles of Jewish Law*, 123–24; M. Chigier, "Codification of Jewish Law," *Jewish Law Annual* 2 (1979), 6–16; Morris Adler, *The World of the Talmud* (New York, 1963), 20–46; Weingreen, *From Bible to Mishna*, 77, 80.

31. Moshe Silberg, *Talmudic Law and the Modern State* (New York, 1973), 83–84; Blenkinsopp, *Wisdom*, 129; R. Travers Herford, *The Ethics of the Talmud: Sayings of the Fathers* (New York, 1962), 19–21; Weingreen, *From Bible to Mishna*, 139; Adin Steinsaltz, *The Essential Talmud* (New York, 1976), 47, 56–57; Prov. 3:18.

32. Alon, *Jews in Their Land*, 212, 230–33, 237; Dorff and Rosett, *Living Tree*, 132–34; Weingreen, *From Bible to Mishna*, 22, 132–42.

33. Zvi Zohar, "The Consumption of Sabbatical Year Produce in Biblical and Rabbinic Literature," in Harvey E. Goldberg, ed., *Judaism Viewed from Within and from Without* (Albany, 1987), 75–76; Dorff and Rosett, *Living Tree*, 227, 230; Baruch M. Bokser, *The Origins of the Seder* (Berkeley, 1984), 77; Salo W. Baron, *A Social and Religious History of the Jews*. Vol. II: *Ancient Times*, Pt. II (New York, 1952), 214, 298, 319–21.

34. Salo W. Baron, *The Jewish Community* (3 vols., Philadelphia, 1942), I, 208–209, 213; Menachem Elon, "Power and Authority," in Daniel J. Elazer, ed., *Kin-*

ship and Consent (Washington, D.C., 1984), 184–85, 205–207; Biale, *Power and Powerlessness*, 58–59, 77–79; Roth, *Halakhic Process*, 126, 133; S. D. Gotein, "The Interplay of Jewish and Islamic Laws," in Ruth Link-Salinger, *Jewish Law in Our Time* (Denver, 1982), 59.

35. Baron, *Jewish Community*, I, 214–15; Biale, *Power and Powerlessness*, 54–56; Leo Landman, *Jewish Law in the Diaspora* (Philadelphia, 1968), 87–96; Dorff and Rosett, *Living Tree*, 516–19; Gotein, "Interplay of Jewish and Islamic Laws," 59; Gil Graff, *Separation of Church and State: Dina de-Malkhuta Dina in Jewish Law, 1750–1848* (University, Ala. 1985), 2.

36. Berkovits, *Not in Heaven*, 85–86, 91–94.

37. Mark Zborowski and Elizabeth Herzog, *Life Is with People* (New York, 1962), 111–12, 116–18, 216–19; Stephen M. Passamaneck and Louis M. Brown, "The Rabbis—Preventive Law Lawyers," *Israel Law R.* 8 (1973), 541–42.

38. Matt. 23:2–39; Shulamith Hareven, "Anatomy of a Deviation," *Jerusalem Q.* 36 (Summer 1985), 120–22; Rivkin, *Hidden Revolution*, 26.

39. Julius Wellhausen, *Prolegomena to the History of Israel* (London, 1885), 402–405, 421–25, 465–68, 497–500, 502, 509–10.

40. For the classic statements, see Albrecht Alt, *Essays on Old Testament History and Religion* (Oxford, 1966), 132; Martin Noth, *The Laws in the Pentateuch and Other Studies* (London, 1966), 87–103; von Rad, *Old Testament Theology*, I, 89–92; Morton Smith, *Palestinian Parties and Politics That Shaped the Old Testament* (New York, 1971), 54–55. Such attitudes help to explain, in the title of Jon D. Levenson's fascinating essay, "Why Jews Are Not Interested in Biblical Theology," in Jacob Neusner et al., eds., *Judaic Perspectives on Ancient Israel* (Philadelphia, 1987) 281–307.

41. Roth, *Halakhic Process*, 9; Hans Jochen Boecker, *Law and the Administration of Justice in the Old Testament and Ancient Near East* (Minneapolis, 1980), 136–38; Moshe Meiselman, *Jewish Woman in Jewish Law* (New York, 1978), 64–65, 185; Ringgren, *Israelite Religion*, 304–305; Blenkinsopp, *Wisdom and Law*, 92; Elon, ed., *Principles of Jewish Law*, 15.

42. Nahum Sarna, *Exploring Exodus* (New York, 1986), 144, 174; Dorff and Rosett, *Living Tree*, 27–28; Falk, *Law and Religion*, 15–20, 53–55; Haim Cohn, *Jewish Law in Ancient and Modern Israel* (New York, 1971), xxxi, 4–5; Deut. 6:18; Lev. 20:22, 26–27; Michael A. Fishbane, *Judaism: Revelation and Traditions* (New York, 1987), 55. As Jews reiterate during festival services: "you have raised us up out of all the nations, set us apart through your commandments, and drawn us close to you."

43. De Vaux, *Ancient Israel*, I, 147–49; Moshe Weinfeld, "Covenant," *Encyclopedia Judaica* 5:1019; Hillers, *Covenant*, 49–53, 64; Harry M. Orlinsky, "The Biblical Concept of the Land of Israel: Cornerstone of the Covenant between God and Israel," in Lawrence A. Hoffman, ed., *The Land of Israel: Jewish Perspectives* (Notre Dame, 1986), 28–35; Sarna, *Exploring Exodus*, esp. 140–41 for the dissimilarities.

44. For a perceptive discussion, see Elliot Salo Schoenberg, "The Constitution and the Religious Life," in Study Guide, "Covenant," 37–38. (For an example of the obliteration of God from the covenantal tradition in order to underscore common features, see Michael Walzer, *Exodus and Revolution* [New York, 1985], 88– 89.) Dorff and Rosett, *Living Tree*, 53, 94–95, 362.

45. Deut. 31:12–13; Ezra 7:10; Neh. 8:8–9.

46. Sol Roth, *Halakhah and Politics: The Jewish Idea of the State* (New York, 1988), 26–28, 40, 66–68, 93; Deut. 12:8.

47. Daniel Pipes, *In the Path of God* (New York, 1983), 35–38, 39, 110; Bernard Lewis, *The Political Language of Islam* (Chicago, 1988), 28–29, 72.

48. Dorff and Rosett, *Living Tree*, 568.

49. *The Works of Flavius Josephus*, trans. William Whiston; *Antiquities of the Jews* (London, 1871), Book XX, Ch. XI, 549.

50. For a recent example that demonstrates the continuing urgency of the effort, see Bernard M. Zlotowitz, "The Biblical and Rabbinic Underpinnings of the Constitution," *Judaism* 37 (Summer 1988), 328–34.

3. PROPHETIC JUSTICE

1. Amos 5:15, 24; Isa. 1:14, 17; Jer. 22:17–18; Mic. 4:3, 6:8.

2. James L. Crenshaw, *Prophetic Conflict* (Berlin, 1971), 93–94, 97, 103; Yehezkel Kaufmann, *The Religion of Israel* (New York, 1972), 157ff.; Sheldon H. Blank, "'Of a Truth the Lord Hath Sent Me': An Inquiry into the Source of the Prophet's Authority," in *Interpreting the Prophetic Tradition* (New York, 1969), 5.

3. Bernhard W. Anderson, *The Eighth Century Prophets* (Philadelphia, 1978), xiii–xv, 2–5, 23; Gerhard von Rad, *The Message of the Prophets* (New York, 1972), 282–84; E. W. Heaton, *The Old Testament Prophets* (London, 1977), 9–10, 142–43, 147; Matt. 9:10–13; Acts 2:16; 21:11, 46.

4. Joseph Blenkinsopp, *A History of Prophecy in Israel* (London, 1984), 27; Ronald E. Clements, *A Century of Old Testament Study* (Guildford, 1983), 2, 62–63; Adolphe Lods, *The Prophets and the Rise of Judaism* (London, 1937), 1.

5. Blenkinsopp, *History of Prophecy*, 25; Clements, *Century of Old Testament Study*, 9–11, 66–69.

6. Julius Wellhausen, *Prolegomena to the History of Israel* (Edinburgh, 1885), 3–4; Clements, *Century of Old Testament Study*, 7–10.

7. Wellhausen, *Prolegomena*, 5, 8–9, 417, 465–70.

8. Ibid., 398, 473–74, 485, 491.

9. Ibid., 5, 402, 421–25, 485, 499–500, 502, 509–10, 538–42, 548.

10. Kaufmann, *Religion of Israel*, 153; Bernhard Lang, *Monotheism and the Prophetic Minority* (Sheffield, 1983), 15; George W. Coats and Burke O. Long, eds., *Canon and Authority* (Philadelphia, 1977), ix–x; Robert R. Wilson, *Prophecy and Society in Ancient Israel* (Philadelphia, 1980), 3; Clements, *Century of Old Testament Study*, 61–2.

11. Ivan Engnell, *Critical Essays on the Old Testament* (Nashville, 1969), 137–38; A. S. Van Der Woude, "Three Classical Prophets: Amos, Hosea, and Micah," in Richard Coggins *et al.*, eds., *Israel's Prophetic Tradition* (Cambridge, 1982), 32; J. Pederson, "The Role Played by Inspired Persons among the Israelites and the Arabs," in H. H. Rowley, ed., *Studies in Old Testament Prophecy* (Edinburgh, 1946), 128; W. Robertson Smith, *The Prophets of Israel* (London, 1882), xlvix–lv, 95–101, 227–28, 271, 275; Joseph Blenkinsopp, *Prophecy and Canon* (Notre Dame, 1977), 187–88; Heaton, *Old Testament Prophets*, 146–47; C. F. Whitley, *The Prophetic Achievement* (Leiden, 1963), 197; Clements, *Century of Old Testament Study*, 63, 174; Kaufmann, *Religion of Israel*, 403; Stephen A. Geller, "Wellhausen and Kaufmann," *Midstream* 31 (Dec. 1985), 39–40.

12. Jakob J. Petuchowski, *Ever since Sinai* (New York, 1961), 18–20; Blenkinsopp, *History of Prophecy*, 28–33; Clements, *Century of Old Testament Study*, 74–80, 84; R. E. Clements, *Prophecy and Tradition* (Oxford, 1978), 3–4; James Muilenburg, "The 'Office' of the Prophet in Ancient Israel," in J. Philip Hyatt, ed., *The Bible in Modern Scholarship* (Nashville, 1965), 89; Dennis J. McCarthy, *Old Testament Covenant* (Oxford, 1972), 36; Robert R. Wilson, "Prophecy and Society in Ancient Israel," in Norman K. Gottwald, ed., *The Bible and Liberation* (Maryknoll, 1984), 203–207.

13. R. E. Clements, "Patterns in the Prophetic Canon," in Coats and Long,

eds., *Canon and Authority*, 50; Kaufmann, *Religion of Israel*, 346–52; Irving M. Zeitlin, *Ancient Judaism* (Cambridge, 1984), 211–14.

14. 2 Kings 17:2, 7–9, 13–15, 18.

15. John Bright, *Covenant and Promise* (London, 1977), 80–82; Blenkinsopp, *History of Prophecy*, 147–48, 164; Gerhard von Rad, *Old Testament Theology* (2 vols., London, 1965), I, 69–70; Amos 1:2.

16. Adam C. Welch, *Prophet and Priest in Old Israel* (Oxford, 1936), 5–6, 148–49; Kaufmann, *Religion of Israel*, 343–44.

17. Jer. 6:16; 29:32. Whether a modern Jew who cites prophetic authority is obligated to remain faithful to its historical context and substantive content can, of course, be vigorously debated. My own position is implicit in the text. It is less a plea for "original intent," in the American constitutional vernacular, than an insistence upon fidelity to history and language. Anything less strikes me as mindless deconstructionism. Certainly new insights may illuminate old admonitions, and should; but indifference to the tradition one claims to interpret, or to its own interpretive canons, hardly inspires confidence in the result.

18. Kaufmann, *Religion of Israel*, 405; Isa. 2–3.

19. Ps. 137:1–2, 4–5.

20. Isa. 42:6; 45:22–23; 46:10–13; Whitley, *Prophetic Achievement*, 42: Blenkinsopp, *History of Prophecy*, 212–15. For a contrary view, see R. E. Clements, *Old Testament Theology* (Atlanta, 1978), 77; Zeitlin, *Ancient Judaism*, 267.

21. Hos. 12:14, 14:2; Blenkinsopp, *Prophecy and Canon*, 1–5; 2 Kings 17:13; Richard Hentschke, "Law and Eschatology in the Message of the Prophets," in Ruth Link-Salinger, ed., *Jewish Law in Our Time* (Denver, 1982), 27–29.

22. R. E. Clements, *Prophecy and Covenant* (London, 1965), 16, 69–71, 123–24, 126–27; Louis Isaac Rabinowitz, "Prophets and Prophecy," *Encyclopedia Judaica* (Jerusalem, 1972), vol. XIII, 1152, 1161; Delbert Hillers, *Covenant* (Baltimore, 1970), 141. For a contrary view, see Anthony Phillips, "Prophecy and Law," in Coggins et al., eds., *Israel's Prophetic Tradition*, 217–22.

23. Isa. 1:2; Hos. 6:6–7; Jer. 11:6; 31:31–32; Ezek. 36:27–28; Clements, *Old Testament Theology*, 102–103.

24. For a listing that matches prophetic accusation to pentateuchal legislation, see Richard V. Bergren, *The Prophets and the Law* (Cincinnati, 1974), 182–83. On the general point of covenantal obligation in prophecy, see Kaufmann, *Religion of Israel*, 165–66; von Rad, *Message of the Prophets*, 207–208; Engnell, "Prophets," 172–73; Brevard S. Childs, *Memory and Tradition in Israel* (Chatham, 1962), 56–67; Walter Brueggemann, *The Land* (Philadelphia, 1977), 92. For an argument for the direct transmission of covenantal fidelity from the Prophets through Christianity to "our liberal democratic tradition," see R. B. Y. Scott, *The Relevance of the Prophets* (New York, 1944), 188–190, 235–37.

25. Mic. 6:1–2, 8; Hos. 4:1, 6–7; Isa. 1:2–3; Jer. 2; 6:9–11; Jon D. Levenson, *Sinai & Zion* (San Francisco, 1987), 54–55; G. Ernest Wright, "The Lawsuit of God: A Form-Critical Study of Deuteronomy 32," in Bernhard W. Anderson and Walter Harrelson, eds., *Israel's Prophetic Heritage* (New York, 1962), 63–66; Hillers, *Covenant*, 124–26, 134, 140–41; Bergren, *Prophets and Law*, 85–86, 126–27.

26. Amos 2:4; Hos. 8:1; Herbert B. Huffmon, "The Covenant Lawsuit in the Prophets," *J.Bib.Lit.* 78 (1959), 285–95; James Limburg, "The Root ריב and the Prophetic Lawsuit Speeches," ibid. 88 (1969), 291–304; George Mendenhall, *Law and Covenant in Israel and the Ancient Near East* (Pittsburgh, 1955), 19ff.; Claus Westermann, *Basic Forms of Prophetic Speech* (London, 1967), 80, 89; Clements, *Prophecy and Tradition*, 18–20, 44, 50; Mal. 3:22–23.

27. Gen. 18:26; Exod. 21:1–23:20; Lev. 24:22; Deut. 1:17; 25:1.

28. Klaus Koch, *The Prophets* (2 vols., Philadelphia, 1983), II, 97–98; Eliezer Berkovits, "The Biblical Meaning of Justice," *Judaism* 18 (1969), 188–89, 197–201; Zeev W. Falk, *Hebrew Law in Biblical Times* (Jerusalem, 1964), 25–26; Chaim Shine, "The Concept of Justice in Jewish Law," in Link-Salinger, *Jewish Law in Our Time*, 49; Hillers, *Covenant*, 130; Helmer Ringgren, *Israelite Religion* (London, 1966), 131–32.

29. Ezek. 5:2–7; J. Lindblom, *Prophecy in Ancient Israel* (Oxford, 1962), 348; Koch, *Prophets*, I, 57–61; Heaton, *Old Testament Prophets*, 65–66; Abraham J. Heschel, *The Prophets* (2 vols., New York, 1962), I, 200–201, 210; Martin Buber, *The Prophetic Faith* (New York, 1949), 1, 101–102.

30. Phillips, "Prophecy and Law," in Coggins *et al.*, eds., *Israel's Prophetic Tradition*, 220–23; F. Charles Fensham, "Widow, Orphan and the Poor in Ancient Near Eastern Legal and Wisdom Literature," *J. Near Eastern Studies* 21 (1962), 129–39; Kaufmann, *Religion of Israel*, 221–38.

31. Shalom M. Paul, "Prophets and Prophecy," *Encyclopedia Judaica*, vol. XIII, 1172; Roland de Vaux, *Ancient Israel* (2 vols., New York, 1965), II, 354–55; Norman W. Porteous, *Living the Mystery* (Oxford, 1967), 52–53; Clements, *Prophecy and Covenant*, 86–88.

32. Hos. 4:6; 6:6–7; 14:2; Amos 5:5; 21:5; Clements, *Prophecy and Covenant*, 86–88.

33. Isa. 1:4, 11, 14; Jer. 7:22–24; Clements, *Prophecy and Covenant*, 94–99; Shubert Spero, *Morality, Halakha, and the Jewish Tradition* (New York, 1983), 36–38.

34. Isa. 6:6–8, 9; Ringgren, *Israelite Religion*, 262, 269–70; Clements, *Prophecy and Tradition*, 38–39.

35. Ezek. 12:1–2; 14:5; 15:8; 36:25–29; Isa. 42:18; 43:24– 5; Heaton, *Old Testament Prophets*, 119; Ringgren, *Israelite Religion*, 284–86; Lindblom, *Prophecy in Ancient Israel*, 384–87.

36. Koch, *Prophets*, II, 186: Hag. 1:8; Zech. 14:20–21.

37. Koch, *Prophets*, II, 159–60; Rex Mason, "The Prophets of the Restoration," in Coggins, *et al.*, eds., *Prophetic Tradition*, 151; Heaton, *Old Testament Prophets*, 127–28.

38. Kaufmann, *Religion of Israel*, 158–59; Engnell, "Prophets," 139–40; Blenkinsopp, *History of Prophecy*, 95; Amos 5:6; Porteous, *Mystery*, 55–56, 67, 124; Lindblom, *Prophecy in Ancient Israel*, 322–23; Ringgren, *Israelite Religion*, 250–55; R. E. Clements, *The Conscience of the Nation* (Oxford, 1967), 39–40; Koch, *Prophets*, I, 96; II, 190–91; Clements, *Old Testament Theology*, 55–56, 113.

39. Deut. 4:8; Boaz Cohen, *Law and Tradition in Judaism* (New York, 1969), 185–86, 192; Saul A. Berman, "Law and Morality," *Encyclopedia Judaica*, vol. X, 1480; Menachem Elon, ed., *Principles of Jewish Law* (Jerusalem, 1976), 153; Clements, *Prophecy and Tradition*, 69–71, 76, 77–80, 125; Clements, *Old Testament Theology*, 121–22, 125.

40. Kaufmann, *Religion of Israel*, 234, 316; Pinhas Peli, "In the Valley of the Dry Bones," *Jerusalem Post*, April 25, 1986, p. 9. It should be noted, however, that Jewish worship, consistent with the normative tradition, subordinates prophecy to law. Only adults can read from the Torah. It is read first, only from the scrolls in Hebrew, and only in the company of a *minyan* of ten adults. The prophetic selection can be read by a minor, in any language, from a printed book. In religious ritual, therefore, the Prophets "stand in the shadow of the Torah." Walter Zimmerli, *The Law and the Prophets* (Oxford, 1965), 15, 22.

41. Deut. 18:15, 18; 34:10–11; Kaufmann, *Religion of Israel*, 212–13, 316–17, 328; Michael Fishbane, *Text and Texture* (New York, 1979), 68–69.

42. Blenkinsopp, *Prophecy and Canon*, 116, 144, 151–52.

43. Deut. 13:2–4; 18:15; Nehama Leibowitz, *Studies in Devarim* (Jerusalem, 1980), 125–33; Clements, *Prophecy and Tradition*, 51–52.

44. Deut. 13:1; 18:15, 20–21; Blenkinsopp, *History of Prophecy*, 24–26; Levi A. Olan, *Prophetic Faith and the Secular Age* (New York, 1982), 56, 57, 59–60; Walter S. Wurzburger, "Modern Jewish Thought," *Encyclopedia Judaica*, vol. XIII, 1179–82.

45. Tom Segev, *1949: The First Israelis* (New York, 1986), x. See also David Ben-Gurion, "Words and Values," *Jewish Frontier* 24 (Dec. 1957), 15. Yet Judah Magnes, an American Reform rabbi who went to live in Palestine after World War I, became chancellor of the new Hebrew University in Jerusalem, and actively resisted the proclamation of Jewish statehood, rested his alternative peace plan upon Hebrew prophecy. Identifying with Jeremiah, he found that "the chief source of my moral being is the Hebrew prophet." Norman Bentwich, *For Zion's Sake* (Philadelphia, 1954), 281, 284–86. For a parallel movement in Islam, the splitting of law and justice into separate spheres, see Bernard Lewis, *The Jews of Islam* (Princeton, 1984), 53.

46. Robert Alter, *The Art of Biblical Poetry* (New York, 1985), 162. A poignant example can be found in a father's acknowledgement of a condolence letter upon the death of his son during the Spanish Civil War: "My boy was actually living . . . some of the ideals of prophetic Judaism. . . . He was an avowed Socialist and an ardent anti-fascist." Lee L. Levinger to Stephen S. Wise, October 15, 1937, Box 46, Stephen S. Wise MSS, American Jewish Historical Society. The liberal journal *Tikkun*, upon its founding in 1986, claimed to speak to those "who are still moved by the radical spirit of the Prophets"—not only Jews ("much less religious Jews"), but all who can hear in prophecy the condemnation of religion as "a cover for economic immorality." Michael Lerner, "Tikkun: To Mend, Repair, and Transform the World," *Tikkun* 1 (1986), 3–4.

4. EMANCIPATION

1. Salo W. Baron, *The Jewish Community* (3 vols., Philadelphia, 1941), I, 155, 208–15; Jacob Neusner, *Death and Birth of Judaism* (New York, 1987), xi, 4, 33–36, 295; Baruch Halpern, *The Emergence of Israel in Canaan* (Chico, 1983), 239.

2. Alain Besancon, "Modern Ideologies and the Jews," *Commentary* 83 (March 1987), 42–43; Nicholas de Lange, *Judaism* (Oxford, 1987), 92, 139.

3. Paul R. Mendes-Flohr and Jehuda Reinharz, *The Jew in the Modern World* (New York, 1980), 104–105, 108; Lucy S. Dawidowicz, *The Jewish Presence* (New York, 1976), 3ff.

4. Mendes-Flohr and Reinharz, *The Jew*, 114; Simon Schwarzfuchs, *Napoleon, the Jews and the Sanhedrin* (London, 1979), 57–58; Franz Kobler, *Napoleon and the Jews* (New York, 1976).

5. Mendes-Flohr and Reinharz, *The Jew*, 116–17, 119. The Assembly did, however, apply the *dina de-malkhuta dina* principle to justify its capitulation. See Gil Graff, *Separation of Church and State: Dina de-Malkhuta Dina in Jewish Law, 1750–1848* (University, Ala., 1985), 88–89.

6. Mendes-Flohr and Reinharz, *The Jew*, 122, 124. "What remained of Jewish legal authority was an emasculated concurrent jurisdiction" in marriage and divorce issues. Before too much longer, under Reform influence, the *dina* principle only protected religious belief from state control. Graff, *Separation of Church and State*, 107, 135.

7. Daniel Pipes, *In the Path of God* (New York, 1983), 108–10; Ismar Schorsch, "Emancipation and the Crisis of Religious Authority—The Emergence of the Modern Rabbinate," in Werner E. Mosse, ed., *Revolution and Evolution* (Tubingen, 1981), 205, 207, 212, 230.

8. David Biale, *Power and Powerlessness in Jewish History* (New York, 1986), 94–95; Baron, *Jewish Community*, I, 9; Schwarzfuchs, *Napoleon*, 179–180, 182–83.

9. Neusner, *Death and Birth*, 75–76, 82; Jacob Katz, *Tradition and Crisis* (New York, 1961), 270–71; Elliot N. Dorff and Arthur Rosett, *A Living Tree* (Albany, 1988), 338–45.

10. Michael A. Meyer, *Response to Modernity* (New York, 1988), 6, 9, 62–63, 67, 82.

11. Naomi W. Cohen, *Encounter with Emancipation* (Philadelphia, 1984), xi–xii; Leon A. Jick, *The Americanization of the Synagogue, 1820–1870* (Hanover, N.H., 1976), 7, 80–81, 96; W. Gunther Plaut, "The Ambiguity of Reform," in Bertram W. Korn, ed., *A Bicentennial Festschrift for Jacob Rader Marcus* (New York, 1976), 424.

12. John F. Wilson and Donald L. Drakeman, eds., *Church and State in American History* (Boston, 1987), xi–xii; Cohen, *Encounter*, 161–162.

13. Jick, *Americanization*, 70, 73, 115, 131, 143, 155; Marc Lee Raphael, *Profiles in American Judaism* (San Francisco, 1984), 34, 38; Jacob Katz, *Out of the Ghetto* (Cambridge, 1973), 68, 130.

14. Dawidowicz, *Jewish Presence*, 15, 93–95; Egal Feldman, "The Social Gospel and the Jews," *AJHQ* 58 (1969), 311–12; Meyer, *Response to Modernity*, 239; Jacob Neusner, ed., *Understanding American Judaism* (2 vols., New York, 1975), II, 85; Jakob J. Petuchowski, "The Limits of Liberal Judaism," in ibid., 49; Wilson and Drakeman, eds., *Church and State*, 88–91, 128; James F. Maclear, "The True American Union of Church and State: The Reconstruction of the Theocratic Tradition," *Church History* 28 (1959), 41–62.

15. James G. Heller, *Isaac M. Wise* (New York, 1965), 78–90, 94; Isaac M. Wise, *Reminiscences* (Cincinnati, 1901), 13, 21–24, 71.

16. Wise, *Reminiscences*, 85–86, 116, 267; Heller, *Wise*, 136–39, 162, 185–93.

17. Heller, *Wise*, 136; Wise, *Reminiscences*, 85–86, 133, 136, 138–39, 143–44, 146; Jick, *Americanization*, 83–84, 125.

18. Wise, *Reminiscences*, 221–24, 317, 331; Heller, *Wise*, 229, 235–37, 552–53, 559; Isaac M. Wise, *History of the Israelitish Nation from Abraham to the Present Time* (Albany, 1854), iv.

19. Jick, *Americanization*, 134, 151, 157; Heller, *Wise*, 237, 277, 408–17, 434, 458.

20. Wise, *Reminiscences*, 295; Heller, *Wise*, 583–86.

21. Sefton D. Temkin, "Kaufmann Kohler," *Encyclopedia Judaica* (Jerusalem, 1972) vol. X, 1142; Kaufmann Kohler, *The Origins of the Synagogue and the Church*, biographical essay by H. G. Enelow (New York, 1929), viii–xv; Kaufmann Kohler, "Personal Reminiscences," in *Studies, Addresses, and Personal Papers* (New York, 1931), 475–76.

22. Alexander Kohut, *The Ethics of the Fathers* (New York, 1885), 8, 11; Cohen, *Encounter*, 180–81.

23. Kohler, "Backward or Forward?" in *Studies*, 201–208.

24. Kohler, "Form or Spirit," ibid., 209–11; "Piety or a Living Religion," ibid., 216, 219; "Is Reform Destructive or Constructive?" ibid., 222, 224, 227.

25. Kohler, "Form or Spirit," ibid., 213; "Palestine or American Judaism?" ibid., 229–30, 232, 234.

26. Meyer, *Response to Modernity*, 266–69; Jonathan D. Sarna, "Review Essay," *AJH* 76 (March 1987), 362–63.

27. Heller, *Wise*, 463–64; "Pittsburgh Platform" (1885), *Yearbook of Central Conference of American Rabbis* (hereafter CCAR *Yearbook*) 1 (1890), 121–22; Plaut, "Ambiguity of Reform," 425–26; Plaut, "The Pittsburgh Platform in the Light of European Antecedents," in Walter Jacob, ed., *The Pittsburgh Platform in Retrospect* (Pittsburgh, 1985), 21.

28. Plaut, "Ambiguity of Reform," 424–25; Jacob B. Agus, "The Reform Movement," in Neusner, ed., *Understanding American Judaism*, II, 10–15; Kohler, "Form or Spirit," 211; Plaut, "Pittsburgh Platform," 22–24. For another view of the Pittsburgh Platform, deemphasizing its antinomianism, see Walter Jacob, "The Influence of the Pittsburgh Platform on Reform Halakhah and Biblical Study," in Jacob, ed., *Pittsburgh Platform*, 27–29, 35–38.

29. Jacob B. Agus, "The Prophet in Modern Hebrew Literature," in Agus, ed., *Interpreting the Prophetic Tradition* (New York, 1969), 45–46, 51, 56–62, 78. For a confirming example, see Sheldon H. Blank, "Hebrew Prophecy: The Challenge and the Hope," in Edward A. Goldman, ed., *Jews in a Free Society* (Cincinnati, 1978), 30–42.

30. Bertram W. Korn, "Introduction: The Jews of the Union," *Amer. J. Archives* 13 (Nov. 1961), 135; [David Einhorn] *Sinai* 6 (June 1861), in ibid., 152, 158, 160–61; Korn, *American Jewry and the Civil War* (Philadelphia, 1957), 20–22, 25, 30.

31. Cohen, *Encounter*, 195–96; Roland B. Gittelsohn, "The Conference Stance on Social Justice and Civil Rights," in Bertram W. Korn, ed., *Retrospect and Prospect* (New York, 1965), 83, 87–88; Leonard J. Mervis, "The Social Justice Movement and the American Reform Rabbi," *Amer. J. Archives* 7 (June 1955), 171–230; Feldman, "Social Gospel and the Jews," 308–22.

32. *Proceedings of the CCAR*, 2 (1891), 5; ibid., 3 (1892), 4, 6; ibid., 6 (1895), 8–10; ibid., 9 (1898), 7; David Philipson, *My Life as an American Jew* (Cincinnati, 1941), 168; Marc Lee Raphael, "Rabbi Jacob Voorsanger of San Francisco on Jews and Judaism," *AJHQ* 63 (1973–74), 189, 192–93, 201.

33. CCAR *Yearbook*, 1 (1890–91), 117–19; Naomi Wiener Cohen, "The Reaction of Reform Judaism in America to Political Zionism (1897–1922)," in Abraham J. Karp, ed., *The Jewish Experience in America* (Waltham, 1969), 149–53.

34. Raphael, *Profiles*, 25–30, 41; Melvin Weinman, "The Attitude of Isaac Mayer Wise toward Zionism and Palestine," *Amer. J. Archives* 3 (Jan. 1951), 5–10; Heller, *Wise*, 605–608; CCAR *Yearbook*, 8 (1897), xi–xii, xli; ibid., 9 (1899), 190; Joseph P. Sternstein, "Reform Judaism and Zionism, 1895–1904," *Herzl Year Book* 5 (1963), 15–16, 21; David Philipson, "Judaism and the Republican Form of Government," CCAR *Yearbook*, 2 (1891), 48, 52–55; ibid., 14 (1904), 188–91; ibid., 18 (1908), 145–46.

35. CCAR *Yearbook*, 2 (1891–92), 85, 87–89, 91–92, 94.

36. Ibid., 94, 115, 128; H. Berkowitz to Bernard Felsenthal, Aug. 19, 1890, Box 1, Felsenthal MSS, AJHS.

37. Jacob Voorsanger to Bernard Felsenthal, August 6, 1883, Box 2, Felsenthal MSS; CCAR *Yearbook*, 1 (1890), 67–69; ibid., 5 (1894), 121–22, 124–27, 129. The titles of these addresses are suggestive of the malaise of the time: "The Relation of the Rabbi to the Congregation"; "The Duties of the Rabbi in the Present Time." What those duties were, no Reform rabbi seemed to know. Their abdication helps to explain the emergence of lay leaders, committed to philanthropic and fraternal activities, in Jewish communal affairs. They even ran the synagogues, with rabbis literally their employees. Arthur Goren called my attention to this development.

38. CCAR *Yearbook*, 7 (1896), 116–18; ibid., 4 (1893), 58, 60–61, 63; David Philipson to Felsenthal, Aug. 1, 1904, Box 2, Felsenthal MSS.

39. Richard J. H. Gottheil, *The Life of Gustav Gottheil* (Williamsport, Pa. 1936),

34; Jerome E. Carlin and Saul H. Mendlovitz, "The American Rabbi: A Religious Specialist Responds to the Loss of Authority," in Marshall Sklare, ed., *The Jews* (New York, 1958), 377–411; Jacob A. Shankman, "The Changing Role of the Rabbi," in Korn, ed., *Retrospect*, 234–39, 243; Bernard J. Bamberger, "The American Rabbi—His Changing Role," *Judaism* 3 (1954), 488–90; Salo W. Baron, "The Image of the Rabbi, Formerly and Today," in *Steeled by Adversity* (Philadelphia, 1971), 148–56; Jakob J. Petuchowski, *Ever since Sinai* (New York, 1961), 109; Abraham J. Feldman, "The Changing Functions of the Synagogue and the Rabbi," in Neusner, ed., *Understanding American Judaism*, I, 103–10; Harold Saperstein, "The Changing Role of the Rabbi: A Reform Perspective," in Gilbert S. Rosenthal, ed., *The American Rabbi* (New York, 1977), 152–54; Schorsch, "Emancipation and the Crisis of Religious Authority," 230.

40. Kaufmann Kohler, *Hebrew Union College and Other Addresses* (Cincinnati, 1916), 8; Kohler, *A Living Faith* (Cincinnati, 1948), 11–12; Kohler, *Studies*, 189–91, 198, 331–32.

41. Nathaniel Katzburg and Walter S. Wurzburger, "Orthodoxy," *Encyclopedia Judaica*, vol. 12, 1486–87; Raphael, *Profiles*, 132–33; Abraham J. Karp, "New York Chooses a Chief Rabbi," *PAJHS* 44 (March 1955), 133–35; Herbert S. Goldstein, ed., *Forty Years of Struggle for a Principle: The Biography of Harry Fischel* (New York, 1928), 12.

42. Karp, "New York Chooses," 137–39, 143–44.

43. Ibid., 146, 155, 173–75, 179–80.

44. Ibid., 191; Carlin and Mendlovitz, "American Rabbi," 383, 385; Bernard Drachman, *The Unfailing Light* (New York, 1948), 198–204.

45. Kohler, *Hebrew Union College*, 207–208.

46. Meyer, *Response to Modernity*, 280; Arnold M. Eisen, *The Chosen People in America* (Bloomington, 1983), 170.

47. Robert Alter, "Emancipation, Enlightenment and All That," *Commentary* 53 (1972), 62–3, 67–68. One might ask why, if the sacred law defined the good life, so many Jews were so eager to repudiate it? The answer (as the question itself suggests) lies in the power of a competing, indeed domineering, authority system to redefine the loyalties of those who wished to benefit from its opportunities.

48. Leon Simon, ed., *Selected Essays of Ahad Ha-'Am*, (New York, 1970), 170, 177, 192–94. Even before Ahad Ha-'Am, Moses Hess and Leo Pinsker had similar insights. See Shlomo Avineri, *The Making of Modern Zionism* (New York, 1981), chaps. 3, 7.

5. THE AUTHORITY OF TRADITION

1. Charles Reznikoff, *Louis Marshall: Champion of Liberty* (2 vols., Philadelphia, 1957), I, Introduction by Oscar Handlin, x–xii, 4–5; Marshall to Jacob Schiff, Oct. 30, 1914, Box 1583, Marshall MSS, American Jewish Archives; Marshall to David A. Reed, April 14, 1926, Box 4, Marshall MSS, AJHS.

2. Reznikoff, *Louis Marshall*, I, 4, 7, 1149.

3. Ibid., I, 4.

4. Moshe Davis, *The Emergence of Conservative Judaism* (Philadelphia, 1965), 218–38; Bernard Drachman, *The Unfailing Light* (New York, 1948), 177–81.

5. Marshall Sklare, *Conservative Judaism* (Philadelphia, 1965), 161–64.

6. Cyrus Adler, *Jacob H. Schiff: His Life and Letters* (2 vols., New York, 1928), II, 53–54; Adler to Solomon Schechter, Aug. 26, 1901, Box 1, Schechter MSS, Jewish Theological Seminary; Adler to Schechter, Oct. 2, 1901, in Ira Robinson, ed., *Cyrus Adler: Selected Letters* (2 vols., Philadelphia, 1985), I, 95; Sklare, *Conservative Judaism*,

165, 191–92; Marc Lee Raphael, *Profiles in American Judaism* (San Francisco, 1984), 88–91; Abraham J. Karp, "Solomon Schechter Comes to America," in Karp, *The Jewish Experience in America* (New York, 1969), 127–28.

7. Marshall to Philip Cowen, April 30, 1900, Box 1571; Marshall to Leonard Lewisohn, May 16, 1901, Box 1571; Marshall to Isidor Lewi, Sept. 17, 1904, Box 1573; Marshall to Mayer Sulzberger, Jan. 2, 1902, Box 1572, Marshall MSS, AJA (unless otherwise noted).

8. Marshall to Sulzberger, April 9, 1901, Marshall to Schiff, Aug. 16, 1901, Box 1571; Marshall to Sulzberger, Jan. 11, 1902; Marshall to Nathaniel A. Elsberg, Jan. 14, 1902, Box 1572; Marshall to Schiff, June 3, 1911, Box 1580; Marshall to Eugene H. Lehman, Feb. 28, 1905, Box 1574, Marshall MSS.

9. Marshall to Adolph Lewisohn, June 17, 1902; Marshall to Elias Asiel, Nov. 22, 1902; Marshall to Abraham Abraham, Aug. 6, 1902, Box 1572; Marshall to Eugene H. Lehman, Feb. 28, 1905, Box 1574, Marshall MSS.

10. Abraham A. Neuman, "Cyrus Adler," *AJYB* 42 (5701; 1940), 69.

11. Neuman, "Cyrus Adler," 44–5, 58–60, 68–70; Karp, "Solomon Schechter" 111–16, 121. For some interesting parallels between the history of the Seminary and the development of Yeshiva University, see Aaron Rafettet-Rothkoff, *Bernard Revel: Builder of American Jewish Orthodoxy* (New York, 1981), 46ff.

12. Karp, "Solomon Schechter," 111; Howard Singer, "The Judaism Born in America," *Commentary* 82 (Dec. 1986), 41; Norman Bentwich, *Solomon Schechter* (Philadelphia, 1938), 24–48, 126–30; Solomon Schechter, *Seminary Addresses and Other Papers* (Cincinnati, 1915), 36; Schechter, *Studies in Judaism*, 2d series (Philadelphia, 1908), 4–7.

13. Bentwich, *Solomon Schechter*, 97, 167; Karp, "Solomon Schechter" 112, 124–25; Neuman, "Cyrus Adler," 59–60; Meir Ben-Horin, "Solomon Schechter to Judge Mayer Sulzberger," *Jewish Social Studies* 25 (1963), Pt. I, 268.

14. Ben-Horin, "Solomon Schechter," 268, 270, 275; Bentwich, *Solomon Schechter*, 98, 115; Schechter to Salomon Solis-Cohen, Aug. 6, 1899, Box 5, Schechter MSS.

15. Charles Hoffman to Schechter, July 15, 1900, Box 3, Schechter MSS; Schechter, *Seminary Addresses*, 1–2, 48–49, 85, 147, 158. As Schechter conceded, his praise for Lincoln had an ulterior purpose: to break the Reform monopoly on American patriotism. Schechter to Sulzberger, Feb. 14, 1909, Box 6, Schechter MSS.

16. Bentwich, *Solomon Schechter*, 198; Schechter, *Seminary Addresses*, 22–23, 133, 235.

17. Schechter, *Seminary Addresses*, 23, 125, 131–34; Bentwich, *Solomon Schechter*, 302–303, 306.

18. Schechter to Marshall, Aug. 27, 1905, Box 44, Marshall MSS; Solomon Schechter, *Studies in Judaism*, 1st series (Philadelphia, 1938), 212.

19. Bentwich, *Solomon Schechter*, 207, 211–12, 281–85; Jacob Agus, "The Conservative Movement: Reconstructionism," in Jacob Neusner, ed., *Understanding American Judaism* (2 vols., New York, 1975), II, 207–209, 211; Schechter, *Seminary Addresses*, 231, 235.

20. Schechter, *Seminary Addresses*, 6, 202–204; Bentwich, *Solomon Schechter*, 302; Schechter to Marshall, March 14, 1905, Box 44, Marshall MSS; Schechter to Sulzberger, March 14, 1905, in Meir Ben-Horin, "Solomon Schechter to Judge Mayer Sulzberger," *Jewish Social Studies* 27 (1965), Pt. II, 85; Schechter to Judah L. Magnes, Jan. 7, 1910, File 115, Magnes MSS, Central Archives of the History of the Jewish People, Jerusalem.

21. Singer, "Judaism Born in America," 42; Karp, "Solomon Schechter," 127–28; Marshall to S. R. Travis, June 7, 1917, in Reznikoff, *Louis Marshall*, II, 879;

Jacob R. Marcus and Abraham J. Peck, eds., *The American Rabbinate* (Hoboken, N.J., 1985), preface; Bentwich, *Solomon Schechter*, 190.

22. Bentwich, *Solomon Schechter*, 216, 219, 239; Schechter, *Seminary Addresses*, 114; Naomi W. Cohen, *Encounter with Emancipation* (Philadelphia, 1984), 297.

23. Bentwich, *Solomon Schechter*, 310–12, 314.

24. Bentwich, *Solomon Schechter*, 314–15; Schechter to Israel Zangwill, Feb. 27, 1904, Box 6, Schechter, MSS.

25. Schechter to Zangwill, Feb. 27, 1904, Box 6, Schechter MSS; Bentwich, *Solomon Schechter*, 319–20; Schechter, *Seminary Addresses*, xiv, 91, 93. Schechter's statement appears in *Seminary Addresses* and also in Arthur Hertzberg, ed., *The Zionist Idea* (New York, 1975), 504–13. Citations below are to the Hertzberg text.

26. Schechter, "Zionism: A Statement," 506–508.

27. Ibid., 506–507, 510.

28. Ibid., 508, 510–12.

29. Ibid., 507, 512.

30. Schechter to Marshall, March 31, 1908, File 115, Magnes MSS; Bentwich, *Solomon Schechter*, 322–23, 329; Schechter, "Zionism," 511; Schechter, *Seminary Addresses*, xii–xiii, xxiv, 249.

31. Adler, *Jacob H. Schiff*, II, 165–66, 168–69.

32. Bentwich, *Solomon Schechter*, 190–91, 194–95; Schechter to Marshall, Dec. 12, 1913, Box 4, Schechter MSS.

33. Schechter to Magnes, March 25, 1908, File 115, Magnes MSS; Schechter to Adler, May 16, 1907, Box 2, Adler MSS, AJHS; Schechter to Richard Gottheil, Nov. 18, 1909, Box 3, Schechter MSS; Schechter to Norman Bentwich, Feb. 26, 1914, Feb. 23, 1915; Schechter to Adler, June 8, 1915, Box 1, Schechter MSS.

34. Schechter to Max Heller, Feb. 4, March 10, 1909; Schechter to Samuel Greenbaum, Feb. 23, 1912, Box 3, Schechter MSS.

35. H. Pereira Mendes to Marshall, June 25, 1913, Box 38, Marshall MSS; Bentwich, *Solomon Schechter*, 253; Marshall to Felix Warburg, Dec. 8, 1917, and Marshall to S. R. Travis, June 7, 1917, in Reznikoff, *Louis Marshall*, II, 876, 880.

36. Agus, "Conservative Movement," 207–11; Bentwich, *Solomon Schechter*, 281–2, 285, 296.

37. Davis, *Emergence of Conservative Judaism*, 6, 159– 60; Jacob Neusner, *Death and Birth of Judaism* (New York, 1987), 173.

38. Marshall to Nathan Straus, Oct. 18, 1924, in Reznikoff, *Louis Marshall*, II, 887; Norman B. Mirsky, "Yavneh vs. Masada," in Bertram W. Korn, ed., *A Bicentennial Festschrift for Jacob Rader Marcus* (New York, 1976), 383–84.

39. Schechter to Samuel Greenbaum, Feb. 13, 1912, Box 3, Schechter MSS; Marshall to Nathan Straus, Oct. 18, 1924, in Reznikoff, *Louis Marshall*, II, 885.

40. See Naomi W. Cohen, *Not Free to Desist* (Philadelphia, 1972), 9–13.

41. Marshall to Adolph Kraus, Dec. 26, 1905; Marshall to Cyrus Adler, Dec. 30, 1905, Box 1574, Marshall MSS.

42. Marshall to D. M. Hermalin, Dec. 12, 1903, quoted in Lucy S. Dawidowicz, "Louis Marshall's Yiddish Newspaper, *The Jewish World*: A Study in Contrasts," *Jewish Social Studies* 25 (1963), 129; Marshall to Edward Lauterbach, July 9, 1912, Box 1581; Marshall to Adler, Jan. 23, 1914, Box 1583, Marshall MSS; Marshall to Herbert Friedenwald, Jan. 17, 1907, AJC Archives.

43. Marshall to President William McKinley, March 14, 1900, Box 1571, written to recommend a Jew for appointment to West Point; Marshall to Magnes, May 21, 1915, Box 1584, Marshall MSS; Marshall to Augusta E. Stetson, Jan. 15, 1927, AJC Archives.

44. Marshall, "The American Jew of To-Day" (Dec. 2, 1905), in Reznikoff, *Louis Marshall*, I, 274–75; II, 794, 808; Marshall Address (Temple Beth Emeth, Albany), Nov. 24, 1905, Box 1619; Marshall to Gustavus Rogers, July 25, 1905, Box 1574; Marshall to Charles P. Taft, Aug. 21, 1908, Box 1577, Marshall MSS.

45. Marshall to William D. Guthrie, April 9, 1926, in Reznikoff, *Louis Marshall*, I, 278; Marshall to David A. Reed, April 14, 1926, Box 4, Marshall MSS, AJHS; Reznikoff, *Louis Marshall*, I, Pt. IV.

46. Arthur Goren, *Dissenter in Zion* (Cambridge, 1982), 8–10; Goren, "Judah L. Magnes' Trip to Przedborz," *Studies in Contemporary Jewry* 1 (1984), 163–67, 174; Yohai Goell, "*Aliya* in the Zionism of an American *Oleh*: Judah L. Magnes," *AJHQ* 65 (Dec. 1975), 102–103; Drachman, *Unfailing Light*, 63, 70–71; Stephen S. Wise, *Challenging Years* (New York, 1949), 26–27.

47. Morton Rosenstock, *Louis Marshall, Defender of Jewish Rights* (Detroit, 1965), 46, 48, 49; Reznikoff, *Louis Marshall*, I, 409; II, 798, 808, 883, 884; Marshall to Schechter, June 13, 1907, Box 1576, Marshall MSS; Marshall to Magnes, July 24, 1912, File 1585, Magnes MSS; Marshall to Joseph Silverman, March 12, 1910, Box 1579; Marshall to David Blaustein, Oct. 7, 1905, Box 1574, Marshall MSS. But Marshall did draw the line of support at Yeshiva University. A Jewish university, he believed, would be "most unfortunate," for it could only be "a Ghetto Institution." Rafettet-Rothkoff, *Bernard Revel*, 98–108.

48. Marshall to Edward Lauterbach, Oct. 1, 1908, Box 1577, Marshall MSS; Marshall to Richard V. Lindabury, Oct. 24, 1919, in Reznikoff, *Louis Marshall*, I, 327.

49. Marshall to Schechter, March 4, 1909, Box 1578, Marshall MSS; Rosenstock, *Louis Marshall*, 104, 106.

50. Marshall to A. D. Lasker, Dec. 3, 1914, Box 1583, Marshall MSS; Marshall to Stephen S. Wise, Nov. 29, 1922, Box 183, Wise MSS, American Jewish Historical Society; Marshall to Bernard G. Richards, May 2, 1924, Box 116, ibid.

51. Marshall to Adolph S. Ochs, April 9, 1904, Box 1573; Marshall to Charles H. Shapiro, Feb. 14, 1911, Box 1580, Marshall MSS.

52. Cohen, *Not Free to Desist*, 11–13; Marshall to Adolph Kraus, Dec. 26, 1905, Box 1574; Marshall to Joseph Stolz, Jan. 12, 1906, Box 1575, Marshall MSS; Simon Wolf to Joseph Jacobs, July 14, 1906; Sulzberger to E. B. M. Browne, Dec. 25, 1910, Sulzberger MSS, AJC Archives.

53. Rosenstock, *Louis Marshall*, 28, 192, 278; Cohen, *Not Free to Desist*, 30.

54. Marshall to Schiff, Aug. 9, 13, 1912, Box 35, Marshall MSS; Marshall to Magnes, July 24, 1912, File 1585, Magnes MSS.

55. Reznikoff, *Louis Marshall*, I, 268, 295–97; Marshall to Mack, April 24, 1915, Box 1584; Marshall to Editor, *American Israelite*, Aug. 23, 1926, Box 1598, Marshall MSS.

56. Joseph Jacobs to Marshall, June 12, 1906, Box 17; Marshall to Simon Wolf, March 4, 1919, Box 1589, Marshall MSS.

57. See the perceptive observations in Evyatar Friesel, "Jacob Schiff Becomes a Zionist: A Chapter in American-Jewish Self- Definition, 1907–1917," *Studies in Judaism* 5 (1982), 85–87.

58. Marshall to Maurice Leon, Dec. 30, 1901, Box 1571, Marshall MSS; Reznikoff, *Louis Marshall*, II, 704; Marshall to Schiff, March 26, 1910, Box 1579, Marshall MSS; Marshall to Julian Mack, March 21, 1914, XVIII/113, Mack MSS, Zionist Archives, New York; "Mr. Louis Marshall on Zionists and Zionism," *Jewish Correspondent* (1917), Box 183, Wise MSS.

59. Marshall to Adler, Nov. 10, 1909; Marshall to Daniel Guggenheim, Nov. 24, 1909, Box 1578; Marshall to Aaron Aaronsohn, Jan. 13, 1910, Feb. 21, 1910,

March 30, 1910; Marshall to Adler, Jan. 18, 1910; Marshall to Schiff, March 22, 1910, Box 1579, Marshall MSS. Two years later, Brandeis met Aaronsohn and, equally taken by him, transformed the Palestinian Zionist into an American pioneer. See chapter 6 below. Aaronsohn, a passionate Zionist, used the field station as a base of espionage against the Ottoman Turks during World War I. He died in an airplane accident; his associates, including family members, were arrested and tortured.

60. Marshall to Harry Friedenwald, Aug. 2, 1915, Box 1584, Marshall MSS; Marshall to Schiff, Nov. 14, 1917 (two weeks after the Balfour Declaration), in Reznikoff, Louis Marshall, II, 711–13.

61. Marshall to Lionel de Rothschild, July 12, 1918, AJC Archives; Marshall to Robert Lansing, April 15, 1918; AJC Statement, April 26, 1918, in Reznikoff, Louis Marshall, II, 714–16.

62. Marshall to David Philipson, April 29, 1918; Marshall to Lionel de Rothschild, July 12, 1918; Marshall to Max Senior, Sept. 26, 1918, in Reznikoff, Louis Marshall, II, 717–18, 720–22; Marshall to David Philipson, Sept. 15, 1918, Box 1/13, Philipson MSS, American Jewish Archives; Marshall to Simon Wolf, March 4, 1919, Box 1589, Marshall MSS.

63. Marshall to Rothschild, July 12, 1918, in Reznikoff, Louis Marshall, II, 719; Marshall to Mack, Aug. 23, 1918, AJC Archives, on Mack's decision to resign from the AJC after his election as president of the Zionist Organization of America.

64. Marshall to Schiff, Nov. 14, 1917; Marshall to Cyrus Adler, Sept. 11, 1919, in Reznikoff, Louis Marshall, II, 711, 725–26; Marshall to Adolph S. Ochs, March 5, 1919, Box 1589, Marshall MSS.

65. Marshall to Mack, July 31, 1916, XII/72, Mack MSS; Marshall to Nathan Straus, Jan. 20, 1914; Marshall to James H. Becker, March 19, 1923, in Reznikoff, Louis Marshall, II, 708, 731; Chaim Weizmann, Trial and Error (New York, 1949), 308-309. Yet American Jewish historians continue to overlook his importance. In a recent survey, only three of eleven respondents named Marshall among "the two greatest American Jewish leaders." See, "The Greatest American Jewish Leaders," AJH 78 (Dec. 1988).

66. Friesel, "Jacob Schiff," 84.

67. Marshall to Wise, Dec. 1, 1905, Box 3, Wise MSS.

6. Louis D. Brandeis

1. Allon Gal, Brandeis of Boston (Cambridge, 1980), 72–77, 92–94; Herbert Friedenwald to Mayer Sulzberger, February 28, 1907, Sulzberger MSS, AJC. Felix Adler, the founder of Ethical Culture, was Brandeis's brother-in-law.

2. Gal, Brandeis of Boston, 124–26; Yonathan Shapiro, Leadership of the American Zionist Organization, 1897–1930 (Urbana, 1971), 31; Jacob deHaas, Louis D. Brandeis: A Biographical Sketch (New York, 1929), 52. DeHaas, who worked closely with Brandeis in the American Zionist movement, wrote that Brandeis's "first real contact with Jews" came during the 1910 strike. "The idea of Zionism, the whole problem of Jewish existence had suddenly and unexpectedly confronted him."

3. The best analysis of the textual differences and modifications is Gal, Brandeis of Boston, 131–36. The interview appeared in the American Hebrew (Dec. 2, 1910) and the Jewish Advocate (Dec. 9, 1910). Gal perceptively notes that Brandeis's prophetic self-identification was with Daniel, who dwelled with his people in Babylonian exile, not with Isaiah, who lived in the land of Israel and prophesied the ingathering of Jewish exiles there (pp. 134–35). See also deHaas, Louis D. Brandeis, 151–52.

4. Gal, Brandeis of Boston, 202; Brandeis to Norman Hapgood, June 16, 1913, in Melvin I. Urofsky and David W. Levy, eds., Letters of Louis D. Brandeis (5 vols.,

Albany, 1971–78), III, 117; Address of May 18, 1913, in Barbara Ann Harris, "Zionist Speeches of Louis Dembitz Brandeis: A Critical Edition" (Ph.D. diss., UCLA, 1967), 85–87.

5. Horace Kallen to Stephen S. Wise, March 16, 1916, Box 112, Stephen S. Wise MSS, AJHS.

6. Gal, *Brandeis of Boston*, 206.

7. Gal, *Brandeis of Boston*, 94–95, 126, 180–81; Melvin Urofsky, "Zionism: An American Experience," *AJHQ* 63 (1974), 223–24; Urofsky, *A Mind of One Piece* (New York, 1971), 100, 103–104; Philippa Strum, *Louis D. Brandeis: Justice for the People* (Cambridge, 1984), x-xi, 237–42, 247.

8. Shapiro, *Leadership*, 65–66, 69; Ben Halpern, "Brandeis' Way to Zionism," *Midstream* 17 (Oct. 1971), 12–13. For a critique of the Shapiro thesis, see Stuart M. Geller, "Why Did Louis D. Brandeis Choose Zionism?" *AJHQ* 62 (June 1973), 391ff.

9. Gal, *Brandeis of Boston*, 157–63, 166, 181; Melvin I. Urofsky, *American Zionism from Herzl to the Holocaust* (New York, 1975), 129; deHaas, *Louis D. Brandeis*, 161, 163.

10. Marnin Feinstein, *American Zionism, 1884–1904* (New York, 1965), 20–21, 24, 26–27, 55; Hyman B. Grinstein, "The Memoirs and Scrapbooks of the Late Dr. Joseph Isaac Bluestone of New York City," *PAJHS* 35 (1939), 53–54.

11. Evytar Friesel, "Brandeis' Role in American Zionism Historically Reconsidered," *AJH* 69 (Sept. 1979), 60–61.

12. Richard Gottheil, "The Aims of Zionism" (1898), in Arthur Hertzberg, ed., *The Zionist Idea* (New York, 1975), 499–500.

13. Ibid., 497, 500.

14. Israel Friedlaender, "The Problem of Judaism in America," in *Past and Present* (Cincinnati, 1919), 260, 262.

15. Ibid., xxiii, 269, 273, 278; Friesel, "Brandeis' Role," 43; Friesel, "Ahad Ha-Amism in American Zionist Thought," in Jacques Kornberg, ed., *At the Crossroads: Essays on Ahad Ha-Am* (Albany, 1983), 133–34, 137.

16. Friesel, "Ahad Ha-Amism," 141; Ben Halpern, "The Americanization of Zionism, 1880–1930," *AJH* 69 (Sept. 1979), 17–22; Arthur A. Goren, *Dissenter in Zion* (Cambridge, 1982), 14–18.

17. Kallen to Wise, Dec. 3, 1914, Oct. 13, 1915, Box 112, Wise MSS, AJHS.

18. Friesel, "Brandeis' Role," 43, 78–80, is the best analysis, and a much needed antidote to the standard Brandeis hagiography. See also Eisig Silberschlag, "Zionism and Hebraism in America (1897–1921)," in Isidore S. Meyer, ed., *Early History of Zionism in America* (New York, 1958), 334–35.

19. Union of American Hebrew Congregations, *Proceedings* 5 (1898), 402; Urofsky, *American Zionism*, 92; Shapiro, *Leadership*, 5–6; *Diaries of Theodor Herzl*, Marvin Lowenthal, ed. and trans. (New York, 1956), entry for Nov. 10, 1895, p. 73. "A man," Herzl wrote, "has to choose between Zion and France."

20. Urofsky, *Mind of One Piece*, 10–11; Strum, *Louis D. Brandeis*, 17.

21. Gal, *Brandeis of Boston*, 180–81.

22. Sarah Schmidt, "The Zionist Conversion of Louis D. Brandeis," *Jewish Social Studies* 37 (Jan. 1975), 20, 24–25; Schmidt, "The *Parushim*: A Secret Episode in American Zionist History," *AJHQ* 65 (Dec. 1975), 121; Horace M. Kallen, *Judaism at Bay* (New York, 1932), 32–41, 63, 66.

23. Schmidt, "Zionist Conversion," 27–29, 31–33; Kallen, *Judaism at Bay*, 39–41; Harris, "Zionist Speeches," 111.

24. Harris, "Zionist Speeches," 100, 103–104, 110–11, 113, 125, 132–33, 142–43,

146, 149, 162–64, 247–50; deHaas, *Louis D. Brandeis*, 161–63. The speeches were delivered on Aug. 30, Sept. 27, Oct. 25, Nov. 8, 22, 1914.

25. Harris, "Zionist Speeches," 209, 219.

26. Gal, *Brandeis of Boston*, 93, 95, 126; Urofsky, *American Zionism*, 427; Halpern, "Brandeis' Way to Zionism," 12–13.

27. Hertzberg, ed., *Zionist Idea*, 517–22.

28. DeHaas, *Louis D. Brandeis*, 184–85, 194, 202–203; Urofsky, *American Zionism*, 130.

29. Brandeis to Kallen, March 4, 1915, A 138/9, Richard Gottheil MSS, Central Zionist Archives; Brandeis to deHaas, Sept. 25, 1920, in Urofsky and Levy, eds., *Letters*, IV, 486; Friesel, "Brandeis' Role," 46–47; Halpern, "Americanization of Zionism," 32–33.

30. Brandeis to Jacob Schiff, Nov. 2, 1917, quoted in Shapiro, *Leadership*, 115.

31. Alfred Zimmern to Frankfurter, Nov. 11, 1920, quoted in Simha Berkowitz, "Felix Frankfurter's Zionist Activities" (D.H.L. thesis, Jewish Theological Seminary, 1971), 277.

32. Brandeis to Wise, May 1, 1919, in Urofsky and Levy, eds., *Letters*, IV, 39; Szold to Frankfurter, March 5, 1919, Folder I/1, Robert Szold MSS, Zionist Archives; Szold to the Executive, Dec. 17, 1920, Box 2, Benjamin Cohen MSS, Zionist Archives; Report of Walter E. Meyers, "The First Direct Message from Jewish Palestine," A 264/2, Frankfurter MSS, Central Zionist Archives; Brandeis to Mack and deHaas, Sept. 21, 1921, XVI/92; Mack to Cohen, Aug. 5, 1921, XVI/95, Mack MSS, Zionist Archives.

33. Brandeis to H. Pereira Mendes, Nov. 10, 1918; Brandeis to Bernard Flexner, Feb. 12, 1919; Brandeis to Alice Goldmark Brandeis, July 1, 1919, in Urofsky and Levy, eds., *Letters*, IV, 329, 361, 379–81, 410.

34. Brandeis to Alice Goldmark Brandeis, July 10, 1919; Brandeis to Chaim Weizmann, July 20, 1919, ibid., 417–20.

35. Allon Gal, "Brandeis's View on the Upbuilding of Palestine, 1914–1923," *Studies in Zionism* 6 (Autumn 1982), 216, 218–19, 220, 222; Harry Barnard, *The Forging of an American Jew* (New York, 1974), 265.

36. Brandeis to Mack, Oct. 24, 1919; Brandeis to Mack *et al.*, Oct. 23, 1920, in Urofsky and Levy, eds., *Letters*, IV, 434, 493.

37. Shapiro, *Leadership*, 135–38, 157–58; Urofsky, *American Zionism*, 273–75.

38. Friesel, "Brandeis' Role," 47, 52–56; Halpern, "Americanization of Zionism," 28–29; Shapiro, *Leadership*, 165–66; Brandeis to Frankfurter, April 10, 1921; Brandeis to Alfred Brandeis, April 23, 1921, in Urofsky and Levy, eds. *Letters*, IV, 484–85, 526–27, 549, 549–50n, 552; Weizmann to Mack, Jan. 6, 1921, A264/34, Frankfurter MSS; *Jewish Morning Journal*, May 5 [1921], in III/17, Mack MSS.

39. Gal, "Brandeis's View," 236; Urofsky, *American Zionism*, 291–93; *The Day* (April 5, 1921), quoted in Shapiro, *Leadership*, 171.

40. Weizmann quoted in Isaiah Berlin, *Personal Impressions* (New York, 1982), 37; deHaas, *Louis D. Brandeis*, 169.

41. Brandeis to Frankfurter, Jan. 11, 1924; Brandeis to Szold, Sept. 17, 1930, in Urofsky and Levy, eds., *Letters*, V, 111, 455; Naomi W. Cohen, *The Year after the Riots* (Detroit, 1988), 69ff. For repeated references to the need for "competent" and "able" lawyers, see File IX/2, 7a, Szold MSS.

42. Friesel, "Brandeis' Role," 35–36, 48–51; Halpern, "Americanization of Zionism," 25.

43. Cyrus Adler to Schechter, Oct. 6, 1915; Schechter to Adler, June 8, 1915,

Box 1, Schechter MSS; Schechter to Marshall, June 10, 1915, Box 44, Marshall MSS; Friesel, "Brandeis' Role," 56–57.

44. Louis Lipsky, *Thirty Years of American Zionism* (New York, 1927), 68–70, 71, 76; Deborah Lipstadt, "Louis Lipsky: The Early Years of His Zionist Career," in Frances Malino and Phyllis Cohen Albert, eds., *Essays in Modern Jewish History* (Rutherford, N.J., 1982), 265–66.

45. Chaim Weizmann, *Trial and Error* (New York, 1949), 41–42; Halpern, "Americanization of Zionism," 32–33.

46. Urofsky, *American Zionism*, 297. See also Strum, *Louis D. Brandeis*, chaps. 13–14; Peter Grose, *Israel in the Mind of America* (New York, 1983), 50–51.

47. Urofsky, *American Zionism*, 315–16; Weizmann, *Trial and Error*, 309–11.

48. Naomi W. Cohen, *Encounter with Emancipation* (Philadelphia, 1984), 63.

49. In a recent study, Brandeis is praised as "the founding father of the Jewish presence in American law," while Marshall is not even cited in the index! Robert A. Burt, *Two Jewish Justices* (Berkeley, 1988), 6.

50. Carl E. Schorske, *Fin-de-Siècle Vienna* (New York, 1980), 146–47, 159, 172–73; Walter Laqueur, *A History of Zionism* (New York, 1972), 132–33; Theodor Herzl, *The Jewish State* (New York, 1946), 145–46.

51. Ahad Ha-'Am, "The Jewish State and the Jewish Problem," in *Ten Essays on Zionism and Judaism*, trans. Leon Simon (London, 1922), 46; Solomon Goldman, ed., *The Words of Justice Brandeis* (New York, 1953), 160.

7. Isaiah's Disciples

1. Joseph M. Proskauer, *A Segment of My Times* (New York, 1950), 30; *Felix Frankfurter Reminisces* (New York, 1960), 35–37; Louis Marshall to William D. Guthrie, April 9, 1926, quoted in Jerold S. Auerbach, *Unequal Justice* (New York, 1976), 122.

2. Stephen S. Wise to Frankfurter, April 26, 1921, Box 108, Stephen S. Wise MSS, AJHS.

3. Harry Barnard, *The Forging of an American Jew* (New York, 1974), 18–35, 45–51, 82–3. Julian Mack and Felix Frankfurter may seem, to some, undeserving of the attention I give to them. They did not mold American Jewish opinion in any distinctive way; nor were they—except briefly for Mack—"leaders." I do not intend to diminish the contributions of Jacob Schiff, Cyrus Adler, or Louis Lipsky, among others. Rather, I chose Mack and Frankfurter to illuminate the ideological constraints that American patriotism and immigrant acculturation imposed upon the next generation of prominent Jewish lawyers.

4. Ibid., 94–99, 172–79, 187–89, 192–93.

5. Ibid., 202, 213–15; Mack to Schiff, Nov. 25, 1917, in Evytar Friesel, "Jacob Schiff Becomes a Zionist," *Studies in Zionism* 5 (1982), 88–89; Julian W. Mack, *Americanism and Zionism* (New York, 1919), 3–5.

6. Yonathan Shapiro, *Leadership of the American Zionist Organization, 1897–1930* (Urbana, 1971), 165–66; Melvin I. Urofsky, *American Zionism from Herzl to the Holocaust* (New York, 1975), 291, 293.

7. *Felix Frankfurter Reminisces*, 19, 26–27, 37–38, 289–90; H. N. Hirsch, *The Enigma of Felix Frankfurter* (New York, 1981), 13, 21, 44; Frankfurter to Emory Buckner, Aug. 2, 1912, quoted in Simha Berkowitz, "Felix Frankfurter's Zionist Activities" (D.H.L. thesis, Jewish Theological Seminary, 1971), 1.

8. *Felix Frankfurter Reminisces*, 26–27, 37.

9. Ibid., 27–28, 37; see Hirsch, *Enigma*, 49, and chap. 2 generally.

10. Frankfurter to Mack, Jan. 31, 1916; Kallen to Brandeis, April 10, 1914; Frankfurter to Jesse Lilienthal, Jan. 20, 1918, quoted in Berkowitz, "Felix Frankfurter," 12, 23, 39; Brandeis to Frankfurter, April 28, 1916, A 264/25, FF MSS, Central Zionist Archives; *Felix Frankfurter Reminisces*, 146–47; Hirsch, *Enigma*, 48–52, 62–64.

11. Frankfurter to deHaas, April 1, 1918; Frankfurter to Mack, April 9, 1918, A 264/26; Frankfurter to David Amram, May 14, 1918, A 264/27; Frankfurter to Max Raisin, June 17, 1918, A 264/28; Unidentified memo [1918], A 264/29, FF MSS, Central Zionist Archives.

12. Frankfurter to Prof. Westermann, March 23, 1919; Frankfurter to Robert Szold, April 7, 1919, A 264/30, FF MSS, Central Zionist Archives.

13. Frankfurter to Woodrow Wilson, May 8, 14, 1919, A 264/7, FF MSS, Central Zionist Archives; Frankfurter Memo of Meeting on June 24, 1919, Box 1, Benjamin Cohen MSS, Zionist Archives.

14. *Felix Frankfurter Reminisces*, 155; Frankfurter to Brandeis, April 3, 1919; Minutes of Zionist Provisional Committee Meeting, March 27, 1914, quoted in Berkowitz, "Felix Frankfurter," 11, 13 n.42, 80, 82.

15. Weizmann to Frankfurter, Aug. 27, 1919; Frankfurter to Weizmann, Aug. 29, 1919; WZO Executive Meeting, May, 1921, quoted in Berkowitz, "Felix Frankfurter," 141–42, 278.

16. Frankfurter to Mack, Oct. 10, 1929; Frankfurter to Philip Potash, Oct. 24, 1930, quoted in ibid., 358–60, 397; Naomi W. Cohen, *The Year after the Riots* (Detroit, 1988), 116, 126–27, 130.

17. *Felix Frankfurter Reminisces*, 290; Frankfurter to Meyer W. Weisgal, Dec. 3, 1929, A 264/9; Frankfurter to Felix Warburg, Nov. 6, 7, 1930, A264/36; Frankfurter to "Ben", Dec. 5, 1930, A 264/29; Frankfurter to Harold Laski, Dec. 15, 1930, A 264/42, FF MSS, Central Zionist Archives; Laski to Holmes, Dec. 27, 1930, in Mark DeWolfe Howe, ed., *Holmes-Laski Letters* (2 vols. Cambridge, 1953), II, 1301–2; Frankfurter, "The Palestine Situation Restated," *Foreign Affairs* 9 (April 1931), 417; Frankfurter to Mack, March 30, 1931, quoted in Berkowitz, "Felix Frankfurter," 425.

18. "Professor Frankfurter's Itinerary" (April 1934); Frankfurter to Haim H. Cohen, March 3, 1958, A 264/46; Frankfurter to FDR, April 14, 1934, in *Roosevelt and Frankfurter: Their Correspondence, 1928–1945*, annotated by Max Freedman (Boston, 1967), 211; deHaas to [Mack], June 19, 1934, III/3, Robert Szold MSS, Zionist Archives; Frankfurter to Harry Zinder, Dec. 23, 1937, A264/47, Central Zionist Archives; Berkowitz, "Felix Frankfurter," 446.

19. Margold to Frankfurter, March 27, 1933, Roll 21, FF MSS, Harvard Law School; Frank to Julian Mack, April 17, 1933; Frank to Frankfurter, April 18, 1933, Frank MSS, Yale University Library; Stevenson to Ellen Stevenson [July 1933], in Walter Johnson, ed., *The Papers of Adlai E. Stevenson* (Boston, 1972), I, 249; Frank letters, quoted in Peter H. Irons, *The New Deal Lawyers* (Princeton, 1982), 126–28; Robert Jerome Glennon, *The Iconoclast as Reformer* (Ithaca, 1985), 30, 79.

20. Auerbach, *Unequal Justice*, 167–72; Freedman, *Roosevelt and Frankfurter*, 27; Frankfurter to Marion Frankfurter, March 12, 1923, quoted in Hirsch, *Enigma*, 86; *Felix Frankfurter Reminisces*, 288.

21. Joseph P. Lash, *From the Diaries of Felix Frankfurter* (New York, 1975), 264. Robert A. Burt, *Two Jewish Justices* (Berkeley, 1988), 60–61, notes that Frankfurter often wore the "wrong" clothes for important occasions: his first Oxford dinner; his first Supreme Court conference. He may overlook the most revealing example, recalled at length by Frankfurter himself: When Roosevelt telephoned with the

news of his nomination to the Court, Frankfurter received the call in his under-wear. *Felix Frankfurter Reminisces*, 282–83. See Michael E. Parrish, *Felix Frankfurter and His Times* (New York, 1982), 276; Conference Minutes, Dec. 22– 23, 1938, in Berkowitz,"Felix Frankfurter," 470. For examples of Frankfurter's expressions of concern to Roosevelt during 1938, see Freedman, *Roosevelt and Frankfurter*, 463, 466.

22. *Minersville School District v. Gobitis*, 310 US 586 (1940), 593–94, 596–97; Hirsch, *Enigma*, 148; Richard Danzig, "Justice Frankfurter's Opinions in the Flag Salute Cases: Blending Logic and Psychologic in Constitutional Decision-Making," *Stanford Law Review* 36 (1984), 690–701.

23. *Schneiderman v. U.S.*, 320 US 118 (1943); Lash, *From the Diaries*, 211–13.

24. *West Va. State Board of Education v. Barnette*, 319 US 624 (1943); Lash, *From the Diaries*, 71–72.

25. Lash, *From the Diaries*, 152, 165, 348–50; Bruce Allen Murphy, *The Brandeis/ Frankfurter Connection* (New York, 1982), 302–303; Shabtai Teveth, *Ben-Gurion: The Burning Ground, 1886–1948* (Boston, 1987), 692, 776–77, 804.

26. Murphy, *Brandeis/Frankfurter Connection*, chaps. 6, 8; David Wyman, *The Abandonment of the Jews* (New York, 1984), 316.

27. Lash, *From the Diaries*, 73, 89–90; Hirsch, *Enigma*, 204.

28. Selma Stern, *The Court Jew* (Philadelphia, 1950), 13, 245–46; Hannah Arendt, *The Origins of Totalitarianism* (New York, 1958), 23–25, 66; F. L. Carsten, "The Court Jews: A Prelude to Emancipation," *Leo Baeck Institute Year Book* (1958), 140–56.

29. Wyman, *Abandonment, passim*.

30. Glennon, *Iconoclast as Reformer*, 30–31, 79; Wyman, *Abandonment*, 316. For a vivid, if dismaying, example of Frank's discomfort as a Jew, see his Anon Y. Mous, "The Speech of Judges: A Dissenting Opinion," *Va. Law R.* 29 (1943), 630, 639, in which he criticized Justice Benjamin N. Cardozo for the "alien grace" of his writing style, which was not "good American" (like the prose of Justices Black, Douglas, and Jackson). Fred Konefsky provided me with this revealing tidbit.

31. Haskell Lookstein, *Were We Our Brothers' Keepers?* (New York, 1985), 33; Wyman, *Abandonment*, 313.

8. RABBI AND LAWYER

1. [SSW] "Luncheon with Dr. Weizmann" (April 26, 1921), Box 122, Stephen S. Wise MSS, AJHS.

2. Melvin I. Urofsky, *A Voice That Spoke for Justice* (New York, 1982), 2–4, 6–7, 10–11.

3. Stephen S. Wise, *Challenging Years* (New York, 1949), 23–24.

4. Stephen S. Wise, "To Aaron Wise," in Sidney Strong, ed., *What I Owe to My Father* (New York, 1931), 161–66; Wise, *Challenging Years*, 23, 26–27. Suggestive of the enduring paternal impact on Wise's emotional life was his own deep fear of dying as he approached the age of his father's death. See Urofsky, *Voice*, 235; Wise, "The Beginning of American Zionism," *Jewish Frontier* (Aug. 27, 1947).

5. Wise, quoted in *New York Herald*, Aug. 31, 1897; Carl Hermann Voss, ed., *Stephen S. Wise: Servant of the People* (Philadelphia, 1969), 7; Wise to Herzl, Oct. 26, 1898, Nov. 28, 1899, Box 111, SSW MSS.

6. Urofsky, *Voice*, 24; Wise to Richard Gottheil, April 2, 1904; Wise to Herzl, May 6, 1904, in Voss, ed., *Stephen S. Wise*, 21–22.

7. Wise to Richard Gottheil, July 11, 1904, in Voss, ed., *Stephen S. Wise*, 24; Urofsky, *Voice*, 40–43.

8. See Arthur Aryeh Goren, "The Wider Pulpit: Judah L. Magnes and the Poli-

tics of Morality," in E. Miller Budick *et al.*, eds., *Studies in American Civilization* (Jerusalem, 1987), 107, 112.

9. Urofsky, *Voice*, chap. 7; Wise to Louise Waterman Wise (1902), in Justine Wise Polier and James Waterman Wise, *The Personal Letters of Stephen Wise* (Boston, 1956), 85–86.

10. Polier and Wise, *Personal Letters*, 86; Urofsky, *Voice*, 193; Goren, "Wider Pulpit," 105.

11. Urofsky, *Voice*, 66–67; Wise, "*Gaudium Certaminus*—Why I Have Found Life Worth Living," *Christian Century* 45 (Oct. 11, 1928), 1224; Adler to Schechter, Dec. 28, 1910, Box 1, Schechter MSS, JTS.

12. Rabbi H. Pereira Mendes to Wise, Oct. 6, 1915, Box 116, Wise MSS; Urofsky, *Voice*, 83; Goren, "Wider Pulpit," 105.

13. Wise to Gertrude Wolf, April 23, 1913; Wise to Henry Morgenthau, Sr., Dec. 14, 1914, in Voss, ed., *Stephen S. Wise*, 54, 63; Wise, *Challenging Years*, 45.

14. Wise, *Challenging Years*, 198, 200–201; Wise to Mack, Aug. 24, 1920, Box 114, Wise MSS; Urofsky, *Voice*, 118–19; Wise to Joseph Goldstein, Nov. 13, 1914, Box 123; Horace M. Kallen to Wise, Nov. 2, 1914, Box 112; Wise to Morris Lazaron, April 3, 1917, Box 46, Wise MSS.

15. Wise to Clarence I. de Sola, June 18, 1917, Box 123, Wise MSS; Wise to Rabbi Max Heller, April 16, 1921, quoted in Yonathan Shapiro, *Leadership of the American Zionist Organization, 1897–1930* (Urbana, 1971), 175.

16. Shapiro, *Leadership*, 175; Wise to Nathan and Lena Straus, March 6, 1919, in Voss, ed., *Stephen S. Wise*, 86; Wise, *Challenging Years*, 33; Urofsky, *Voice*, 123–24, 276–77.

17. Urofsky, *Voice*, 162–63, 219–20. Mack reiterated Wise's point: "many of us—like you and I and plenty more—are so situated that we can't give our entire time to the cause." Mack to Wise, Dec. 31, 1930, Box 114, Wise MSS.

18. Urofsky, *Voice*, 268.

19. Wise to Frankfurter, Sept. 8, 1932, Box 108, Wise MSS; Urofsky, *Voice*, 254.

20. Wise to Mack, March 8, 1933, Box 115, Wise MSS; Wise to Brandeis, March 23, 1933, in Voss, ed., *Stephen S. Wise*, 181.

21. Wise to Mack, March 29, 1933, Box 115, Wise MSS; Wise to John Haynes Holmes, April 3, 1933, in Voss, ed., *Stephen S. Wise*, 183; Urofsky, *Voice*, 265.

22. *New York Times*, March 28, 1933. See Moshe Gottlieb, "The First of April Boycott and the Reaction of the American Jewish Community," *AJHQ* 57 (1967–68), 516–56.

23. Wise to Mack, March 29, 1933, Box 115, Wise MSS; Urofsky, *Voice*, 266, 403 n.23; Voss, ed., *Stephen S. Wise*, 183.

24. Wise to Mack, April 15, 1933, Box 115, Wise MSS; Wise to Richard W. Montague, April 18, 1933; Wise to George Alexander Kohut, April 26, 1933; Wise to Mack, April 15, 1933, in Voss, ed., *Stephen S. Wise*, 184–86.

25. Wise to Mack, April 16, April 28, May 4, 1933, Box 115, Wise MSS.

26. Wise to Mack, May 4, 1933, Box 115; Wise to Horace Kallen, June 1, 1933, Box 112, Wise MSS; Urofsky, *Voice*, 271; Wise to John Haynes Holmes, Oct. 19, 1933; Wise to Mack, Oct. 20, 1933; Wise to Nahum Goldman, Feb. 9, 1934, in Voss, ed., *Stephen S. Wise*, 196, 202, 208.

27. Urofsky, *Voice*, 283–84.

28. Wise to Irma Lindheim, Nov. 18, 1936, in Voss, ed., *Stephen S. Wise*, 217; Wise to Robert Szold, June 16, 1937, X/15, Robert Szold MSS, Zionist Archives; Wise to Roosevelt, May 10, 1939, Box 68, Wise MSS; Wise to Otto Nathan, Sept. 17, 1940, in Voss, ed., *Stephen S. Wise*, 242; Urofsky, *Voice*, 288–89.

29. Wise to Frankfurter, Oct. 10, 1941, Box 109, Wise MSS; Wise to Frankfurter, Oct. 10, 1936, X/14, Szold MSS; Wise to Szold, Feb. 10, June 16, Oct. 29, 1937, Box 121, Wise MSS.

30. Wise to Abraham Cohen, Oct. 23, 1939, Box 106; Wise to Samuel Rosenman, Aug. 24, 1943, Box 78, Wise MSS.

31. Wise, "I Am an American," *Opinion* 12 (July 1942), 5; Wise to A. B. Horwitz, Jan. 19, 1939, in Voss, ed., *Stephen S. Wise*, 231–32; Wise to Leo Fassberg, April 14, 1942, quoted in Urofsky, *Voice*, 360.

32. Wise, "I Am an American," 5.

33. Haskel Lookstein, *Were We Our Brothers' Keepers?* (New York, 1985), 216.

34. Henry L. Feingold, "Stephen Wise and the Holocaust," *Midstream* 29 (Jan. 1983), 45; Walter Laqueur and Richard Breitman, *Breaking the Silence* (New York, 1986), 143–53.

35. Ibid., 154–63; Wise to Roosevelt, Dec. 2, 1942, Box 68, Wise MSS; *Zionist Review* 7 (Dec. 11, 1942), 2; Urofsky, *Voice*, 318–19. See David S. Wyman, *The Abandonment of the Jews* (New York, 1984).

36. Urofsky, *Voice*, 321–23, 331; Feingold, "Stephen Wise," 47.

37. Henry L. Feingold, "Who Shall Bear Guilt for the Holocaust? The Human Dilemma," in Jonathan D. Sarna, ed., *The American Jewish Experience* (New York, 1986), 241, 255, 258.

38. Wise to Mack, March 29, 1933, Box 115, Wise MSS; Wise to Mack, April 15, 1933, in Voss, ed., *Stephen S. Wise*, 184.

39. For the World War I episode, see Urofsky, *Voice*, 136–40, 141; Feingold, "Stephen Wise," 47.

40. Wise to Roosevelt, May 13, 1941; Roosevelt to Wise, June 9, 1941, Box 68, Wise MSS.

41. Wise to Frankfurter, Sept 16, 1942; Wise to James Waterman Wise, Feb. 16, 1943, in Voss, ed., *Stephen S. Wise*, 250, 257; Wise to Roosevelt, Dec. 2, 1942, Box 68, Wise MSS.

42. Benny Kraut, "Living in Two Civilizations: Hope and Confrontation," *Modern Judaism* 4 (Oct. 1984), 328; Selig Adler, "The Roosevelt Administration and Zionism: The Pre-War Years, 1933–39," in Melvin I. Urofsky, ed., *Essays in American Zionism* (New York, 1978), 134–35; Wyman, *Abandonment*, 181–86; Saul Friedman, *No Haven for the Oppressed* (Detroit, 1973), 225.

43. Wyman, *Abandonment*, 84–92, 346–47; Urofsky, *Voice*, 336–37.

44. Wyman, *Abandonment*, 90, 92; Feingold, "Stephen Wise," 48. Zionist leaders, according to Wyman (p. 346), even tried to get Bergson drafted, or deported. It is hardly coincidental that Wyman, standing outside the liberal Zionist consensus, has been one of the few historians to reject the conventional historiographical position on this issue, which can be found in Melvin I. Urofsky, *We Are One!* (New York, 1978), 75–81.

45. Wise to Nathan Straus, April 22, 1920, in Voss, ed., *Stephen S. Wise*, 99. Perhaps, Arthur Goren suggests, the war emergency impelled the Zionist organization, with its loyalty concerns, to restore clergymen to positions of prominence. Clearly, there was a rhythmic ebb and flow, during the twentieth century, from rabbis to lawyers (and back again). Neither has yet eradicated the influence of the other in American Jewish affairs.

46. Urofsky, *We Are One!*, 24–30; Urofsky, *Voice*, 339; Wise, *As I See It* (New York, 1944), 67.

47. Wyman, *Abandonment*, 171–74; Urofsky, *Voice*, 343–45; Wise to Roosevelt, Dec. 12, 1944, Box 68, Wise MSS; Wise to Julius Livingston, Dec. 18, 1944, in Voss,

ed., *Stephen S. Wise*, 267; Wise to Emanuel Neumann, Feb. 23, 1945, Box 117, Wise MSS.

48. Urofsky, *Voice*, 355; Frankfurter Message, Feb. 21, 1944, Box 109, Wise MSS.

49. Urofsky, *Voice*, vii–viii, 359–60.

50. See Arnold A. Offner, *American Appeasement* (Cambridge, 1969).

51. Joseph M. Proskauer, *A Segment of My Times* (New York, 1950), vii, 12–13, 18, 152; Alfred Kazin, *New York Jew* (New York, 1978), 42. Biographical data about Proskauer can be found in Louis M. Hacker and Mark D. Hirsch, *Proskauer: His Life and Times* (University, Ala., 1978).

52. Proskauer, *Segment*, 21–25; Hacker and Hirsch, *Proskauer*, 192. For virtually identical "civilizing" experiences, see Mary Antin, *The Promised Land* (Boston, 1912), 249–50; Norman Podhoretz, *Making It* (New York, 1969), 11–13; Theodore H. White, *In Search of History* (New York, 1978), 49.

53. Proskauer, *Segment*, 260.

54. *New York World Telegram*, Feb. 5, 1935; Proskauer to Rabbi Louis I. Newman, Oct. 2, 1933, Bernard G. Richards MSS, Jewish Theological Seminary, New York.

55. Morris Waldman to Dr. Alfred Cohen, May 23, 1933; Cyrus Adler memo of Hull interview [May 1933]; I. M. Rubinow to Waldman, June 2, 1933, American Jewish Committee MSS, New York.

56. Morris Waldman, *Nor by Power* (New York, 1953), 210–27; Proskauer to Waldman, April 29, 1942, Proskauer MSS, Proskauer, Rose, Goetz, and Mendelsohn, New York. Proskauer's anti-Zionism also made him an appealing prospective leader for the militantly anti-Zionist American Council for Judaism, which tried to persuade him to join its cause. Louis Wolsey to Morris Lazaron, Jan. 19, 1943, Wolsey MSS, American Jewish Committee.

57. Alexander Kohanski, ed., *The American Jewish Conference* (New York, 1944), 60, 101, 169; Proskauer memo, Dec. 28, 1943, AJC MSS; Cordell Hull to Proskauer, Dec. 2, 1943; Proskauer to Welles, Oct. 18, 1943; Proskauer to Rosenman, Feb. 8, 1944, Proskauer MSS; Rosenman to Watson, March 17, 1944, PPF 5029, FDR MSS, Hyde Park.

58. Proskauer address, Nov. 24, 1948, Proskauer MSS; Max Gottschalk to Waldman, March 10, 1949; Jacob Blaustein memo, Aug. 16, 1946, AJC MSS; Waldman, *Nor By Power*, 276–79. Proskauer's switch paralleled Marshall's earlier response to the Balfour Declaration, when support for Zionist objectives became, at least temporarily, American government policy.

59. Proskauer to Jack Lampl, Nov. 7, 1946; Proskauer to Robert Lovett, Feb. 13, March 1, 1948; Dean Rusk to Proskauer, April 22, 1948; Proskauer to Moshe Shertok, April 27, 1948; Proskauer to Ben- Gurion, April 30, 1948, Proskauer MSS. AJC colleagues continued to express their dismay over Proskauer's unilateral negotiations with State Department and Zionist officials, which expressed his determination not to be left outside the government consensus. See Blaustein to Proskauer, May 15, 1948, Proskauer Papers.

60. See Proskauer, *Segment*, 242–61.

61. See Proskauer to Wise, Aug. 10, 1944; Wise to Proskauer, Aug. 13, 1944, Proskauer MSS. For the conspicuous exception, when they each claimed Roosevelt's favor months after the president's death, see Proskauer to Wise, Nov. 13, Dec. 5, 1945; Wise to Proskauer, Nov. 21, 23, 1945, Proskauer MSS.

62. Daniel Jeremy Silver, ed., *In the Time of Harvest* (New York, 1963), 1–4, 34–35; Abba Hillel Silver, *Vision and Victory* (New York, 1949), 10, 21, 83, 123.

63. Silver, *Vision and Victory*, 75, 211–12.

64. Ibid., 130, 153ff, 223, 226.

EPILOGUE

1. For an analysis of the ambiguities, see Harold Fisch, *The Zionist Revolution* (New York, 1978), 79–85.

2. Naomi W. Cohen, *American Jews and the Zionist Idea* (New York, 1975), 115.

3. Ben-Gurion to Abe Feinberg, Dec. 30, 1948; Ben-Gurion to Jacob Blaustein, Nov. 14, 1951, Ben-Gurion MSS, Ben-Gurion Research Institute and Archives, Sde Boker.

4. Louis E. Leventhal to Ben-Gurion, Sept. 27, 1949; Abba Eban to Moshe Sharett, Oct. 10, 1949; Ben-Gurion to Proskauer, Nov. 1, 1949, Ben-Gurion MSS; Joseph M. Proskauer to Ben-Gurion, Oct. 5, 1949, RG 17-10, AJC MSS. Ben-Gurion claimed that his Histadrut statement was misquoted.

5. Ben-Gurion Address, Aug. 23, 1950, Ben-Gurion MSS. See Naomi W. Cohen, *Not Free to Desist* (Philadelphia, 1972), 311– 13.

6. The Ben-Gurion–Blaustein exchange appears in *AJYB* 53 (1952), 564 ff; Blaustein quoted in Cohen, *Not Free to Desist*, 314. See Charles S. Liebman, "Diaspora Influence on Israel: The Ben Gurion–Blaustein 'Exchange' and Its Aftermath," *Jewish Social Studies* 36 (1974), 271–80.

7. Blaustein to Ben-Gurion, Aug. 19, 1951; Ben-Gurion to Blaustein, Aug. 12, 1951, RG 17-10, AJC MSS; Ben-Gurion to Blaustein, Nov. 14, 1951, Ben-Gurion MSS. For persistent American demands and Israeli responses, the last of which occurred in 1961 and provoked an Israeli cabinet motion of censure for Ben-Gurion's deference to American sensibilites, see Cohen, *Not Free to Desist*, 314–15. See also Zeev Tzahor, "David Ben-Gurion's Attitude toward the Diaspora," *Judaism* 32 (Winter 1983), 21 ff.

8. Nathan Glazer, *American Judaism* (Chicago, 1957), 114.

9. Philip Roth, "Eli, The Fanatic," in *Goodbye, Columbus* (New York, 1960), 251.

10. Ibid. 255–56, 258, 261–62, 267, 277–78, 287, 298.

11. Abraham Joshua Heschel, *Israel: An Echo of Eternity* (New York, 1969), 195–96, 198–99; *The Seventh Day* (Harmondsworth, 1971), 220, 308; Meir Ben-Dov et al., *The Western Wall* (Israel, 1983), 148.

12. Charles E. Silberman, *A Certain People* (New York, 1985), 185–99.

13. Charles S. Liebman, *The Ambivalent American Jew* (Philadelphia, 1973), vii, 24–25, 27.

14. Eugene B. Borowitz, *The Mask Jews Wear* (New York, 1973), 29, 31, 33, 40 74–75.

15. *Jerusalem Post*, Jan. 11, 13, 14, 1983; *New York Times*, Jan. 16, 1983.

16. Edward Alexander, "Where is Zion?" *Commentary* 86 (Sept. 1988), 47; Albert Vorspan, "Soul-Searching," *New York Times Magazine* (May 8, 1988), 40 ff. For some striking similarities in the responses of American Jews to Arab riots in 1929 and 1988, see Naomi W. Cohen, *The Year after the Riots* (Detroit, 1988), 15, 87–88, 93, 99–100, 106–10; and Jerold S. Auerbach, "Are American Jews, Once Again, Debilitated by Cold Feet," *Jewish Advocate* (July 21, 1988), 9, 20. See also Ruth R. Wisse, "Israel & the Intellectuals: A Failure of Nerve?" *Commentary* 85 (May 1988), 19–25.

17. Silberman, *A Certain People*, 10, 23–24, 29, 366.

18. Ibid., 25, 269–72, 358.

19. Ibid., 95, 99–101, 244-47.

20. Jonathan S. Woocher, *Sacred Survival* (Bloomington, 1986), viii, 27, 37, 65,

88, 97–98, 102, 162–63, 200–201. It might be noted that the "timeless injunction" of *tsedekah* (p. 86) came belatedly to denote "charity," a quite narrow rendition of its fuller meaning as "righteous acts." The Deuteronomic command, "Justice, only justice shalt thou pursue" (Deut. 16:20), from which the injunction comes, cannot fairly be rendered as "Charity, only charity, shalt thou donate." See J. H. Hertz, ed., *The Pentateuch and Haftorahs* (London, 1978), 820–21.

21. Leonard Fine, *Where Are We?* (New York, 1988), xx, 32, 133, 233.

22. Ibid., 172–73, 176, 233, 235–36. The recent literature is replete with similar examples. Among the more suggestive, in addition to those discussed in the text, are Jacob Neusner, *Stranger at Home* (Chicago, 1981); Steven M. Cohen, *American Modernity and Jewish Identity* (New York, 1983); and Calvin Goldscheider, *Jewish Continuity and Change: Emerging Patterns in America* (Bloomington, 1986). After a while, however, the reader may begin to feel imprisoned in a house of mirrors, for every analysis of compatibility invariably strengthens the myth of compatibility. A conspicuous exception and a subtle exploration of the idea of "chosenness" for American Jews, is Arnold M. Eisen, *The Chosen People in America* (Bloomington, 1983). In illuminating how chosenness has solidified the link between Judaism and Americanism, Eisen never falls into the trap of taking the claim at face value.

23. Howard Singer, "Rabbis & Their Discontents," *Commentary* 79 (May 1985), 57.

24. Eisen, *Chosen People*, 119, 169–70.

AFTERWORD

1. Gen. 32:25, 29.
2. Hos. 8:14, 9:17-10:1, 11:10-11.

Bibliographical Note

Manuscript Collections

Cyrus Adler, American Jewish Historical Society (AJHS), Waltham; American Jewish Committee (AJC), New York; David Ben-Gurion, Ben-Gurion Research Institute and Archives, Sde Boker; Benjamin Cohen, Zionist Archives (ZA), New York; Bernard Felsenthal, AJHS; Jerome Frank, Yale University; Felix Frankfurter, Central Zionist Archives (CZA), Jerusalem; Harvard Law School (HLS), Cambridge; Richard Gottheil, CZA; Julian W. Mack, ZA; Judah L. Magnes, Central Archives of the History of the Jewish People, Jerusalem; Louis Marshall, American Jewish Archives (AJA), Cincinnati; AJHS; David Philipson, AJA; Joseph M. Proskauer, New York; Bernard G. Richards, Jewish Theological Seminary (JTS), New York; Franklin D. Roosevelt, Hyde Park; Solomon Schechter, JTS; Mayer Sulzberger, AJC; Robert Szold, ZA; Stephen S. Wise, AJHS; Louis Wolsey, AJC.

The secondary sources that I found most insightful and challenging are grouped below by chapter.

American Zion.

For an understanding of the Christian content of the identification of colonial America with biblical Israel: Sacvan Bercovitch, *The Puritan Origins of the American Self* (New Haven, 1975); John F. Berens, *Providence and Patriotism in Early America* (Charlottesville, 1978); Ursula Brumm, *American Thought and Religious Typology* (New Brunswick, N.J., 1970); Conrad Cherry, ed., *God's New Israel* (Englewood Cliffs, N.J., 1971): Nathan O. Hatch, *The Sacred Cause of Liberty* (New Haven, 1977); Mason I. Lowance, Jr., *The Language of Canaan* (Cambridge, 1980); Harry S. Stout, *The New England Soul* (New York, 1986). For a sensitive and subtle exploration of the attraction of constitutional law to immigrant Jews, see Alfred S. Konefsky, "Men of Great and Little Faith: Generations of Constitutional Scholars," *Buffalo Law Review* 30 (Spring 1981).

The Rule of Sacred Law.

Perspectives on Jewish law that take it seriously within its own categories of analysis include: Gedaliah Alon, *The Jews in Their Land in the Talmudic Age* (2 vols., Jerusalem, 1980); Eliezer Berkovits, *Not in Heaven* (New York, 1983); Joseph Blenkinsopp, *Wisdom and Law in the Old Testament* (Oxford, 1983); Boaz Cohen, *Law and Tradition in Judaism* (New York, 1969); Elliot N. Dorff and Arthur Rosett, *A Living Tree* (Albany, 1988); Menachem Elon, ed., *The Principles of Jewish Law* (Jerusalem, 1976); Ze'ev W. Falk, *Law and Religion: The Jewish Experience* (Jerusalem, 1981); Michael Fishbane, *Biblical Interpretation in Ancient Israel* (Oxford, 1985); Delbert R. Hillers, *Covenant: The History of a Biblical Idea* (Baltimore, 1969); Yehezkel Kaufmann, *The Religion of Israel* (New York, 1972); Jon D. Levenson, *Sinai and Zion* (San Francisco, 1987); Jacob Neusner, *A Life of Rabban Yohanan ben Zakkai* (Leiden, 1962) and *From Politics to Piety* (Englewood Cliffs, N.J., 1973); E. W. Nicholson, *Deuteronomy and Tradition* (Oxford, 1967); Joel Roth, *The Halakhic Process* (New York, 1986); Sol Roth, *Halakhah and Politics* (New York, 1988); Shubert Spero, *Morality, Halakha, and the Jew-*

ish Tradition (New York, 1983); Ephraim E. Urbach, *The Sages*, trans. Israel Abrahams (Cambridge, 1987). There is no substitute, of course, for a direct encounter with the biblical text. I have used *The Jerusalem Bible*, with English text revised and edited by Harold Fisch (Jerusalem, 1984).

Prophetic Justice.

For attentiveness to the relationship of prophecy and law in Jewish tradition: Bernhard W. Anderson and Walter Harrelson, eds., *Israel's Prophetic Heritage* (New York, 1962); Richard V. Bergren, *The Prophets and the Law* (Cincinnati, 1974); Joseph Blenkinsopp, *A History of Prophecy in Israel* (London, 1984) and *Prophecy and Canon* (Notre Dame, 1977); R. E. Clements, *Prophecy and Covenant* (London, 1965) and *Prophecy and Tradition* (Oxford, 1978); Richard Coggins *et al.*, eds., *Israel's Prophetic Tradition* (Cambridge, 1982); E. W. Heaton, *The Old Testament Prophets* (London, 1977); Herbert B. Huffmon, "The Covenant Lawsuit in the Prophets," *Journal of Biblical Literature* 78 (1959); Klaus Koch, *The Prophets* (2 vols., Philadelphia, 1983); James Limburg, "The Root ריב and the Prophetic Lawsuit Speeches," *Journal of Biblical Literature* 88 (1969); Gerhard von Rad, *The Message of the Prophets* (New York, 1972); Julius Wellhausen, *Prolegomena to the History of Israel* (Edinburgh, 1885); Robert R. Wilson, *Prophecy and Society in Ancient Israel* (Philadelphia, 1980).

Emancipation.

For the relationship of emancipation, Reform Judaism, and the loss of rabbinical authority: Robert Alter, "Emancipation, Enlightenment & All That," *Commentary* 53 (1972); Jerome E. Carlin and Saul H. Mendlovitz, "The American Rabbi: A Religious Specialist Responds to the Loss of Authority," in Marshall Sklare, ed., *The Jews* (New York, 1958); Naomi W. Cohen, *Encounter with Emancipation* (Philadelphia, 1984); Walter Jacob, ed., *The Pittsburgh Platform in Retrospect* (Pittsburgh, 1985); Leon A. Jick, *The Americanization of the Synagogue, 1820–1870* (Hanover, N.H., 1976); Jacob Katz, *Out of the Ghetto* (Cambridge, 1973) and *Tradition and Crisis* (New York, 1961); Franz Kobler, *Napoleon and the Jews* (New York, 1976); Michael A. Meyer, *Response to Modernity* (New York, 1988); Ismar Schorsch, "Emancipation and the Crisis of Religious Authority—The Emergence of the Modern Rabbinate," in Werner E. Mosse, ed., *Revolution and Evolution* (Tubingen, 1981); Simon Schwarzfuchs, *Napoleon, the Jews and the Sanhedrin* (London, 1979).

The Authority of Tradition.

It is astonishing that there has not been a single scholarly biography either of Solomon Schechter or Louis Marshall, whose influence on American Jewish life, in both its religious and secular dimensions, was profound. For background, I drew upon Norman Bentwich, *Solomon Schechter* (Philadelphia, 1938); Moshe Davis, *The Emergence of Conservative Judaism* (Philadelphia, 1965); Abraham J. Karp, "Solomon Schechter Comes to America," in *The Jewish Experience in America* (New York, 1969); Jacob Agus, "The Conservative Movement: Reconstructionism," in Jacob Neusner, ed., *Understanding American Judaism* (2 vols., New York, 1975); Marc Lee Raphael, *Profiles in American Judaism* (San Francisco, 1984); Charles Reznikoff, ed., *Louis Marshall: Champion of Liberty* (2 vols., Philadelphia, 1957); Morton Rosenstock, *Louis Marshall, Defender of Jewish Rights* (Detroit, 1965); Solomon Schechter, *Seminary Addresses and Other Papers* (Cincinnati, 1915); Howard Singer, "The Judaism Born in America," *Commentary* 82 (1986); Marshall Sklare, *Conservative Judaism* (Philadelphia, 1965).

Louis D. Brandeis.

By contrast, even Brandeis's belated and constricted attachment to Zionism has been endlessly recounted, invariably within Brandeis's own terms of Americanization. Most of the critical detachment has come from Israeli scholars. See Naomi W. Cohen, *The Year after the Riots* (Detroit, 1988); Evytar Friesel, "Brandeis' Role in American Zionism Historically Reconsidered," *American Jewish History* 69 (Sept. 1979); Allon Gal, *Brandeis of Boston* (Cambridge, 1980); Ben Halpern, "The Americanization of Zionism, 1880–1930," *American Jewish History* 69 (Sept. 1979); Barbara Ann Harris, "Zionist Speeches of Louis Dembitz Brandeis: A Critical Edition" (Ph.D. diss., UCLA, 1967); Isidore S. Meyer, ed., *Early History of Zionism in America* (New York, 1958); Sarah Schmidt, "The Zionist Conversion of Louis D. Brandeis," *Jewish Social Studies* 37 (Jan. 1975); Yonathan Shapiro, *Leadership of the American Zionist Organization, 1897–1930* (Urbana, 1971); Melvin I. Urofsky and David W. Levy, eds., *Letters of Louis D. Brandeis* (5 vols., Albany, 1971–78).

Isaiah's Disciples.

For Julian W. Mack there is Harry Barnard, *The Forging of an American Jew* (New York, 1974). The most insightful glimpses of Frankfurter appear in Simha Berkowitz, "Felix Frankfurter's Zionist Activities" (D.H.L. thesis, Jewish Theological Seminary, 1971); Richard Danzig, "Justice Frankfurter's Opinions in the Flag Salute Cases: Blending Logic and Psychologic in Constitutional Decision-making," *Stanford Law Review* 36 (1984); *Felix Frankfurter Reminisces* (Harlan B. Phillips ed., New York, 1960); H. N. Hirsch, *The Enigma of Felix Frankfurter* (New York, 1981); *Roosevelt and Frankfurter: Their Correspondence*, Annotated by Max Freedman (Boston, 1967). See also Jerold S. Auerbach, *Unequal Justice* (New York, 1976); Peter H. Irons, *The New Deal Lawyers* (Princeton, 1982); and Selma Stern, *The Court Jew* (Philadelphia, 1950).

Rabbi and Lawyer.

For Stephen S. Wise, see Melvin I. Urofsky, *A Voice That Spoke for Justice* (New York, 1982). For Joseph M. Proskauer, see Louis M. Hacker and Mark D. Hirsch, *Proskauer: His Life and Times* (University, Ala., 1978); and Jerold S. Auerbach, "Joseph M. Proskauer: American Court Jew," *American Jewish History* 69 (Sept. 1979). For American Jews and the Holocaust, see Walter Laqueur and Richard Breitman, *Breaking the Silence* (New York, 1986); Haskel Lookstein, *Were We Our Brothers' Keepers?* (New York, 1985); and especially David S. Wyman, *The Abandonment of the Jews* (New York, 1984).

Since 1948.

Although there is an abundant literature that celebrates the congruence of Americanism and Judaism, and a proliferating critique of Israel by disillusioned American Jews, the more complex interactions between American Jewry and Israel have yet to be explored. With the exception of Charles S. Liebman, *The Ambivalent American Jew* (Philadelphia, 1973), Eugene B. Borowitz, *The Mask Jews Wear* (New York, 1973), and Arnold Eisen, *The Chosen People in America* (Bloomington, 1983), there are few books to provoke thoughtful analysis of the process of American Jewish acculturation. I offer *Rabbis and Lawyers* in an effort to fill that void, before the memory loss of American Jewry becomes even more debilitating than it already is.

Index

J   E   R   O   L   D   S.   A   U   E   R   B   A   C   H

is the author of *Labor and Liberty, Unequal Justice,* and *Justice without Law?* His articles have appeared in *Commentary, Harper's, Judaism, The New Republic,* and *The New York Times.* He has been a Guggenheim Fellow, Fulbright Lecturer at Tel Aviv University, and Visiting Scholar at Harvard Law School. He is Professor of History at Wellesley College.